Richard H. Jones

SIMON DE MONTFORT

OXFORD UNIVERSITY PRESS
AMEN HOUSE, E.C. 4
LONDON EDINBURGH GLASGOW
LEIPZIG NEW YORK TORONTO
MELBOURNE CAPETOWN BOMBAY
CALCUTTA MADRAS SHANGHAI
HUMPHREY MILFORD
PUBLISHER TO THE
UNIVERSITY

MONTFORT L'AMAURY FROM THE CASTLE, LOOKING EAST

SIMON DE MONTFORT
EARL OF LEICESTER
1208–1265

BY

CHARLES BÉMONT

Membre de l'Institut (Académie
des Inscriptions et Belles-lettres)

A New Edition
translated
by

E. F. JACOB

OXFORD
AT THE CLARENDON PRESS
1930

Printed in Great Britain

À LA MÉMOIRE
DE MES VÉNÉRÉS MAÎTRES
GABRIEL MONOD ET
PAUL MEYER

I DEDICATE THIS
NEW EDITION TO

MY WIFE

Ch. B.

AVANT-PROPOS

J'AI le très agréable devoir d'adresser mes remerciements à
tous ceux qui m'ont aidé à faire paraître une nouvelle édition,
très remaniée, de mon étude sur Simon de Montfort. Ils vont
en première ligne à mon éminent collègue et confrère, M. Gabriel
Hanotaux. C'est lui en effet qui, spontanément, m'a offert
ses bons offices auprès de ses amis à l'ambassade de la Grande-
Bretagne à Paris; grâce à lui, j'ai trouvé le plus obligeant accueil
auprès de M. J. R. Cahill, conseiller, délégué aux affaires com-
merciales, et de M. Arthur H. S. Yeames, deuxième secrétaire.
Ces deux Oxford men ont bien voulu s'intéresser à mon livre
et l'ont recommandé aux administrateurs du Clarendon Press
en des termes que j'ignore, mais dont j'ai éprouvé aussitôt
les heureux effets: je n'ai pas tardé en effet à savoir que l'on con-
sentait à faire imprimer et publier mon ouvrage, à cette seule
condition qu'il fût traduit en anglais. Je ne puis dissimuler que
j'éprouvai une certaine déception, craignant de ne plus recon-
naître mon œuvre sous un vêtement étranger; mais le vêtement
était si bien apprécié dans le monde savant que je me résignai
facilement aux avantages certains que je devais en retirer. Je
n'ai eu en effet qu'à me louer du soin avec lequel les épreuves
ont été exécutées et corrigées à l'imprimerie.

A cette première bonne fortune de paraître dans une des
maisons d'édition les plus justement célèbres dans le monde
entier, s'en ajouta une autre d'un prix infini. On m'annonça
que mon livre serait traduit par l'érudit qui, sans doute, connaît
le mieux l'époque où vécut le comte de Leicester et qui même
venait de publier tout un livre sur le mouvement réformateur
des années 1258–67 où mon personnage a joué un si grand rôle.
Me permettra-t-on un souvenir personnel concernant Sir Paul
Vinogradoff? Sir Paul m'avait fait l'honneur de me prendre en
amitié. A son avant-dernier passage à Paris, il voulut bien me
faire savoir qu'il lui serait agréable de causer avec moi. Dans
notre entretien et comme je lui parlais de mon livre, il m'apprit
qu'un de ses meilleurs élèves, M. Ernest F. Jacob, allait faire
paraître dans sa collection *Oxford Studies in Social and Legal*

History un livre intitulé *Studies in the Period of Baronial Reform and Rebellion, 1258-1267,* livre dont il tenait en main les épreuves déjà mises en pages. Grâce à lui j'ai pu consulter l'ouvrage avant même son apparition et le mettre à profit pour le mien Or, c'est précisément M. Jacob à qui l'on voulait confier la traduction. Je ne pouvais que me louer d'un choix aussi qualifié. En fait, M. Jacob a été pour moi plus qu'un traducteur, presque un collaborateur, en tout cas le conseiller le plus compétent que je pusse désirer. Il m'a évité plus d'une erreur et j'aurais certainement amélioré mon livre en acceptant toutes ses suggestions, si je n'avais craint de paraître m'emparer du bien d'autrui. Qu'il veuille bien ne pas m'en savoir mauvais gré. Les érudits qui liront mon livre et qui auront des critiques à lui faire voudront bien me considérer comme le seul coupable de mes fautes ou omissions.

Je ne saurais oublier enfin l'obligeance avec laquelle les fonctionnaires du Public Record Office, et le Deputy Keeper tout le premier, ont bien voulu répondre aux questions que je me suis permis de leur poser. Ils ont fait plus. Ayant eu la bonne fortune de retrouver dans leur admirable dépôt plusieurs documents relatifs au gouvernement de Simon de Montfort en Gascogne, ils se sont empressés de m'en envoyer des photographies avec un commencement de déchiffrement. Les parchemins retrouvés étaient pour la plupart en un tel état de mutilation qu'il a été bien difficile de les utiliser en toute sécurité ; pour certains d'entre eux, il a fallu renoncer à faire imprimer des lignes ou des mots que même les meilleurs paléographes (je veux dire ceux du Public Record Office), n'avaient pas réussi à déchiffrer. Leur science et leur patience ont été mises à une rude épreuve et méritent une reconnaissance toute particulière.

CH. BÉMONT

MAIN ENTRANCE TO THE CASTLE OF MONTFORT
L'AMAURY, LOOKING NORTH

CONTENTS

3463   b

LIST OF ILLUSTRATIONS

INTRODUCTION

IN December 1884 I presented at the Sorbonne for the degree of Dr.-ès-Lettres two theses entitled: *De Johanne sine terra Parisiis anno 1202 condemnato*, and *Simon de Montfort, comte de Leicester: sa vie, 120?–1265, son rôle politique en France et en Angleterre.* On the former I need not comment: it has been partly rewritten, and its conclusions have been confirmed with the aid of more solid and exhaustive arguments by Stubbs's learned commentator, M. Charles Petit-Dutaillis.[1] But my biography of the Earl of Leicester, more than forty years old now, is out of print and no longer up-to-date. I have therefore decided to rewrite it, making full use of the numerous documents and important historical works which have been published during the last fifty years.

The *pièces justificatives* that occupied more than a hundred pages in my thesis have not been reproduced here. The saving of space thus effected has enabled me to increase the bibliographical references and textual citations in the foot-notes. The general plan of the book has been modified. I hope that in its present form it will be thought better adapted to the complexity of the subject.

SOURCES

It is first and foremost in the matter of archives that our knowledge has increased. Reference will here be made successively to texts derived from French, British, and Papal archives.

I. *French Archives.* First must come the archives of the *comté* of Montfort, which can, I believe, be reconstructed, at any rate partially. The chief constituent of such an attempt is to be found in a MS. of the Bibliothèque Nationale, *fonds Clairembault*, no. 1188 (former title 'Ordre du Saint-Esprit, no. 78, Montfort').[2] As this MS. is

---

[1] *Revue historique*, cliv.

[2] Pierre Clairembault, genealogist of the royal orders, appointed in 1698, and later given the task of classifying and listing the Gaignières and d'Hozier collections, set himself to write a history of the Order of the Holy Ghost, and for this purpose brought these documents together. He amassed a considerable number, 266 volumes with two of Indexes. His nephew, Nicolas Pascal Clairembault, succeeded him in the work (1740), but shortly afterwards sold

described only in a few very summary lines in the catalogue of this class drawn by M. Lauer,[1] I ought to describe it in detail. It comprises 96 folios, unmethodically arranged. Folio 1 entitled 'Liasse cotée prieuré de Montfort l'Amaury', formerly bore the number 87; it contains an 'Extrait no. 15', which is the copy of an Act of king Philip I extracted from the cartulary of S. Magloire. Then follows a group of folios, paged from 2 to 40, bearing the old pagination 6569–6702. The Acts copied on to the folios of this category relate to the lords and counts of Montfort. I shall return to them later on. Folio 41 begins a new series headed 'Tiltres qui sont a Dampierre, communiquez par Monseigneur le Duc de Chevreuse au mois de juin 1707'. There is another similar heading to folio 42 (formerly 6653): 'extrait de plusieurs tiltres originaux en parchemin qui sont dans le trésor de Dampierre. Ils ont été tirés de Saint-Denis lorsque le Cardinal de Lorraine acquit Beaurain pour le joindre au duché de Chevreuse. Communiquez par Mgr. le duc de Chevreuse en juin 1707'. The deeds described as 'original' are in reality no more than copies of two diplomata of Charlemagne and Charles the Fat. Then comes a series of folios in which several deeds, this time really original, have been pasted, all relating to Montfort, and each bearing a consecutive number, from 70 to 89. No. 71 is missing, and so too no. 77, but a note in Léopold Delisle's hand indicates that the fragment of the charter here has been added to another fragment of the same charter bound up in MS. *latin* 9016. The two fragments make up the piece numbered 6 in that MS. (I may be allowed to add that it was upon my information that these two fragments were connected, a course clearly indicated.) The volume ends with six folios (90–6) containing, as before, copies of several deeds and obituary notices relating to Montfort. Volume 1188 therefore contains (i) modern copies and original deeds of the thirteenth and fourteenth centuries, relative to the county of Montfort in particular, and (ii) copies relating to the duchy of Chevreuse as a whole.

At the end of the seventeenth century the two lordships (Montfort and Chevreuse) belonged to the same family. After being in the

the whole collection to the king (1755). After the decree of 1792 extinguishing titles of nobility it suffered serious losses. See L. Delisle, *Le cabinet des manuscrits de la Bibl. Nat.* (1874), pp. 19–24. There is an inventory of the seals in this collection by G. Demay, *Doc. inéd.*, t. i (1885); but in MS. 1188 the Gaignières documents show representations only, not the original seals, and consequently these do not figure in his inventory.

[1] Philippe Lauer, *Catalogue des manuscrits de la collection Clairembault*, see t. ii (1924), p. 352.

possession of the father and the eldest brother of the earl of Leicester, the county of Montfort (l'Amaury) passed into the house of Dreux, later of Brittany. The duchess Anne, wife of Louis XII, transmitted it to her daughter Claude, who by her marriage with Francis I brought it into the demesne of the French Crown. In 1692 Louis XIV exchanged it for the greater part of the duchy of Chevreuse,[1] and the Duke,[2] who thus acquired the county, came as a matter of course into possession of its archives. We saw above that the contents of the 'trésor des chartes' of the county, which were communicated by the duke for the first time in 1707, as the heading of the *dossier* tells us, were again communicated in the following year, as can be seen in the title of the *dossier* paged 2 to 40. We read to this effect at the top of folio 2 r.: 'Extrait des tiltres . . . fait sur les originaux communiquez par Mgr. le duc de Chevreuse au mois de Janvier 1708. Ces tiltres estoient autrefois à Montfort.'[3] Clairembault, who gives this information, explains how afterwards the title-deeds were stolen, then restored, without saying when or how they came into his hands. It would be interesting to know with what object the archives of Montfort were thus communicated in 1707 and 1708, and why they are to be found finally deposited among the documents of the Order of the Holy Ghost.

[1] The contract of exchange and letter of ratification are given in le Père Anselme, t. v, pp. 684, 697. Cf. La Martinière, *Grand dictionnaire géographique, historique et critique* (1726–1730) *s.v.* Montfort.

[2] Then Charles Honoré d'Albert, duc de Luynes, intimate friend and colleague of the duc de Beauvillier.

[3] It may be found useful to reproduce here the complete text of the heading and the information added by Clairembault. 'Liasse cotée Prieuré de Montfort. Cet extrait fait sur les originaux communiquez par Monseigneur le duc de Chevreuse au mois de janvier 1708. Ces tiltres estoient autrefois à Montfort. Le lieutenant général de Montfort, qui se nommoit le sieur de Goussainville, se trouva de la connoissance d'Haudiquier, auquel il les presta. Haudiquier avoit une maitresse qui luy estoit commune avec quelques autres. Ce lieutenant la vit par occasion et, ne luy ayant pas déplu, Haudiquier entreprit de les marier ensemble. Il fit en sorte que le Lieutenant allast voir cette fille, laquelle, d'intelligence avec Haudiquier, fit paroiste sur sa toilette de faux billets payables au porteur. Elle fit l'embarrassée sur l'usage et l'emploi de ces billets; elle consulta le lieutenant et les luy confia pour les porter a son notaire auquel on avoit fait le bec, et duquel Haudiquier se servoit pour déposer de fausses minutes. Le Lieutenant donna dans le paneau, et ne fut pas moins charmé des billets que de la belle. Il fait l'amour en forme, va au [word illegible] à Haudiquier et à son notaire, et se marye promptement, de crainte de manquer sa proye. Il fut aussi peu de temps à découvrir la fourberie; il devint fou et mourut. Les tiltres de Montfort restérent à Haudiquier jusqu'à son emprison-nement à la Bastille.' This note, M. Lauer tells us, is written wholly in the hand of Clairembault, who had the deeds collected by Gaignières copied.

I shall return presently to parts of volume 1188 which are concerned solely with the county, the lords and counts of Montfort. The *dossier* formed by folios 2–31 contains, as I remarked, only copies. The deeds entered there, eighty-one in number, are arranged, with a few exceptions, in chronological order. They run from 1209 to 1286, excluding the first, which is of 1089, and the last, dated 1324, which immediately follows another of 1286. After 1324 no order is observed. It may be helpful to append the indications of their sources given by the copyist or the copyists of this group of documents. Folio 3 (formerly 6571) recto, charter of Simon, father of the earl of Leicester, dated, during the siege of Toulouse, 10 Kal. Jun., 1211: 'tiltre de l'abbaye du Val près Pontoise.' Similarly folio 26 (formerly 6614 verso), two deeds of 1217 and 1218. Folio 6 (formerly 6577), charter of 1239: 'l'original est à Montfort, chez le curé administrateur de l'Hostel Dieu.' Folio 27, 'tiltres de l'abbaye de Saint-Mesmin près Orléans'; after which, in a space left blank, has been inserted an extract from 'l'ancien obituaire de Nostre-Dame du Val près Pontoise'. Folio 28 (formerly 6617 verso) extracts of obituaries from Nostre-Dame de Port-Royal-des-Champs. Folio 93 verso, several rough inventories at the end of which are the words 'Jean Doublet, garde du sel de la châtellenie de Montfort. Selé dudit sel, 1333, 17 may', together with a rough impression of the seal. These indications may perhaps help in the recovery of other deeds from the lords and counts of Montfort.

To the documents collected in volume 1188 (Clairembault) should be added other pieces found indifferently in several MSS. in the Bibliothèque Nationale, in the boxes [*Layettes*] of the Archives Nationales, and finally in the British Museum, all of which certainly hail from the ancient archives of the county.

Leicester had to undergo two suits at law: the first was before the King's Court in England, to which the complaints of the Gascon lords and communities against the rigours of his administration were brought in 1252; the second was before the king of France, chosen to arbitrate in the disputes between Henry III of England and his brother-in-law Leicester (1261), notably in matters concerning the preliminaries and the execution of the Treaty of Paris (1259). The grievances of the plaintiffs and Simon's replies are to be found (*a*) in the Bibliothèque Nationale, *MSS latin* 9015, 9016, (*b*) in the British Museum, which in 1839 acquired a considerable part of the collection by Joursanvault, and in 1856 several other documents through the Moore sale. I have published all these documents among the *Pièces justificatives* in my thesis. The Additional Charters in the British

Museum have likewise supplied me with eleven documents relating to the same subject.[1] Other isolated documents which bear every likelihood of coming from the Montfort archives are to be found in the boxes of the *Trésor des chartes* at the Palais Soubise marked J 1028 (recto) no. 13 and J 1031 no. 5. In J 628, no. 14 is a piece of parchment (60×15 cm.) bearing the transcriptions : i. (recto) of seven documents to be found in the *Layettes du Trésor* ;[2] ii. (verso) of two other documents so far unpublished [3] which are exclusively concerned with the earl's possessions in England. In J 1024, no. 14 is an original charter by which Richard, king of the Romans, Henry III's brother and Simon's brother-in-law, undertakes (6 September 1265) to remain the loyal friend of his sister Eleanor, Leicester's widow, and of all hers. This document, issued a month after the death of the earl at Evesham, had the effect of a safe-conduct for his widow, who was then being pursued by the enmity of the victors, and we may well believe that she was still treasuring it in the convent of the nuns of St. Dominic at Montargis where she died in 1275. Was it from Montargis that the documents in the *Trésor des chartes* came ? Yet how did they get there and when ?

In my thesis I dealt in sufficient detail with the diplomatic of the earl's chancery. I showed that the style employed in drawing up the deeds that emanated from him is the 'Easter' style. I further discussed the two seals he used, and pointed out several forgeries which have deceived historians.[4] This should be enough : but before leaving the Montfort archives I ought to mention a precious document published long ago and undoubtedly belonging to that class, the book, or a fragment of the book of the household expenses of the countess. This fragment runs from 19 February to 29 August 1265, with several

---

[1] Nos. 3298, 3299, 3300, 3301, 3302, 3303, 11234, 11236, 11237, 11238, and 11240.

[2] *Layettes du Trésor des chartes*, ii (1866), nos. 2088, 2151, 2190, 2366, 2789, 28452, and 28453.

[3] Here are the texts of the two charters on the dorse and in another hand :
i. Universis has literas inspecturis Herebertus filius Mathei, salutem. Noveritis me recepisse de dono S. de Monteforti XX marcatas terre in dominico suo de dominico suo (*sic*) de Hakeleston ; ita scilicet quod, si dictum dominicum magis quam XX marcate terre secundum extensionem fuerit, ego, Herebertus, et heredes mei dicto Simoni et heredibus suis reddere et restaurare tenemur. Et in huius rei testimonium huic scripto sigillum meum apposui. ii. H. dei gratia etc. Sciatis quod concessimus dilecte sorori nostre A., comitisse Leyrc., castrum meum de Kenilleworth cum pertinenciis, tota vita sua custodiendum. In cujus rei testimonium literas nostras fieri fecimus patentes. Teste me ipso, apud Westm. IX die jan., anno regni nostri XXXj°. Cf. *C. P. R. 1247–1258*, (9 January 1248).

[4] *Simon de Montfort*, pp. v-vi.

other scattered entries, the last of which is of 1 October. It belongs
to the most troubled period in the life of Simon and his wife, the
period in which the fortunes of his house collapsed after the disaster
at Evesham. The smallest domestic details at that time take on an
almost tragic significance.

II. *British Archives.* We may deal first with the Leicester records,
secondly with those to be found in the innumerable shelves of the
Public Record Office in London.

Half a century ago, upon the recommendation of Samuel Rawson
Gardiner and thanks to the kindness of William Kelly, I was permitted to work alone and unsupervised in the store-room where the
ancient archives of Leicester were kept. I was then only able to copy
hastily and under somewhat unfavourable conditions the few pieces
which figure in the Appendix to my thesis.[1] Several of these were
already known, but only through the lists of contents given them by
Cordy Jeaffreson in the reports of the Historical Manuscripts Commission. In actual fact, the text of all that early material can now be
read in Miss Mary Bateson's fine edition. I had the satisfaction of
proving my copies to be accurate transcripts of the originals; but
with the complete collection of these valuable documents now at
hand, I have found it necessary to rewrite in entirety the section of
my book that deals with the relations of earl Simon with the town
and, to a certain degree, with the earldom of Leicester. We shall see
later on that the interest of this study goes considerably beyond the
limits of local history.

In London the administration of the Public Record Office offers
priceless opportunities for study, thanks to the order and method
with which the sources are classified, as well as to the publications of
texts and inventories which it is constantly putting at the disposal of
scholars.[2] The decisions taken by the king, often with the help of his
Council, affecting the general business of the kingdom were given
written form in the office of the Chancery, which sent out the
sealed originals after having copied them.[3] These copies were transcribed upon skins of parchment (*membranae*), one sewn to the end
of another, so as to form at least a single *rotulus* for each year. The
series which have been most worked upon owing to the importance
and variety of the documents there transcribed are those of the

---

[1] *Simon de Montfort*, pp. 257–365.

[2] See the *Guide* by M. S. Giuseppi.

[3] For the details of its working, see the very important work of Sir H. C.
Maxwell Lyte, *Historical Notes on the Use of the Great Seal of England* (1926),
and *Revue historique*, t. clvi, pp. 399–402.

Charters, the Letters Patent, and the Letters Close. Charters were employed when the king wished to grant to individuals or communities 'liberties', privileges or immunities, lands, fiefs, &c. These concessions, normally characterized by perpetual validity, were drawn up in the most solemn terms and bore at the end the attestation of the persons present or who were deemed to have given their consent to the royal act. This list of witnesses is absent from the *litterae patentes* which were simply addressed 'to all who shall see these present letters'. The *patentes* served the most various purposes: royal prerogatival action, diplomatic correspondence, truces and treaties, letters of protection and of safe-conduct, &c. In the case of *litterae clausae*, the letters sent to individuals and bearing a more individual character, the diplomatic formulae contained scarcely more than what was necessary to designate the addressee and to date the document. On the other hand, it is the Letters Close which contain most information on the personalities and the little facts that interest historian and biographer. Warm thanks are therefore due to the administration of the Public Record Office for continuing to publish them *in toto*, though the series has, unfortunately for my purpose, ceased for the time being at the end of 37 Hen. III (October 1253). For the Charters from 1216 and Letters Patent from 1232 we must rest content with the resumé given in the Calendars, instructive publications which facilitate the researcher's task by means of their excellent indexes, but are not a complete substitute for the originals. The reader must not be surprised to find here and there in the present work extracts from the texts of Letters Patent from 1237 and Letters Close after 1253: these are copies which I made some time ago, and in consequence are still valuable. I should add that the series of Letters Patent and Close, utilized long ago when they were deposited in the Tower of London, furnished a number of important entries for Rymer's *Foedera*, and from the same source Shirley drew the majority of his documents published in the two volumes of his *Royal Letters*, which are particularly interesting to the biographer of Simon de Montfort; for Shirley then had it in mind to write the earl's life, and this aim must have guided his choice. Side by side with the three great series just referred to should be mentioned that of the *Rotuli finium*, into which the Chancery Clerks copied royal mandates conferring, in return for various money payments, public offices, granting territorial concessions and privileges, ordering the recovery or complete remittance of the debts contracted by individuals towards the Crown, &c. There is still no more than an Index of them: recently a *Calendar* has been started, and, until it goes farther, the

most profitable course is to consult the extracts published by
Sir T. D. Hardy and Charles Roberts for the reign of Henry III.
Recently the P.R.O. has discovered a roll relating to the year 1242-3,
of direct interest for Leicester's biography.[1]
From the biographical point of view, the edition of the *Rôles
Gascons* has also been especially useful. In 1884 it was still only
possible to utilize the very incomplete and incorrect inventory of
Thomas Carte, and the unmethodically published texts in the
Archives historiques du département de la Gironde which were taken
from the copies made in the eighteenth century at the Tower of
London under the direction of Bréquigny. In 1885 Francisque-
Michel published the first volume of the Rôles, containing precisely
the years of Leicester's government in Gascony. In 1896 a supplement to the first volume added the letters patent sent in the name of
Prince Edward, whom his father had commissioned to restore order
in the province: these have a direct bearing upon the earl's biography,
while vols. II and III which relate to the reign of Edward I contribute practically nothing.

The archives concerned more particularly with the internal administration of the country we may view under the heads of justice,
finance, and feudal tenures:

Plea Rolls, Assize Rolls, &c. Were it possible to consult anywhere
else than in the Public Record Office in London the rolls of pleas
before the king's court (*curia regis*), the supreme organ of jurisdiction,
a mass of priceless information would accrue. But the records so far
published have not passed John Lackland's reign, and no Calendar
exists for Henry III. So for the moment, with our present subject,
the stormy years 1258-65 especially in view, we have to rely upon
the results gained by the researches of a careful historian, Mr. E. F.
Jacob. Sir Paul Vinogradoff, who wrote the preface to Mr. Jacob's
book,[2] stated the position very truly: 'A thorough examination of
these [plea rolls] has enabled Mr. Jacob to supplement the description
of the political struggle in the great centres and to show how the
parties were grouped and organized in the country at large. As a
result of these studies controversies as to important points of the
constitutional movement have received a new orientation.'

We are rather better situated for understanding the work done by
the justices itinerant (justices in Eyre) whom the king sent out into
the counties to make inquiries about all sorts of juridical and

---

[1] Ch. Bémont, *Un 'rotulus finium' retrouvé (1242–1243)*. *Bulletin du Comité
des travaux philologiques et historiques* (1926).

[2] See the Bibliography at the end of this Introduction.

administrative matters, in order to control the action of the agents of the central government from the sheriff down to the humblest bailiff of the royal domain, and even, in certain cases, of the seignorial liberties. These inquiries were conducted in each hundred before the juries convoked by the judges, the verdicts of which were entered upon their rolls. Thence we derive various series of assize rolls and hundred rolls. Under Miss Cam's scrutiny,[1] they have given us a great number of facts which, in conjunction with those brought to light by Mr. Jacob, help to make us better acquainted with the administrative and social life of the time.

For a text of these legal documents we have nothing more at our disposal than a single official publication, the *Placitorum abbreviatio*; but its compiler only included a relatively small number of cases, and these are mainly represented by mere extracts. As for the proceedings before the judges itinerant, the period when earl Simon begins to be prominent is covered by Bracton's invaluable Note Book, which Vinogradoff first identified as such, and which was later edited by Maitland with all the authority that attaches to his great name. Other Assize Rolls are to be found printed in the scattered publications of local record societies.

Financial administration was the proper sphere of the Exchequer. There, before the great officers of the King's Household and the chief functionaries of the place, called Barons of the Exchequer, the sheriffs and the bailiffs of 'liberties' or 'franchises' (the lordships normally exempt from the sheriff's interference) would appear twice a year to give account of their receipts and expenditure. The audit completed, the result of these transactions was entered on a roll called the *Magnus rotulus pipae* or Great Roll of the Pipe. The series of these records has been preserved nearly intact from 1154 to 1832. The Society founded to publish the complete text has not yet finished with the reign of Richard I; but it has had the roll of 1230 edited already, and an American scholar, Mr. Henry L. Cannon, has published that of 1241–2. The second of these two volumes has a considerable bearing upon Leicester's biography. An analysis of these great rolls, unhappily of all too summary a character, is to be found in Sir James Ramsay's last work.[2] The exchequer dealt judicially with all questions that arose out of the ingathering of the revenue. Two secretaries (Remembrancers), of the King and of the Treasurer respectively, entered notes of them on their Rolls (Memo-

---

[1] 'Studies in the Hundred Rolls' in *Oxford Studies in Social and Legal History,* vi, pp. 109–10.
[2] See Bibliography at the end of this Introduction.

randa Rolls) which later formed two distinct[1] series in the Public
Record Office. Certain public services like the Navy came under the
direct personal control of the king; they formed a department of the
royal Wardrobe and constituted a separate series, the *Foreign
Accounts*, which in the thirteenth century were still entered upon
the Pipe Rolls at the end of the sheriffs' accounts, under the special
rubric 'Rotulus compotorum'.[2] Professor Tout has made excellent
use of these 'Foreign' rolls in his *Chapters in Medieval Administrative History*, when demonstrating the importance of the part played
in the government by the Chamber and the Wardrobe, acting side by
side with the public offices and entering sometimes into conflict with
them. These were instruments of personal government more or less
tolerated by the baronage, but always powerful.

The king discovered extra sources of income in impositions like
the carucage, a contribution levied on all lands freed from military
service; tallage, the payment due from all dwellers on royal demesne
and from the burgesses of the king's towns; scutage paid to replace
the military service of the tenures in chivalry; the extraordinary
taxes of the tenth and fifteenth on goods and movables, &c. The
Church was affected no less than the laity, and we shall see later on
how it had to contribute in 1254 for a crusade that had been decided
upon, but was never carried out, and what resistance it offered to the
demands of the Crown. By a use of exchequer documents Mr. Lunt
has made this point fully clear.

The monarchy had its roots deep in the feudal system; it was in
consequence obliged to supervise the whole feudal mechanism, to see
to the dues payable by, and to the transmission of fiefs. Every now and
then it ordered inquests to be made into knights' fees and serjeanties.
These inquests were preserved in compilations like the *Liber Feodorum*, better known under the enigmatic title of the *Testa de Nevill*,
where are to be found the returns of royal fiefs, of widows and
heiresses of the immediate vassals of the Crown whom the king could
marry, under certain liabilities, to his favourites, lists of lands confiscated as the result of actions permitted by feudal law (*escaetae* or
escheats), or of political events like the confiscation of the lands of
Normans who after 1204 had remained faithful to the king of France
(*terrae Normannorum*). Such lists made it possible for royal administration to ascertain the origin and importance of the lordships,
liberties, baronies, &c., constituting the fortune of a great lord like

---

[1] Differences between the two sets of rolls first make their appearance in
52 Hen. III. The P.R.O. is proceeding with a typed and indexed abstract of
the Lord Treasurer's Remembrancer's Memoranda Rolls.

[2] See Giuseppi, *Guide*, i. 72, 123.

the earl of Leicester, and consequently help us to understand the resources of which he could effectively dispose. In each county escheators (*excaetores*) were entrusted with the taking of the *Inquisitiones post mortem*, which were concerned not only with the inheritances of tenants-in-chief, great and small, after their decease, but also with questions in dispute over dower, proof of age, goods belonging to outlaws, &c. The first volume of the Calendar of Inquisitions *post mortem*, relates to Henry III's reign. This was the source used by Charles Roberts to compile his *Calendarium genealogicum*, where we can trace the destinies of the noble families more or less closely connected with Simon de Montfort's career.

III. The Vatican archives are of interest to all countries of Christendom. The bulls despatched by the Papal Chancery were transcribed in the Registers; and since an enlightened decision of Pope Leo XIII opened the Papal archives to students, this precious source of information has been methodically exploited. The French School of Archaeology at Rome has played a foremost part here in publishing the entries made in the thirteenth-century Papal registers, especially those of interest for French affairs. They directly concern the subject of our biography. Gregory IX (d. 1241) had been asked to intervene on the subject of Simon's marriage with Eleanor, Henry III's sister; after him Innocent IV (1243–54), Alexander IV (1254–61), Urban IV (1261–4), pope during the Barons' War, had many opportunities of intervention, whether in the earl's private affairs or in English politics at large. Urban's legate, Guy, who succeeded him as Clement IV, was the active instrument of the Papal diplomacy hostile to the reforming party led by Simon, which initiated the civil strife. A similar selection of these registers has been undertaken from the English point of view, but in the form of a Calendar. Volume I edited by the late W. H. Bliss is a useful complement to the volumes produced by the French scholars. The *Regesta* of Potthast are also an indispensable repertory of facts.

This archive material provides the dry bones of history: to make it live we must have recourse to the contemporaries who recounted the events they themselves witnessed. I need do no more than allude to what I have already written on the valuable correspondence of two friends of the earl, Robert Grosseteste, bishop of Lincoln, and the Franciscan Adam Marsh; and I shall deal very rapidly with the English chroniclers of the thirteenth century. In the front rank stand the chronicles composed at St. Alban's Abbey. These were, as all know, the work of the Benedictine monk Roger of Wendover

(d. 1236), later of Matthew Paris (d. 1259), and finally, of an anonymous writer, long endowed with the imaginary name of Matthew of Westminster, whose work ends in 1307. It will be scarcely necessary to mention Wendover, who died before Simon de Montfort began to play a prominent part in English life. It is otherwise with Matthew Paris, who in his *Chronica majora* sets down a great number of facts directly bearing upon Simon's personality and work. Matthew Paris, who loved to adorn a tale, was in a position to acquire a great mass of information both at his own convent, which was visited by great numbers of persons, as well as at the court, where the king himself was sometimes glad to provide the material. His word cannot, of course, be accepted literally on all occasions: Matthew had a touch of the superficial about him; he only saw the outside of persons and events, he had his prejudices and his antipathies. None the less he remains the most prolific and the most appetizing of contemporary chroniclers. Had he never written, the central part of the thirteenth century would have lacked for us much of its colour and charm.

A continuation of the *Chronica majora*, from 1259–1307, has been attributed to William Rishanger, another monk of St. Alban's, though the section 1259–72 may well be the work of another compiler. Whatever may be the truth here, the continuation served as the basis of the *Chronicon de duobus bellis apud Lewes et Evesham*, where it is evident that the pen of an anonymous writer has made such remarkable transformations in the text of the continuation, so that biography now comes to sound like hagiography. The author of the continuation is a more concise and trustworthy guide.

Of considerable value are six of the ten narratives in the form of annals edited by Luard under the general title *Annales Monastici*. These are the annals (1) of Tewkesbury (1066–1263), important only for certain events relating to the king's victorious counter-offensive in 1263; (2) of Winchester, original and wholly contemporaneous for 1267–77; (3) of Burton-on-Trent (1004–1263), which have preserved the text of the Provisions of Oxford (1258); (4) of Waverley, original for the period 1219–66; (5) of the Priory of Dunstable, compiled by the prior himself, Richard de Morins, for the years 1201–42, and then by various anonymous writers, 1242–97; (6) of Osney, copied up to 1259 by a monk of the monastery, Thomas Wykes. An original authority from 1258, Wykes becomes of considerable importance after 1263; thenceforward he is one of the most valuable contemporary chroniclers. All of them are in fact more or less favourable to Simon de Montfort and his cause; Wykes on the contrary is strongly attached to the royalist party and writes his chronicle in honour of

SEALS OF SIMON DE MONTFORT AND AMAURY VI
DE MONTFORT

Prince Edward, whose activity prepared the definitive triumph of the royal cause. True, he wrote some time after the events, since he did not take the habit at Osney till 1282; the annalist who was his predecessor stands quite near these events: but how drily he relates them! A chronicle formerly belonging to the Priory of Dover and attributed on the strength of a single manuscript to a certain Henry de Silgrave (of whom nothing else is known) contains a number of useful particulars about the Barons' War. At Battle Abbey an anonymous writer compiled a *Brutus abbreviatus, cum continuatione usque ad mortem Simonis comitis Leycestrie*, the last pages of which I published as an appendix to my thesis. It contains some details not met with elsewhere on the baronial movement in the years before Evesham.

The *Chronicle of Lanercost* is the work of two different hands, as Mr. Little has shown.[1] The author of the first was a Franciscan who lived not far from the Scotch frontier at Haddington, and it was he who composed the part between 1201–97: this was afterwards recopied, interpolated, and continued by another Franciscan, brother Richard of Durham, Canon of Lanercost. Richard of Durham has nothing to say about Simon de Montfort. His predecessor, on the other hand, pretends to have learned about the earl, especially on the subject of his marriage with Eleanor the king's sister, particulars which are not merely mistaken, but preposterous. He does not scruple to repeat what he has ascertained, he says, 'from a man who set himself to penetrate secrets of either party, husband and wife, to the effect that Pope Gregory IX granted them a dispensation to marry, although the earl, faithful servant of the Church, abstained from any knowledge of his wife for twelve years'.[2] This is a gross error, and only to be explained by the fact that the Franciscan chronicler, writing far from the court, puts the marriage in 1228, i. e. ten years too early. Information on the massacre of the royalists beaten at Lewes (1264) was given him 'by a noble who had been there'; but it is no more trustworthy than the other.[3] Another passage describing the fury with which the earl charged his enemies at Evesham,[4] merely bears witness to the desire that urged the chronicler to represent Simon less as a hero than a martyr. The

---

[1] *E. H. R.* xxxi. 269–79.

[2] *Chron. Lanercost*, ed. Stevenson, pp. 34–40: 'licet idem bonae fidei comes, ob conscientiae teneritudinem, duodecim annis ab uxoris suae amplexu abstinuerit, sicut ego ipse accepi ab homine qui utrorumque secreta rimari consuevit.'

[3] The number of corpses was so great that in the chronicler's own day there were still to be found in the marshes bodies of men 'armati, equis insidentes, oculis apertis et gladiis exortis, velut vivi essent, brachia rigida protendentes'; and the chronicler adds: 'protestante mihi uno nobili qui ibidem fuerat' (p. 74).

[4] P. 76: 'attestante mihi uno illorum qui adversus eum dimicabant.'

chronicle here is hagiography rather than history. At all events, let us carefully note the fact that the writer was a Franciscan, a member of the religious order with which Simon was on most cordial terms and which always showed him the most friendly consideration.

London played a very active part in the war between the king and the barons. It would therefore be of considerable importance to know what the people felt, how important was the democratic party that became all powerful in the City for several years, and what its projects were. Unhappily our sources of information are few, and the annalists tell us little. The Chronicle of the Mayors and Sheriffs begins as a chronological succession of these magistrates from 1188: from 1240 short notices are added to their names. Dry as they are, these notes have their value in showing the popularity the earl seems to have enjoyed among the Londoners, particularly during the mayoralty of Fitz Thomas. As for the Chronicles of London, drawn up in French (1260-1345), it is very hard to get any helpful information out of them.

Finally, we may mention, as evidence of the painful impression produced by Leicester's tragic death among a section of the people, a collection describing the numerous miracles done at his tomb. Several of them are dated, and show that thirteen years after his 'martyrdom' and in spite of royal prohibition, people were making pilgrimages to the spring which had, as was believed, broken from the ground on the place where Simon had fallen and been mutilated. This theme of the martyrdom is to be found in several Latin and French poems which I have already described.[1] The most important of such documents, one partially belonging to the literature of hagiography, is the Song of Lewes, to be read in the edition of the late Mr. Kingsford, with its abundant notes. These bear witness to popular credulity, no doubt, but the historian ought not to neglect them: besides, it sometimes happens that the credulous and ignorant take the right view, when they recognize and honour those who have laboured and succumbed in the cause of the oppressed.

One of the most useful of helps to study is the *Dictionary of National Biography*. I have used it a good deal more than my book might indicate. The earliest biography proper of earl Simon, to my knowledge, is the one given by Sambrook Nicholas Russell in his 'Memoirs of the Earls of Leicester' which figures in the voluminous *History of the County and the Town of Leicester* by John Nichols. These occupy no less than a hundred folio pages, double column and

---

[1] *Simon de Montfort* (1884), pp. xvi-xix.

very close print. It is a work by no means lacking in merit, especially
for that period; but beyond the fact that it contains many useless
digressions, there is no evidence that its author has consulted the
archives of the town, which could easily have been placed at the
disposal of Nichols or of Russell. Mr. Billson, who has given so many
circumstantial details about these compilers, has perhaps scarcely
laid sufficient stress on this lack of scientific curiosity. The biography
of Simon by Reinhold Pauli (1867) is foremost a study of his political
activity; and the work of (Sir) G. W. Prothero was written from the
same point of view (1877); but in the ten years' interval between
them had appeared the masterly work of William Stubbs on English
institutions, and Prothero, with a more adequate documentation,
had far more fully grasped and could far better convey the importance of Simon's role in constitutional history. The documents published for the first time in my thesis and the intensive research into
English archives which I sketched above have been cleverly utilized
by Mr. Bateman, the latest biographer of earl Simon (1925). Nor
must we forget the life of Eleanor of Leicester by Mrs. Alice Everett
Green: in her work she drew upon archives which enable us to add
considerably to our knowledge of the facts.

For the background of our subject some important monographs
deserve mention. Among histories of the county of Leicester, and of
the town itself, Miss Bateson's edition of the municipal archives
(referred to above) is a work of the first importance. For the earl's
government in Gascony the articles which I published on the towns
of this district, whose institutions all more or less underwent the
influence of the *Établissements de Rouen*, allowed me to add a good
deal to the contents of my thesis, and the recent works on the subject by Mr. Marsh and Miss Lodge[1] may be read with profit. On the
Barons' War Blaauw's book (1871) retains its interest, even side by
side with that of Richardson, and something is to be learned from
Sir Charles Oman's opinion about the military talents of the victor of
Lewes. On the religious movement, with which Simon sympathized
with all the ardour of his belief, the works of the late Cardinal
Gasquet and the books of Mr. Stevenson and Mr. Little contain many
noteworthy observations; and as regards Robert Grosseteste, we should
not forget the Register of his episcopal visitations edited by Canon
F. N. Davis for the Canterbury and York Society. But it is above all on
the subject of administrative organization, the interpretation and the
tendency of the reforms imposed upon the king by the Barons who
revolted in 1258-9, and the social disorganization produced by the

---

[1] See Bibliography, pp. xxxviii.

royal counter-offensives, by Leicester's momentary triumph, by the
reprisals of the royalists after Evesham, that the works of Professor
Tout, Miss Helen Cam, and Mr. Jacob have thrown the greatest
light. These scholars have opened new horizons. Lastly, the general
history of the thirteenth century has found in Sir James Ramsay a
well-informed guide, especially for matters concerning the army, war,
and finance. On institutions, though Stubbs remains master of the
field, works like those of M. Pasquet and Professor Pollard have
penetrated still farther into the early history of Parliament, with
which the earl's name remains for ever connected.

Simon de Montfort's personality may be described with some
degree of certainty, and I have made my attempt at it here. But
what of his physical appearance? We have no figure of him that is
in the least trustworthy. His effigy on the seals which have come
down to us affords no guarantee of likeness. It has been thought that
Simon is seen represented in a window in Chartres Cathedral. In the
inventory of designs executed for Roger Gaignières and preserved in
the *Cabinet des Estampes* of the Bibliothèque Nationale, the late
Henry Bouchot pointed out (t. i, p. 5) a series of windows concerned
with the family of our Simon and Simon himself. Under no. 85 is
represented Pierre de Courtenay, husband of Perronelle de Joigny,
who was connected with the Montforts; in no. 87 appears Amaury,
Simon's elder brother; no. 88, the inventory says, is our Simon, a
figure identical with that of Amaury, with this difference, that the
helm of the elder brother is closed and that of the younger open. The
Gaignières reproductions have been severely criticized by Canon Yves
Delaporte and M. Étienne Houvet, the authors of an admirable
monograph on the windows of Chartres.[1] These authors had facilities
for work which their predecessors did not possess and which will never
be repeated; for during the Great War the windows were taken down
and photographed, and it was then noticed that the helm of the
second brother was closed like the first. In reconstructing the history
of the Cathedral M. Delaporte showed that the church, which was for
the greater part destroyed by fire in 1194, was almost completely
restored in the thirty years that followed, and he drew up the list of
donors who contributed to reset the admirable series of windows.
If this is true, how could our Simon, born in 1208, have figured in this
gallery of portraits? But is it true? The persons portrayed in the
window of the Cathedral and identified by Gaignières and later by

---

[1] *Les Vitraux de la Cathédrale de Chartres. Histoire et description par Yves
Delaporte, archiviste diocésain, reproduction par E. Houvet, gardien de la
Cathédrale.* Chartres, 1926, 1 vol. of text and 3 albums of photographs.

the learned Benedictine Montfaucon,[1] are all immediate contemporaries of our Simon. Pierre de Dreux, count of Brittany, the crusader, died in 1250. John, his son and successor, was to die at Tunis in 1270. His daughter Yolanda, John's sister, wife of Hugh XI le Brun, count of la Marche and Angoulême (†1250), died in 1272. Peter de Courteney died in Egypt after the battle of Mansourah (1250); his brother Raoul served under Charles of Anjou in Italy and died as count of Chieti in 1271. It may well have been after the disastrous expedition of 1239–41 which cost Simon's eldest brother, Amaury VI, his liberty and his life, that the effigy of the younger brother was set side by side with that of the elder and so many other crusaders. This may also perhaps have been the time when the arms of Montfort were sculptured in Westminster Abbey, alongside of those of Clare, Bigod, and Warenne.[2] Canon Delaporte thinks that the figure in the window he had studied is not that of Simon, earl of Leicester, but of his father, the conqueror of the Albigensians, who, it should be noted, had personal relations with the bishop Renard de Mouçon, during whose prelacy (1182–1217) the work of restoration was mainly carried out. Conversely, no trace of any special relations between Simon or his wife Eleanor and Chartres or its bishop has been discovered.[3] Several obituary notices gathered together in the Clairembault, vol. 1188 (fols. 3 and 28) indicated at the beginning of this introduction, show that certain members of the de Montfort family were reckoned among the benefactors of the abbeys of Val near Pontoise and of Port-Royal-des-Champs;[4] none of these, however, bears any relation to Chartres and its cathedral. When Simon's widow had taken refuge in France after Evesham, she lived and died among the nuns of St. Dominic at Montargis,[5] and in her will, left the nuns of St. Antoine near Paris all that might accrue to her

[1] Bernard de Montfaucon, *Les monuments de la monarchie françoise, avec les figures de chaque règne que l'injure du temps a épargnées*, t. ii (1730), p. 168, planche II.

[2] *Royal Commission on Hist. Monuments: An Inventory of the Historical Monuments in London;* vol. i., *Westminster Abbey* (1924), p. 153 d., plate 102.

[3] Montfaucon remarks that in 1234 Amaury made a donation to the chapter of Notre-Dame: 'le titre', he says, 'est conservé dans le chartrier de cette église, scellé et contre-scellé comme il est dit ici.'

[4] A. de Dion, *Cartulaire de l'abbaye de Porrois, au diocèse de Paris, plus connue sous le nom mystique de Port-Royal* (1903). Cf. Comte d'Armancourt, *Chartres, notes héraldiques et généalogiques* (1908), p. 190.

[5] See Guillaume Morin, *Histoire du Gastinois* (1630), p. 24; Fr. Chapotin *Histoire des Dominicains de la province de France* (1898), pp. 348–62; Rohault de Fleury, *Les couvents de Saint Dominique*, t. ii (1903). Fr. Menestrier (*Le véritable art du Blason, ou L'usage des armoiries*, 1873, pp. 166–8), recalls the vow of chastity made by the countess Eleanor after the death of her first

of her dowry in Ireland and in Wales.[1] We may therefore accept the identification of a figure of Leicester in a painted window of Chartres, the view generally adopted from the time of Gaignières to the present day. But it is of small importance for our purpose. Even if this identification had the highest credentials, even if the earl's helm was open and not closed, we should not be able to discover the slightest personal characteristic. It is exactly the same with the seal that shows us a Simon de Montfort on horseback, dressed for the chase and sounding his horn, with no armour to conceal his features. At the most we can say that he had no beard. Under these conditions any and every picture of him must be purely imaginary.

husband; he then adds: 'c'est peut-être la cause pourquoy elle a voulu estre représentée vestue en religieuse sur son tombeau, tenant son coeur entre les mains, comme si elle l'offrait au Ciel. Aux costez de sa représentation sont les armoiries de ses quatre fils: les deux plus hautes sans brisure, l'un pour l'aisné de la maison [Henry] qui portoit les armes pleines; l'autre pour un d'église [Amaury] et qui par conséquent ne brisa point. Le troisième écusson est semé de croisettes pour brisure [a feature reserved for cadets] et le quatrième chargé de lambel de quatre pendants. Tous quatre sans ornements . . .' This tomb has no inscription: but apart from the armorial bearings of the house of Montfort, a certain argument that it is the tomb where Eleanor's heart is buried, there is an old inventory of the furniture of the abbey which bears the words: 'on the heart of the countess of Leicester one coverlet each day, one on festivals, one for Lent.'

[1] *Calendar of Charter Rolls*, vi (1927), 1427–1516; Eleanor's will is analysed in a letter addressed by K. Edward I to the Treasurer and Chamberlain of the Exchequer, who receive an order to pay the abbey and the nuns of St. Antoine a sum of 62*l.* 20*d.*, equivalent to 220*l.* 16*s.* of Paris money (*op. cit.*, p. 289).

On the relations of the Montfort with St. Dominic, Montargis and St. Antoine of Paris, see the *Cronica Ordinis* by Gérard de Frachet, who refers to his *Vitae fratrum ordinis praedicatorum*, ed. by Reichert. The relevant passage runs thus: 'Illo quoque tempore (after a mention of the year 1205) comes Montisfortis pugnans contra hereticos gladio materiali et beatus Dominicus gladio verbi Dei, in partibus illis, facti sunt adeo familiares quod voluit comes quod ipse beatus Dominicus benedictionem faceret in nupciis filii sui [G] . . . apud Carcassonam, et filiam quamdam suam baptizaret que usque hodie vivens, et priorissa apud Sanctum Antonium Parisius, religiosissima et magne sanctitatis habetur . . . Unde usque hodie genus illud [the family of de Montfort] dileccionem et familiaritatem habet ad ordinem, in tantum quod quedam filia comitis predicti [Simon de Montfort] scilicet domina Amicia de Joviniaco [Joigny] magni nominis et sancta mulier, voluit multociens quod filius suus unigenitus [Jean de Joigny] . . . intraret ordinem, si fratres voluissent. Et in extremis agens ipse apud Cyprum in exercitu regis Francorum habitum nostrum suscepit et factus est frater.' But the mother, unable to become a friar, was anxious to become a sister of the Dominican order, and 'fecit domum sororum de Montargis et bene dotavit . . . inter quas et ipsa sepulta requescit . . .' (*Monumenta ord. fr. Praedicatorum historica*, p. 321). This passage has been utilized in the chronicle of brother Galvagni de la Flamma (*ibid.*, t. ii, p. 1, 1897). Cf. the *Registers* of Innocent IV, 8 April 1245; Potthast, no. 16624.

BIBLIOGRAPHY

THREE categories, Works of Reference, Sources, and Secondary Works (monographs, special studies, &c.) are adopted here. Abbreviations used henceforth in the text are given in italics and within brackets. The commonest are: P.R.O., to designate the Records of the Crown preserved in the Public Record Office; R.S., the series of texts published by the above office and known under the general title of the Rolls Series; Cal. S.P. the Calendars of records published by the P.R.O.; C.S., the texts published by the Camden Society; Rec. Com., the publications of the Record Commission, 1801–36; and *E.H.R.*, English Historical Review.

I. WORKS OF REFERENCE

Dictionary of National Biography (D. N. B.), edited by Leslie Stephen and Sidney Lee. 63 volumes, 1885–1900. New edition in 24 volumes, 1908–10, with three volumes of Supplement. Additions and Corrections, with a view ultimately to a complete revision of the work, have been appearing since 1925 in the *Bulletin of the Institute of Historical Research*.

GIUSEPPI, M. S. *Guide to the Manuscripts preserved in the P. R. O.* 2 vols. 1923–4. This work resumes, corrects, and completes the three editions of the Guide edited by Scargill-Bird under a rather different title: *A guide to the principal classes of documents preserved in the P. R. O.* 1891–1908. (Giuseppi, *Guide*).

GROSS, Charles. *The Sources and Literature of English history . . . to about 1485.* 1900. 2nd edition (preferable) 1915. (Gross, *Sources*).

—— *A Bibliography of British Municipal History*, 1897.

HARDY, Thomas Duffus. *Descriptive Catalogue of materials relating to the history of Great Britain and Ireland.* 3 vols. in 4, 1862–71. Vol. iii contains the chronicles and other sources of a narrative character compiled c. 1200–1327.

WINFIELD, Percy H. *The Chief Sources of English Legal History*, 1925.

II. SOURCES

ABBADIE, François. See *Livre de Dax.*

Actes du Parlement de Paris 1254–1328. 2 vols. ed. Edgar BOUTARIC. 1863–7. Archives de l'Empire.

Annales monastici, ed. H. R. LUARD. 5 vols. 1864–9. The material used here is almost exclusively confined to:

vol. i. Annales monasterii de Theokesberia. Annales monasterii de Burton.

vol. ii. Annales monasterii de Wintonia (Winchester): Annales monasterii de Waverleia (Waverley).

vol. iii. Annales prioratus de Dunstaplia (Dunstable).

vol. iv. Annales monasterii de Oseneia (Oseney): Chronicon Thomae Wykes; Annales prioratus de Wigornia (Worcester).

Annales sex regum Angliae, 1135–1307, by Nicholas TREVET. Ed. Thomas OGG. Eng. Hist. Soc., 1845.

Archives historiques du département de la Gironde (from 1859). Deux tables générales, i. pour les tomes 1–20; ii, pour les tomes 21–39.

Archives municipales de Bayonne. *Livre des établissements,* 1892.

Archives municipales de Bordeaux. *Livre des coutumes.* Ed. Henri BARCK-HAUSEN, 1890.

BALLARD, Adolphus. *British Borough Charters.* 2 vols. 1913–23. Vol. ii by Ballard and James Tait contains the charters of 1216–1307.

BALME, Father François. *Cartulaire ou Histoire diplomatique de Saint Dominique.* 1891–9. Contains 140 charters relating to the founder of the Order of the Friars Preachers. There is a genealogical tree of the Montfort family on p. 348.

BATESON, Mary. *Records of the Borough of Leicester.* 3 vols. 1899–1905. Vol. i relates to the years 1103–1327 (Bateson, *Records*).

BERGER, Élie. See *Layettes du Trésor des chartes,* and *Registres d'Innocent IV.*

BEUGNOT, Count. See *Olim.*

BLISS. See *Calendar of Entries.*

Book of Fees. See *Liber feodorum.*

BOTFIELD, Beriah. *Manners and Household expenses of England in the XIII and XV century.* Roxburgh Club. 1841. At the beginning of this volume is to be found the *Rotulus hospitii Alienorae comitissae Leicestriae, 1265.*

BRACTON, Henry de. *De legibus et consuetudinibus Angliae libri quinque.* Ed. Sir Travers Twiss. R.S. 6 vols. 1878–83; also (up to fol. 159 b) ed. G. E. Woodbine. 1915, 1922.

—— *Notebook.* A collection of cases described in the king's courts during the reign of Henry III. Ed. F. W. MAITLAND. 3 vols. 1887.

Brutus abbreviatus. BÉMONT. *Simon de Montfort,* p. xiv.

Bullarium ordinis fratrum predicatorum. Ed. by the Rev. Frs. Thomas RIPOLL, and Antonin BRÉMOND. Vol. i. 1215–80. 1729.

BURTON. See *Annales Monastici.*

Calendar of Entries in the Papal Registers relating to Great Britain and Ireland. Papal Letters. Vol. i. Ed. W. H. BLISS. 1893 (*Papal Letters*).

—— *of the Charter Rolls.* Vols. i and ii. 1226–1300. Cal. S.P. 1903, 1906. (*C. Ch. R.*).

—— *of the Inquisitions post mortem* and other analogous documents. Cal. S.P. Vol. i (1904) relates to the reign of Henry III. (*C. Inquis.*).

Calendar of the Patent Rolls. 3 vols. (without numeration) 1232–66. Cal. S.P. 1906–10. (*C. P. R.*).

—— *of the Plea Rolls of the Exchequer of the Jews.* Ed. J. M. RIGG. 1905–10.

Calendarium Genealogicum for the reign of Henry III and Edward I. Ed. Charles ROBERTS. 2 vols. 1865.

CAM, H. M., and JACOB, E. F. Notes on an English Cluniac Chronicle. *E.H.R.* 1929, 87 f.

Cartulaire de Saint-Dominique. See BALME (Father François).

Cartulaire normand de Philippe Auguste, Louis VIII, Saint Louis et Philippe le Hardi. Ed. Léopold DELISLE. Mémoires de la société des Antiquaires de la Normandie, t. xvi.

CHAMPOLLION-FIGEAC. See *Lettres de rois et reines.*

Chartes des libertés anglaises, 1100–1305. Ed. Charles BÉMONT. 1892.

Chronicon de duobus bellis. See RISHANGER.

—— *de Lanercost,* 1201–1346. Ed. Joseph STEVENSON. Maitland and Bannatyne Clubs. 1839.

Chroniques de London, 1259–1343. Ed. G. J. AUNGIER. C.S. 1844.

Close Rolls. 6 vols. (without numeration) 1227–53. Cal. S. P. 1903–22. (*C. R.*).

Commission, Royal, on Historical Manuscripts. See Appendix II of GROSS, *Sources.*

Cronica maiorum et vicecomitum Londoniarum. See FITZ THEDMAR.

De necessariis observantiis scaccarii dialogus, commonly called Dialogus de Scaccario, by Richard, son of Nigel, treasurer of England and bishop of London. Ed. Arthur HUGHES, C. G. CRUMP, and C. JOHNSON. 1902.

Dignity of a Peer. See *Reports from the Lords' Committees.*

Documents illustrative of the social and economic history of the Danelaw. Ed. F. M. STENTON. British Academy. 1920.

DOUAIS, Abbé G. *Les frères prêcheurs en Gascogne au XIIIe et au XIVe siècle.* Archives historiques de la Gascogne. 1885.

DUNSTABLE. See *Annales monastici.*

ECCLESTON, Thomas de. *De adventu fratrum minorum in Angliam.*
    Ed. (1) by J. S. BREWER, *Monumenta Franciscana.* R.S. 1858;
    (2) by A. G. LITTLE, *Tractatus fratris Thomae, vulgo dicti de Eccleston, de adventu fratrum minorum in Angliam.* 1909.

English Coronation Records. Ed. L. G. Wickham LEGG. 1901.

Excerpta e rotulis finium, 1216–72. Ed. Charles ROBERTS. 2 vols. Rec. Com. 1835–6.

FITZ THEDMAR, Arnold. *De antiquis legibus liber.* Cronica majorum et vicecomitum Londoniarum, 1183–1274. Ed. Thomas Stapleton. C.S. 1846.

Flores Historiarum.
    (i) See WENDOVER, Roger de.
    (ii) Ed. H. R. LUARD, 3 vols., R.S. 1890. This is a continuation of the Cronica majora of Matthew Paris, wrongly attributed to 'Matthew of Westminster'.

GERARDI DE FRACHETO, O. P. *Vitae fratrum ordinis praedicatorum, 1203–54.* Edited by Fr. Bendit Marie Reichert. *Monumenta ordinis fr. praedicatorum historica.* 1897. At the end of the *Vitae* has been printed a 'Cronica ordinis' which is not, as Quetif and Échart supposed it to be, the work of Humbert de Romans. In reality, as Father Denifle proved, it is the sixth book of the *Vitae.*

HALL, Hubert. See *Red Book of the Exchequer.*

Hundred Rolls. See *Rotuli Hundredorum.*

JEAFFRESON, John Cordy. *The Corporation of Leicester.* This is an abridged inventory of the municipal archives, with a certain number of texts published *in extenso.* See *8th Report* of the Historical Manuscripts Commission.

KINGSFORD, C. L. See *Song of Lewes.*

Layettes du Trésor des Chartes, t. ii. 1223–46, publié par Alexandre TEULET (1886); t. iii. 1247–60, publié par Joseph de LABORDE (1876); t. iv, 1260–70, publié par Élie BERGER (1902); t. v (containing the Supplement to the Trésor des chartes, 632–1270), publié par H. F. DELABORDE, with a masterly introduction upon the constituents of the Trésor by the same scholar.

LEGG, L. G. Wickham. See *English Coronation Records.*

Lettres de rois, reines et autres personnages des cours de France et d'Angleterre depuis Louis VII jusqu'à Henri IV, tirées des archives de Londres par Bréquigny et publiées par CHAMPOLLION-FIGEAC, t. i. 1162–1300. Documents inédits sur l'histoire de France. 1839.

Liber Feodorum. The Book of Fees, commonly called 'Testa de Nevill', 1198–1293. Ed. Sir H. MAXWELL-LYTE. 3 vols. Cal. S.P. 1923–8. This text should be consulted in preference to that of the old edition, by Caley and Illingworth. Rec. Com. 1807.

Liber rubeus. See *Red Book of the Exchequer.*

Livre des établissements. See Archives municipales de Bayonne.

Livre noir et Établissements de Dax. Ed. by François ABBADIE. 1902.

Lords' Reports. See *Reports from the Lords' Committees.*

LUARD, H. R. See *Flores Historiarum* and MATTHEW PARIS.

MATTHEW PARIS. See PARIS.

MATTHEW OF WESTMINSTER. See *Flores Historiarum.*

Monumenta Franciscana. Ed. J. S. BREWER. R.S. 1858. Contains (i) Thomae de Eccleston, De adventu fratrum minorum in Angliam (Eccleston); (ii) Adae de Marisco Epistolae (Marsh); (iii) Registrum fratrum minorum Londoniae.

Monumenta ordinis Praedicatorum historica. Ed. B. M. REICHERT. 1897.

Munimenta Gildhallae Londoniensis. Ed. H. T. RILEY. 3 vols. in 4 parts. R.S. 1859–62. Contains (i) *Liber custumarum,* 1320; (ii) *Liber Horn.*

Olim, Registres des arrêts rendus par la cour du roi sous les règnes de Saint Louis, de Philippe-le-Hardi, de Philippe-le-Bel, de Louis-le-Hutin et de Philippe-le-Long. Publié par le Comte BEUGNOT. 3 vols. in 4. Documents inédits. 1839–48.

Papal Letters. See *Calendar of Entries.*

PARIS. *Mathaei Parisiensis monachi Sancti Albani Chronica majora.* Ed. Henry Richards Luard. 7 vols. R.S. 1872–83.

—— French translation by Huillard-Bréholles. 9 vols. 1840–1; t. vi contains a genealogical table of the Montforts.

—— *Historia Anglorum.* Ed. Sir Frederic Madden. 3 vols. R.S.

Pipe Rolls. Second series of the publications of the Pipe Roll Society. Vol. ii, *The Great Ro of the Pipe for the third and fourth years of the reign of King Richard I.* Ed. Doris M. STENTON, 1926. Vol. iii, 5 *Richard I,* Michaelmas, 1193. 1927. Vol. iv, *for the fourteenth year of the reign of king Henry III,* Michaelmas 1230. Ed. Chalfant ROBINSON. 1927. Vol. vi, 6 *Richard I,* Ed. D. M. STENTON. 1928. [Not in the series] *The Great Roll of the Pipe for the 26th year of king Henry III, 1241–2.* Ed. Henry Lewis CANNON. 1918.

Placitorum Abbreviatio, Richard I–Edward II. Rec. Com. 1811.

POSSE, Otto. *Analecta Vaticana,* Extracts from the Regesta vaticana, 1254–87, and from the Acta vaticana, 1255–1272. 1878.

POTTHAST, A. *Regesta Pontificum Romanorum.* Vol. ii. 1875.

Recognitiones feodorum in Aquitania. Recueil d'actes relatifs à l'administration des rois d'Angleterre en Guyenne au XIIIe siècle. Publié par Charles BÉMONT. Documents inédits. 1914.

Record Commission. The list of publications from the Public Records authorized by this Commission (1801–36) is in GROSS, *Sources,* no. 538.

Red Book of the Exchequer (Liber rubeus de Scaccario). Ed. Hubert HALL. 1 vol. in 3 parts. R.S. 1896.

Registres des papes, publiés par l'école française de Rome. Gregory IX, ed. by Lucien AUVRAY, 2 vols., 1227–39 (1896–1907); *Innocent IV,* by Élie BERGER, 4 vols., 1243–54, and vol. 5 consisting of indexes (1921); *Alexander IV,* t. i, by Bourel de La RONCIÈRE, 1254–6 (1907), t. ii. 1256–61, by Joseph de LOYE et Pierre de CENIVAL 1254–7; *Urban IV,* ed. L. DOREZ and Jean GUIRAUD,3 vols. 1261-4 (no index); *Clement IV*, ed. E. JORDAN, 1265-6; *Gregory X*, ed. Jean GUIRAUD and L. CADIER, 1276-7; *Jean XXI*, ed. Jean GUIRAUD; *Nicolas III*, ed. Jules GAY, 1277-5; *Martin IV*, ed. SŒHNÉE, 1281-3; *Honorius IV*, ed. Maurice PROU (complete); *Nicolas IV*, ed. Ernst LANGLOIS (completed, no index).

Reports from the Lords' Committees appointed to search all matters touching the dignity of a Peer. Parliamentary Papers. 3 vols. 1820-9.

Reports of the Deputy Keeper of the Public Records (from 1870). List in GROSS, *Sources*, pp. 672-703.

RISHANGER, William de. *Chronica*, 1259-1306. Ed. H. T. Riley. R.S. 1865. A continuation of the Chronica majora of Matthew Paris (who figures in the first editions of the chronicle).

—— *Chronica de duobus bellis apud Lewes et Evesham*, 1263-7. Ed. (1) J. O. Halliwell. C.S. 1840; (2) H. T. Riley. R.S. 1876.

Rôles gascons. 3 vols., t. i. 1242-54, publié par Francisque MICHEL, 1885. Supplément, 1254-5, publié par Charles BÉMONT. Documents inédits. 1896.

Rotuli clausarum. Rolls of letters close preserved in the P.R.O., examined by Bémont, but not yet published in the edition of the Close Rolls.

Rotuli finium. One roll of fines, 1242-3, has been published by Ch. BÉMONT. Bulletin du Comité des travaux philologiques et historiques. 1924.

Rotuli hundredorum tempore Henrici III et Edward I. 2 vols. Rec. Com. 1812-18.

Rotuli Roberti Grosseteste, episcopi Lincolniensis 1235-53. Ed. F. N. DAVIS. Canterbury and York Society. 1907-9.

Rotulorum originalium in curia scaccarii abbreviatio. Rec. Com. 1805-10.

Rotulus hospitii Alienorae, comitissae Leicestriae. See under BOTFIELD above.

Royal and other Historical Letters of the reign of Henry III. Ed. W. W. SHIRLEY. 2 vols. R.S. 1862-6 (*Royal Letters*).

RYMER, Thomas. *Foedera . . . et . . . acta publica inter reges Angliae et alios quosque reges.* 1st ed., 17 vols. 1704-17. 3rd ed. The Hague, 10 vols. 1739-45. 4th ed. Rec. Com. vols. i-iii. 1816. Vol. iv of this edition stops at 1383. The *Syllabus of Rymer's Foedera*, ed. T. D. Hardy, Rec. Com., is a useful summary.

Select Cases before the King's Council, 1243-82. Ed. I. S. LEADAM and J. F. BALDWIN. Selden Society, 1919.

Select Charters. See STUBBS.

Song of Lewes. See KINGSFORD.

SILEGRAVE, Henry, de. Chronicon. Ed. C. Hook, 1849.

STENTON, F. M. See *Documents*.

STUBBS, William. *Select Charters.* 9th ed. by H. W. C. Davis. 1913.

Testa de Nevill. See *Liber foedorum*.

Tewkesbury. See *Annales monastici*.

TREVET or TRIVET, Nicholas. See *Annales sex regum Angliae*.

Waverley, Winchester, Worcester. See *Annales monastici*.

WENDOVER, Roger de. *Flores Historiarum*-1235. Ed. (1) H. O. Coxe. Eng. Hist. Soc. 4 vols. 1841-4. (2) H. C. Hewlett. R.S. 1866-9.

WRIGHT, Thomas. *Political Songs of England from the reign of John to that of Edward II.* C.S. 1839.

WYKES. See *Annales monastici*.

III. SECONDARY WORKS

ADAMS, George Burton. *Council and Courts in Anglo-Norman England.* 1926.
—— *The origin of the English Constitution.* 1912.
ANSELME, Father. *Histoire généalogique et chronologique de la maison de France.*
   Edition of 1726–33. 9 vols. For Montfort, see t. vi.
AVEZAC MACAYA, A. d'. *Essais historiques sur le Bigorre.* 2 vols. 1823.
BALASQUE, Jules. *Études historiques sur la ville de Bayonne.* 3 vols. 1862–75.
BALDWIN, James Fosdick. *The King's Council in England during the Middle
   Ages.* 1913.
BALLARD, Adolphus. *The English Borough in the XIIIth century.* 1914.
BATEMAN, Somerset. *Simon de Montfort, his Life and Work.* 1923.
BÉMONT, Charles. *La Guyenne pendant la domination anglaise, 1152–1453:*
   Esquisse d'une bibliographie methodique. 1920.
—— Art. *Simon de Montfort in the Grande Encyclopédie.*
—— *Simon de Montfort,* 1884.
BERGER, Élie. *Histoire de Blanche de Castille, reine de France.* 1895. See
   Registres d'Innocent IV and *Layettes du trésor des chartes.*
BILLSON, Charles James. *Medieval Leicester.* 1920.
—— *Leicester Memoirs.* 1924. Contains a chapter on the early historians of the
   town and county.
BIRCH, Walter de Gray. Catalogue of Seals in the Department of MSS. in the
   British Museum, 6 vols. 1887–1900. See vol. ii (1892).
BLAAUW, William Henry. *The Barons' War, including the Battles of Lewes and
   Evesham.* 2nd ed. 1871.
BOLLAND, Willian Craddock. *The General Eyre.* 1922.
—— *A Manual of Year Book Studies.* 1925.
BOUCHOT, Henri. *Inventaire des dessins exécutés pour Gaignières et entrés au
   département des estampes à la Bibliothèque Nationale.* 1891.
BOUTARIC, Edgar. *Saint Louis et Alfonse de Poitiers.* 1870.
CAM, Helen M. *Studies in the Hundred Rolls. Some Aspects of thirteenth-century
   Administration.* Oxford Studies in Social and Legal History, vol. vi. 1921.
CARTELLIERI, Alexander. *Philipp II August, König von Frankreich.* 4 vols.
   1899–1921.
COTTON, Charles. *The Grey Friars of Canterbury.* 1924.
CREIGHTON, Mandell. *Life of Simon de Montfort, earl of Leicester.* 1876.
CURTIS, J. *A topographical history of the County of Leicester.* 1831.
DEGERT, Abbé A. *Histoire des evêques de Dax.* 1903.
DELABORDE, H. François. *Étude sur la constitution du Trésor des chartes.* 1909.
DEMAY, Germain. Inventaire des sceaux de la collection Clairembault à la
   Bibliothèque Nationale. Documents inédits, 1885–6.
DOREZ, Léon. Catalogue de la collection Dupuy (Bibl. Nationale). 2 vols.
   Table alphabétique par S. Solente 1928.
DORING, Ernst Friedrich. *Studien zur Verfassungsgeschichte Leicesters; ein
   Beitrag zur Geschichte englischer Stadtverfassung bis zur Zeit Edwards I.*
   1907.
DOÜET D'ARCQ, Louis. Collection de sceaux. Archives de l'Empire. Inventaires
   et documents. 3 vols. 1863–8.
DUGDALE, William. *Monasticon Anglicanum.* 3 vols. 1655–73. Last ed.
   6 vols. 1817–30.
—— *The Baronage of England.* 1675–6. Additions and corrections in Nichols,
   Collectanea historica et geographica. 1834–43.

EHRLICH, Ludwig. *Proceedings against the Crown, 1216–1377.* Oxford Studies in Social and Legal History, vol. vi. 1924.

EXPILLY, Abbé Jean-Joseph. *Dictionnaire géographique, historique et politique des Gaules et de la France.* 1762–70.

FELTEN, Joseph. *Robert Grosseteste, Bischof von Lincoln; ein Beitrag zur Kirchen- und Kulturgeschichte des XIII Jahrhunderts.* 1887.

GASQUET, Cardinal Aidan. *Henry III and the Church.* 1905.

GAVRILOVITCH, Michael. *Étude sur le traité de Paris de 1259.* Bibliothèque de l'École des Hautes Études, no. 125. 1899.

GIERKE, Otto. *Political Theories of the Middle Age.* Tr. F. W. MAITLAND. 1900. Tr. into French by le Comte Jean de Pange, *Les théories politiques du moyen-age.* 1914.

GIRY, Arthur. *Les Établissements de Rouen; études sur l'histoire des institutions municipales de Rouen, Falaise, Pont-Audemer, Verneuil, La Rochelle, Saintes, Oléron, Bayonne, Tours, Cognac, Niort, Saint-Jean d'Angely, Angoulême, Poitiers, etc.* 2 vols. Bibl. École des Hautes Études, no. 55.

GLASSON, Ernest. *Histoire du droit et des institutions politiques, civiles et judiciaires de l'Angleterre, comparés au droit et aux institutions de la France.* 6 vols. 1882–3. t. iii is entitled: The Great Charter, the fusion between Saxons and Normans.

GNEIST, Rudolf. *Das Englische Parlament.* 1886.

—— *Englische Verfassungsgeschichte.* 1882.

—— *Simon von Montfort, Graf von Leicester.* 1864.

GREEN, Mrs. Mary Anne Everett. *The Lives of the Princesses of England.* 6 vols. 1849–55. Vol. ii contains the life of Eleanor of Leicester (pp. 48–169).

GROSS, Charles. *The Gild Merchant.* 2 vols. 1890.

GUINODIE, Raymond. *Histoire de Libourne et des autres villes et bourgs de son arrondissement.* 3 vols. 1845.

HALL, Hubert. *Studies in English Official Historical Documents.* 1908. See also *Red Book.*

HARCOURT, L. W. Vernon. *His Grace the Steward.* 1907.

HARRIS, Edwin. *Simon de Montfort, or the third siege of Rochester Castle.* 1902.

HEMMEON, Morley de Wulf. *Burgage Tenure in Medieval England.* 1914.

HOLDSWORTH, W. S. *History of English Law.* 3rd ed. 9 vols. 1922–7.

—— *Sources and Literature of English Law.* 1925.

HUTTON, Edward. *The Franciscans in England, 1224–1238.* 1926.

—— W. H. *Simon de Montfort and his Cause. 1251–1266.* 1888.

JACOB, Ernest F. *Studies in the Period of Baronial Reform and Rebellion, 1258–1267.* Oxford Studies in Social and Legal History, vol. viii. 1925.

JAURGAIN, Jean de. *La Vasconie, étude historique et critique sur les origines du royaume de Navarre, du duché de Gascogne, des comtés de Comminges, d'Aragon, de Foix, de Bigorre, d'Ayala et de Biscaye, de la Vicomté de Béarn et des grands fiefs du duché de Gascogne.* 2 vols. 1898–1902.

JENKINS, Claude. *The Monastic Chronicler and the Early School of St. Albans.* 1922.

JESSOPP, Augustus. *The Coming of the Friars.* 1889.

JULLIAN, Camille. *Histoire de Bordeaux.* 1895.

KELLY, William. *Ancient Records of Leicester.* Leicester Literary and Philosophical Society. 1855.

KINGSFORD, Charles Lethbridge. *The Song of Lewes*. 1890.
—— *The Grey Friars of London*. British Society of Franciscan Studies, vol. vi. 1915.
LAUER, Philippe. *Bibliothèque Nationale. Catalogue des manuscrits de la collection Clairembault*. 2 vols. 1923–4.
LITTLE, Andrew G. *The Grey Friars of Oxford*. Oxford Historical Society. 1892.
—— *Roger Bacon*. Essays. 1914.
—— *Studies in English Franciscan History*. 1917.
See also *Eccleston*, Thomas de.
LODGE, Eleanor C. *Gascony under English Rule*. 1926.
LONGNON, Auguste. *La formation de l'unité française*. 1922.
McKECHNIE, William Sharp. *Magna Carta*. 2nd ed. 1914.
MADOX, Thomas. *Baronia Anglica; an history of land-honours and baronies, and of tenure in capite*, 1736.
—— *Firma burgi, or an historical Essay concerning the cities and boroughs of England*. 1726.
—— *The History and Antiquities of the Exchequer of England, 1066–1327*. 1711. 2nd ed. 2 vols. 1769.
MAITLAND, Frederick William. *Collected Papers*. Ed. H. A. L. Fisher. 3 vols. 1911. See *Bracton, Gierke, Pollock*.
MARCA, Pierre de. *Histoire de Béarn, contenant l'origine des rois de Navarre, des ducs de Gascogne, marquis de Gothie, princes de Béarn, comtes de Carcassonne, de Foix et de Bigorre*. 1640. New ed. 1894 (t. i, the only one yet issued, has not gone beyond the eleventh century).
MARSH, Frank. *English Rule in Gascony, 1199–1259*. 1912.
MAXWELL-LYTE, Sir Henry C. *Historical Notes on the use of the Great Seal of England*. 1926.
MEDLEY, Dudley Julius. *A student's manual of English Constitutional History*. 6th ed. 1925.
MITCHELL, Sydney Knox. *Studies in Taxation under John and Henry III*. 1914.
MOLINIER, Auguste. *Catalogue des actes de Simon et Amaury de Montfort* in Bibl. de l'École des Chartes, t. xxxiv. 1873.
MUGNIER, François. *Les Savoyards en Angleterre au XIIIe siècle, et Pierre d'Aigueblanche, évêque de Hereford*. 1891.
NEILSON, George. *Trial by Combat*. 1890.
NICHOLS, John. *The History and Antiquities of the Town and County of Leicester*. 8 vols. 1794–1815. The passages relating to the earls of Leicester are the work of Nicholas Russell.
NORGATE, Kate. *John Lackland*. 1902.
—— *The Minority of Henry III*. 1912.
—— Artt. 'Amaury, Eleanor, Guy, Simon, de Montfort' in *D.N.B.*
OLLARD, S. L. and CROSSE, Gordon. *A Dictionary of English Church History*. 1912.
OMAN, Sir Charles W. C. *A History of the Art of War in the Middle Ages*. 2nd ed. 2 vols. 1923.
PASQUET, D. *Essai sur les origines de la chambre des communes*. 1914. Tr. R. G. D. Laffan, *An Essay on the Origins of the House of Commons*. 1925.
PAULI, Reinhold. *Geschichte von England, 1154–1509*. 3 vols. 1853–8.
—— *Geschichte des Bischofs Robert Grosseteste und Adam Marsh; ein Beitrag zur älteren Geschichte der Universität Oxford*. 1864.

PAULI, Reinhold. *Simon von Montfort, Graf von Leicester, der Schöpfer des Hauses der Gemeinen.* 1867. Tr. Una M. Godwin. 1876.

PIKE, Luke Owen. *A Constitutional History of the House of Lords.* 1894.

PLEHN, Hans. *Der politische Charakter von Mathaeus Parisiensis; ein Beitrag zur Geschichte der Englischen Verfassung und des Ständetums im XIII Jahrhundert.* 1897.

POLLARD, A. F. *The Evolution of Parliament.* 2nd ed. 1926.

POLLOCK, Sir Frederick and MAITLAND, F. W. *The History of English Law before the time of Edward I.* 2nd ed. 2 vols. 1895.

POWICKE, F. M. *The Loss of Normandy, 1189–1204.* 1913.

—— *Stephen Langton,* 1928.

PROTHERO, Sir G. W. *The Life of Simon de Montfort, earl of Leicester, with special reference to the Parliamentary History of his times.* 1877.

RAMSAY OF BAMFF, Sir J. H. *The Angevin Empire, 1154–1216.* 1903. *The Dawn of the Constitution,* 1216–1307. 1908. *A History of the Revenues of the Kings of England.* 2 vols. 1925.

RHEIN, André. *La seigneurie de Montfort-en-Iveline, depuis son origine jusqu'à son union au duché de Bretagne au XIVe siècle.* 1910. Contains the acts of the lords of Montfort.

RICHARDSON, Oliver H. *The National Movement in the reign of Henry III and its culmination in the Barons' War.* 1897.

STEPHENS, W. R. W. *The English Church, 1066–1272.* 1901. Vol. ii of *The History of the English Church,* ed. W. R. W. Stephens and W. Hunt, 9 vols. 1899–1910.

STEVENSON, Francis Seymour. *Robert Grosseteste, bishop of Lincoln.* 1899.

STUBBS, William. *The Constitutional History of England.* 3 vols. 1875–8. Vol. ii, 4th ed. 1906. French tr. by G. Lefebre, 3 vols., 1907–27, with supplementary studies by Charles Petit-Dutaillis. This translation with its essays and detailed index should be carefully studied.

—— *Registrum Sacrum Anglicanum.* 2nd ed. 1897.

SUSSMANN, Stanislaus. *Das Budget-Privileg des Hauses der Gemeinen.* 1909.

TOUT, T. F. *Chapters in the Administrative History of Medieval England: the Wardrobe, the Chamber and the Small Seals.* 4 vols. 1920–28.

—— *Wales and the March during the Barons' War.* Owens College Historical Essays. 1907.

VAISSETE, Dom J. *Histoire générale du Languedoc.* 5 vols. 1730–45. Ed. Dulaurier, 15 vols. 1872–92. Tt. vi–viii in this edition relate to the years 1165–1271.

VEILLET, Chanoine René. *Recherches sur la ville et sur l'église de Bayonne.* Ed. by the Abbés V. Dubarat et J. B. Daranatz. t. i. 1910. Contains the history of the bishops of Labourd and Bayonne.

WALLACE, Wilfred. *Life of St. Edmund of Canterbury, from original sources.* 1893.

WURSTEMBERGER, L. *Peter der Zweite, Graf von Savoyen.* 4 vols. 1856.

I

BIRTH AND ANCESTRY. SUCCESSION TO
AMAURY DE MONTFORT'S ENGLISH LANDS

S IMON III of Montfort, the famous leader of the Albigensian
Crusade, had four sons and three daughters. With the latter
we are not concerned. The sons were Amaury, count of Montfort and marshal of France; Guy, later count of Bigorre;
Simon, the subject of our biography; and Robert, who has left
no trace upon history except his name.[1] The date of the third
son's (our Simon's) birth is uncertain. In a charter of February
1199 (old style?) the father merely mentions his sons Amaury
and Guy, and the name occurs in another charter of 1207;[2]

[1] The pedigree of the Montforts has not been traced definitively. See Fr.
Anselme, *Histoire généalogique*, t. vi; *l'Art de vérifier les dates*, t. ii (ed. 1783),
pp. 6 and 671; a note of Huillard-Bréholles to his translation of the Chronicle
of Matthew Paris, t. vi, p. 576 (following Fr. Anselme), as well as André Rhein,
La Seigneurie de Montfort en Iveline, pp. 59–63. Among other points, there is
some divergence of opinion on the order in which the numerous Simons and
Amaurys succeed each other. Without dealing with the problem of their
origin, I need go no further back than Amaury III, lord of Montfort and count
of Évreux, who married Agnès de Garlande about 1120. Then follow Amaury
IV, who died childless in 1140, and his younger brother, heir to his fiefs,
Simon II (III), who died in 1180. This Simon married the elder sister of the
last of the Beaumont earls of Leicester, Robert IV (d. 1204), of whom more
later on. Her name was Amicia; she had three sons by her husband: Amaury
V (who had no issue), Guy and Simon III (or IV?), the father of our Simon.
On Amicia, see *E. H. R.*, xxii, 1917, p. 248.
[2] *Cartulaire des Vaux-de-Cernay*, t. i, p. 71. It ends thus: 'Ego autem, Simon
de Monteforti, . . . dona omnia que dederunt antecessores mei concessi et
confirmavi, concedentibus et laudantibus uxore mea Eva et filiis meis Amaurico
et Guidone, et fratre meo Guidone.' Cf. Auguste Molinier, *Catalogue des actes
de Simon et d'Amauri de Montfort*, no. 28[a]. The name Eva is doubtless a
copyist's error, for everywhere else she is called Alix; thus, in the same cartulary, p. 188, we read in a charter of 1213: 'Simon, comes Leycestrie . . . concedentibus A., comitissa, uxore mea, et filiis nostris A. et G. . . .' (note that
here too Amaury and Guy alone are named); in 1217, in a charter of the Abbey
of Val-près-Pontoise (copy in Clairembault 1188, fol. 27), occurs the phrase:
'Ego Adeliga (*sic*), comitissa Tolosana et domina Montisfortis . . . assensu
ipsius domini mei et mariti et liberorum nostrorum Amaurici, Guidonis, Simonis
et Roberti. . . .' So too in a charter of 1218: 'Ego Matheus de Montemoren-
ciaco, . . . domina Aalidis, soror mea . . .' and (vol. cit. fol. 3), 'Amauricus de
Monteforti . . . et Guido, Bigorre comes' approve a donation made to the
Abbey of Val by their mother Alix: 'concesserunt etiam fratres nostri Simon
et Robertus.' This charter is dated June 1218. Simon III was killed on 25 June
that year in front of Toulouse.

3463   B

this suggests that Simon was not yet born. Now the chronicler Pierre de Vaux-de-Cernay, so well informed about the crusading hero's family, says in 1209 that God had blessed the countess by giving her 'filios multos et pulcros',[1] which leads us to suppose that she had more than two. We may thus agree to put the date of Simon's birth in 1208.[2]

We know nothing of Simon's early years and training. He seems to have had a thorough education, and perhaps even understood Latin,[3] for we shall find him later on corresponding acceptably with scholars and learned men. His parents we know better: his mother, a vigorous and active woman, took a most energetic share in the Albigensian war; his father, Innocent III's lieutenant in southern France, an ambitious and fanatical general, won imperishable renown. In his childhood, Simon must have received a lively impression of the tragic events in which his parents played the leading part, and he inherited their crude virtues. He was as ambitious, as talented as his father: but he never fought for a cause that was to end in the ruin of a brilliant civilization; in him Englishmen still venerate, and rightly venerate, one of the founders of their political freedom.

When Innocent's lieutenant died before Toulouse, his entire inheritance passed to his eldest son, Amaury de Montfort. The dead leader's titles had included the earldom of Leicester and the stewardship of England. These he held from his mother

---

[1] *Histor. de France*, t. xix, p. 23. Is the epithet 'pulcros' justified? In the chronicle of John of Oxenedes (R.S., p. 144) there is an epitaph in English upon Simon, the famous victim of the siege of Toulouse, translated thus:

Dantur item facto, casuque cadunt iterato,
Simone sublato, Marsque, Parisque, Cato.

On which the chronicler comments: 'Alter Mars fuit, quia bellicosus, alter Paris, quia formosus, alter Cato, quia bonis moribus adornatus.' If the father was as beautiful as Paris, the children may have inherited that quality. The chronicler of Lanercost says of our Simon: 'erat miles strenuus, in corpore procerus et facie formosus' (p. 39).

[2] The date accepted by Miss Norgate in *D. N. B.*

[3] This seems to be borne out by Adam Marsh's correspondence. Prothero notes (p. 39) that Amaury, Simon's elder brother, was taught by Master Nicholas, one of the best mathematicians of his time, as Roger Bacon observed. Cf. Little, *Roger Bacon*, p. 159. On his arrival in England, says the Lanercost chronicler, Simon could not speak English (p. 77): 'cum in Angliam anglicanae linguae inscius prima pube venisset.' Did he learn it later?

Amicia, the elder sister and heiress of Robert, fourth earl of Leicester after the conquest, who died childless in 1204; but he never made use of them. His English property had been confiscated, just in the same way as Philip Augustus had confiscated the property of the Norman lords who had established themselves in England and remained faithful to King John.[1] From 1207 to 1215 the 'honour' of Leicester, or at any rate the half which came to Simon de Montfort,[2] was administered to the profit of the royal treasury by several agents who had no scruple in committing large depredations. In 1215 it was assigned to Ranulf, earl of Chester, nephew of Simon III.[3] Ranulf, who had rallied to John Lackland's cause, received it in full ownership, with all its dependent rights and emoluments. These measures of reprisal have some light thrown upon them by a remarkable passage in the Dunstable Annals. In 1210 King John was returning from his Irish expedition undertaken with the object of bringing to reason the English vassals discontented with his arbitrary policy.[4] At this moment, says the chronicler, the Welsh united to invade the March, then occupied in military force by the English. 'Upon this news the king marched with his army to Nottingham; there he learned that his barons were conspiring against him, and that they had elected Simon de Montfort king.'[5] This unique piece of information has little to substantiate it, but it is at least worth remembering as testimony to the fame won by the earl's

[1] *Rot. litt. claus.*, ed. Hardy, i. 77, 93, 99, 106.

[2] Robert IV left his property to his two sisters: Amicia, wife of Simon de Montfort, and Margaret, wife of Saer de Quincy, earl of Winchester (Ramsay, *Dawn*, p. 471); the important Norman possessions of the deceased could not be divided equally between two heiresses holding from different and mutually hostile suzerains, and so were sequestrated, the count of Montfort having to compensate his brother-in-law with forty librates of land taken from within the English fiefs. The performance of this succession settlement was to be long delayed.

[3] Beyond the sons mentioned above, Simon II had a daughter, Bertrada, who married Hugh, earl of Chester (d. 1180): their son was Ranulf. Ranulf married Constance of Brittany, widow of Geoffrey, Henry II's second son, and, in right of his wife, took the title of count or duke of Brittany. In 1215 he did faithful service to John Lackland, who rewarded him by giving him custody of the county of Leicester; J. H. Round, *D. N. B.*, *s.v.* Blundevill, Ranulf de. Cf. Harcourt, *His Grace the Steward*, c. iii.

[4] K. Norgate, *John Lackland*, pp. 152, 252.

[5] *Ann. Dunstable*, p. 33.

victories over Raymond VI of Toulouse; Simon, as a matter of fact, would have found it impossible to gratify the English wishes, since his presence was urgently needed in Languedoc. Amaury made several protests, 'in all humility',[1] he says, against the sequestration of his property, always proclaiming himself to be the vassal, the 'knight' of Henry III. Then, doubtless understanding that his title of constable of France ruled out any pretension on his part to occupy concurrently a similar rank at the court of a hostile monarch,[2] he came to terms with his younger brother. Here is Simon's version[3] of the facts:

'My brother Amaury released to me our brother's whole inheritance in England, provided that I could secure it; in return I released to him what I had in France. I went over to England and asked the lord king to restore to me my father's inheritance. He answered me that he could not do it, because he had given it to the earl of Chester and his heirs. Whereupon I left without having found grace at his hands. The following year[4] [1230] my lord the king crossed to Brittany with the earl of Chester, who possessed my inheritance; I went and found the earl at the castle of St. James of Beuvron.[5] He received my request in friendly fashion and, in the

---

[1] *Layettes*, no. 2088: Request of Amaury to the king, February 1231: 'Vestre regie majestati multociens supplicavi humiliter et devote quod mihi terram meam et jus meum . . . mihi, militi vestro, redderetis. . . .'

[2] Harcourt, *His Grace the Steward*, p. 77, convinced himself that Amaury had 'the wild idea' of holding both titles.

[3] Bémont, *Simon de Montfort*, p. 333.

[4] Simon's journey must therefore be placed in 1229. If he was born in 1208, he had just attained his majority. Harcourt wrongly thinks that Simon left France to escape the anger of the Queen-regent, Blanche of Castille; but Guillaume de Nangis (*Histor. de France*, t. xx, p. 58) and Nicholas Trevet (*Annales sex regum Angliae*, p. 226), his authorities, put this detail in the year 1239. We shall discuss the true date later on; but here we may take the opportunity of correcting another mistake, this time Wendover's, who says that Simon claimed the county of Toulouse at the council of Bourges in 1226. The chronicle of Tours, edited by Ph. Labbe (*Sacrosancta concilia*, t. xi, Ière partie, p. 291) rightly puts the name of Amaury in place of that of his brother. Prothero had already pointed out this confusion; p. 40, n. 1.

[5] In 1230 Wendover, after mentioning an agreement between the Pope and the Emperor in August, adds: 'eodem tempore, comes Cestrensis Ranulphus munivit castellum apud S. Johannem de Beverona, quod ad jus uxoris suae comitissae jure hereditario pertinebat, militibus, alimentis et armis. Reddiderat enim illi castrum illud comes Britanniae Henricus (*sic*) quando, confederatus regi Anglorum, omnia jura sua in regno Angliae, rege concedente, recepit' (vol. iii, p. 6). The count of Brittany of whom Wendover is speaking

following August [1231], took me to England with him. He asked the king to receive my homage because, said he, I had more right than he to my father's inheritance; he then renounced everything that the king had given him, and so the king of England received my homage.'

Is this statement of a date thirty years later (1261) complete and accurate? We know that Simon had made no secret of his intentions from the beginning of 1230, at the very moment when the English king, in alliance with the count of Brittany, was planning an expedition to France. Henry III was at Reading on Easter Day (7 April), and on the morrow he informed Simon by letter that he had received one of the earl's knights, Amaury de Maintenon, bearing overtures expressive of his desire 'to enter the king's service both in England and abroad'; he therefore granted him an annual revenue of four hundred marks out of the receipts of the exchequer 'until he had recovered the earldom of Leicester, in accordance with the agreements made between them when Simon came to find him in England'.[1] If we may judge thirteenth-century people according to modern ideas, our verdict would be that it was not a fortunately chosen moment for a Frenchman to transfer his homage to a king about to invade France;[2] but the feudal mind did not boggle at these transactions; the knight's home-country was determined by his oath of fealty. At any rate, the change had begun. The king was agreeable, and it now remained to settle with Earl Ranulf and to give Count Amaury de Montfort his lawful compensation. Ranulf's reception of Simon has just been described:[3] Amaury, for his part, wrote to the

here was Pierre de Dreux, whose alliance John Lackland bought in 1215 (Norgate, *John Lackland*, p. 241).

[1] *Royal Letters*, i. 362. Cf. *C.R. 1227–1231*, 316.

[2] Élie Berger, *Histoire de Blanche de Castille*, p. 200, and 'Les préparatifs d'une invasion anglaise et la descente de Henry III en Bretagne, 1229–1230,' in *Bibl. de l'École des Chartes*, 1893, pp. 1, 34. Henry embarked at Portsmouth on 30 April (Wendover, ii. 383).

[3] Harcourt supposes (p. 83) that later on Ranulf somewhat regretted his generosity, as Saer de Quincy had done on a similar occasion under John Lackland. His death supervened (28 October 1232) to set aside any possible difficulties on this score. With Amaury there were long negotiations. Simon seems to have surrendered to his brother his French properties 'sicut ea tenebat' and had obliged himself to pay him fifteen hundred pounds in Paris money the following year: 'Nos vero conventiones istas juravimus super

English king (August 1231) saying that he was granting his brother 'all his land and all his right'. Amaury further promised to make no claims upon Simon, when he had been put in possession, 'if the king receives him for his man, on this present occasion when Simon goes to him'.[1] Everything in fact had been so well arranged ahead that on 13 August Henry III declared that he had 'taken homage' from Simon, and instructed his officials to put him in immediate possession of his inheritance and the Honour of Leicester.[2] The relief was paid,[3] and Simon, invested with his fiefs and doubtless with his dignities,[4] found himself henceforth attached to the service of

sacrosancta evangelia inviolabiliter observare, salvis tamen quibusdam convencionibus quas prius [Simon] habebat nobiscum' (*Layettes*, no. 2366, letter of Amaury from St. Léger-en-Iveline). Before the end of the year 1235, Amaury requested and obtained (4 October) a safe-conduct to go on pilgrimage to the tomb of Thomas Becket; *C. P. R. 1235–1247*, 119. Was not this journey dictated by another aim, the definite settlement of the business? Amaury made a solemn renunciation at Westminster before the papal legate on 11 April 1239 (*Layettes*, no. 2739), and died two years afterwards. Thus at least on two occasions death worked to Simon's advantage.

　[1] *Layettes*, no. 2151: 'vos rogantes quatinus de omni jure nostro quod habemus et habere debemus in Anglia seisietis eundem et cum de ipsa seisitus fuerit, nos absolvimus vos super hoc et quietamus . . . , si ipsum de jure nostro in hominem receperitis hac vice qua ad vos proficiscitur in presenti.'

　[2] *Royal Letters*, i. 401; *C. R. 1227–1231*, 543 (13 August): 'Rex cepit homagium Simonis de Monteforti de tota terra quam S. de M., pater ejus, quondam comes Leicestrie, de rege tenuit de honore Leicestrie.' Cf. *ibid.*, p. 560 (22 September).

　[3] *Excerpta e rotulis finium*, p. 27: 'Memorandum de relevio Simonis de M., cujus homagium rex cepit de honore Leicestrie, sicut plenius in rotulo clausarum.' The Annals of Dunstable noted the fact under 1231: 'Eodem anno, comes de Muntford recuperavit seisinam de Leicestria et de medietate comitatus sui' (p. 128).

　[4] Nichols, Miss Bateson, and Harcourt all tried to determine the exact moment when Simon officially assumed his English title or titles. The quest is unprofitable, for one prospective fact is plain: at the beginning of August 1231 Simon received investiture of his fiefs and his rights. Nichols says that Simon did not take the title of earl till after the death of Ranulf of Chester (25 October 1232). This is uncertain in view of the fact that in June 1232, four months before Ranulf's death, Amaury in confirming the cession to his brother of his English estates gives him the title of earl of Leicester. He makes it clear, when he says: 'Quicquid ad . . . patrem nostrum accidere potuit de hereditate Amicie, heredis et sororis comitis Roberti Leicestrie primogenite, *cum senescalcia Anglie tocius*' (*Layettes*, no. 2190). But during same month (15 June) letters patent of Henry III in Simon's favour thus address this address only: 'dilecto et fideli nostro Simoni de Monteforti;' *Royal Letters*, i. 497; *C. P. R. 1225–1232*, 481. In a charter dated at St. Léger-en-Iveline (April 1235) Amaury still gives his brother the title of earl, which was quite natural in the case of a deed drawn

the English king. It had taken two whole years to reach this final result.

It seems that until now everything had gone very smoothly between the king and the head of the family of Montfort. The light-hearted, extravagant monarch of twenty-four enjoyed his power, and had made up his mind to exercise it in complete independence, with the approval of the officials devoted to his person. A contemporary chronicler has drawn Henry, and the picture must have been taken from the life. 'The king', he says, 'was of middling height. He had a narrow forehead: one of his eyelids was half-closed and almost hid the dark of the pupil. Strong in physique, he was impulsive in action.'[1] If only we had as vivid a portrait of Simon! It would be pleasant to know whether feelings of friendship had helped to bring together these two young men of practically the same age and possibly similar tastes. The information given by the chroniclers is wholly impersonal. They agree in telling us that Henry III liked to surround himself with aliens. The English barons, jealous to defend their privileges recently confirmed by the Great Charter, were hostile to arbitrary government; they aspired to wield a preponderating influence in the counsels of the Crown. Henry III on the other hand thought that people from without, established at court and enriched by him, would not be venal in their loyalty; but his choices, inspired by the influence of women, were not happy. His mother Isabella of Angoulême had married, as her second husband, Hugh X le Brun, count of la Marche,[2] and it was she who encouraged the

up in the chancery of a French lord (*Layettes*, no. 2366). Harcourt (*ibid.*, p. 81) declares that this charter is an 'impudent' method of transferring the possession of a title: that may be true in regard to English law, but Amaury was not bound to take cognizance of it or to know if the office of steward was or was not transmissible to the heir. In a charter drawn up in the English Chancery, is the *Inspeximus* on 1 August 1237 (*C. Ch. R.*, i. 230) of a charter whereby Simon de Montfort, earl of Leicester, and steward of England, grants his friend John of Ferentino, papal chamberlain, for his good services, forty marks of rent in the vill of Chauton (co. Bedford).

[1] Rishanger, *Chronica*, p. 75.

[2] Hugh X married Isabella, widow of John Lackland, in 1220. She gave John two sons: Henry (who was Henry III) and Richard, earl of Cornwall, and two daughters: Isabella, who married the emperor Frederick II, and Eleanor, who was the wife of Simon de Montfort. The countess-queen brought her second husband nine children: prominent among them in England were

'Poitevins' to seek their fortunes in England. Later Henry III's wife, Eleanor of Provence, brought in the 'Provençals'. Doubtless Simon profited from the king's predilection for 'alienigenae'. He too was an alien,[1] but he was scarcely a *parvenu*; for he had legal right to the handsome inheritance which he had just recovered, and even to the dignity which brought him straight into the foremost rank of the English baronage. If his arrival at first provoked their jealousy and distrust, the place he was destined to occupy among them could scarcely be regarded as a usurpation.

William de Valence, the ancestor of the earls of Pembroke of the second line, and Aymar, bishop-elect of Winchester. Cf. Delisle, *Bibl. de l'École des Chartes*, 4ᵉ série, t. ii, p. 541; and *Bulletin de la Société archéologique de la Charente* (1886). Valence is a hamlet in the commune of Couhé (Vienne, arr. Civray). In 1226 the count of la Marche founded a Cistercian abbey there, of which interesting remains survive.

[1] In the chronicle of Melrose there is a wise observation on Simon's peculiar position: 'alienigenarum inimicus et expulsor, quamvis ipse natione unus esset ex illis.' This passage is cited and commented on by Kingsford, *Song of Lewes*, p. 79.

II

POSITION AND PERSONALITY

BEFORE we study Simon de Montfort's military and political exploits, we ought to understand what was involved in the titles of earl of Leicester and steward of England, how the possessions, revenues, and privileges which he enjoyed were derived, and to form some idea of the influence exerted by his family and his friends upon his mind and his career.

The earldom. Since the conquest the earl had lost most of the effective authority exercised by the Danish jarl and the Anglo-Saxon earl. When the county court met to transact judicial and administrative business, in theory the earl took the first place there alongside of the bishop, but in practice the county was governed by the sheriff (*vicecomes*), who held his dignity from the king alone. The earl retained scarcely any other material advantage except the third penny, i.e. a third of the profits of justice. The title of earl was none the less a desirable and coveted one, partly because of its ancient glories, partly because it was only borne by very few, ten great feudatories at the most, and because the holder was almost necessarily a member of the King's Council. In addition, it was normally accompanied by numerous privileges.[1]

In the ninth century the Danes had organized a kind of confederation, the 'Five Boroughs' including, exclusive of Leicester, the towns of Lincoln, Nottingham, Stamford, and Derby. The impress of Scandinavia was long felt there.[2]

The office of steward. The position of the earls exercising the stewardship after 1066 was at first somewhat uncertain. The first three[3] did not take the title of *comes*, but on the

---

[1] Did the earl of Leicester regularly receive the product of the third penny? No doubt on the point is possible in view of *Pipe Roll, 34 Hen. II* (1187–88), which shows the sheriff rendering account of 4 l. 'de tercio denario comitatus Legrecr.'quas comes Legercestr. renuit accipere' (p. 119). A similar passage occurs in *Pipe Roll, 2 Richard I*, p. 44.

[2] Stenton, *Documents*, p. xix.

[3] The list of earls after the conquest runs thus: 1. Hugh de Grandmesnil, who

C

other hand they performed in the Royal Household the function described in normal twelfth-century Latin by the word *dapifer*, and in Henry III's time by the expression *senescallus*. As the word indicates, the *dapifer's* duty was to hand the king, at ceremonial feasts, meats and drinks and even napkins. This office, well known in France at the courts of Charlemagne and the Capetians, and of the dukes of Normandy also, was equally in existence under the Anglo-Saxon kings. Under Edward the Confessor there were as many as three *dapiferi* in his service simultaneously. William .I organized his household on the Capetian and English models combined: he too had three *dapiferi*, two for himself and one for the queen. When their names occur among the attestations to royal charters, they are generally placed in a subordinate position. This inferior situation, originally lacking in prestige but not in profit (since it brought its holders into frequent contact with the king), lasted without notable change as far as the end of Henry I's reign. The *Constitutio domus regis* composed a little before Henry

had at least 5 sons and 5 daughters (*D. N. B.*, *s.v.* Hugh [de Grantmesnil]). 2. Ivo, third son of Hugh, who died in 1102 after returning from pilgrimage in the Holy Land; his inheritance then passed to Roger de Beaumont [-le-Roger]. 3. Robert de Beaumont, son of Roger and of Adelina de Meulan; as count of Meulan he fought at Senlac, was later in favour with William II and Henry I, and received the earl's third penny of Leicester without however bearing the title; he died on 5 June 1118 (*D. N. B.*, *s.v.* Beaumont). He had married Isabel or Elisabeth de Vermandois, who gave him five daughters and three sons, two of whom were twins. 4. Robert II the Hunchback, born after 1104; married Amicia, granddaughter of William FitzOsbern, died 1168. His widow took the veil at the abbey of Nuneaton, her own foundation. 5. Their son, Robert III White-hands, married Perronelle (Eng. Parnel), the heiress of Grantmesnil. He started on Crusade and died in Greece (1190). He had three sons and two daughters: Amicia, who married Simon III de Montfort, and Margaret, wife of the earl of Winchester, Saer de Quincy (a bull of Innocent IV, 1 December 1247 mentions a Robert 'de Kenci', cousin of Simon de Montfort: *Papal Letters*, i. 239). 6. Robert IV FitzPerronelle (Eng. FitzParnel), who married Loretta or Laurencia, daughter of William de Briouze. Taken prisoner at Rouen by Philip Augustus in 1193, he was set at liberty in 1196 and died childless in 1204 (20 October, according to the *Chronicon coenobii Lyrensis* in *Histor. de France*, t. xviii, p. 352). His widow, a recluse at Hackington near Canterbury was still thought to be alive in 1265. Cf. Little, *Thomas de Eccleston*, p. 26, and Charles Cotton, *The Grey Friars at Canterbury*, p. 9. After him the earldom passed to his brother-in-law Simon III (*D. N. B.*, *s.v.* Beaumont; cf. Bateson, *Records*, i. xiv, and Harcourt, *His Grace the Steward*, pp. 72–5).

died [1] attests the fact. Certain of these *dapiferi*, however, succeeded through their personal merit or by the royal favour in winning a public position: William FitzOsbern of Normandy became in 1067 earl of Hereford; [2] and at the same period Hugh de Grandmesnil is both *dapifer* and *vicecomes* (later we shall call him earl) of Leicester.[3] To be *dapifer* tended to increase the influence of officials holding that office; then, as happened so often in the Middle Ages, the fact created the legal right and the function became hereditary. The so-called 'anarchy' of Stephen's reign without any doubt assisted this slow elevation of the office. We can witness the Empress Matilda in process of disputing the crown with her cousin the king, confer upon Humphrey de Bohun (1144) 'dapiferatum suum in Anglia et Normannia' on the same conditions as in the time of Henry I,[4] and later her son Henry, while only duke of Normandy, restore (1153) [5] the dapiferate to Robert II the Hunchback. Immediately upon his accession Henry II nominated Hugh Bigod earl of Norfolk; it was his intention that Hugh and his heirs should hold the office of *dapifer* on the same conditions as under his grandfather Henry I. The office had therefore at least two functionaries at the same time, the earl of Leicester and the earl of Norfolk, as in the times of the Confessor and the Conqueror. It had as many as three when Henry II held his court at Guildford in 1186. On that occasion the earls of Leicester, Arundel, and Norfolk 'served the king at table for the

[1] Tout, *Chapters*, i. 13. The *Constitutio* is printed in the *Red Book of the Exchequer*, pp. 807–13.

[2] Harcourt, pp. 14, 30. Ordericus Vitalis gives him these titles: Herfordensis comes et regis vicarius, Normannie dapifer et magister militum bellicosus.

[3] *Ibid.*, p. 5, and Bateson, p. xiii.

[4] Harcourt, p. 57.

[5] Harcourt has published two versions of this charter. The first (p. 58) addressed 'Roberto comiti Leycestrie et heredibus suis' restores and grants him 'totam terram quam tenuit Robertus, comes de Mellent, pater suus, in Anglia'; the second (p. 59) from File J 219 of the Trésor des chartes, addressed 'Rodberto, filio comitis Legrecestrie et heredibus suis', grants him 'totam terram Rodberti comitis, patris sui, de Anglia, sicut Rodbertus de Mellent, avus suus, eam melius et liberius tenuit'. In the former case it is certainly a question of Robert II the Hunchback, son of the count of Meulan; but the later relates to Robert White-hands, grandson of Robert de Beaumont. How could the duke of Normandy have given the son all the possessions of his father while still alive? Harcourt mildly calls this (p. 37) 'a source of quite unnecessary perplexity to genealogists'.

service that pertained to them at coronations and solemn feasts'.[1] Thus the dapiferate had been divided, but was become hereditary, a fact that made it still more desirable, though it changed the primitive character of the institution. No surprise will be felt when we see the Montforts and the Bigods struggling to possess it. This is what happened at the coronation of John Lackland. The details of the controversy we do not know, but it appears that Roger Bigod gave up his claims on condition of receiving in exchange ten knights fees promised by Robert of Leicester.[2] This was because in their eyes the office of *dapifer*, or steward as we may now call it,[3] served as the stepping-stone to the highest ambitions.

In the twelfth century, when the king was absent from his kingdom, when, for example, he went to war in France, he entrusted the care of government to regents normally called *justiciarii*. Thus at the beginning of his reign Henry II gave the justiciarship to Robert II the Hunchback,[4] and during the time when he employed him thus, the office was shared by him with Richard de Lucy.[5] Was this, as Harcourt imagines, in imitation of the Norman practice, by which several great feudatories bear the title of 'dapifer et justitia totius Normannie'?[6] Are we to consider, as he does, that the treatise of Hugh de Clère on the claims of the counts of Anjou to the title

[1] Benedict of Peterborough (R.S.), ii. 3, cited by Harcourt, p. 42.

[2] Harcourt, p. 73. At the same period we find Saer de Quincy, brother-in-law of Robert IV, with the title of 'senescallus domini regis' (Bateson, p. 18) which corresponds exactly with that found in a charter of Henry III 'de senescalcia hospitii regis' (1 May 1221, Harcourt, p. 77 n.). This is an allusion to a domestic *dapifer*, not to the great public official.

[3] Harcourt says on p. 72, 'On the coming of Richard I the expression *dapifer*, which served to designate the Steward of the King's household, began to be replaced by that of "Steward". A last act of tacit assumption added later the ambitious definition "Steward" of England' (Tout, *Chapters*, i. 90 and 170, n. 2). Besides, 'Senescallus Anglie' could mean seneschal *of* England quite as much as seneschal *in* England, just as the 'senescallus Normannie' was the seneschal of the king in Normandy.

[4] Harcourt, p. 48, 'Roberto, comite Leycestrie, justiciario meo' (Charter dated between 1155 and 1162); 'tunc temporis capitali justicia mea tocius Anglie' (*ibid.*, p. 44, n. 3).

[5] Harcourt warmly eulogizes these two associates. The *Dialogus de Scaccario* speaks of Robert as 'virum discretum, litteris eruditum et in negociis forinsecis exercitatum' (pp. 103, 198).

[6] Harcourt, p. 46.

of Grand Steward of France [1] exercised more or less direct influence on those of the high dignitaries of the English Crown? The parallel is ingenious, if a trifle arbitrary. We may venture another suggestion. On several occasions Simon de Montfort complained that the privileges of steward with which he had been invested had been cut down—but in what respect? If we may trust a document nearly fifty years later than Simon's death, the office of steward must have been an extremely important one.[2] It must have consisted in supervising and governing, immediately under the king, the English kingdom and all ministers whose duty it was to administer the laws, both in peace as in war; if there were evil counsellors round the king and the king accepted evil counsel, the steward had to confer with the constable, the nobles and the commons of the realm with the object of inviting these evil counsellors to leave the king. 'If the king refuses to get rid of them himself, it is permitted to the Steward and the Constable of England, the nobles and commons of the realm, to unfurl the royal banner in the name of king and kingdom, to put the recalcitrant counsellor in prison until a new Parliament, to seize his goods, revenues, and all his other possessions, until he had been brought to judgement before Parliament. This is what happened in the time of Edward the Confessor to Godwin, earl of Kent, who was deprived of his earldom and exiled on account of his perverse conduct and evil counsel. The same happened to Hubert de Burgh, earl of Kent, who for similar motives was arrested by the Steward and other barons, and then deprived of his earldom by the decision of the whole Parliament. So also it was done in

---

[1] Harcourt, p. 68. Professor Tout (*Chapters*, i. 202, n. 4) observes that in letters close (1221) the Chancery still uses the restricted expression 'senescalcia hospicii domini regis'. It is in Amaury's charter that the term 'senescallus Anglie' appears for the first time, but from the pen of a French scribe. The tradition, or, if it is preferred, the assumption, took official form in several charters granted by Simon to Leicester after 1254. It is only when he was master of the king and country after Lewes that the title appears in all its emphasis in the charters emanating from the royal Chancery.

[2] Reprinted by Harcourt, pp. 164–7. At his coronation Edward II ordered researches to be made into Exchequer archives in order to find out 'que et cujusmodi feoda quondam comites Leycestrie, temporibus quibus ipsi comites senescalli progenitorum regis quondam regum Anglie de feodo extiterint, ratione senescalcie illius percipere consueverunt, et que et cujusmodi feoda ad eandem senescalciam pertinuerunt temporibus supradictis. . . .' *Ibid.*, p. 142.

the case of Piers Gaveston, who was banished from the king's lands, both at home and abroad; and when Gaveston dared, even after his second sentence, to return to England, he was seized by the Steward, the Constable and the other barons of England, treated as a public enemy of king and realm and beheaded.' [1]

Now of course we must be careful not to suppose that the rights exercised by the steward of England under Edward II were regulated with such precision and emphasis under Henry III, or that Simon de Montfort could claim the same power as Thomas of Lancaster; [2] but it is difficult to believe that such an assertion of the rights of the stewardship made by Thomas of Lancaster, himself one of the 'martyrs' of English liberty, was a work of pure imagination, or that Simon de Montfort at the time of his greatest power, tried to secure the establishment of his rights simply in order to satisfy his vanity and not to strengthen his political position. Doubtless these rights were obscure, since both Henry III and the earl of Leicester were reduced to appealing to the memory of a recluse in order to ascertain what they were.[3] But does this not prove that they had existed? The document analysed above summarizes them under two heads: the steward must (*a*) see that justice is properly administered; (*b*) supervise the king's counsellors and get rid of them, even by force, if they fail to do their duty. Surely this is exactly the part played by the earl of Leicester during what it may be permitted to call his protectorate. If on several

---

[1] It is not a question here of the further similar example of the Despensers. Probably therefore the document we are analysing was drawn up between 1311 and 1322.

[2] Thomas, earl of Lancaster and Leicester, steward of England, was the son of Edmund Crouchback, son of Henry III, who after Evesham secured the titles and dignities of Simon de Montfort.

[3] Letter of Henry III to Lauretta, recluse of Hackington, 29 April 1265: 'quia vos nostis pre ceteris, ut dicitur, que jura et libertates pertinent ad senescalciam Anglie racione comitatus et honoris Leycestrie, nos, volentes super hiis per vos plenius certiorari, vos attente requirimus et rogamus quatinus in presentia dilectorum nobis in Christo abbatis Sancti Augustini Cantuariensis et prioris ecclesie Christi ejusdem ville dicta jura et libertates exponatis. . . .' (*Close*, 49 Hen. III, m.6.d.). It has been supposed that this Lauretta may have been the wife of Robert IV of Leicester (cf. Harcourt, p. 125), and thus in a position to be well informed. Her age (she was a widow in 1204) must in 1265 have been over eighty, but this is not an obstacle.

occasions he complained of encroachments on the rights of his office, if three months before his death at Evesham, he once more insisted on knowing 'what privileges belong to the office of steward of England by reason of the earldom and honour of Leicester', was it not because he considered this office to be the legitimate foundation of the authority he claimed to exercise in the State? True, research has gone further than this and it has been supposed that after the victory of Lewes Simon took among other things this title of *justiciarius Anglie*; but this is a mistake into which Reinhold Pauli [1] and Sir James Ramsay [2] were led by a faulty transcript of an act printed in Rymer.[3] Mr. Harcourt proved this conclusively. In official deeds Simon never took any other official title than that of *senescallus Anglie*,[4] which was quite enough for his ambition.

The town, borough, and guild of Leicester. The map at the end of Miss Bateson's introduction to the Leicester archives shows clearly the difference that existed between the town and the borough. The town was enclosed within a rectangular enceinte, one side of which was formed and protected by the course of the Soar,[5] a fair-sized river, slow, shallow and much choked with

[1] *Geschichte von England*, iii. 270.　　　[2] Ramsay, *Dawn*, p. 235.

[3] In *Foedera* (edd. 1739 and 1816) under 17 January 1265, there is a patent delivered 'per regem, Simonem de Monteforti comitem Leicestrie, justiciarium, et Rogerum de Sancto Iohanne', which is exactly reproduced in the analysis given in *C. P. R. 1258–1266*, 400; but the fact is that the scribe omitted to give the name of the justiciar, who was Hugh le Despenser. Hugh was summoned to the 'great parliament' of January 1265 thus: 'Hugo le Despenc. justic. Anglie' (*Lords Reports*, iii. 34, quoted *D. N. B.*, *s.v.* Despenser, Hugh le. Cf. Harcourt, pp. 123–6, and App. IV). One must however notice the comments in modification of this suggested by Tout, *Chapters in Med. Admin. History*, i. 296 and 307–9.

[4] Harcourt, p. 123, rightly insists on the importance which this title had in Simon's eyes. After the earl's death, the stewardship underwent a transformation: it resumed its primitive household characteristics; and the fact that it was hereafter conferred on a prince of the blood made it all the more illustrious. Harcourt printed (pp. 192, 201) the texts showing its transmission first to the Leicester earls, then to the Lancastrian.

[5] Latin, Sora. The following passage, i. 361, in the Borough Records edited by Miss Bateson, though it relates to 1298, gives useful details on the topography: On 16 November, at midnight Geoffrey Curlevache 'surrexit amens et demens et ebrius et ambulavit ad Soram extra portam borealem in vico fullonum'. The Fullers' road is called Walker Lane in the fourteenth century, and Soar Lane from the fifteenth. See Billson, *Mediaeval Leicester*, p. 17 and the plan facing p. 16.

rushes. The plan of the place resembled a Roman camp; [1] two principal roads intersected at right angles, forming the boundary of each quarter, [2] divisions which, for several centuries, enjoyed a sort of administrative independence. It was at their intersection that the Town Hall was built. At their extremities were four gates, N. E. S. and W.; the western outlet commanded the passage of the Soar; the principal street led to the northern and southern gates. [3] In the south-western angle, a small rise, perhaps an artificial 'motte', bounded by the natural moat that was the river, formed a bastion clearly indicated as the site of a strong castle and the lord's dwelling-place, quite near the parish church of St. Mary of the Castle. The quarters contained besides several parishes and other churches, a hospital of St. John of Jerusalem, [4] and later on friaries founded by the Franciscans and the Dominicans. Leicester having been till 1094 the seat of a bishopric (moved that year to Lincoln) it naturally possessed during a certain period, and retained, the title of 'civitas'.

Outside the walls was the *banlieue*, which extended to the limit of three 'hundreds', administrative divisions from which the town of Leicester was completely excluded. This *banlieue* comprised a great forest touching the northern wall, arable lands and pastures. The forest and the river as well, which worked the mills, [5] supplied the inhabitants, subject to the earl's consent, with everything needful for their sustenance and the building and warming of their houses. The arable lands were divided into three 'fields', [6] in which unenclosed strips, divided among heads of families, were cultivated in common according to the well known three-field system, and were subject to manorial custom.

[1] On Roman Leicester see *V. C. H. Leicestershire*, vol. i.

[2] Billson, p. 12. In one of the charters printed by Mr. Stenton (*Documents*, no. 347) mention is made of a 'mansura' situated 'in magno vico' and of another 'extra portam de West'. 'Magnus Vicus' is to-day High Street.

[3] See the diagrams in Billson, pp. 1, 16, and 18. The parish of St. Leonard was founded by a brother of Robert IV, called William, who was a monk of Évreux (Round, *D. N. B., s.v.* Beaumont).

[4] Bateson, p. 9.

[5] *Ibid.*, p. 8.

[6] The description of these open fields is given by Bateson, p. xi. On p. 47 we find the mention of a place situated 'in campo australi'.

The town and the *banlieue* constituted the borough. This is not the place to enter into the origin of English boroughs or their peculiar characteristics. Ballard's collection of documents and Professor Tait's introduction (to vol. ii) have thrown much light upon matters that were for long time controversial.[1] The example of Leicester might serve to demonstrate that the borough was not necessarily a fortified town, since the walls never enclosed anything but the city itself; it is further known that many boroughs were simply rural agglomerations, without any means of defence. The borough was up to a certain point an artificial creation, endowed with very varying privileges by the lords who possessed the land, the king or his vassals. More than a hundred and eighty boroughs are mentioned in Ballard's work, and of these about half owed their privileges to lords who were not necessarily important personages.[2] The borough of Leicester, which was in existence long before the Conquest, belonged to the earl who held from the king, but ruled there, if one may use the term, without the king's agents, sheriffs, or other officials having the right to intervene in his relations with his own subjects.[3] It was a mediatized fief. Still, the earl was not the sole possessor of the lands, houses and burgesses (for the burgesses could equally well belong to the temporary holder of the fief). According to Domesday Book 'the king had 39 houses in Leicester, perhaps built and maintained by him, perhaps those of burgesses who commended themselves to him for his protection. Hugh of Grantmesnil had 17 houses attached to three of his manors; two distant abbeys had 13 houses, and the archbishop of York, two, with "sac and soc", belong to a manor of his. Several lesser lords owned a few houses, and rights of jurisdiction over them lay in their neighbouring manors. Two lords had one burgess.'[4] Finally the bishop of Lincoln had his 'fee' which substantially corresponded with what was

---

[1] In addition to *British Borough Charters*, cf. the summary of the same writer, *The English Borough in the Twelfth Century* (1913), which has a useful bibliography, and Professor Tait's *The Study of Early Municipal History in England* (British Academy Publications, 1921).

[2] J. Tait, Introduction to *British Borough Charters* (ii), p. cxxv.

[3] Bateson, p. xii. 'The Leicester of Domesday book stood, as a free borough should, on no man's land and in no Hundred.'

[4] *Ibid.*, p. xiii.

later the parish of St. Margaret outside the Walls.[1] In 1101
Leicester was still under four masters: the bishop, Earl Simon
de Senlis, the widow of the Anglo-Saxon earl Waltheof, and
Ivo the son and heir, as we have seen above, of Hugh of Grantmesnil. Ivo, a traitor to his king, pillaged and destroyed part
of the town; when condemned to pay a heavy penalty, he put
himself under the protection of one of Henry I's principal
counsellors, Robert de Beaumont, who succeeded him. Robert
managed to get his authority universally recognized, except
over the 'bishop's fee', and it was this lordship finally en-
franchised that he transmitted to his descendants, henceforth
admitted without challenge to be the earls of Leicester.

Robert I built up the ruins of the town or city. He granted
the chapter of Austin Canons of St. Mary of the Castle, his own
foundation, all the churches in the place, save that of St.
Margaret which was a prebend of Lincoln.[2] Robert II built outside the northern gate the Abbey of St. Mary in the Meadows to
which he transferred the chapter and the prebends of the Castle
Church (1144).[3] An educated man greatly appreciated by
Henry II 'whose interests he protected as much as his person',[4]
Robert II played a considerable part until his death. His son
Robert III (White-hands) nearly gave the position away by
taking arms with the king's enemies. His revolt brought a new
disaster upon the town: 'on the fifth of the nones of July [3 July
1173] it was besieged by order of Henry II. When it had been
nearly burned, the burgesses sued for peace; they offered to
purchase for 300 marks the privilege of withdrawing whereso-
ever they would. This condition having been accepted, they
were dispersed throughout the royal towns and castles. After
their departure the gates were battered down and the walls
partly destroyed. The defenders of the castle obtained a truce

---

[1] Bateson, p. xviii.

[2] In the list of the churches in the county drawn up by Sister Elspeth in
V. C. H. Leicester, i. 357, Robert Grosseteste, future bishop of Lincoln, is
mentioned as an archdeacon and prebendary (1225–31).

[3] Dugdale, *Monasticon*, vi. 466. The Rev. H. E. Salter (*Chapters of the
Augustinian Canons*, pp. 1–2) has printed a bull of Innocent III (29 February
1216) ordering the holding, at the Octave of All Saints 'apud monasterium
S. Marie de Pratis Leicestrense', of the chapter due under the recent decree of
the Lateran Council to be held every three years.

[4] *Dialogus de Scaccario*, p. 103.

and the siege was thus ended on the fifth of the kalends of August' [28 July].[1] It had lasted more than three weeks, a proof that the place was not valueless from a military point of view.[2] The earl made his peace four years later; [3] the town extricated itself from the difficulty as best it might.

With Robert IV surnamed Filius Petronille (in English Fitzparnel) [4] the line of the Beaumonts came to an end, and his inheritance, as we said above, devolved in part upon his elder sister Amicia, the mother of our Simon. At this period begins the series of acts preserved in the town archives, especially the rolls of the guild merchant which throw such curious light upon the social and economic position of the bourgeoisie of the town. This period too saw the reign of 'the great charter-monger', as John Lackland has been termed.[5] John freely gave away municipal 'liberties' for pecuniary reasons, and his example was followed by many a lord of mediatized towns.[6]

As long as Leicester was in the possession of several lords, it seems that the burgesses remained in the state of the semi-serfdom evidenced in Domesday Book and persisting in many

[1] Wendover, i. 94.

[2] Of Leicester Castle to-day we can see nothing more than the shapeless remnants; a narrow, low door and a few remains of the ramparts are all that survive of the exterior defences. A bowling green marks the place of the dungeon. Visitors are shown a vast underground cellar which was used to store the provisions of the garrison. The great hall, now occupied by administrative offices, alone survives.

[3] At the assembly of Northampton (11 January 1177) Henry II restored to him 'totam Leicestriam et forestam que jurate erant per commune sacramentum comitatus esse debere de dominico suo' (Benedict of Peterborough, i. 134). See the charter of donation made by the Countess Petronilla (*Rep. on the MSS. of the late Reginald Rawdon Hastings, Hist. MSS. Com., 1928*, pp. 36–7.

[4] Because his father had, as we remarked above, married Petronilla (Perronelle), heiress of the Grantmesnils.

[5] Bateson, p. xv: 'King John, the great charter-monger.' Henry III was also a great 'charter-monger' like his father, and for the same reason: during the first ten years of his reign, as long as he was under tutelage, the Chancery issued no borough charters; as soon as he came of age, 'the flood-gates opened again'. We have twenty-five borough charters for 1227, and then the supply is checked till 1255–7, the period of financial distress, when fifty charters were granted. Ballard and Tait, *British Borough Charters*, ii. xviii.

[6] We may note incidentally that this ability to purchase step by step such privileges as they coveted helps, to explain why the communal movement in England was generally a peaceful one. Violent revolts similar to those related by Augustin Thierry as taking place in the more disturbed France of the early Capetians were rare in the Anglo-Norman State.

manors until the end of the twelfth century. At the beginning
of this period they were still bound to harvest for the earl; they
had to pay if they pastured their cows in the specially reserved
meadow (the 'defensa'), if they brought their corn to other mills
than his.[1]   Robert II remitted these duties and obligations.[2]
After this they were allowed to go freely and without charge
along the roads that traversed his fields, to pass through his
forest in order to transport building materials gathered from
neighbouring woods.[3] They bought the pasturage of Cowhay
situate outside the southern gate, together with the right to
pass through the lands of the earl's demesne.[4] To 'his burgesses
of Leicester and to all those who wished to live in common with
them', Robert granted the privilege, so often mentioned in
municipal charters, that their suits might be pleaded within,
instead of without, the town, and in the 'church-yard'.[5] Finally
they obtained the right to 'hold their merchant guild' under the
most advantageous conditions,[6] and were enabled to secure

[1] Bateson, p. 8. Along with the mills should be mentioned the seignorial
bakehouse (*ibid.*, pp. 8, 10, 40). With regard to specially reserved or 'defended' lands, Simon gave the church of St. Mary in the Meadows and its
canons 320 acres of land and the reserved portion (defensa) of his forest. The
limits are given at length in the deed. This part is to be held by the canons in
frankalmoign, that is to say it was to be subject to no feudal dues. They could
enclose it, could cultivate it or exploit it as they liked; but if the earl's deer
entered this enclosure, the earl, members of his family or his bailiffs could enter
by the common gate and secure the said deer without committing any depreda-
tion. Among the witnesses to this deed are mentioned Stephen de Segrave,
Thomas de 'Meynill', steward of the earl, Ernald du Bois and Ralph Basset
(a person often met with in his service), William the falconer, and Reginald who
was then keeper of the forest. The act was confirmed by the king on 6 November 1252. Cf. *C. Ch. R.*, i. 408.
[2] Bateson, pp. 3, 4. To Miss Bateson's documents should be added the
numerous particulars furnished by the archives of the seignorial family of
Hastings preserved at Ashby La Zouche, a manor situate in the county of
Leicester (cf. Report, *sup. cit.*, 1928).
[3] Bateson, p. 3.
[4] *Ibid.*, p. 4: 'in pastura que dicitur Kowheye, jacente in campo australi
Leycestrie'; cf. p. 38.
[5] *Ibid.*, p. 4: 'quod neque per placitum neque per aliquam consuetudinem
eant extra Leycestriam, set tantummodo ad coumecherchiam, sicut antiquitus
constitutum fuit.' In an early English translation of this text Miss Bateson
found the gloss 'Portemanmote' relating to the unintelligible 'Coumecherchiam'; consequently she proposed to correct the Latin word into 'touncher-
chiam' or 'communecherchiam', which she translates by 'church yard'.
[6] *Ibid.*

legal validity in the assembly of burgesses (Portmanmoot) for all purchases and sales regularly carried out.[1]

An inquest of 1253 explains somewhat fancifully the establishment in earl Robert of Meulan's days of the tax known as 'gavel-pence' and the 'bridge-toll'.[2] Two burgesses, cousins, were disputing possession of certain lands; they were compelled to have recourse to the judicial battle which was, we know, a method of procedure imported from Normandy. One of the combatants, forced by his opponent on to the bank of a ditch which he did not see, was on the point of falling in when the other warned him of the danger. The information was doubtless given out of charity, but it was certainly illegal, and gave rise to such an uproar that the earl heard the noise from the castle. When he heard the details of the business, he decided to abolish —in return for a money payment—a procedure that was doubtless repugnant to older inhabitants attached to the pre-conquestual methods of proof. He agreed with them that they should pay three pence a year for every house with a gable (*gablus*) in the main street; in return they secured that their pleas should be tried in the town by the 'twenty-four jurats who had been long established at Leicester', that is, by the *Portmanmoot* mentioned above, whose composition is now for the first time defined.[3]

Such in brief was the condition of the 'free burgesses' of Leicester at the moment when the town passed under the suzerainty of Simon de Montfort. Shortly after the solemn renunciation made by his brother Amaury (11 April 1239), he confirmed (3 May) the cession of the pasture at Cowhay in return for an annual rent of three shillings a head on cattle and a colt of a hundred shillings' value once for all.[4] Two undated

---

[1] Bateson, p. 7.　　　　　　　　　　[2] *Ibid.*, pp. 40–3.

[3] *Ibid.*, pp. 40–2. Cf. Neilson, *Trial by Combat*, p. 66, and Holdsworth, *Hist. Eng. Law*, i. 308 f. The Portmanmoot or Portmote was in origin no more than a seignorial tribunal sitting at the manor, the judicial and financial centre of the lordship: Ballard and Tait, ii. xxix.

[4] Bateson, p. 38: 'pro hac autem remissione, relaxacione et quieta clamatione, dederunt mihi predicti burgenses mei unum pullum precii centum solidorum pre manibus.' Miss Bateson translated the word 'pullum' correctly by 'colt' or 'foal', meaning the young of an animal. Here it is clearly a case of a valuable beast, a thoroughbred. The translation 'chicken' which I gave in my thesis (*Simon de Montfort*, p. 58) is out of the question.

charters supplement these grants: by the first, Simon remits to 'his men' of Leicester all the moneys paid annually for the earl's harvest, as well as for the admission of their beasts into the 'defensa' of Leicester, 'and for carts carrying the corn of townsmen to other mills than the earl's';[1] in return the burgesses were to pay him fifteen marks silver. The second acquits these burgesses of 'all dues exacted at the bridge or bridges of the town (Briggesiluir) and of all imposts upon houses within the town (Govelpennii) on condition of their paying an annual rent of 56s. 8d.[2]

Like many English towns, Leicester had retained a very ancient custom, probably Celtic in origin, by which the father's inheritance passed not to the first-born, but to the last of his sons, the one who for reasons of age was supposed to stand most in need of assistance. This custom, termed inappropriately enough *Borough English*, ran contrary to feudal notions[3] that favoured the eldest born, as the one able most speedily to defend the hereditary fief; in the thirteenth century it was doubtless still considered as a mark of servile tenure,[4] a survival of the time when the English had been brought under serfdom. It disappeared from Leicester under the government of Simon de Montfort. On the 22 October 1255, in the presence of the earl of Winchester (Roger de Quincy), Ralph and William Basset, Richard de Havering and Thomas of Eastley, knights, of three burgesses and several clerks assembled at Westminster, the earl 'yielding to the requests and applications of the burgesses, for the common profit of the town which was daily declining because heirs were of too tender an age to recover their heritages',[5] granted that in the future 'all the first-born sons, the

---

[1] Bateson, p. 39: 'de carectis et vecturis portantibus bladum hominum de Leycestria ad alia molendina quam ad molendina mea de Leycestria, salva tamen michi et heredibus meis multura, dum tamen ad molendina mea de Leycestria invenire possunt (*sic*) multuram sine impedimento et dilacione.'

[2] *Ibid.*, p. 46 (*c.* 1254): 'et pro hac remissione et quieta clamacione, maior et burgenses nostri de communitate Leycestrie dederunt quinquaginta sex solidos et octo denarios . . . percipiendos in villa nostra et in campis Leycestrie.'

[3] Ballard and Tait, ii. lxxix, and 93–4.

[4] Maitland's opinion (*Hist. Eng. Law*, i. 279), referred to by Miss Bateson, p. xvi, n. 8.

[5] In the deed of 1255 (Bateson, p. 49) we read: 'propter defectum heredum et debilitatem eorum'; in the royal confirmation (*ibid.*, p. 51), 'per defectum

issue of lawful marriage in the town and its suburb, should be held for lawful heirs on the death of their fathers, and should freely enter into possession of their paternal inheritances and dwellings'.

It has been rightly observed [1] that, generally speaking, municipal autonomy was much less favoured in mediatized than in royal boroughs. Was this the case with Leicester? Miss Bateson, the author of remarkable works on urban history,[2] reveals to us how the municipality of the town was slowly organized, and the part which Simon de Montfort took in the process. We have already seen the existence of the *Portmanmoot*, the tribunal in which the lord gave his orders and administered his justice; in the time of Robert I this court was transformed into an assembly of burgesses which, later still, we see composed of twenty-four 'jurats'. Side by side with this functioned the merchant guild. The earliest acts of the guild which have come down to us are dated 1196;[3] they are now well known to us through Miss Bateson's fine work. In its own sphere, every guild enjoyed a practically complete autonomy, and it must not therefore be expected to discover instances of the earl's interference very easily in Leicester;[4] but the close relation that existed in the thirteenth century between the guild and the

---

heredum et teneram etatem eorundem.' Miss Bateson translated correctly: 'on account of the feebleness and youthfulness of the heirs,' and, 'through the weakness of heirs and their tender age.'

[1] Ballard and Tait, ii. lxxxi.

[2] Notably on the Norman customs of Breteuil and English borrowings from them: *E. H. R.*, xv, xvi, and xvii. Cf. however M. de W. Hemmeon, *Burgage Tenure in Medieval England*, (Harvard, 1921) pp. 166–72 for a criticism.

[3] The guild was in existence in the time of Robert White-hands, since he confirms a donation made to the nuns of Easton granting them two 'mansuras' at Leicester, 'salvo omni servitio meo et omnibus consuetudinibus meis ad gildam mercatoriam pertinentibus' (Stenton, *Documents*, no. 347; cf. no. 392). The earliest roll begins with these words dated 9 October, 1196: 'Item isti,' showing clearly that it is a continuation, not a beginning. The date is given by the context: 'Item isti intraverunt in Gildam Merchatoriam die festi beati Dionysii primo post aduentum comitis in Angliam post deliberacionem suam de capcione sua in Francia.' We said above that Robert IV, taken prisoner in 1193, did not recover his liberty till three years afterwards.

[4] Note however the Letters Patent by which Henry III (30 May 1257) 'at the request of the earl exempts his burgesses of Leicester, for seven years, from all exactions made to their detriment on their cloths at fairs and markets in his kingdom' (*C. P. R. 1247–1258*, 357).

town administration demands that we should scrutinize the position carefully.

Conditions of entry into the guild were not severe. The newcomer, if he did not succeed his father, had to furnish two sureties and pay an entrance fee, not to speak of certain extraordinary contributions which are not clearly specified. On these conditions the candidate was henceforth 'quietus de ansis et omnibus rebus'; but he had to swear loyally to observe the rules of the guild, to obey the mayor's orders, to inform the mayor and the 'good men of the commune' if he knew of any merchant not affiliated to the guild, so that he could be made to enter it. The guild had its bell and its records,[1] which gave it a duly authorized personality.

A number of very significant texts enable us to follow, throughout our Simon's life, the parallel development of *portmanmoot* and guild, and the late fusion of two municipal offices —that of the alderman, whose name proclaims its English ancestry, and that of the mayor, a French importation. In 1209 occurs the first mention of an 'alderman of the Guild', called William de Liverie, termed simply 'alderman' in 1214. About 1225 Simon Curlevache and John Warin are jointly 'aldermen'. The following year this Simon alone is named, but with the title 'alderman of Leicester', and from henceforth he fulfils the duties of the office conjointly with William de St. Lô (1234–42). Lastly, William of St. Lô and Peter, son of Roger, are termed mayors, and Peter is sole mayor from 1251 to 1256. In August 1257 the mayoralty was confiscated and entrusted to a 'keeper' who put in an 'attorney'. The latter, accompanied by a burgess, went in search of the earl to ask him to choose a mayor; which actually took place, for on 23 January 1258 Henry de Ruddington received the mayoralty from the hands of the earl. He is called 'alderman' in a slightly earlier list of councillors of the guild, and this Henry was in office on and off till 1270. From the list which Miss Bateson drew up,[2] the interesting fact seems to

---

[1] 'Notandum quod campana empta fuit in Morwenspeche vigilia Sancti Marci evangeliste pro vj d. de Ricardo Coco, ad communam Gilde, et tradita fuit in manum Ade de Wintonia anno quo Damiata ciuitas capta fuit a christianis' (Bateson, p. 33). Damietta was taken by assault on 6 November 1219.

[2] Pp. xliii. 1–4, 12–25. P. 41, 'per xxiiii jurati qui erant in Leicestria antiquo tempore statuti'; p. 50: 'ad instantiam communitatis burgensium de

emerge that the alderman and the mayor were really the same municipal magistrate under different nomenclatures. It is tempting to make a similar approximation between the acts of the guild and those of the Portmanmoot, which do not begin till 1260,[1] but which unquestionably cannot emanate from the manorial court, the earl's tribunal. The two assemblies were probably composed of the same persons, that is, all the burgesses and, by preference, those who were engaged in commerce.

All these details are valuable, but we should like to be able to discuss the personal influence exerted by the earl and his officials in his relations with the clergy on his demesne or with his vassals, his burgesses and his agricultural tenants. We know very little about it. In ecclesiastical matters only one reference occurs to the right possessed by the earl to authorize an abbatial election.[2]

The earl's officials are sometimes enumerated in his charters, as for example when he addresses 'his sheriff and all his ministers and agents at Leicester, French and English',[3] or 'the stewards, bailiffs and foresters of the forest of Leicester';[4] but

Leicestria'; p. 51 'concessi Petro filio Rogeri, majori Leicestrie, et burgensibus commune Leycestrie . . .' &c. Miss Bateson rightly says, p. xlvi: 'the evidence points to the fact that the 24 Jurats of Portmanmoot and Gild were identical'. The list of mayors is given on p. 401. The mayor was nominated on 29 September each year, but he was re-eligible indefinitely.

[1] Bateson, p. 116.

[2] Notley Abbey, co. Bucks., a house of Austin or 'Black' Canons, noted in a list printed by the Rev. H. E. Salter, *Chapters of the Augustinian Canons*, p. 277. Cf. *Rotuli Roberti Grosseteste*, p. 381: 'Frater Johannes de Grendon [Long Crendon], canonicus de Nutlei, petita prius licencia eligendi a domino Symone de Monteforti et optenta, per priorem et conventum suum electus est.'

[3] Bateson, p. 4: 'Vicecomiti suo et omnibus justiciariis et ministris suis de Leycestria, Francigenis et Anglis.'

[4] *Ibid.*, p. 6: 'senescallis suis et omnibus ballivis et omnibus forestariis de foresta Leycestrie.' In a charter dated between 1251 and 1255 (p. 52) the name of Richard Havering occurs at the head of a list of witnesses, 'tunc senescallo Leicestrie,' and he occurs in letter 143 of Adam Marsh. In 1257 Paris relates (v. 634, 677) a plea 'coram rege et magnatibus' about an 'invasion' carried out by William de Valence, the king's half-brother, into the lands of the earl, which was repulsed by his steward. On the subject of the steward, who stood first and foremost in the earl's court, Miss Bateson gave numerous details (p. xxxviii f.) of a date subsequent to the earl's death. His bailiffs of the manor and hundred of Odiham secured (14 January 1251) the right to the liberty enjoyed by the burgesses of Leicester, 'de returno brevium regis', the right to receive royal commands and return them directly to the king without the intermedium of the sheriffs (*C. P. R. 1247–1258*, 400). On 30 January 1250,

we know little of their conduct as administrators. Doubtless matters did not always go smoothly; for the frequent and lengthy absences of the earl must have told in favour of abuses of power by these officials;[1] only very scanty traces of such conduct are found in the archives, and the chronicles are practically silent about them. Matthew Paris, however, noted the severity met with by one of the burgesses, Simon Curlevache. It was in 1239, at the time when Simon was getting ready to go on crusade and sold the abbey of St. Mary in the Meadow his 'noble forest' of Leicester.[2] Curlevache was a leading citizen, whose name we have noticed above. The earl, says the chronicler, 'extorted' from him a considerable sum of money for those days, 500 marks.[3] The incident seems to have aroused criticism, as may at least be inferred from a letter written by Robert Grosseteste to the earl, which probably concerns Curlevache: 'We have learned that you are thinking of punishing S., your burgess, with a severity disproportionate to his offence. Let not your severity be turned against him, or your justice be unappeased, but let pity mercifully exalt your judgment, so as to give an example of kindness instead of cruelty.'[4]

No less pointed are certain remarks of Adam Marsh, though addressed not to the earl, but to his lieutenant: 'It is not without good reason', he wrote to Simon in Gascony (April 1250) 'that I counsel and conjure you immediately to write to Richard de Havering and forbid him to allow your officials (*ministeriales*), the guardians of your property in England, to destroy souls for whom the Author of Life laid down His own.'[5] But at another moment Adam is acting as the accredited inter-

letters close commanded the sheriff of Surrey to take an inquest in order to find out who had seized the earl's carts which had fallen into the water near Dorking, and to have their contents restored to his bailiffs, *C. R. 1247–1251*, 261. The bailiffs of the earl should be distinguished from those of the town: the provost was a municipal officer.

[1] Bateson, p. xxxix.

[2] *Chron. maj.*, iv. 7.

[3] See this name in Bateson's index, vol. i.

[4] *Letters of Robert Grosseteste*, p. 141. The initial S. may well denote Simon Curlevache.

[5] Adam Marsh, Letter CXLIII, p. 276. Richard de Havering is mentioned as steward of the earl of Leicester in a Letter Close of 27 December 1249 (*C. R. 1247–1251*, 248). Cf. *Royal Letters*, ii. 56, where he is called Ralph, clearly by an error; *Rôles gascons*, t. i, Suppl., cxix.

mediary between the earl and the bishop of Lincoln, to whom he commends the cause of Simon de Montfort. 'I appeal to your good will, my brother, when I ask that in the very tiresome affair which will bring before you the bailiffs and men of the earl of Leicester you use moderations and kindliness, so as to assist our excellent and worthy earl without damaging the rights of ecclesiastical dignity'[1] (May 1252). At the same period in another matter of litigation 'touching the men of Leicester' Simon expressed the desire that, instead of its being entrusted to the arbitration of three persons, the archdeacon of Oxford, John de Crakhale and Robert de Wynkele, it might be settled by the bishop of Lincoln personally.[2] In these various exchanges we can detect a certain degree of hostility on the part of the moralist bishop of Lincoln, a latent note of censure for the harsh and uncompromising conduct of his friend Leicester.

On one point however the bishop and Simon de Montfort seem to have been perfectly in accord: in 1231 Robert Grosseteste advised the countess of Winchester, Margaret de Quincy, not to receive the Jews 'whom the lord of Leicester had driven out from his town, to prevent them crushing its Christian inhabitants under the weight of usury'.[3] At the same time, we should observe, he recommended a course of moderation towards these Jews. Later, in a charter granted to the burgesses of Leicester (1253), Simon stipulated 'that at no time during his life or the lives of his heirs, and to the end of the world', might any Jew or Jewess dwell or find means to dwell within the boundaries of the liberty of Leicester.[4] Would the bishop of Lincoln have blamed the earl, had he seen him ten years later [5]

---

[1] Adam Marsh, Letter XVIII, p. 103.

[2] Letter XXV, p. 110.

[3] *Letters of Robert Grosseteste*, p. 33.

[4] Nichols, ii, Appendix, p. 38. Cf. Stevenson, *Grosseteste*, p. 97 and *passim*.

[5] Wykes, p. 148, and Worcester, p. 448. Robert Grosseteste probably had no love for the Jews, but he desired their conversion. In one of his most famous treatises *De cessatione legalium* (1231), he sets forth the arguments capable of bringing Jews to Christianity, a writing which has been called a sort of 'Epistle to the Hebrews' (Stevenson, *Grosseteste*, p. 105). In the same year Robert founded the 'domus conversorum Judeorum' in London, on the place where the P.R.O. now stands (*ibid.*, p. 99). On the condition of the Jews during these troubles immediately after the baronial revolt against the royal despotism, see E. F. Jacob, *Studies*, p. 236, and his references to Rigg, *Calendar of the Plea Rolls of the Exchequer of the Jews*, pp. 133, 139, 146, 148.

taking his share of the spoils of the Jews massacred at London and at Worcester (1263–6) ? Before this decree of banishment, the Jews, execrated by the inhabitants, had found a refuge in the ruins of the old Roman wall, then called 'the Jews' Wall'.[1] They were forced to leave this miserable shelter, a place where more than a few burgesses probably resorted to solicit money for redeeming debts, when market day or term for payment came round.[2]

The earl of Leicester's lands and revenue. To maintain his rank in society the earl, like all great feudal lords, drew upon two sources of revenue: the issues of his fiefs and domains, and the gifts and pensions he received from the king.

About his territorial wealth we need very precise information, if we are to know whether the earl was right when he complained of not having sufficient private fortune to meet the expenses of his household, the administration of his lands, or the cost of the offices and missions on which he was employed. Minute researches into collections of texts and archives not yet fully explored would doubtless reveal a very lengthy list of the fees in his possession,[3] but their value is seldom indicated with any

[1] On the Jews' Wall see *Archaeological Journal*, xxxii. 325, and *The Journal of the British Archaeological Association*, vi. 116. Cf. Billson, *Mediæval Leicester*, p. 161.

[2] On the persecutions in which the Jews were victimized in several towns see Ballard and Tait, ii. lxix. Cf. Cunningham, *The Growth of English Industry and Commerce*, i. 187, and *C. R. 1251–1253*, 312–13: 'de provisione facta per regem de Judeis Anglie.'

[3] Documents concerning the origin and character of these fiefs abound. I take examples from two famous and easily accessible collections, the *Rotuli Hundredorum* and the *Book of Fees*. 1. *R. H.* (i) Manor of East Sutton, hundred of Eyhorne, co. Kent: the jurors of inquiry say 'quod manerium de Sutton fuit dominicum domini regis H., patris regis nunc [Edw. I], qui dedit manerium domino Willelmo, comiti marescallo, in maritagium suum, cum domina Elianora sorore sua. Et, mortuo dicto Marescallo, dominus Simon de Monteforti duxit dominam predictam in uxorem, et habuit cum ea illud manerium. . .' (ii) The vill of Sproughton, hundred of Samford, co. Suffolk: 'Comes de Leicestria tenet in villa de Sproutune X libratas terre de terra Normannorum (cf. *C. R. 1247–1251*, 156) . . . Jurati de Samford dicunt quod Johannes de Formanvill, Normannus, tenuit xj marcatas terre in Sprowton cum advocacione ecclesie et, quando Normanni recesserunt ab Anglia a fide domini regis, Basilia, uxor dicti Johannis, tenuit dictas xj marcatas terre cum advocacione ecclesie, nescitur quo warranto' (ii. 1736). 2. *Book of Fees*. Inquest in the hundred of Badbury (Dorset): 'Dominus rex Henricus primus dedit comiti de Meulent Kingeston cum pertinenciis . . . Et ipse comes dedit

exactitude, and it would be impossible even approximately to compute the revenue drawn from them. All we can do is to bring together here certain information, somewhat restricted in scope, in order to describe in general terms what composed the 'honour' of Leicester, what was the importance of Eleanor's dower and of the donations which the couple owed to the king, and whether Henry made them out of charity or out of interest.

The Honour of Leicester.[1] The honour of Leicester being divided between the two sisters of Robert IV,[2] we shall only be concerned with the half inherited by Simon. A financial document[3] gives us precise information: when Henry III married his eldest daughter, Margaret, to the king of Scotland (26 December 1251), he exacted from his vassals in accordance with art. 12 of the Great Charter, an aid of 20 shillings or 1*l.* on the knight's fee. Now Simon had to pay 60*l.* 14*s.* for his 'honoor';

honorem Roberto, filio ejus postnato, qui post fuit comes Leicestrie. Et descendit Roberto, filio suo, in hereditario; et de illo descendit Roberto, filio suo, qui extremo obiit. Et ille Robertus dotavit uxorem suam Lorette de manerio de Kingeston . . . Honor iste partitus est per . . . comitem Simonem et comitem Seher . . .' pp. 91–2. Lorette is mentioned again on pp. 254, 257, 261. 'Nomina illorum qui tenent feoda militaria in comitatu Kancie et de quibus ipsi tenent. . . . Feoda comitis de Leycestria . . .' (p. 680). 'Rotulus de feudis militum in comitatu Wiltes . . . Feuda Comitis Lecestrie. . . .' (p. 730), &c.

[1] Pollock and Maitland, *History of English Law*, i. 238–9, find it very difficult to trace the distinction between honour and barony. In Dr. Farrer's work, *Honours and Knights' Fees* (3 vols., 1922–6) where the citations are given with scrupulous accuracy, the two expressions constantly occur as synonyms.

[2] See in the *Report on the MSS. of R. R. Hastings*, cited above, a highly detailed inquest upon the division of the goods which had belonged to Robert IV, now inherited by the two sisters, one married to the earl of Leicester, the other to the earl of Winchester (i. 334–41): an extremely curious and instructive document.

[3] Printed in Thomas Madox, *Exchequer*, i. 414. Madox (*Firma Burgi*, p. 85) further published a list of 'Milites honoris comitis Leicestrie' owing 55*l.* 'de auxilio vicecomitis'. On 11 February 1257, the king confirms a donation made to the earl of Leicester, by Hereward 'de Marisco' and his wife 'Rainette', of the barony of Embleton (co. Northumberland); in this barony and its dependencies the earl and his heirs are to enjoy all the 'liberties' granted by king John to earl Robert [IV], who 'held the whole honour of Leicester in lands and fiefs'. The act enumerates all the privileges (*C. Ch. R.* i. 462). On 19 February 1248, the king orders the sheriff of Berks 'quod habere faciat S. comiti Leic' seisinam de terra quam Simon le Normaunt tenuit de Ildesle (Ilsley) de honore Leicestrie, et quam Johannes Maunsel postea tenuit de dono regis (*C. R. 1247–1251*, 31).

he held therefore at least sixty knights' fees.[1] All the same such a figure does not indicate the real number of the fees held by the vassal, but only the number on which he could be assessed for taxation by the barons of the Exchequer. We may add that the fiefs mentioned as belonging to the 'honour' of Leicester were situate in at least a dozen different counties; and perhaps the most numerous and the most important were not in Leicestershire itself.[2] Letters close of 6 October 1242 enumerate those on which he had to pay his first scutage at the Exchequer as lying in at least twenty different counties.[3]

The Dower of the countess of Leicester. William Marshal, second earl of Pembroke and Striguil, first husband of Eleanor, Simon de Montfort's wife, left when he died (6 April 1231) a rich inheritance to be partitioned between four brothers and five sisters.[4] This inheritance comprised (*a*) practically the

---

[1] In *Pipe Roll 1241–1242* we read, p. 180, in the account of the sheriff of Warwick and Leicester: 'Simon de Monteforti reddit compotum de 50*l*. de relevio suo. In thesauro nichil. Et in perdonis ipsi Simoni 50*l*. per breve regis. Et quietus est.' This means that the king had presented him with a sum equal to the relief he owed, and he was therefore discharged in regard to the Exchequer. The sums were in blanch.

[2] *C. R. 1237–1242*, 491. Cf. *Book of Fees*, pp. 939–40. In *Royal Letters*, ii. 394, Shirley printed letters close of 5 July 1256 ordering the sheriff of Buckinghamshire to inquire whether 'the vill of Hudden is of the honour of Leicester'.

[3] Like the majority of lords possessing fees, the earl of Leicester enjoyed certain privileges or liberties very characteristic of the feudal régime. Three letters close bear this out. 1. 21 August 1248: 'quia rex concessit per cartam suam S. de M. comiti L., quod, non obstante eo quod libertates in eadem carta contente hactenus non fuerint usitate', the king wills 'quod ipse et heredes sui omnibus eisdem libertatibus decetero libere et plenarie utantur', and orders the sheriff of Leicestershire 'quod predictam cartam in pleno comitatu suo legi et firmiter faciat teneri' (*C. R. 1247–1251*, 80). 2. 18 November 1249: the king commands the sheriff of Leicestershire and Warwickshire not to molest Simon de Montfort or his people 'contra libertates quas idem comes habet per cartam predecessorum regis et confirmationem regis (*ibid.*, p. 343). 3. 15 January 1251: the king commands the sheriff of Hampshire to allow the earl's bailiffs 'uti libertatibus de returno brevium regis in manerio et hundredo de Odiham, sicut iidem ballivi antea usi sunt,' (*ibid.*, p. 400; cf. p. 398): that is, the earl's bailiffs were authorized to return the writs they received direct to the Exchequer, without passing them through the normal intermediary, the sheriff. Cf. P. & M. i. 558–82.

[4] The four brothers were: Richard, third earl, d. 16 April 1234 of wounds received in Ireland sixteen days earlier; Gilbert, fourth earl, who died by falling from horseback in a tournament (27 June 1242); Walter, fifth earl, m. Margaret de Quincy, widow of John de Lacy, earl of Lincoln, d. 24 November 1245;

whole of the ancient Irish kingdom of Leinster, conquered in the twelfth century by Richard de Clare, earl of Pembroke, 'Strongbow'; (b) the Welsh earldom of Pembroke; (c) the hereditary office of marshal of England. This last was granted to Hugh Bigod ; Pembroke went to William of Valence ; and on the death of the last male heir, the five daughters shared Leinster among themselves. Gilbert de Clare got, in right of his wife, 1520l., the seven coheirs of Sibyl de Ferrières 217l. each, the three coheirs of Eva de Briouze each 506l. As for Eleanor, her dower had been principally composed of Irish lands ; but her brother-in-law Richard, who detested her, sold the widow's property to pay her dead husband's debts. Henry III found it necessary to intervene. In 1233 Richard promised to pay the countess an annual sum of 400l., and the king promised to convert this rent into real property in England.[1] This latter promise was not completely carried out. In 1256 Henry III gave his sheriffs orders to compel the heirs and heiresses of the marshal to pay to the royal treasury the part of the 400l. rent promised to the countess that was contingent upon each, which the king had been forced to pay on their behalf for seven years.[2]

Anselm, sixth earl, who died a few days only after Walter ; he had m. Matilda, daughter of Humphrey twelfth earl of Hereford. None of them left descendants. The five daughters were Matilda, m., in 1206, Hugh Bigod, third earl of Norfolk ; Johanna, who m. Warin or Guérin de Montchesney, whose daughter brought the earldom of Pembroke to her husband William de Valence, half-brother of Henry III ; Isabella, who m. (1) 1217, Gilbert, seventh earl of Clare, from whom she had six children ; (2) 1231, Richard, earl of Cornwall, younger brother of Henry III ; Sibyl, wife of William de Ferrers, earl of Derby, to whom she presented seven daughters ; Eva, wife of William de Briouze. See the preface to the *Liber de antiquis legibus*, p. xvii f. ; *Journal of British Archaeological Association*, v. 197 ; *D. N. B., s.v.* Marshal.

[1] On 16 June 1251 the king ordered the barons of the exchequer to ensure payment by the heirs of the deceased earl of Pembroke 'de portione singulorum ipsorum contingente de 400 l. quas solvere debent per annum Simoni de M., com. Leic., et Alienore, uxori ejus, pro dote ipsius Alienore in Hybernia, unde sumus plegii' (*Excerpta e rotulis finiium*, ii. 107). Cf. Green, *Lives of the Princesses of England*, ii. 61. These 400l. were but a small compensation. The revenue of the countess seems in reality to have amounted to 1300l. Two thirds of her property were thus retained. *Ibid.*

[2] The countess of Lincoln owed 1000 marks ; the earl of Gloucester 426l., 1 mark ; Roger de Mortimer and Henry de Bohun 42l., 4s. 5d. each ; the earl of Winchester, Agnes de Vescy, Sibyl de Bohun, Reginald de Mohun, William le Fort, Joan, widow of John de Mohun 60l. 19s. each : Close, 43 Hen. III, m. 5 d. ; cf. Roberts, *Cal. genealog.*, i. 227 (inquest of 1275).

Finally, three years afterwards, several manors were assigned to Simon de Montfort and Eleanor his wife in lieu of the annual rent of 400*l.*; they were Gunthorpe and Kingshay (Nottingham), Melbourne (Derby), Dylun, Lugwardine, and Mawurdyn (Hereford), Bere Regis (Dorset), Redley and Minsterworth (Gloucester), Easingwold (York), &c.[1] The question, as wearisome for us as it was important for the earl, had not even then finished.[2]

Late as it came, an annual income of 400*l.* was a welcome addition to the personal revenue of the earl, who was under the necessity of keeping up a large household. And this was not all. On several occasions Henry III enfeoffed his brother-in-law with castles and manors, granted him pensions, made him presents of different sorts,[3] conferred privileges upon him. Among his manors, there were Chawton and Odiham in Hampshire, Hungerford, Compton, and Collingburn in Wiltshire, Kenilworth in Warwickshire,[4] and Widford in Essex.[5] Several of these manors were important by reason of the fortress defending them. Fortified castles were at this time comparatively rare in England. The first Norman kings had had the majority destroyed, and although the nobility had used the troublous period during the war of succession between Stephen and Matilda to build their walls again, Henry II had put into force the designs of his predecessors with equal energy and success.

[1] Bibl. Nat. MSS. Clairembault 1188, pp. 12–15. This volume contains a copy of six documents relating to this long discussion. They are dated 25 June and 27 July 1259, when the conclusion of the Treaty of Paris was imminent.

[2] *Royal Letters*, ii. 393.

[3] See below, p. 33.

[4] On 13 February 1244 the king put into Simon's custody (commisit) the castle of Kenilworth 'ad placitum regis' (*C. P. R. 1232–1247*, 419). Three years earlier the king had given expensive orders for the decoration and painting of the castle chapel, the repair of the roofs and walls, and the doing up of the bedrooms: 'camera regine ibidem lambruscanda et lineanda, et fenestris eiusdem camere frangendis et maioribus faciendis, et caminis camere regis et regine reparandis . . . ; quadam etiam nova portica ante cameram regine cum quadam trappa facienda, quadam etiam fenestra in capella regis ex parte boreali et ponte tornitio faciendis. . . .' (*Great Roll of the Pipe 1241–1242*, 177). On 9 November 1253 the king gave the earl and his wife Eleanor the manor of Odiham and the castle of Kenilworth for life (*Rôles gascons*, 1, no. 2160; *C. P. R. 1247–1258*, 5, 58). There is a description of the castle in an article by G. T. Clark in *Archaeological Journal*, xxix. 331, and the same for Odiham (*ibid.*). Cf. A. Hamilton Thompson, *Military Architecture in England during the Middle Ages* (1912).

[5] L. O. Pike, *Year book 14–15 Edward III*, p. 351.

Henceforth the nobility had to possess the express or implied authorization of the monarch to have these fortresses at all. In this respect Simon de Montfort was well situated. In Kenilworth and Odiham he had strongholds of the first rank. Odiham with its octagonal dungeon, the walls ten feet thick and sixty in height; Kenilworth, a still more redoubtable stronghold, built on the edge of a tarn deep enough to make approach dangerous and defence a simple matter, as Henry III was one day to discover to his cost. It was in Kenilworth that the earl and countess of Leicester most frequently resided, at Kenilworth that their eldest son was born; it was there that Eleanor normally lived during her husband's absences, there that after the battle of Lewes several of the noble prisoners captured that famous day were imprisoned; there that the happy conqueror celebrated with royal magnificence the Christmas of 1264. It was for Kenilworth that he was making after his disastrous campaign in Wales (1265), when he was beaten and slain at Evesham. It was in Kenilworth that his last supporters found a refuge which only starvation could ultimately unbar.

In addition to these Simon had certain other sources of income, whether ordinary like the third penny, or extraordinary like escheats (*escaetae*). By the latter term was understood the whole category of goods, movable or immovable, that passed for reasons of crime, forfeiture or on other grounds into the grasp of the royal treasury.[1] The king often disposed of them in favour of certain persons whom he desired to reimburse, honour or recompense. Thus he assigned the earl the revenues of the lands of the Normans lying within the 'honour' of Leicester.[2] After 1232 he confirmed in Simon's favour the concession made

---

[1] Du Cange, *s.v. Escaeta.*

[2] *Royal Letters*, ii. 380. In *C. R. 1247–1251*, 156, we find under 27 April 1249: 'Quia rex accepit per inquisicionem quam a vicecomite Suff' fieri precepit, quod manerium de Sprouton' est de feodo Leyc', mandatum est eidem vicecomiti quod S. de Monte Forti, comiti Leyc', cui rex concessit omnes terras Normannorum que sunt de feodo suo, de predicto manerio plenam seisinam habere faciat.' Sproughton is a little way from Ipswich in Suffolk. Cf. *C. P. R. 1247–1258*, 36, and Roberts, *Cal. Genealog.* i. 121. On the 'terrae Normannorum' confiscated by the king of England 'until the time when the lands of England and Normandy shall be united', see E. F. Jacob in *Trans. Roy. Hist. Soc.*, 1927, pp. 30–1. The formula just quoted continued to be used by the chancery even after the Treaty of Paris in 1259.

by the executors of Ranulf, earl of Chester, of Dodford manor
in Worcestershire, to be held until the son and heir of William
de Cahagnes[1] reached his majority. In 1245 he granted him the
wardship of the son and heir of one of the principal barons in
northern England, Gilbert de Umfravill, with the right of
marriage over this heir,[2] the advowsons of churches, knights'
fees, and all other dependencies and escheats belonging to this
inheritance, saving a reasonable dower for the widow.[3] To these
we must add payments in money or in kind coming from the
villeins cultivating the demesne or the plots which they held
from the earl, the profits of his markets,[4] his bake-houses, his
mills, his fish-ponds, the profits of justice and amercements &c.
But on these points there is an almost complete absence of
precise facts. The charters and letters close from the royal
chancery throw light on one matter alone, rights of hunting.
There are frequent mentions of grants of bucks or does to stock
the earl's or the countess's parks,[5] or of permissions to enclose

---

[1] *Pipe Roll 1241–1242*, 305: 'Heres Willelmi, filius Radulfi de Caagnes
. . . Simon de Monteforti, qui tenet Dodeford, 6*l*. 6*s*. 4*d*. pro eodem herede.'
Caagnes is doubtless Cahagnes, Calvados, arr. Vire, c. Aunay.

[2] On marriage rights, see Bracton, ii. 12–22. Gilbert de Umfravill (the name
is derived from the Norman locality Amfreville-sur-Iton, arr. Eure, c. Louviers),
who died in 1245 (*Chron. maj.*, iv. 415) had as wife Matilda, daughter and
heiress of Malcolm, earl of Angus. His son (d. 1307) was also named Gilbert,
who was a year old when his father died (*D. N. B.*, *s.v.* Umfraville).

[3] Defined in Bracton (ii. 39, 49, 56) as the third of the lands possessed by her
husband. Simon's purchase of this wardship for 10,000 marks, payable in
twenty years by annuities of 500 marks, was counter-balanced by the annual
payment of a like sum to him by the Exchequer (*Excerpta e rotulis finium*, i. 436;
cf. *C. P. R. 1247–1258*, 493, 22 August 1256). One can understand why
Richard, the king's brother, was annoyed at seeing a wardship which he
coveted ('quod moleste tulit comes R. ipsam desiderans' says Paris) escape
him. Did Simon abuse the royal favour? A letter of Henry III (28 June 1246)
ordered him to put the heir of a certain Roger in possession 'de omnibus terris
et tenementis que idem Rogerus tenere debet de herede Gilberti de Umfraun-
vill, et que sunt in manu sua, occasione terrarum que fuerunt ipsius Gilberti in
manu ipsius comitis.' *C. R. 1242–1247*, 436.

[4] *C. Ch. R.* ii. 1; charter of 13 December 1251, relative to a weekly market
taking place at Elmedon (? Elmdon, co. Warwick).

[5] A few examples from *C. R. 1242–1247* will suffice: 18 July 1244 the king
orders his justice of Bedwin forest (co. Wilts.) to get the countess of Leicester
six stags and six does (p. 214); 19 November, he directs that Simon shall have
from Chute forest (co. Wilts.) twenty bucks and does 'ad parcum suum de
Everley (co. Wilts.) instaurandum' (p. 268); on another occasion the same park
profits by a grant of three stags and ten does, alive, taken in the royal forest of

these parks or preserves for the purpose of game, even in the middle of the royal forests,[1] protected as they usually were by the most tyrannous of codes.[2]

As an off-set to these sources of income and receipts from so many different quarters, it would be necessary to enumerate the expenses incurred in the cultivation of the land, in the upkeep of the houses where the earl and countess normally resided, or in the course of their daily existence; but we possess only a few references to the household administration of the countess Eleanor, a household organized like that of the king, the queen and the great lords; and these very sparse entries relate only to a few months in 1241 [3] and 1265.[4]

There remain to be considered the continental lands, privileges and claims that Simon possessed in his own or in his wife's right. Before the conquest of Normandy by Philip Augustus the earls of Leicester had both vassals and domains in the country of their origin.[5] Robert IV having remained faithful to King John was forced before he died to see these fees confiscated by the victorious French king; they were from henceforth lost eternally to his successors. The name 'Fee of the earl of Leicester' lasted on some while, as the designation of an estate of private dwelling houses at Rouen, near the Porte-Massacre (i.e. the

Savernake (p. 288). The countess secured a grant of twenty oaks from that forest 'ad capellam suam reedificandam' (p. 458).

[1] 3 May 1246, the king authorizes the earl to enclose his wood of 'Bauteleg', a part of the royal manor of Hungerford (Berks.) and to convert it into a park, although situate within the limits of Savernake Forest (*C. Ch. R.* i. 293). Robert IV of Leicester had already granted the nuns of Nuneaton, a foundation of Fontevrault, 'quiectanciam pannagii et herbagii in bosco meo de Hungeforda' (Stenton, *Documents* no. 323; cf. letters patent of 29 August 1256, *C. P. R. 1247–1258*, 525), and a 'charter' (*C. Ch. R.*, i. 460) authorizing the earl to enclose his wood of 'Shypleg' in the royal forest of Northampton, and to convert it into a park as far as the limit of the deer's bounding, the earl and his heirs having power to possess it free from interference from the royal foresters.

[2] Further on is a list, far from complete, of the numerous gifts of money made by the king to his sister Eleanor and the earl her husband. Several trifling details may further be gleaned from *C. Inq. post mortem*, i, nos. 558, 586, 797.

[3] In *The Great Roll of the Pipe, 1241–1242*, 177.

[4] The valuable document published by Botfield. Simon and Eleanor each had a private household organization, and this was the case with all the great seignorial families.

[5] Several are listed in L. Delisle's *Cartulaire Normand*, as well as in his *Catalogue des Actes de Philippe Auguste*.

slaughterhouse) and the church of Notre-Dame de la Ronde;
but this fee, bought from Philip Augustus by the burgesses of the
place in 1220, had no further connexion with Simon de Montfort
nor any of his descendants.[1] When the Treaty of Paris (1259)
re-established peace between France and England, Louis IX
may have been anxious to indemnify the earl of Leicester for the
fees now confiscated for fifty years by granting him an income
of 500*l.* (*Paris*), one part of it drawn from the town and rents
of Remi.[2] The point is uncertain; but one little fact should not
go unnoticed: the name of Remi, town and lordship in the
county of Clermont (Beauvaisis) surely recalls the memory of
Philippe de Beaumanoir, who may have been a page in Simon de
Montfort's service about 1263–5.[3] The French conquest formed
a powerful obstacle to the right of Henry III's sister ultimately
to succeed to her father John Lackland's continental possessions.
The fact was clear, when in 1258 the definitive conclusion of
peace had to be retarded by Eleanor's claims, though in the end,
as we shall see later, she abandoned all her rights in the Treaty
of Paris. The countess also had a long suit to maintain against
her brothers-in-law, the sons of Hugh de la Marche, relative to
their mother's inheritance, the countess-queen Isabella; she
pleaded unsuccessfully before the court of the French king in
1261 and 1262.[4] The judgement was given in 1269 and went
against her.[5] In both processes Simon was energetic in protecting his wife's interests, and his advocacy did not fail to bring
him both disappointments and enmities. Farther on we shall
notice the disturbance which the succession of Bigorre caused
him. In spite of the considerable gaps in our authorities, it is
clear that Simon's personal position, brilliant as it outwardly
seemed, was in fact a complex and a difficult one. Not but what
we may draw one general conclusion: though a great landed

---

[1] L. Delisle, *Cartulaire Normand*, no. 647, n. 24, corrects the erroneous information on this point given by Chéruel in his *Histoire de Rouen*, i. 122.

[2] Act of December 1266, in the Registre du Trésor des Chartes JJ41, fol.
lxxxiii r.; Bibl. Nat., Clairembault, 1188, fol. 25.

[3] This is the ingenious suggestion of Henri Bordier in his study *Philippe
de Remi*, pp. 25–32. It has been adopted after some hesitation by Hermann
Suchier in his Introduction to *Œuvres poétiques de Beaumanoir* (Société des
anciens textes français, 1884), i. x.

[4] The principal documents of this process are in Clairembault 1188.

[5] See Du Cange, *s.v. Apanamentum.*

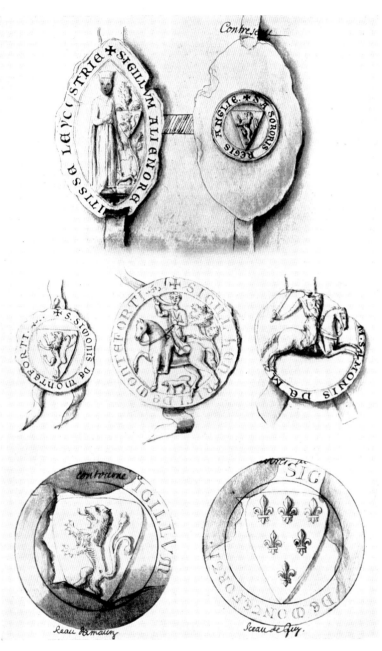

SEALS OF ELEANOR DE MONTFORT; SIMON THE YOUNGER
AND HENRY DE MONTFORT; AMAURY AND
GUY DE MONTFORT

From the drawings of Roger Gaignières

proprietor holding numerous fiefs of the king, in turn the suzerain of vassals who owed him homage and fealty, Steward of England into the bargain, the earl did not derive from honours or property the means of playing a great political part on his own. His wealth was scattered piecemeal throughout a realm strongly centralized governmentally, and therefore it could not constitute a homogeneous mass capable of forming a check or counterpoise to the royal power. It was the same with the other barons whose vassals were considered and treated more or less directly as the king's subjects. The great feudatories of England cannot be compared with those of the French king; the earldom of Leicester, for example, with the county of Champagne. Individually the English barons could do very little; united they could do a great deal, and individual action only availed if it was based on party support. Simon belonged to such a party, as we shall presently observe.

But before coming to this, we must give some account of his character and his ideas. First, then, some words on his immediate circle, his wife, children, and household.

What influence, for joy or sorrow, had the countess Eleanor, the king's sister, upon her husband? Though there were seven children of the marriage,[1] the couple did not always live on the happiest terms. We may call to witness the simple and kindly Adam Marsh, their counsellor and friend—perhaps one might almost call him their spiritual director. The countess had gone with Simon to Gascony. Adam wrote to her from England a long and animated letter of advice. 'To fly into a temper,' he says,[2]

[1] Five sons and two daughters. The sons were Henry, godson of Henry III; Simon and Guy, who dishonoured their father's name by the murder of their cousin Henry of Almain (1271); Richard, of whom we know nothing; and Amaury. Of the two girls, one, Eleanor, was to have the troubled future related below (p. 261); the other, whose existence the Abbé Douais has made known to us (Les frères prêcheurs en Gascogne) died while still a child and was buried in a chapel of the Dominican convent in Bordeaux. From the accounts of the house the Abbé Douais extracted the following passages: p. 265: 'nobilis vir Symon de Montforti fieri fecit propriis sumptibus dormitorium infirmatorii valde pulchrum, cujus una filia parvula jacet in capella Sancti Petri apostoli ad sinistram; p. 276: 'Simon, magni Simonis Montisfortis filius, Aquitannie prorex, prestat sumptus ad construendum infirmatorii nostri dormitorium. Apud nos sepelit unam ex filiabus suis.'

[2] Monumenta Franciscana (R.S.), i, Letter CLIX, p. 294. This is undated, but apparently of the winter 1249–50.

'destroys the peace of the household, and breaks the bonds which God willed to strengthen when he said 'let us make for man a companion like unto him'. In anger the heart palpitates, urges on the arm to strike, impels the tongue to slander, destroys the intelligence, engenders hatred between beings better made to love each other, and breaks the pact of friendship.' Was this mere rhetoric ? 'Please God,' the Franciscan continues with severity, 'that this execrable taint do not throw your soul into the detestable ignominy of sin.' Later on, 'Let not the asperity of my words astonish you. Yet why this excessive cult of your person, these enormous expenses and insensate taste for unnecessary ornaments which provoke the divine majesty?'[1] On another occasion, however, he adjures her to make her husband listen to counsels of prudence and moderation.

'If', he writes, 'the illustrious earl, your husband, has for the honour of God and the safety of the Church, for the king's service and the good of the people, and confiding in the Saviour's aid which, I trust, will never fail him, magnanimously undertaken the perilous and almost desperate task of preserving the province of Gascony to the king your brother and to his heirs, you and all those bound by friendship to the earl ought to break out in joyful thanksgiving.[2] If, however, through injudicious actions, themselves the product of praiseworthy intentions, he has observed certain agreements less strictly than he should have done, if he has had recourse to excessive measures,[3] it is for you, considering the fact that he has been manifestly driven to them by necessity, to display all your industry and tact in putting an end to these irritating disputes and in bringing him gently, by your sweetness and good advice, to conduct himself more prudently in the future.'

Beneath the mild terms of this letter we seem to find an indication of the disputes referred to above. Did those 'irritating disputes' have some influence on Simon de Montfort's character? Did they make him more imperious, more headstrong

[1] Letter CLXI, p. 297. Compare what Robert de Sorbon was saying at the same time of the queen of France, Margaret of Provence, wife of St. Louis; Hauréau, *Bulletin de l'Académie des Inscriptions et Belles Lettres*, t. xxvii, p. 53.

[2] Had the countess shown some traces of discontent over Gascon affairs ?

[3] These words surely constitute the condemnation of the oppressive character of Simon's government in Gascony.

than he naturally was? Did the countess Eleanor take part for or against her brother, or did she remain neutral between the king and the steward of England? There is nothing to tell us. We can only note that Simon took up all his wife's grievances, whether against Henry III on account of her dowry, or against her half-brothers the Poitevins, with whom she was disputing part of the inheritance of their mother, the countess-queen Isabella. It should also be added that during the Barons War the countess shared her husband's destiny, and after Evesham mourned his loss with all proper dignity. The human heart is an impenetrable complex

Though it is hard to penetrate the veil covering the private life of Simon and Eleanor, several of the earl's friends are known to us. There were many of them, and—a fact of some importance—the most illustrious were churchmen: seculars like Robert Grosseteste, or regulars, belonging especially to the two new religious orders, the Franciscans and the Dominicans.

The Franciscans who arrived in England in 1224, not long before the young Simon, were immediately given a remarkable welcome, which is to be explained by the moral laxity among the monastic orders. These were the words used by the bishop of Lincoln in conjuring Pope Gregory IX to receive the Minorites into his favour:

'Know that they diffuse among us benefits that no tongue can express. For they illuminate all our land with the brilliant light of preaching and teaching. Their most holy lives vehemently excite to contempt of the world and voluntary poverty, to maintaining humility even in dignity and power, to showing all obedience to prelates and the head of the Church, to patience in tribulation, to abstinence in the midst of plenty, and, in a word, to the performance of all virtues. If only your holiness could see with what devotion and humility the people ran to hear from them the word of life, to confess their sins, to be instructed in rules of living, and what an advance the Church and religion have made by their example. Truly you would say that "for them who dwell in the shadow of death has a light arisen".'[1]

To the bishop of Coventry and Lichfield he wrote less elaborately, but in the same strain: 'Know what services the Brothers

[1] Letter LVIII, pp. 179–80.

Minor are rendering to the people among whom they live, by
their preaching, by the example they give of a holy, celestial
life, by their continual and unwearied intercessions; they bring
peace, illuminate the land and go far to supply what prelates
lack.'[1] Vowed to poverty, clad in coarse garments, the Grey
Friars, as they soon came to be called, had to beg for their
living, to beg in order to raise the dwellings destined to replace
the hovels where they had first wanted to reside in a town like
London. Gifts flowed in from all quarters, so that thirty years
after their arrival they disposed of forty-nine houses (*loci*).[2]
These were not convents, as the brothers were not cloistered
monks but persons commanded to mix with the world around
them. Furthermore they did not content themselves with bringing spiritual comfort to the poor or to the piously inclined;
they also addressed themselves to all desirous for knowledge as
well as for belief. From their circle arose scholars of eminence.
The first Chancellor of the nascent University of Oxford,
Robert Grosseteste, christened the 'magister scholarum', taught
the brothers (1229–35) until his election to the episcopate.
Adam Marsh, the 'doctor mirabilis' was a disciple of St.
Francis. The brothers established 'lectors' at London, Canterbury, Hereford, Bristol, and Leicester.[3] 'The gift of wisdom
overflowed at this time in the province of England so much that
before the deposition of William of Nottingham there were
thirty teachers in the country and their regular succession in
the Universities was assured.'[4]

[1] Letter XXIV, p. 121.

[2] Thomas de Eccleston, ed. Little, p. 14: 'anno ab adventu fratrum in
Angliam xxxij⁰ numerati sunt viventes fratres in Anglia in xlix locis m. cc. xl. ii.'
Cf. *Ibid.*, p. xxviii.

[3] There were Franciscans at Leicester already by 1230. *Thomas de Eccleston*,
ed. Little, p. 47. Thomas of Eccleston speaks of 'frater Villelmus de Leycestria'
lector at Hereford (p. 62); 'fr. Gregorius de Bosellis [lector] Leycestrie' (p. 63);
'fr. Robertus de Leycestria' (p. 70); 'fr. Petrus de Swynesfeld', who was
buried at Leicester (p. 146). Leicester was part of the custody of Oxford.

[4] *Ibid.*, p. 53: 'ita inundavit in provincia Anglie donum sapientiae, ut ante
absolutionem fratris Willelmi de Nothingeham essent in Anglia XXX lectores
qui solemniter disputabant, et tres vel quatuor qui sine disputatione legebant.
Assignaverat enim in universitatibus, pro singulis locis, studentes qui, dece-
dentibus vel amotis lectoribus, succederent . . .; Oxonie legit primus frater
Adam de Marisco. . . .' The part played by Leicester in this enumeration is to
be noted. William of Nottingham was elected provincial minister in 1240;
deposed that same year by the general of the order, John of Parma, in spite

Although St. Dominic's disciples, the Friars Preachers, had preceded the Minorites in England by some years, they never reached the same degree of influence or of popularity. It was not their business, as it had been in Languedoc, to preach or to pursue heretics; they had the more modest and more humane task of being primarily teachers. To facilitate the study of the Bible, where all science was to be found, they drew up the famous concordances (indexes to all words and phrases in the sacred text), the *concordanciae majores,* still called *concordancie anglicanae.* Their moral treatises on the seven commandments, on the Vices and the Virtues, on the *Paternoster,* had an immense vogue throughout the Middle Ages, a fact attested by the numerous manuscripts of them preserved in European libraries to this day. One at least of these treatises, *De vitiis et virtutibus,* mentioned among the works of the Dominican Guillaume Péraud,[1] was to be found in the 'library' of Simon de Montfort.[2]

Memories of his childhood and his youth were, we may surmise, the chief reason that bound the earl to the Dominicans, the zealous helpers of his father in heretical Languedoc. They may perhaps have been his preceptors. His grandmother, Amicia de Joigny, founded the church of Dominican canonesses at Montargis, which served as a burial-place for several members of his family. It was there that after her husband's death the countess Eleanor sought refuge, there that she found her long repose.[3] The close relations of Simon with the Franciscans are explained by the relatively large numbers of Friars Minor belonging to Leicester and by the friendship that early bound him to

of the unanimous vote of the brothers, he was soon afterwards absolved at the Council of Metz in 1251, and died shortly afterwards. See Little's article on him in *D. N. B.* (*s.v.* Nottingham, William of) and the same writer's *The Grey Friars of Oxford* (Oxford Hist. Soc.).

[1] See Father Mortier, *Histoire des grands-maîtres de l'ordre des frères prêcheurs,* i. 511. Guillaume Péraud (or Perrault), died in April 1260. Cf. Ch. V. Langlois, *La vie en France au Moyen Âge,* iv. 133.

[2] Bibl. nat. MSS. Clairembault 1188, fol. 29 v.: 'A tous ceaus qui ces lettres verront, seur Guie, prieuse, et lou couvent des sereurs de l'ordre de Saint Dominique de lez Montargis, saluz en Notre Seigneur. Sachiez que nous avons receu de monsegneur Amarri de Montfort, tresorier d'Eurwyck [York] une *summe de vices et de vertuz* qui fu a mon seigneur lou conte de Leycestre, son pere. Et prometons en bone foy que nos le garderons por li et a li la rendrons la ou il voudra, a son mandement, quand il li plera . . . ' (18 March, 1270).

[3] See below, c. x, for the relations of the Montforts with the convent of Montargis.

one of the most eminent adepts of the new order, Adam Marsh, and to Robert Grosseteste. Upon arrival in England Simon made the acquaintance of the future bishop of Lincoln, for Robert was then archdeacon of Leicester.[1] A priest of exemplary life, as bishop he was the glory of his time. He was doubtless the intermediary through whom Simon got to know not only Adam Marsh but also John of Basingstoke, the friend of the chronicler Matthew Paris, and successor of Grosseteste in his archdeaconry, one of the few scholars of that epoch who like Grosseteste knew some Greek;[2] together, that is, with William of Nottingham, the provincial of the Franciscans,[3] and Walter Cantilupe, bishop of Worcester, all his life one of the earl's most faithful partisans.

Of all these friendships Adam's presents the fewest difficulties. His correspondence is not doctrinaire nor dogmatic, like that of Robert of Lincoln, but more vivid, affording us a better idea of the earl's personality, his character and ambitions. We noticed above the pious asperity, natural to Christian preachers and letter-writers, wherewith Adam Marsh reproached the countess for her immoderate taste for luxury and expense. He has no less scruple on occasion in blaming the earl of Leicester, though he does it more deferentially. Simon had taken with him to Gascony the vicar of the chancellor of Salisbury, the parson of Odiham. Adam wrote to him (October 1248) with a certain liveliness of tone: 'This priest will be for long separated from the mass of his parishioners who will thus be deprived of him.

---

[1] He had earlier been 'rector S. Margaritae de Leicestria' (Luard, p. xxxv and p. 1). In MS. Cotton Claudius, C. IV, fols. 124–5, there is a modern copy of a 'Carta Roberti Lincolniensis episcopi, de militibus suis feofatis'. It is of 1253 and consequently emanates from Grosseteste. It is addressed to Henry III: 'Sciat, domine, excellentia vestra subscriptos milites de beata Maria Linc' feffatos esse, et quantum unusquisque eorum debeat vobis, scripto meo significo'. Then come the names of forty-two knights, among whom the earl of Leicester is mentioned as owing service of two knights. 'Omnes jam dicti milites feofati fuerunt tempore Henrici regis, aui vestri [Henry II], excepto comite Leicestr' et Willelmo de Chahame (sic), qui post coronationem vestram fefati fuerunt. Et de hiis debeo vobis sexaginta milites'.

[2] *Chron. maj.*, iv. 322 and v. 284. Cf. *D. N. B.*, *s.v.* Basingstoke. On the knowledge of Greek in England during the thirteenth century, see Stevenson, *Bishop Grosseteste*, pp. 21–3, and C. H. Haskins, *Studies in the History of Mediaeval Science* (1924).

[3] See Luard's preface to his edit. of Grosseteste's letters.

Moreover he has not given any proof of his affection or his zeal, and it is dangerous to deliver one's renown over to the mercy of a man whom even his master does not know.'[1] But his letters are generally those of a man devoted to the interests of the house he serves. He is anxious about the health of his patrons; he gives them news of their children, left in the guardianship of the bishop of Lincoln while the earl and countess are away.[2] He takes a sympathetic view of the earl's troubles: 'Thanks to the eternal mercy of God,' he writes to the bishop of Worcester, 'a new light of heavenly justice seems to rise in the king's mind for the affairs of the earl of Leicester.'[3] 'The king,' he writes on another occasion to Simon himself, 'the archbishop of Canterbury, the queen, Earl Richard and the other prelates and magnates of the kingdom (blessed be the God of peace and love!) have conceived towards your person, as numerous conversations lead me to believe, far more friendly feelings than usual.'[4] He becomes Simon's intermediary with the king and queen: 'The king,' he writes, 'has spoken to me of your affair. I think that he will be pleased to trust in your advice, for he has great confidence in your devotion, if only his immediate circle favours you. I have also talked with the queen, who replied to me in all with friendliness, because she also relies greatly upon your services.'[5] He recommends Simon to the prelates who value his correspondence—to the bishop of Lincoln, the archbishop of Rouen,[6] &c. When he can do nothing else, he bids the earl to be resigned, and points out to him suitable passages for reading that might engender humility in a spirit impatient of all restraint. 'I draw this letter to a close. In the middle of all the cares weighing upon you I do not want to read you a lesson and so weary your ears that have to listen to a multitude of business. I know too that your excellency's energy and zeal will gather from these few lines much instruction for your safety. Work, I beg you, to gain the salutary comfort of the divine words, and meditate often upon the Holy Scriptures. It is, I think, very necessary for you to study, with all the attention of which heaven has made you capable, Chapters 29,

Letter CXXXVI, p. 262.   [2] Letter XXV, p. 110.
[3] Letter LXXII, p. 178.   [4] Letter CXLVI, p. 281.
[5] Letter CXL, p. 268.   [6] Letter XVIII, 104; VI, p. 86.

30, and 31 of the book of Job, and everything in that same book that relates to your position, with the gentler dissertation of St. Gregory.' [1]

These sparse details are precious: it would be desirable to date them with greater precision, for then they would be even more valuable. But too often we lack the means of so doing; and, worse still, the information given by Adam about the state of opinion in England, about the plans of reform discussed with intimate secrecy between Simon de Montfort and his friends, excites our curiosity, but does not satisfy our longing for exact information. 'I return to your lordship,' he writes to the bishop of Lincoln, 'your own abbreviation of the *de principatu regni et tyrannidis*, as you sent it me, sealed with the seal of the earl of Leicester.' [2] What work of Robert Grosseteste's is alluded to here we have no means of telling. We have a good notion of the bishop's views on ecclesiastical reform, but are much less well informed about his political ideas. The passage translated above is perhaps the only one of its kind in all Adam's correspondence —to the great grief of Simon's biographers; in all other contexts it is the question of the salvation of souls which forms the subject of the earl's constant reflection. 'What noble rewards, illustrious earl, will you receive in the kingdom of God for the happy solicitude with which you plan to purify, enlighten and sanctify the Church of God by a government that well befits it!' [3] Adam further writes to Master Ralph of Canterbury: 'The noble earl of Leicester, devoured by ardent desire for the honour of God and the good of the country, a disposition on which, for reasons both open as well as secret, depends, as is known, the salvation of many, earnestly wishes the help of your presence; thus I appeal to your zeal and ask you to go and find the earl,

---

[1] It may not be too risky to compare with this letter (p. 268) one of Robert Grosseteste (no. LXXV) addressed 'nobili viro et amico in Christo, carissimo domino Symoni de Monteforti . . .' exhorting him to bear 'tribulation', which he now suffers, with constancy, 'sicut congruit proprietati vestre cognominationis, in cacumen montis fortis, hoc est Christi, qui est mons in vertice montium'. But it is impossible to discover what is intended by this 'tribulation'. Luard simply dates the letter 'about 1239'.

[2] 'Remitto dominationi vestre abbreviationem illam quam scripsistis de principatu regni et tyrannidis, sicut misistis signatam signo comitis Leycestrie'. Letter XXV, p. 110. Cf. Pauli, *Simon de Montfort*, p. 27.

[3] Letter CXXXVII, p. 264.

and give your friendly consent to his pious requests.'[1] To Robert Grosseteste he expresses himself more frankly: 'The earl of Leicester spoke to me about a salutary and marvellous project which heaven has inspired in your heart for the salvation of souls; he has given it unmeasured approval, embraces it warmly, and is quite ready to put it into execution with his helpers, if he can find any; but disturbed about the bad state of your health, he affirms that you ought not to oppose yourself personally to such great dangers.'[2]

Other passages, equally enigmatic in character, at least have the advantage of being dated. During the early months of 1250, perhaps when Simon was at Lyon, at the Papal curia,[3] where he found his habitual counsellors—the bishop of Lincoln, the bishop of Worcester, Gregory de Bosellis[4]—Adam told the earl of his anxiety, and besought him to put his trust in God, who would enfold him with his protection; the earl is surrounded with danger, but if he remains in the path of virtue, the saying shall be fulfilled against his enemies: 'The wicked flieth with none to pursue him, but the just, sure of himself like the lion, shall be without fear;[5] if the high-souled leader, marked out for the salvation of men, happens to succumb, what action will ever be thought more glorious, more noble and more salutary than to find death in extending life to others?[6] I hide the sense of my words, because in other letters I have explained myself, if not elegantly, at least with clarity. . . . As touching this work of salvation which it is so necessary to carry out in the kingdom of England, and the delay of which is certain to involve the greatest dangers, my regret is infinite to see it, I know not how, abandoned in the judgments of the All-highest.' Adam finishes the letter by recommending to the earl the greatest caution in his speech.[7]

In another, of March or April the same year, he expresses himself thus: 'It is greatly annoying to me not to have been

---

[1] Letter XCIX, p. 225.   [2] Letter XXV, p. 111.

[3] We know that he went there twice: see *Revue historique*, t. iv, p. 254.

[4] For Gregory 'de Bosellis', see *Thomas de Eccleston*, p. 53 n.

[5] *Proverbs*, xxviii. 1.

[6] 'Quid unquam estimabitur aut gloriosius, aut decentius, aut salutarius quam, propter causam vivendi, vivendi finem facere?' (p. 274, cf. Juv., Sat. viii, l. 84).   [7] Letter CXLIII, p. 275.

able, up till now, to talk with you and the countess, as I could have desired. . . . Besides, on the matter of the affair you know, I shall not write anything to you this time, especially when it is a question of a very important matter, from which great salvation is to be obtained, but which makes one fear the greatest dangers. Do not take offence, because I know not how to avoid something maladroit which might give away my letter and thus cause irreparable harm to the work of salvation.' [1] A little later the situation painted so black in this letter (there is no record of it in the chroniclers) seems to have brightened: 'Your wisdom [2] knows the state of the kingdom. There has been faithful work done these days to make it better, and our wavering confidence is becoming more assured; I shall take no rest until I have learned the success of your cause.'

The information that can be extracted from this correspondence can be reduced to a small compass: a frequent exchange of views, reforming plans of a religious rather than political nature; on Simon's side a resolve—cut short—to take in hand the cause of these reforms and to give his life for the salvation of England; great dangers threatening him, the declared hostility of the king and his entourage. All these data go to make up a lively and dramatic picture, but the outline is indistinct and the personalities do not show up lucidly from the background.

We may interrogate the public life of Grosseteste, his writings and his correspondence, for the secret of his theories, adopted with such zeal and self-sacrifice by the earl of Leicester. We know that he struggled ceaselessly for the independence of the clergy both as regards Rome as well as the royal power. He was anxious to forbid churchmen to accept administrative functions, especially those of itinerant judges,[3] and declared that ecclesiastical tribunals were alone competent to take cognizance of the misdemeanours committed by clerks; jealous of the rights of episcopal authority, he did his utmost to bring the whole of his clergy into subordination, to secure the recognition by the Holy See of his absolute right to visit the chapters and religious

---

[1] Letter CXLIV, p. 277.

[2] Letter LIII, addressed to Robert Grosseteste, and hence anterior to the prelate's death (9 October 1253).

[3] *Letters of Robert Grosseteste*, pp. 349, 353, &c.

houses of his diocese.[1] He loved to surround himself with Dominicans and Franciscans,[2] those latest children of the religious life, who brought to the long neglected work of preaching and teaching the ardent and infectious enthusiasm of youth.[3] We also know that part of the clergy, the monks and the schools of Oxford declared for Simon and remained faithful to him till the end; [4] but these are facts, not doctrines. Yet even when we consider the facts, do we know to what extent the bishop of Lincoln viewed with approval a revolution in State or in Church? The acts of the Council of Lyons (1245) show him attacking the Pope with a violence full of bitterness, and Matthew Paris depicts him as a fervid apostle of episcopal autonomy. While there is no need to go so far as to consider him, on the strength of certain letters whose authenticity has been unreasonably doubted,[5] a precursor of Wiclif and reform, or to think that the picture drawn by Matthew Paris is at every point a faithful one, Robert Grosseteste may be imagined as a boldly speculative spirit, passionately defending his own ideas, a monarch in the affairs of his own diocese. By his qualities as much as by his defects he was able to exercise a great influence over the earl of Leicester, and to assist in giving him an unshakeable confidence in himself.[6] But once more we have no clear idea of his actual doctrine and principles, and we do not know if the earl of Leicester was to enter the civil war with a plan that

---

[1] *Letters of Robert Grosseteste*, pp. 367, 376, &c. See also his *Rotuli* (Cant. and York Society). [2] *Ibid.*, pp. 132, 134.

[3] His affection for the Friars doubtless sprang from the irritation caused him by the moral laxity of the monks and nuns: 'Idem Robertus in religiosos terribiliter et in religiosas terribilius consueuit fulgurare. . . . Confidenter tamen assero quod Deo placerent ipsius virtutes quamdiu excessus displicuerint.' Cf. the statement of Thomas of Eccleston: 'frater Agnellus impetrauit a sancte memorie Roberto Grosseteste ut legeret ibi fratribus'; ed. Little, p. 60.

[4] *Chron. maj.*, v. 419; Little, *Studies in English Franciscan History*, p. 51 f.

[5] By M. Jourdain in *Bulletin de l'Académie des Inscriptions et Belles-Lettres*, 2e série, t. iv (1868), p. 13; but see Stevenson, p. 316.

[6] Robert Grosseteste was the friend and counsellor of Richard Marshal, earl of Pembroke, who died in Ireland (1234). Two letters of Robert's correspondence (6 and 7) are addressed to him. Mr. Stevenson seems disposed to believe (p. 93) that Robert had wished to see him place himself at the head of the party hostile to Bishop Peter des Roches and favourable to the principles earlier maintained by Stephen Langton. This was in the spirit of the Great Charter, which he tried later to inculcate into the earl of Leicester.

had been frustrated. Personally I do not think so, though I have no evidence for my opinion. Simon had no bishop of Lincoln to rely on at the moment when (only half reconciled with the king) he returned from Gascony, free henceforward to give sustained attention to the debates that were agitating the country and dividing Parliament, and ready to forget the last counsel of his illustrious friends—to remember kindnesses and forget injuries.

Outside the clergy, Simon de Montfort had a certain number of devoted helpers, who remained faithful to him till death. Here we can but mention their names; the majority have their life stories bound up with the earl's. They are Peter de Montfort, who came of a Norman family established in England since the Conquest, was in Simon's suite in Gascony and constantly at his side during the civil war;[1] the Bassets and the Segraves, who served him in the administration of his property. Simon was furthermore allied to the families of Bigod, Quincy, and Clare, among whom he found as many supporters as enemies. In the royal family itself he was held more in esteem than in affection. His energetic, resolute character was rightly valued; his military gifts were put to good service, but he was feared rather than loved. The violence of his fits of passion and his intemperate language combined to alienate his royal brother-in-law, to whom he owed everything. The king's intimate counsellors carefully fostered these rancid feelings in their master. John Mansel was the earl's secret enemy before becoming his most bitter public opponent.[2]

The queen apparently did not share the king's animosity against Simon. More than once she acted in such a way as to conciliate them. There was real affection between her children and Simon's—at least between the two eldest, Edward and Henry. They were practically the same age, had grown up together; they were destined to be found in arms against each other at Evesham, and it was not Prince Edward's fault that his cousin Henry was killed. With the queen's relatives Simon de Montfort

[1] Dugdale, *Baronage*, i. 408.

[2] Matthew Paris speaks much of John Mansel. For his biography see *D. N. B.*, *s.v.* Mansel; Tout, *Chapters*, i. *passim*; and N. Neilson, *The Cartulary and Terrier of the Priory of Bilsington*, Kent (Records of Social and Economic History, vii) 1928, *passim*.

seems at first to have been on friendly terms. He fell out with Thomas of Savoy as the result of circumstances related below, but his early relations with his brother Peter of Savoy, the 'little Charlemagne' were pleasant. In the two serious affairs of Sicily and the Treaty of Paris, Peter and Simon are found giving the king the same wise and moderate advice; on the eve of the Oxford parliament they were to bring all their personal influence jointly to bear upon the king in the direction of a less arbitrary line of conduct. But Peter of Savoy was an alien : this was a crime, and Simon was to abandon him without regret to the hostility of the national party.

Wholly different were his relations with the king's half-brothers. The insolence of the Lusignans made a striking contrast with Peter of Savoy's moderation. Their rapid rise to prosperity, the pernicious influence they exercised over Henry III's mind had aroused as much hostility as it had given them impertinent assurance. William de Valence and his brother Aymer, elected to the See of Winchester [1] in 1250, but not consecrated by the Pope, were in the front rank of Leicester's enemies. On one occasion, in full parliament, William and Simon actually had to be prevented from coming to blows. 'This William, because he was the uterine brother of the king, thought he might act as he pleased against his neighbours. On one occasion he did not scruple to invade the lands of the earl of Leicester and to return thence with the booty he had captured; but the earl's steward relieved him of it. Furious with rage, William heaped insults, both in act as well as in words, upon the earl. The case was brought before the king and their quarrel nearly raised a fight. For William publicly, in the presence of the king and the nobles, gave Simon the lie and called him traitor, which is the most damaging outrage that can be done to a knight ; the earl rushed upon him and would have pierced him with his sword, had the king not interposed in time; but henceforward their mutual hatred and loathing could not be dissipated.' [2]

Thus with the king and his *entourage* Simon de Montfort met

[1] *Chron. maj.*, v. 183. Cf. *D.N.B.*, *s.v.* Aymer de Valence. The king had him forcibly elected on 4 November 1250; his election was confirmed by the Pope on 14 January 1251 ; but he had to wait for long before being consecrated.

[2] *Chron. maj.*, 634 (1257). Cf. a similar scene at the parliament of London, April 1258, *ibid.*, p. 676. Can this be the same ?

with more enmity than sympathy. He found his friends, his counsellors and masters among those members of the higher clergy and nobility whose aim was to reform the government or the standards of society. Leicester was with them, heart and soul. We shall shortly realize how circumstances were to test his ideas and his character.

III

THE EARL OF LEICESTER FROM 1231–1240. MARRIAGE
WITH THE KING'S SISTER (7 JANUARY 1238). FIRST
QUARREL WITH HENRY III. SIMON AS CRUSADER
(1240) AND IN GASCONY (1242–1243).

WE know little of Simon in the years immediately following
his definite establishment in England. It would be interesting to trace the course of his conduct during the troubles
of 1233, when Richard, the second son of the great Marshal and
his brother Gilbert took up arms against the 'evil counsellors'
of the king;[1] a precedent which, as we suggested, Robert
Grosseteste may have cited as an example to Simon de Montfort.[2] In 1234 Simon recommended Stephen de Sancerre to the
king who granted him a safe-conduct to go on pilgrimage to
Thomas Becket's tomb.[3] He was present at the Westminster
parliament (12 October) when modifications were made in the
legal status of bastards.[4] In 1236 he performed his official
duties as steward at the marriage of Henry III with Eleanor
of Provence (14 January 1236).[5] In 1237 he was one of the two
negotiators ordered by the king (27 March) to Doncaster to
meet the messengers of the king of Scotland, and he was present
at the negotiations which took place at York in the presence of

---

[1] Wendover, iii. 48–53. A curious passage in the *Flores Historiarum* of the
pseudo-Matthew of Westminster relates that the king 'de consilio alienigenarum
et quorundam jam dictorum indigenarum' refused to render justice to Gilbert
Basset; certain barons decided to resist; but, not daring to attack the royal
person ('in personam regis per casum aliquando desevisse hoc nolentes'), fell
upon his officials and pillaged their property all the winter.

[2] See above, p. 47.

[3] *C. P. R. 1232–1247*, 45. I felt some hesitation in seeing Stephen de Sancerre in the person described from the place-name 'de Sacro Cesario'.

[4] Bracton, ed. Twiss, ii. 606. In the list published there for the first time
Simon is placed immediately after those who are described as earls. Cf.
Bracton's Notebook, i. 107, and P. & M., ii. 395.

[5] At the moment when the king sat down to table, Simon presented him
with water in a basin. See *Red Book of the Exchequer*, p. 757, the passage which
Matthew Paris borrowed for his account of the scene: 'servivit eo die de
senescalcia Simon de Monteforti, comes Leicestrie, cui de iure competit illud
officium, licet contradiceret Rogerus Bigod, comes Norff.' Cf. Wickham
Legg, *English Coronation Records*, p. 108.

the legate Otto (September 1237).[1] In the list of forty-four
witnesses he occupies the twelfth place after the earls of
Lincoln, Aumale, and Winchester, but before the earl of Pembroke. Cardinal Otto's legation was also to give Simon the
opportunity of manifesting his devotion to the king. Otto had
come once before, but then simply as nuncio, in 1225–6, and he
had left a somewhat bitter memory behind on account of his
'exactions'.[2] This time he appeared as legate, at the request, it
was said, of the king himself; and Matthew Paris echoes with
indignation the fears and suspicions which his arrival excited
among the clergy.[3] The papal letters which he brought with
him assigned to him the duty of reforming the church,[4] and it
was feared that he would also ask for money.[5] The Council
convoked by him opened at St. Paul's on 10 November, and
when it was learned that he was prepared to condemn members
of the clergy who were pluralists, 'noble by birth and by
possessions,' he could hear angry cries and threats from the inn
where he was staying; but certain great lords, such as the earl
Marshal (Gilbert), the earl of Lincoln (John de Lacy) and the
earl of Montfort, as well as a number of the king's household,
armed themselves with swords and cudgels to protect his coming
and going.[6] This is the occasion on which Matthew Paris, ready
as ever to catch and record the gossip of court and countryman
alike, wrote: 'at this time the king cruelly wounded the hearts
of his nobles. He had also counsellors of evil fame and suspicion

[1] The negotiations took place on 14 September, the day fixed by the English
king (*Chron. maj.*, iii. 413), and on 25 September, the day fixed at the beginning
of the treaty itself, for their final termination (Rymer ad. ann. 1237).

[2] Wendover, reproduced by Matthew Paris, *Chron. maj.*, iii. 97–109.

[3] *Chron. maj.*, iii. 395; 'venit (29 June 1237) legatus in Angliam, nescienti-
bus regni magnatibus'; then Paris states with some astonishment that the
legate conducted himself 'prudenter ac modeste', even going so far as to refuse,
'contra consuetudinem Romanorum,' the majority of the rich presents offered
to him (p. 403).

[4] *Ibid.*, 404, 'de reformatione ecclesiae anglicanae tractaturi', and pp. 414–15.

[5] We might be tempted to think that this was in fact one of the objects of
the legation, since we find in Rymer, just before the treaty of peace with
Scotland and dated round about 7 July 1237 a bull of Gregory IX demanding
from the king of England the tribute of 1,000*l.* sterling due to the Roman
Church. But this bull is really of 9 July 1236 (anno decimo). Cf. Potthast,
no. 10201, and Auvray, *Les Registres de Grégoire IX*, no. 10201. The mistake
has not been corrected in Hardy's *Syllabus*.

[6] *Chron. maj.*, iii. 418.

who encouraged him in his extravagances; the nobles hated hem because they themselves were of English origin, yet these were John earl of Lincoln, Simon earl of Leicester, and brother Geoffrey of the Temple'.[1] But the event which best proves the favour enjoyed by Simon with the king was his marriage with Henry III's own sister.

Simon had in fact twice already explored the possibility of marriage with a rich heiress abroad. There had been two widows: Mahaut, countess of Boulogne, and Joan, countess of Flanders. Mahaut, daughter of Renaud, the count of Dammartin who had been taken prisoner by the French at Bouvines, had been affianced in 1201 to Phillip le Hérissé (Hurepel), son of Philip Augustus and of Agnes of Meran, who died about 18 January 1234, only having one daughter, Joan, married later to Gaucher de Châtillon.[2] For reasons unknown to us, Simon's request for marriage was not granted, and Mahaut married Alphonso of Portugal in 1239.[3] With Joan of Flanders matters went farther. She was the daughter of Baldwin IX, count of Flanders, who was Emperor of Constantinople in 1204 and died a prisoner of the Bulgarians in 1205. In 1212 she married a Portuguese prince, Ferdinand or Ferrand, son of King Sancho. Ferrand was also captured at Bouvines; he was shut up in a tower of the Louvre, and only regained his liberty in 1227 after having accepted the oppressive terms of the treaty of

---

[1] *Chron. maj.*, iii. 412. We may note in this connexion the official acts attested by Simon during 1237: 28 January, confirmation of the Great Charter (Tewkesbury, p. 103);—18 February, remission to K. of 1,000 marks by his almoner (present, the archbishop of York, Richard of Cornwall, John de Lacy, and Simon, *C.P.R. 1236–1247*, 176);—24 March, confirmation by K. of the privileges of Exeter (*Munimenta Gildhallae Londoniensis*, ii. *Liber Custumarum*, p. 669. Like Leicester, Exeter was a mediatized borough, holding from the earl of Cornwall; Ballard and Tait, ii. lxxxv. Cf. J. W. Schopp. ed., *The Anglo-Norman Custumal of Exeter* (1925));—1 Aug., Inspeximus and confirmation of a charter by which Simon, termed here earl of Leicester and steward of England, gave his friend John, son of Luke of Ferentino, for his liege service, 40 marks rent in the parish of Chauton (*C.Ch.R.*, i. 230);— 3 August, Simon, together with the archbishop of Bordeaux, the bishop-elect of Valence, and John de Lacy, attest a royal charter establishing a free fair at Bayonne (*Lettres de rois, reines, &c.*, i. 52, after an inspeximus of Henry VI transcribed on the Rôles Gascons of his reign).

[2] Élie Berger, *Blanche de Castille*, p. 212.

[3] L. Delisle, *Mémoires de la Société des Antiquaires de France*, t. xxxi, p. 189. Cf. Élie Berger, *Blanche de Castille*, p. 323.

Melun. He remained faithful to Blanche of Castille and stood up for her against Pierre de Dreux, count or duke of Brittany, the most consistent enemy of the Regent, whom Joan had wanted to marry after having obtained the annulment of her first wedlock.[1] Ferrand died at Noyon on 27 July 1233, and Simon sought out his widow; but Queen Blanche, fearing fresh intrigues against herself and her son, had the arrangements broken off at an early stage: on 12 April 1237 Joan had to swear that she had never 'made a marriage' with Simon and that 'she would never make one'.[2] Simon did not, however, escape the quite justifiable suspicions of the Regent, and had to return somewhat quickly to England.[3] The chronicler Aubry of Trois-Fontaines thus characterizes these negotiations: 'the intriguing enemies of the king of France had secretly procured the marriage of the countess of Flanders with Simon de Montfort, brother of Count Amaury. Simon was suspected at the court of France because of his English wealth and of the fealty which he had sworn to Henry III. And so he lost this marriage, just as he had lost that of the countess of Boulogne. But God gave him compensation in the sister of King Henry III.'[4] This double rebuff may have helped to win him favour in the eyes of a king naturally hostile to the French crown. Simon hastened to take advantage of the promising situation.

Eleanor was the third daughter of John Lackland.[5] Born in 1215, she had been married when quite a child to William the Young, earl of Pembroke, the eldest son of the great Marshal (23 April 1224).[6] She had been brought up by Cecily de Sanford, 'noble by birth and by character,' who had lost her husband William de Gorham. The young Countess Eleanor in 1231 was,

[1] Kervyn de Lettenhove, *Histoire de Flandre*, ii; Élie Berger, *Blanche de Castille*, p. 210, and pp. 330–3.

[2] *Layettes*, nos. 2478, 2491–509, 2519–56, 2583–7.

[3] Guillaume de Nangis, *Chronicon*, ed. Géraud, i. 192. Trevet (ed. Hog, p. 226) may be exaggerating a little, when he says: 'reginam Blancam . . . sibi timens offensam, aufugit in Angliam.' Leroux de Lincy alludes to the fact in his *Chants historiques français*, i. 192.

[4] *Histor. de France*, xxi. 619; *Mon. Germ. Hist. S. S.*, xxiii. 940–1; and certain lines, vv. 99, 422–9, 427, of Philippe Mousket, *Histor. de France*, xxii. 61.

[5] See the list of John's children in *D.N.B.* and the genealogy of the Pembroke family in *Liber de antiquis legibus*, p. xvii f.

[6] *Chron. maj.*, v. 235.

like her, a widow without children. Under the stroke of a common calamity, she and her former governess took vows of chastity before the archbishop of Canterbury. They did not take the veil, but wore the ring that united them for ever to the mystic bridegroom, Jesus Christ.[1] Eleanor remained at the court of her brother, who, in 1236, married Eleanor of Provence, sister of Margaret, now wife of Louis IX. It is known that Simon was there at the wedding, and he may then have studied her closely. He certainly fell in love with her—the story even went that he seduced her, and the statement is not improbable. Eleanor was an attractive flirt,[2] not the least intended for the semi-religious life to which she had vowed herself in the stunned condition of bereavement. Moreover, if she was to blame, her brother also was aware of it, for he had the marriage celebrated by his own chaplain at Westminster (7 January 1238) in an atmosphere of domestic secrecy. 'Himself he placed his sister's hand in the earl's; and the earl took her with pleasure because of the love he felt for the princess, for her beauty and illustrious birth.'[3] It will be no injustice to his memory to suggest that he did very well for himself. These were the facts. But whether the king wanted to save his sister's honour or to assert his authority by giving her to one of his favourites,[4] his arbitrary conduct was to raise a storm among the magnates. Had not the king on many occasions sworn to take no important decision without asking their advice, and had not the barons a legitimate

[1] *Chron. maj.*, v. 235.

[2] See above (pp. 37–8) for the reproaches addressed to the countess by Adam Marsh.

[3] Matthew Paris (*Chron. maj.*, iii. 470) carelessly writes that the marriage was celebrated 'solempniter'; but he contradicts himself when he gives precise details of the whereabouts, 'in parvula capella regis que est in angulo camere,' and about the celebrant, 'dictante verba et missam celebrante Waltero, capellano Sancti Stephani, apud Westmonasterium.' Besides, if the ceremony had not been semi-private in character, how would it be possible to explain the annoyance of the barons who had not been invited and whose grievances were conveyed to the king by his own brother? Cf. Tewkesbury, p. 106: 'desponsata fuit in parvula capella regis apud Westmonasterium,' and the writer gives the date, the 19th before the Calends of February—14 January. Matthew Paris gives 7 January: 'in crastino Epiphanie, scilicet die Jovis,' in the twenty-second year of Henry III's reign, which began on 28 October 1237.

[4] Simon witnessed, 22 January 1238, letters patent by which the king confirmed a donation made by his grandfather Henry II to St. Pierre of Cluny (*Bibliotheca Cluniacensis*, fol. 1400).

right of control over the marriage of the most noble heiress in the kingdom? Thus when Eleanor's 'secret' marriage was known, they showed lively irritation. Their complaints, energetically seconded by the burgesses of London, were presented to the king by his own brother Richard, now (through his possession of the earldom of Cornwall) the richest lord in Christendom. Why did he surround himself with the foreigners he had sworn to banish? Why did he listen only to Simon de Montfort and John de Lacy, and set aside all the others from his counsels? The legate intervened, and the king ended by promising to submit the case to weighty persons; but while discussion was still in progress, the earls of Leicester and of Lincoln took measures to purchase Richard's good will, by swearing to give him complete satisfaction, and so the storm died down.[1]

Having extracted himself by gifts, and at the price of some humiliation too, from an extremely unpleasant quandary, Simon hastened to Rome in order to regularize his marriage in accordance with canon law. Did he escape thither in disgrace,[2] as Matthew Paris supposes? At all events he carried with him letters patent addressed to the Pope and cardinals (27 March 1238). In them Henry III announced that he was sending his 'dear brother, and faithful subject, Simon de Montfort,'charged with negotiating certain matters touching the honour and the interests of his person as well as of his kingdom, and asked them to give credence to any communications he was bidden to make to them.[3] Armed with these recommendations to the sovereign pontiff, with a strong backing of money to be dispensed when necessary, and with the support of the emperor Frederick II,[4] then in the heyday of the power recently acquired at Cortenuova, Simon secured from Gregory IX the absolution which was his objective. In view of the contradictory reports which

---

[1] Paris deals with this matter at length: *Chron. maj.*, iii. 475-8.

[2] *Chron. maj.*, iii. 479: 'arrepta galeia, clanculo transfretavit.'

[3] *C.P.R. 1232-1247*, 214. This letter, of which the Calendar gives no more than an analysis, was printed by Turner, *Manners*, p. xv, n. 3.

[4] In July 1235 Frederick had married Isabella, second daughter of John. Simon was thus his brother-in-law. Matthew Paris appears to believe that Simon began 'to fight under his orders in order to secure his favour' (p. 430). He certainly had time to pay a passing visit to the army and offer them his services: 'cum gratia imperatoris et literis supplicatoriis . . . et effusa et promissa infinita pecunia,' as Paris says, p. 487.

had reached him, the Pope notified (10 May) the king's sister, in awkwardly-sounding phrases, that there was no obstacle to the validity of a marriage contracted 'in faciem ecclesiae', and he ordered the legate to pronounce solemn sentence in the earl's favour.[1] The decision was, it is true, censured by more rigidly-minded people like the Dominican William of Abingdon, for, as they said, although Eleanor had not taken the veil, she was indissolubly united to Christ by the ring.[2] But Matthew Paris maliciously remarks: 'Rome had designs too subtle for our understanding.' The chronicler seems to have forgotten the embarrassing position into which the struggle against the emperor and the appeal coming from the Holy Land had put the Holy See, the Tartar invasion in Hungary,[3] the rising of the Greeks against Baldwin IX, emperor of 'Romania'. He might have known that Simon had taken the cross,[4] and that

[1] This letter, to which R. Pauli drew attention for the first time (*Simon von Montfort*, p. 83; Eng. tr., p. 36), has been printed, but only in part, by Auvray in *Registres de Grégoire IX*, no. 4889. It is followed by another identical letter addressed to Leicester (no. 4330). It is not in Potthast's *Regesta*. The essential passage runs: 'super matrimonio quod inter te et nobilem virum S. de M., c. L., in facie ecclesie intelleximus esse contractum, nobis et fratribus nostris sunt a diversis diversa relata per que non vidimus contra jus contractum matrimonium presumendum.' Heinrich Weber (*Das Verhältniss Englands zu Rom während der Zeit der Legation des Cardinals Otho 1237–1241*, thesis, Berlin, 1883) suggested that one of the reasons why Henry III commended his brother-in-law's cause at Rome was personal interest: if the earl was going to have progeny while the queen as yet was childless, and if the marriage was invalidated, the children would be reckoned illegitimate and so incapable of succeeding to the crown (p. 58). A complicated and fragile hypothesis.

[2] *Chron. maj.*, iii. 487. On brother William of Abingdon and his skill at extracting alms from the faithful, see Thomas of Eccleston, p. 58. Henry III treated with levity his sermons which, he said, were very fine, but always ended with the refrain: 'da, da, da'; he called him 'the serpent, the tempter.'

[3] *Chron. maj.*, iii. 488–9.

[4] On 25 February 1238 the Pope was writing Simon, 'qui se proposuerat in terre sancte subsidium crucem assumere,' that the moment was badly chosen, since the kingdom, now threatened from all sides, 'ejus auxilio et consilio destitutum,' would be endangered by his absence. He accordingly enjoined upon him 'quatinus idem regnum auxilii salutaris exhibitione muniens, insidientium ludos prudentius et fauces elidens, iter in terre predicte subsidium nequaquam arripiat. . . .' Simon had therefore to await the order to start, under penalty of losing the benefit of the indulgences granted to crusaders (*Reg. Grégoire IX*, no. 4094). Similar letters were sent to Richard of Cornwall, to William Longspee, earl of Salisbury (*ibid.*, nos. 4095, 4096), and doubtless to others. A series of papal letters dated 18–23 April were written with the same object, viz. to prevent Richard of Cornwall, the archbishop of Canterbury,

Gregory IX, who had obviously been informed by his legate of the difficulties of the English government, was dissuading the crusaders from starting. These facts allow us also to conjecture that, if the earl of Leicester was in no hurry to return to England, it was because his stay in Italy might be of value to the emperor, who was now his brother-in-law into the bargain. It is possible that he went to join the English contingent[1] then being taken by Henry de Turbervill to Frederick for the siege of Brescia. He had left his wife with child, and returned (14 October) when her time drew nigh. He was received with rejoicing by Henry III and his household, Paris tells us,[2] but he made haste to return to the royal castle of Kenilworth, where the countess, eleven months after her marriage, gave birth to a son (28 November).[3] The infant was baptized by the bishop of Lichfield, Alexander de Stavensby, who hoped by this means to recover in full the king's good graces.[4] So strong then was the friendship uniting the two brothers-in-law, and it is clear that the king, acting as godfather, must have consented to the child's receiving the name of Henry; clear too that it was to please his sister that Henry III decided to confer upon Simon official investiture as earl of Leicester. The ceremony took place on the day of the Purification, 2 February 1239.[5]

&c., from starting, when the kingdom needed them for its defence (*ibid.*, nos. 4267–78). Simon is not mentioned here, evidently because, being then in Italy, he was in a position to be directly informed of the decisions taken by the Holy See. Bliss, *Papal Letters*, vol. i, drew attention to this instructive correspondence, but it is better to consult the texts and analysis given by Auvray.

[1] Paris writes that, when in Italy, Simon began to fight for the emperor: 'prius militans imperatori'; it is more likely that this was after the absolution on 10 May.

[2] *Ibid.*, p. 498: 'quem rex suscepit in osculo cum magna gaudio, et omnes regales.'

[3] *Ibid.*, p. 518: 'ad regni robur et solatium: timebatur enim ne regina sterilis esset'; but the king and queen had only been married three years, and they were still young. Their first child, the future Edward I, came into the world on 17 or 18 June 1239; doubtless he had already been conceived when Henry de Montfort was born.

[4] *Ibid.*, p. 518: 'episcopus Cestrensis A. . . . ut sic magis sibi regis gratiam compararet.' The king had borne him ill-will because of his too close relations with Richard Marshal (*ibid.*, p. 268). The see of Chester for several centuries alternated between Chester, Coventry, and Lichfield. Bishop Alexander was a friend of Robert Grosseteste. He founded a Franciscan house at Lichfield, and died on 25 December 1238.

[5] *Ibid.*, p. 524: 'vocato prius comite Almarico . . . et pacificato.'

CASTLE OF MONTFORT L'AMAURY. PART OF SOUTH-EAST
ANGLE OF THE KEEP

Amaury, the count of Montfort, was invited to the festivities, but only arrived two months later. At Westminster (11 April 1239),[1] in the presence of the king, the legate, the earls of Cornwall, Lincoln, Hereford, and Essex, and of several lords, he made the final renunciation of his English inheritance. These were happy days for Simon. Absolved by the Pope, strengthened in his position both materially and morally, he could regard the future with confidence. His success was early in coming; but it was based upon the favour of a frivolous and impulsive king, and so was destined to be ephemeral.

Purely material interests were a disturbing element from the very beginning. The earl may have had good reasons for rejoicing in the royal favour; he certainly also had legitimate grounds of complaint, for his earldom had been returned to him in a ruinous condition. Its guardians from 1207 to 1231 had exhausted its revenues, mortgaged its lands, cut down its forests and squandered the resources which it had been their duty to administer. Our proof of this is not only the legal claims of the aggrieved,[2] but several accounts rendered to the Exchequer for the years 1209 to 1210.[3] Simon had indeed the honour of being steward, but it was one shorn of a number of its privileges; he had indeed received Henry III's sister in marriage, but without a marriage-portion; even the dowry of the countess was disputed against him by other heirs of the earl of Pembroke, and Simon complained of his poverty, as if it had been an act of injustice.[4] So strong were the poisoned germs of discontent that before long were to embroil the brothers-in-law and in the end to disturb England. The first occasion came without delay.

While the succession to Ranulf of Chester's earldom was being settled (Ranulf died on 28 October 1232), Simon found himself[5]

[1] Rymer, under this date; *Layettes*, no. 2789; Harcourt, pp. 112–13. Amaury's charter is confirmed in an Inspeximus of Henry III of 17 April, in C. Ch. R., i. 243.

[2] *Simon de Montfort*, p. 333.

[3] Harcourt, *His Grace the Steward*, p. 79, and esp. pp. 99–104.

[4] Green, *Lives of the Princesses of England*, ii. 61.

[5] This is to be concluded from letters patent stating (7 June 1237) that Simon owed 200*l*. to Ranulf, earl of Chester; he had promised to pay the money to Peter of Brittany; the king had approved this settlement of account and promised to have the money paid to the duke of Brittany by the executors of the deceased. *Royal Letters*, ii. 379; cf. *C.P.R. 1232–1247*, 185. Mrs. Green,

in debt to Peter Mauclerc, count (or duke) of Brittany, who had taken the cross in 1235. By a bull dated at Anagni, 10 September 1238,[1] the Pope ordered Jacques de Basoches, bishop of Soissons, to find out if it was true that the earl of Leicester had neglected to refund Peter Mauclerc within the prescribed period a loan of 2,080 silver marks; if it was the case, the legate was to lay the interdict upon Simon's property and constrain him to pay under penalty of excommunication. The business was long protracted, so much so that on 1 May following (1239), the bishop transferred the powers delegated to him by the Pope to the treasurer of the church of Soignies; and the creditor was now Thomas of Savoy, count of Flanders by his marriage with the countess Joan, Simon de Montfort's old flame. We have two accounts of what happened in this awkward business, with its serious consequences for Leicester's career; these agree and confirm each other on several points. One comes from Simon himself and is set forth in a plea made before the French king in 1262; the other is from the chronicler Matthew Paris. First, the most interested party shall state his case: [2]

'The king of England', Simon said, 'honoured me by giving me his sister; but shortly afterwards he was incensed by a debt which my lord Thomas, count of Flanders,[3] was claiming from me and for

---

Princesses of England, ii. 77 (from Liberate Roll 23 Hen. III, m. 6) explains the king's annoyance by adding that the earl of Leicester already owed the king the considerable sum of 1,565*l.* 6*s.* 8*d.*, without reckoning in the 15*l.* which he had just lent his sister.

[1] This bull, transcribed in the letter to the bishop of Soissons, has been printed in *Archives de la Chambre de comptes de Lille*, p. 270, no. 671. It is not mentioned in Auvray's collection, which, however, contains a good many bulls relating to payments owing to Peter of Brittany for the Crusade.

[2] *Simon de Montfort*, p. 333.

[3] Thomas of Savoy was the younger son of Thomas I, count of Maurienne and Savoy; the eldest, Amadeus XIV, reigned from 1235 to 1253. Two other brothers played a notable part in England under Henry III: Peter, nicknamed the 'little Charlemagne', and Boniface, archbishop of Canterbury from 1245 to 1270 (Wurstemberger, *Graf Peter von Savoyen*; Mugnier, *Les Savoyards en Angleterre*; *D.N.B.* under 'Boniface' and 'Peter of Savoy'). In letters patent of 8 December 1239, Henry III gave instructions to the proctors he had appointed at the Roman Curia to defend the interests of the count of Flanders 'in causa que inter nobilem virum P., quondam comitem Britannie, et S. de Monteforti, vertitur in partibus transmarinis' (*Royal Letters*, ii. 16). At the date when this was written, Peter Mauclerc was no longer count of Brittany; he had resigned his duchy to his son, John I the Red, who was the heir (18 November 1237).

which he sued me at the court of Rome.[1] The king wished me to
pay; to which I replied that I was ready to do so, if I was legally
the debtor; but I asked that justice should be done to me, as to the
poorest man in his kingdom. He refused, with ugly and shameful
words which it would be painful to recall.[2] Then, the same day that
he had invited us to the queen's churching, he ordered the men of the
Commune of London to arrest me in the inn where I was lodging and
to take me off to the Tower; but the king of Almain[3] who was there
would not allow that to happen at that moment. Seeing his great
wrath and that he would not listen to reason, I left the country.
When his annoyance was over, he said that he would pay 500 marks,
and did so;[4] but as for the 500 remaining to be paid, he had them
realised from my lands, to my great detriment, the more so because
I was on the eve of starting for the crusade; I had to sell part of my
land and of my forest.'

Now for Paris. He first recounts [5] the fact that on 28 June,
Henry III's eldest son was baptized by the legate at Westminster, and was 'taken up from the font' by three bishops, three earls, of whom Simon de Montfort was one, and
three other great people. At that date there was no change in
the friendly feelings of the king towards his brother-in-law. The
storm broke suddenly on 9 August, the day when the ladies of
the nobility came to London to be present at the churching of
the queen.[6] The earl of Leicester was there with his wife;
suddenly the king burst out in anger upon him, and treating
him as excommunicate forbade the pair to be present at the
festival; as his abusive language continued, the earl and his wife
took a boat, so as to return quickly to their quarters (Henry

---

[1] We have just observed that the process at the Curia was still pending at
the end of 1239.

[2] The terms used by Simon in his plea 'e me dit assez de ledes paroles et de
honteuses que sont dures a recorder' recall Paris's expression, p. 566: 'cum
multiplicaret convitia.'

[3] The king of Almain was no other than Richard of Cornwall, the king's
brother, elected 13 January 1257; we may remember that Simon's plea was
in 1262.

[4] Paris in fact tells us (iii. 616) that about the time of the Assumption
(15 August) the count of Flanders came to England with the French king's
authority. He was received by Henry III with demonstrations of joy which
seem to have excited the laughter and mockery of Henry's subjects. A short
while afterwards, 'quia licentia domini regis Francorum diu non extendebatur,'
he returned; 'quingentas marcas a rege receptas asportavit.'

[5] *Chron. maj.*, iii. 540.   [6] *Ibid.*, iii. 566–7.

had leased them the palace of the late bishop of Winchester);[1] but the king had them forcibly ejected.[2] Weeping and groaning, they returned to his presence, without being able to appease his wrath. Addressing himself to the earl, Henry cast these words in his face: 'You seduced my sister before the wedding; to avoid scandal I gave my consent, in my own despite. You went to Rome to secure that the vow she had taken should not prevent the marriage, and you corrupted the Curia in order to obtain that which was forbidden. The archbishop of Canterbury, here present, told the Pope what was the truth, but truth was conquered by the avarice of the Romans and the presents which you lavished on them. Ay, you have failed to pay the money which you promised to return, and that is why you have deserved excommunication. To crown your folly, you cited me as security by an act of perjury and without telling me aught of it.' At these words the earl blushed, and, at close of day, embarked on the Thames in a small craft, with his wife, and hastened to cross over to the Continent.

If an expedition to the Holy Land could not avail to sweeten these bitter feelings, it might at any rate suspend their legal consequences. The Crusade that Gregory IX had been preaching for some years[3] was to get Simon out of a difficulty and open up for him a new sphere of action. In England there was a general readiness to start in the early months of 1238, and Frederick II asked his brother-in-law, Richard of Cornwall, to pass through his Italian kingdom, the easiest and most opportune route, he urged, for getting to Palestine.[4] But the following

[1] Peter des Roches died on 9 June 1238, and the see remained vacant for five years.

[2] Simon is more precise here: 'la nuit maimes . . . il comanda que je fuisse pris e mené à la Tour de Londres e que le cumuns de Londres fust semons por mai prendre a mon ostel ou j'estaie herbergez, mais li Rais d'Alemaingne qi la fu ne vout pas ce souffrir a cele nuit'. *Simon de Montfort*, p. 334.

[3] See Élie Berger, *Blanche de Castille*, pp. 239–46, 250, &c.; Lenain de Tillemont, *Vie de Saint Louis*, ii. 249; Bliss, *Papal Letters*; *Les Registres de Grégoire IX*.

[4] Huillard-Bréholles, *Historia Diplomatica Frederici II*, ii. 165, letter of 11 February 1238: 'Volumus et rogamus ut . . . per nos et nostrum regnum Sicilie . . . transitum faceretis, maxime cum regnum nostrum sit taliter institutum quod per illud ad partes transmarinas facilior et opportunior' (the letter is transcribed by Matthew Paris, iii. 469–72). On 25 February, the Pope notified Simon de Montfort, Richard of Cornwall, William Lungspee, earl of

year, the Pope came into conflict with the emperor, whom he excommunicated, and endeavoured to get the crusaders to help the emperor of 'Romania', Baldwin IX, against his revolted Greeks. A good many of them received this order with some irritation. Doubtless they remembered what had happened not so long ago, in 1202, when the Crusade had been turned aside from its object and diverted to Zara and Constantinople. It may have been out of desire to follow the example of his father who refused to be associated with Innocent III's projects, that Amaury de Montfort, constable of France, left for the Holy Land at the head of the French contingent. In Sicily the emperor took care to give him an impressive welcome.[1] He had

Salisbury (*Reg. Grég. IX*, nos. 4094–5), that he had received from the king of England a letter setting forth the dangers which his kingdom might run if he was deprived at that moment of their aid and counsels; he consequently orders them to 'defend the kingdom by manifesting a salutary zeal, to combat the intrigues and snares of its enemies', and he forbids them 'to start for Palestine before receiving the formal word of command from the Pope'. Otherwise they would not be able to avail themselves of the indulgence granted to crusaders by the General Council. On 20 October 1238 another bull appeared, in which the Pope told the king the reasons why it was necessary for Richard of Cornwall to delay his departure (no. 4267); other bulls were written with the same object to various crusaders (nos. 4268–78). On this occasion Simon is not named, for the adequate reason that during this month of April he was in Italy over the affair of his marriage. Other bulls of 21 April, 4 May, &c., concern the redemption of crusaders' vows (nos. 4265–79, 4316); and in one of 25 November 1238, the Pope advised Richard of Cornwall to renounce his expedition to Palestine and to apply the sums already collected to aid the emperor of 'Romania', Baldwin IX, whom the Greeks had deprived of part of his estates (no. 4608). On 9 March 1239, he again notifies the leaders of the French crusaders to modify their aims 'quia in proximo imperii Romani imminere videtur excidium' (no. 4741). Cf. *Chron. maj.*, iii. 488, 518.

[1] Huillard-Bréholles, *op. cit.*, v. 474: letter from the emperor (1 November 1239) to his principal officials in Sicily bidding them to give a handsome welcome to the constable of the king of France: 'comes Americus de Monteforti cum quibusdam nobilibus et crucesignatis applicuit in regnum nostrum. . . .' Is the date correct? If Amaury was still in Sicily on 1 November, could he have arrived in Palestine in time to march against the Turks twelve days afterwards and to get himself captured near Gaza on 13 November? Röhricht ('Die Kreuzzüge des Grafen Theobald von Navarra und Richard von Cornwall's nach dem heiligen Lande', in *Forschungen zur deutschen Geschichte*, xxvi. 1886) fixes the dates as follows: 2 November, the army leaves Acre and reaches Jaffa; 4 November, Peter Mauclerc captures a caravan; the Count Henry de Bar, believing there to have been only a thousand Turks at Gaza, thought he could take the place by surprise and assembled his army on 12 November, but it was he who suffered surprise and was defeated on the morrow (pp. 73–5). On the battle of Gaza, see 'L'Estoire de Eraclès', caps. 44–5, *Rec. des histor.*

only just arrived in Palestine when he let himself be dragged unprepared into an engagement with the Turks, and was made prisoner on 13 November. Almost the same day (12 November) in England the crusaders assembled at Northampton swore to depart for Palestine before a year was up 'in order honestly to accomplish their vow and to avoid shedding their blood in Italy and in Greece'. Their leader, Richard, took the oath first at the great altar of All Saints' church. Many others, 'shoulder to shoulder, heart to heart,' prepared courageously for the service of the Cross.[1] A letter addressed by the unfortunate Amaury to his wife and forwarded by her to the earl of Cornwall[2] naturally served to hasten their preparations.

It may have been this letter which determined Simon to return to England. He was there on 1 April 1240. At the cost of great sacrifices he procured the money necessary for so lengthy an adventure,[3] and, following the example of his father and elder brother, he left England shortly after Richard.[4] They took different routes: while Richard traversed France and Provence preparatory to embarking at Marseilles, Simon accepted Frederick II's invitation and passed through Lombardy and Apulia; he took ship at Brindisi. The countess of Leicester, now expecting her second child, accompanied her husband with his eldest son, but stayed at Brindisi in a castle with a vast domain which had been granted to her. The army collected without loss at Acre in October 1240.[5]

The Crusade was notoriously poor in warlike exploits. Earl Richard spent considerable sums in fortifying Ascalon and ransoming Christian prisoners; and that was how Amaury de Montfort came to be set free.[6] Nothing is known of the part played by Leicester himself; all we have is a curious letter addressed to the Emperor Frederick II by the 'barons, knights and citizens of the kingdom of Jerusalem', asking him to give them the earl as governor, until the young Conrad reached his majority. They will swear to obey him 'as it had been the emperor's person'; they will suppress the bell, the councils and

des Croisades, Hist. Occid., ii. 143–415, the continuation of William of Tyre (ibid., pp. 538–48); Les Gestes des Chiprois, ed. G. Raynaud, pp. 118–20.
[1] Chron. maj., iii. 620. [2] Ibid., iv. 25. [3] Ibid., 7.
[4] Röhricht, op. cit., pp. 33–4. [5] Chron. maj., iv. 44; Dunstable, p. 151.
[6] 23 April 1241. See Röhricht, op. cit., p. 84.

the captains of the commune, 'saving those who were there before the emperor was master of the country' (7 June 1241).[1] There could have been no better choice; but whether he declined the honour which it was proposed to do him, or whether the emperor did not consent to confer upon him the guardianship of his son during the minority, or whether for some other motive, the letter of 7 June remained without effect. At the beginning of the following year Leicester returned to France with the duke of Burgundy.[2]

During this time Henry III had been persuaded by his mother, the turbulent countess of La Marche, and against the opinion of his Parliament, to renew against France the attempt attended with such ill success in 1230; for the second time he took up arms and tried to recover the conquests of Philip Augustus and Louis VIII. He disembarked at Royan, summoned to him his loyal Gascon subjects, knights, and dwellers in the communes. The summons reached Leicester in Burgundy. Simon immediately set off for Poitou; but if his services were required, they would have to be paid for. He declared to the king that 'recently arrived from overseas, he was by no means disposed to stop with him, by reason of several acts of injustice which the king had done him. In order to retain his services, Henry had to promise him as much money as he had levied from his lands to pay Thomas of Savoy, and a hundred marks more, so that it could not be called a simple indemnification'.[3] At such a price Simon remained.

[1] Turner, *Manners and Household Expenses*, p. xix n.; *Archives de l'Orient latin*, i. 402.

[2] *Simon de Montfort*, p. 334. Cf. *Chron. maj.*, iv. 180. Richard of Cornwall left Palestine on 3 May 1241 with Amaury de Montfort and the other French prisoners whom he had rescued from captivity. After an unpleasant passage he put in to Trapani on 1 June. Amaury died shortly afterwards at Rome. Richard disembarked at Dover on 7 January 1242; cf. *Chron. maj.*, iv. 180. The duke of Burgundy was Hugh IV (1218-72). In a formulary of the Roman penitentiary compiled by Thomas of Capua, cardinal priest of St. Sabina (f. 1243) and edited by H. C. Lea, Mr. Haskins has drawn attention to the case of a sinner, who, for his penance, was condemned to take the cross with Simon de Montfort ('The sources of the history of the Papal Penitenciary,' in *American Journal of Theology*, ix, 1905, 431); cf. the same writer's 'Robert le Bougre and the beginning of the Inquisition in Northern France'. in *American Historical Review*, vii. 639, n. 6.

[3] *Simon de Montfort*, p. 334. From a *Rotulus finium* recently discovered in the

We are well informed about the details of the campaign begun so light-heartedly by the king of England, and know what part the earl of Leicester took. When the English arrived before Saintes (22 July 1242), they were surprised by the advance-guard of the French.[1] They resisted bravely and entrenched themselves in the vineyards. In the thick of the *mêlée* was the earl of Leicester with the earls of Salisbury and Norfolk; 'even the French admit,' said Matthew Paris, 'that their fierce valour would have changed the issue of the battle, if the number of English knights had only equalled that of their opponents.[2] The English were hurled back into the town. For a moment Henry III made as if he would defend it, a dangerous resolution in view of the risk he ran of being surrounded and doubtless compelled to capitulate with all his men. Simon condemned the idea most emphatically; the king, he said, should be treated in the same manner as Charles the Foolish: at Windsor there were 'houses with iron bolts good for keeping him securely within'.[3] Simon's language was violent, but he was right, and it was decided to abandon the town (24 July): the king beat a hasty retreat to Bordeaux; the French army was stopped by the fortifications of Blaye and decimated by sickness. The campaign was over.[4]

P.R.O., I published a mandate addressed by the king to the Barons of the Exchequer, from Saintes, 2 July 1242. There it is stated that the earl was bound to pay the Exchequer a debt of 400 marks a year; but that the king had pardoned him the sum of 600 marks for the first terms (*Bulletin du Comité des travaux historiques*, 1924, p. 229).

[1] At Taillebourg itself there was no fighting; cf. *Chron. maj.*, iv. 211–12, and *Annales du Midi*, v. (1893).

[2] *Chron. maj.*, iv. 213. Letters close of Henry III (3 July 1243) authorize Simon de Montfort to retain for himself the ransom of 100 marks 'per quas redemit quendam prisonem apud Xanctonam', in spite of the custom which attributed to the king the ransom of all prisoners taken in his presence (*C. R. 1242–1247*, 31. Cf. *Lettres de rois et reines*, i. 53.) These 100 marks probably served to pay the like sum due to Thomas of Savoy. It may be relevant to remember that the husband of Joan of Flanders had arrived in England a short while previously, and that the king had laden him with gifts: 'opimis oneratus regis muneribus,' remarks Paris, iv. 20.

[3] *Simon de Montfort*, p. 341: 'Le roi dit ke le conte li dist a Seintes. . . .' I do not think that these words can apply to another episode.

[4] *Chron. maj.*, iv. 209 f. Sir George Prothero, in relating to this campaign a satirical poem attributed by Wright to 1264 (*Political Songs*, p. 63), treated one of Wright's arguments too lightly; in fact, the poem speaks of Edward as a 'bold knight'; but Henry III's son was only three years old in 1242.

The winter was spent amid negotiations and festivities. Henry III made preparations to renew hostilities in the spring; but during that time at Bordeaux he ruined both himself and his followers—of whom Simon was one. When the fighting season came round, the king was found without alliances and faced by an empty treasury. He agreed to conclude with Louis IX a truce for five years (7 April 1243).

During this period, Leicester was learning to know the people whom he was to govern six years later on; learning to understand the enmities that engendered perpetual war between the lords and the factions that rent the towns. Everywhere he saw authority powerless to repress disorder and brigandage. There in Gascony he discovered alliances which were to be of service later and met with hatreds which were to prove an obstructive influence. In the south, where his father had won such great renown, he had many affinities: a Montfort was reigning at Castres; Alice, a daughter of his brother Guy, had married Jourdain III, the lord of Chabanais, whom she had presented with two sons, Esquivat and Jourdain, and several daughters. Alice's mother, Perronelle, countess of Bigorre, had wedded in 1242 (the fifth occasion) Boso de Matha, a native of Saintonge, and the daughter of this match had just married Gaston de Béarn, who was in devoted attendance on Henry III, during the winter of 1242–3. Thus Simon had connexions on all sides. On the other hand there was no lack of enemies. Raymond VII, count of Toulouse, and the king of Aragon had not forgotten Muret nor the violent conquest of Languedoc. At Bordeaux, where they made their appearance at the same time as the vicomte of Béarn and his 'monstrous' mother, they attempted to do Simon de Montfort a disservice with the king. So we learn from a letter of Adam Marsh written about this time to the superior of the Trinitarians at Paris. 'Trusting in your invariable friendliness,' he told him,[1] 'I beg you to go and find the excellent Queen Blanche and beg her serene clemency, whose influence, lowly as I am, I have long felt, to establish peace between our lords the counts of Toulouse and Leicester. I have found the spirit of the count of Toulouse inclined towards this peace, in accordance with my desire; the earl of Leicester

[1] Letter CCXV, p. 381.

is disposed to agree, also. I should myself have written of it to the queen, if her greatness had not stayed my humility.' We do not know the effect of these negotiations; at any rate the intrigues of the count of Toulouse did not succeed in getting Simon de Montfort into disgrace.

On the contrary, when the earl came back to England [1] it appears that there was no cloud of any sort between him and the king. At the request of countess Beatrice of Provence, Henry III's mother-in-law, who came to England at the end of 1243 with her youngest daughter Sanchia, the fiancée of Richard of Cornwall,[2] the king consented to perform certain 'acts of bounty' towards his sister, the countess of Leicester: 'he was wont to give to so many people towards whom he had few obligations.' [3] Letters patent and close for the years 1243–8 contain much that witnesses to the royal liberality towards Simon de Montfort and his wife Eleanor.[4]

But the earl was soon to be placed in a delicate position. The

[1] It is not known whether this was before or after the king, who reached Portsmouth on 9 October 1243. Mrs. Green thinks that it was before; *Lives of the Princesses of England*, ii. 81.

[2] *Chron. maj.*, iv. 261: 'circa idem tempus scilicet kalendis Decembris, applicuit apud Doveram . . . comitissa . . .'; then he says that the solemn entry of the countess into London took place on St. Martin's Octave (18 November). On this Luard remarks that the anonymous continuator of Matthew Paris, the author of the 'Flores Historiarum', gives the date as the 18th of the kalends of December (= 15 November). It would be sufficient to make a slight addition to the text of Paris and to read 'scilicet [XVIII] kal. Dec.'. Richard of Cornwall was the widower of Isabella, daughter of William Marshal the Great, who died 16 January 1240. His marriage had naturally led him to range himself among the territorial opposition to the king. His second marriage with Sanchia, the queen's sister, brought him nearer to the court and to the Savoyard party; this change of front left the field open to Simon de Montfort (*D. N. B. s.v.* Richard, earl of Cornwall).

[3] *Simon de Montfort*, p. 335. The Countess Beatrice, on learning that the king had given his sister 'ne mariage ne moeble', asked him to do her 'aucune bonté'. Henry thereupon gave 'a mai e a li [Aliénor] v^c mars de rente en tieu manere qe les iii^c fussent a nos e a nos airs . . . e les ii^c a nostre vie'.

[4] On 7 January 1244 Henry III excused Simon and his wife 1,000*l.* out of the debts contracted by Eleanor and her first husband (*Excerpta e rotulis finium*, i. 410);—on the 8th he went security for 40*l.* of annual rent which Walter, earl of Pembroke, owed the countess, as compensation for her dowry in Ireland (*C. P. R. 1232–1247*, 416);—on the 10th, he undertook to assign her a reasonable dowry out of the lands of her deceased husband, if Walter ceased to pay her this rent (*Excerpta*, p. 424); on 12 February he remitted Simon and his wife the debts claimed by the Exchequer, i. e. the reliefs due from the earl for half a knight's fee; 20*s.* and a cask of wine 'de primo scutagio',

campaign of 1242 had brought the king nothing but debt, and he needed money. The parliament which met at London on 2 February 1244 nominated a commission of twelve members charged to negotiate with the king. They comprised six ecclesiastics, among them the bishops of Lincoln and Worcester, Simon's great friends; the six laymen were the earls of Cornwall, Leicester and Norfolk (Bigod), the earl Marshal, Richard of Montfichet and John de Balliol. The demands of these commissioners were imperious. The king must, for example, swear to observe the Great Charter, to accept a justiciar and a chancellor nominated by parliament, to depose officials that were suspected or superfluous. The king refused, and the parliament was prorogued for three weeks. Henry took advantage of this delay to try his blandishments upon individual members of parliament and to persuade them to grant singly what they had refused corporately, but in vain. He received a further check, when he tried to detach the clergy from the opposition. The clergy, without letting themselves be affected by a bull of Innocent IV exhorting the prelates and the whole clergy of the realm to accord their sovereign an aid in money, unanimously decided that the reply to the papal bull should be deferred till the next meeting of the parliament. Henry III, however, was anxious to try still one further expedient. The earl of Leicester, Peter of Savoy, the queen's uncle, and three close counsellors,

50 marks 'de judaismo'; 165*l.* de pluribus praestitis ei factis de garderoba regis per fratrem G., quondam elemosinarium regis; 6*l.* 6*s.* 'de precio septem penularum de bissis e prestito'; 620*l.* due from the earl and countess 'de prestito eis de thesauro regis anno xxij⁰ (1237–8); 180*l.* 'de alba firma de Westcumbe et Bedewind'; 200 *m.* 'de prestito eidem comitisse facto anno eodem [the year of her marriage]; 15*l.* 'de prestito eidem comitisse facto per manum ejusdem fratris Galfridi'. The barons of the Exchequer consequently received a prohibition to claim anything from Simon and Eleanor for these debts and loans (*C. R., 1242–1247*, 159). This act with its interesting detail is valuable as pointing to the existence of a dual financial administration, both Exchequer and Royal Household.—On 7 May 1245 the king placed at the disposal of the earl and his wife 300 marks owed by William Marshal (*C. P. R. 1232–1247*, 453);—on 28 May he assigned them an annual sustenance rent of 500 marks, and another 300 marks for their heirs, with power to convert them into lands or wardships (*C. Ch. R.*, i. 278); on 15 June he gave the earl the wardship of the Umfravill heir mentioned above (p. 34); on 18 August 1246 the countess was released of 30*l.* owed by her each year for the farm of the manor of Wexcumb received by her as her dower (*C. P. R. 1232–1247*, 485), an act confirmed on 21 January 1248 (*Excerpta*, ii. 27).

Ralph FitzNicholas, William de Cantilupe and John Fitz Geoffrey went by order to reveal to the prelates the plight of the treasury and the expenses necessitated by the war in Gascony and in Wales; then the king suddenly appeared on the scene and addressed them with the most earnest requests. He received the chilling reply that they would think about it, and retired, completely confounded. On the morrow the clergy broke up without having undone their purse-strings.[1] The king had thus to submit; at the second session of parliament (the end of February) he promised to observe the liberties which he had so many times sworn to maintain; at this price alone could he obtain the aid that he was soliciting.[2] It is necessary to dwell on this episode, since certain historians have maintained that it was in the parliament of 1244 that Simon de Montfort made his début in the opposition. We have already made clear our answer to this allegation, all the more inaccurate because for three years beyond this date Simon can be seen practically entirely occupied in the king's service. In 1245 he followed Henry in an expedition to the Welsh frontier.[3] If he gave his approval to the letter whereby the bishops, abbots, priors, earls, and barons protested in 1246 against the oppressive treatment of the Church of England by the papacy, it should be noted that this letter was actually sent at the demand and with the consent of the king, who was not unhappy to take advantage of the Council then in session at Lyons in order to combat the encroachments of the Roman Church.[4] In 1247 he was sent to France by the king, on

---

[1] It was Robert Grosseteste, bishop of Lincoln, who induced the clergy not to separate their case from that of the barons, 'proferens hanc theologie auctoritatem: non dividamur a communi consilio, quia scriptum est: 'si dividamur, statim omnes moriemur' (*Chron. maj.*, iv. 366).

[2] For the whole of this episode, see *Chron. maj.*, iv. 362 f.

[3] *Chron. maj.*, iv. 423: The king summoned to the army all owing him military service. In the *Annales Cestrenses* (ed. Christie, 1886, p. 64) we read that Simon rejoined Henry III on the Ides of August (13th) and left him the Sunday following (20th). The expedition had as its sole result the construction in the neighbourhood of Snowdon of the fortress of Gannoc, which was 'like a thorn in the eye of the Welsh' (*Chron. maj.*, iv. 486). That same year the earls of Cornwall, Leicester, and Norfolk were charged to assess the amends due to the king from Ralph de Camoys and several other lords guilty of participating in a tournament 'contra prohibicionem regis' (*C. R. 1242–1247*, 363).

[4] The letters addressed to the Pope are given at length in Matthew Paris, *Chron. maj.*, iv. 529–536. Cf. Potthast, no. 12038 (26 March). In the letter of

'very secret business',[1] and he returned on 13 October, just in time to be present at the festival to which Henry had invited him in honour of his 'dear saint', Edward the Confessor.[2] The one topic of interest at this time was the imminent departure of Louis IX for the Crusade. Following his example, Simon, his

the earls, Simon's name comes immediately after that of Richard, the king's brother. In 1246 the countess Eleanor, who had a peculiar affection for the Abbey of Waverley, was specially authorized by the Holy Father to enter its gates. She had with her her husband ('piissimum maritum suum') and two of her sons, Henry and Simon, with three servants. She offered a precious stuff as an ornament for the high altar on the day of the monstrance of the relics; she listened to the sermon pronounced in the chapter, and after kissing a fragment of the true cross, withdrew (Waverley, p. 236). 'Later on', adds the annalist who carefully recorded these details, 'she gave us 50 marks, and 18 more for the fabric, and a subsidy to allow us to acquire 150 acres of land at Netham.' In the text, these facts are attributed to 1244, but 'Palm Sunday, 1 April' necessitates a correction in the year.

[1] What business? The king may have thought it opportune to calm the suspicions of the king of France, in consideration of the fact that he had summoned to him his three uterine brothers and their sister Alice, who were then quitting Poitou so as to avoid the miserable plight in which they had been left by the French king (Chron. maj., iv. 627-8). But another explanation may be suggested. Edmund Rich, archbishop of Canterbury, had died in voluntary exile, in France, 16 November 1240. He was canonized on 11 January 1247 and his body was transported to Pontigny where it was buried on 7 June (Chron. maj., iv. 631). Richard of Cornwall would have desired to be present at the great pilgrimage to which the ceremony gave rise; he first stopped with Louis IX, and had a long and familiar conversation with him about the business of Normandy. It was said that before leaving to go on Crusade, the king of France wished to unburden his conscience of all sin and perhaps to restore to the English king the duchy of which he had been unjustly despoiled forty years previously (ibid., p. 646); but the opposition of the French magnates had overcome the saintly king's scruples. Now for the following autumn Louis IX had ordered a vast inquiry into abuses committed by the prévôts and bailis in the regions conquered by Philip Augustus and by Louis VIII (ibid., p. 638). Was not Henry III in a position to turn the occasion to profit by taking up negotiations at the point where earl Richard had failed, and was it not in such a manœuvre that Simon was most likely to have been 'secretly' employed?

[2] Chron. maj., iv. 640; the king invited all the great persons of his kingdom to the translation of Edward the Confessor, 'great king and martyr'; the festival was celebrated with the primary object of giving a worthy reception to a 'portion of the blood of Our Lord', secondly in order to dignify the knighting of William de Valence. This triple ceremony was celebrated on one day, 13 October (ibid., p. 644). Matthew Paris describes at length the procession in which the king's childlike devotion was made manifest; he speaks (p. 642) of the gifts which he made 'Deo et ecclesiae S. Petri Westmonasterii et caro suo Aedwardo et sacro conventui'. Doubtless it was to be present at these festivities that Simon returned to England on that same 13 October (p. 645).

wife, knights, and many others of his household took the cross also.[1] Simon was to command the English contingent. In a bull of 12 June 1248, recalling the services done to the Church by Simon and his ancestors, the Pope asked the English clergy to provide him the necessary funds;[2] he could not as yet have known that six weeks earlier[3] Henry III had decided to send his brother-in-law into Gascony, with full powers to re-establish the royal authority, now compromised by the insubordination of the lords and the towns.

[1] It is strange to read in Matthew Paris that Simon took the cross in order to expiate the sin he had committed in marrying a widow who had taken the veil: 'ut peccatis absolutus ad coelos avolare mereretur' (*ibid.*, iv. 1). He evidently forgot in 1248 what he had written ten years earlier.

[2] *Registres d'Innocent IV*, no. 3475 and 3523; *Papal Letters*, i. 239. In August 1248, the bishops of Lincoln and Worcester made assignment to the earl of an aid of 4,000 marks to be collected in view of his departure to Palestine. This assignment was carried out in view of a bull of Innocent IV, dated Lyons 'secundo idus junii, pontificatus nostri anno quinto' (12 June 1248), which is reproduced complete in the charter of August 1248. It contains this passage: 'sane, cum ipse comes, zelo fidei et devotionis accensus, proposuerit assumere signum crucis et in Terre Sancte subsidium transfretare, nos . . . rogamus . . . quatenus de votorum redemptione et aliis . . . que in manus vestras pervenient, . . . comiti memorato pro se et pro aliis quae in sua duxerit comitiva, . . . subventionis dexteram porrigatis.' B. N. Clairembault, 1188, fol. 7. This bull is not indicated in Potthast, and has not been copied into the papal registers. See Adam Marsh, Letter CXLI, p. 270.

[3] Roughly the time taken for a courier to cover the journey between London and Rome. See Friedrich Ludwig, *Untersuchungen uber die Reise- und Marsch-Geschwindigkeit im xii. und xiii. Jahrhundert*, 1897. It could however be done at express speed in 30½ days; cf. R. L. Poole, *The early correspondence of John of Salisbury* (Brit. Acad. Proc. xi), p. 5.

IV

SIMON DE MONTFORT IN GASCONY,[1] 1248–1254

THROUGHOUT the first half of the thirteenth century
Gascony was a source of continual anxiety to the English
king. The whole country was a prey to civil strife. In the rural
districts nobles held merchants to ransom; the towns, strengthened by the municipal privileges which they had won, had
secured their freedom from feudal control, and, as in the case of
the Lombard communes,[2] were the scene of disputes between
armed factions. At Bordeaux the Rostein and the Colom
families were openly declared enemies, and their quarrels
divided the town into two camps. In Dax, La Réole, Bazas,
similar dissensions were witnessed. At Bayonne, a democratic
party recruited primarily from the sea-faring population was
coming into existence to combat an aristocracy that aimed at
reserving municipal office for members of a few privileged
families. The larger mercantile interests felt the need of maintaining friendly relations with England, always provided that
the king emphasized his authority and his continual need of
money as little as possible; while the feudal nobility wavered
between the fealty they had sworn and their desire for independence. So disturbed a country was bound to excite the covetous
desires of its neighbours. In the south, the king of Navarre[3]

---

[1] For this chapter as a whole I should like to refer readers to the detailed
studies written by me since my thesis was published: 'Simon de Montfort,
comte de Leicester; son gouvernement en Gascogne, 1248–1253,' *Revue
historique*, t. iv; 'Les institutions municipales de Bordeaux au Moyen Âge; la
mairie et la jurade', t. cxxiii. 'La mairie et la jurade dans les villes de la Gascogne anglaise: Bourg et Blaye, Saint-Émilion et Libourne,' *Revue historique de
Bordeaux*, 1917, and 'La Réole', *Annales du Midi*, 1919. It is also necessary
to consult the *Rôles gascons*, supplement to t. 1 (1896), and the *Recueil d'actes
relatifs à l'administration des rois d'Angleterre en Guyenne au XIII*e *siècle* (1914):
these documents have been already utilized by Frank Burr Marsh for his work,
English Rule in Gascony, 1199–1259 (1912), and by Dr. Eleanor Lodge, *Gascony
under English rule* (1926).

[2] An analogy suggested by the declaration of its obligations towards the
king of England made in 1274 by the mayoralty of Bordeaux (*Livre des
Coutumes*, p. 506).

[3] Thibaut IV, the Poet, count of Champagne, had succeeded his uncle,
Sancho VII, king of Navarre. See H. d'Arbois de Jubainville, *Hist. des ducs
et comtes de Champagne*, iv. 265.

made perpetual incursions into the rich valley of the Adour; he was supported by the nobility of Béarn and Labour, who did homage to the king of England or the king of Navarre as it suited them. Aragon and Castile[1] claimed to have rights over Gascony itself; and there was some fear that the French king might take the offensive again after the expiry of the truce made in 1243.

Henry III had had occasion to form his own opinion upon the insufferable turbulence of his Gascon subjects, and to estimate how great was the danger that threatened the province, if no energetic measures were taken to establish order. Only a few miles away from his capital he had been obliged to storm the church of Veyrines,[2] where highwaymen had barricaded themselves, entirely undeterred by his presence. He had been compelled to march in person against the king of Navarre, and to lay siege to the castle of Gramont. And what had come of it all? Having spent all his money and borrowed considerable sums from a number of burgesses, he had left the province without reducing it to order. After his departure, risings broke out everywhere. King Thibaut resorted to arms; he was checked by the seneschal, Nicholas de Meulles[3] (1244), a marshal of the king's household; and then, three years later, Nicholas was replaced by Guillaume de Bueil, 'a great talker like all Normans,' but in other ways incompetent.[4] Consequently Gaston, the vicomte of Béarn, could ravage with impunity the territories of the very sovereign who two years earlier had laden him with presents. Dax was one of his victims.[5] The vicomtes of Gramont, Soule, Tartas, his vassals or allies, conspired with the

---

[1] The pretensions of Castile over Gascony arose from the marriage of Eleanor, daughter of Henry II of England, with the Castilian king Alfonso VIII (1170). In 1248 the reigning sovereign in Castile was Ferdinand the Saint. The king of Aragon, James I, could also invoke the rights of his wife Eleanor, daughter of Alfonso IX of Castile and Bérengère, who on her side was the eldest daughter of Alfonso VIII and Eleanor of England.

[2] *Chron. maj.*, iv. 236. Cf. *Revue critique d'histoire et de littérature*, 1897, premier semestre, p. 188, and Leo Drouyn, *La Guienne militaire*, ii. 313.

[3] Meulles is in Calvados, arr. Lisieux, c. Orbec.

[4] *Chron. maj.*, iv. 630: ' Juxta patriae suae consuetudinem, qui Neuster erat, magniloquus, factus est sterilis et pusillus '. Bueil is in Eure, arr. Évreux, c. Passy-sur-Eure.

[5] Balasque, *Études sur Bayonne*, ii. 280.

men of Navarre to ravage Labour; [1] whence disturbances spread little by little all over the country. Close upon the gates of Bordeaux, Bertrand de Bouville, Bernard de Podensac and Guillaume Séguin de Rions spread fire and destruction over each other's lands; a pitched battle was fought over the town of Blaye between Amaubin de Barès and the vicomte of Fronsac.[2] The towns of La Réole, Castillon, and Bazas were also torn by civil war.

The situation was troublesome in every respect; above all, it had the effect of interfering with commerce, the fruitful source of wealth for England and Gascony alike. Henry III resolved to make an end of it. He entrusted extraordinary powers to Richard de Grey, and commissioned him to bring the province to order.[3] But Richard, who had been there before, was soon discovered—or discovered himself—to be inferior to this heavy task, and the earl of Leicester was approached. Simon did not immediately accept. In the first place, as we saw, he had taken the cross; and furthermore, he foresaw the great difficulties ahead, and would only take the post on condition that he had all material means of achieving his end. On a later occasion he explained his reasons at some length: Gascony, he said,[4] was in danger of being lost for the king and his heirs, 'si hastif conseils n'i fust mis', especially now that the truce between the kings of France and England was shortly to expire.[5] Then, 'li Rois et sis conseils et ma dame la Royne proierent le comte de Leyc. qu'il i alast.' Not wishing 'commencer une chose qu'il n'eust tens d'achever', Simon asked for the custody of Gascony for seven years, with the absolute disposal of its revenues and with the further condition that the king should 'deliver to him

[1] *Royal Letters*, ii. 58: letter addressed to the king about 1249 by the 'probi homines' of the castle of Uza (Landes, arr. Dax, c. Castets).

[2] *Simon de Montfort*, p. 286.

[3] On 26 February 1248 Henry III gave Richard the custody of Gascony for two years. He was to receive all its revenues and maintain all necessary military operations, except any against the kings of France, Aragon, Castile, Navarre, and against the count of Toulouse (*C. P. R. 1247–1258*, 10); cf. *D. N. B.*, *s.v.* Grey, Richard, second baron Grey of Codnor. He was one of Simon's supporters even after Evesham.

[4] *Simon de Montfort*, p. 341.

[5] The 'five years' truce concluded 7 April 1243 (*Layettes*, no. 3075) was due to expire at Michaelmas 1249.

at his own expense' fifty knights a year, two thousand marks, and take responsibility for any war that might eventually arise against the four neighbouring kings. 'And the king, by the advice of the good men of his council made the delivery in this manner.' We have indeed the original patent of Henry III granting the earl (1 May 1248) everything he asked.[1] One point of capital importance should be noted: Simon's government was to last seven years; the task in front was seen to be long and difficult.

Simon therefore set out for his governorship armed with full powers, not as 'an official removable at his lord's will, but as his lord's representative in everything up to the end of the seventh year aforesaid'.[2] While Henry III was getting together the promised contingent,[3] he repaired to the court of France, and at Lorris concluded with the regent[4] a truce of three months (20 September). Finally he reached Bordeaux. The Rostein

---

[1] *Simon de Montfort*, p. 264. This patent is not mentioned in the *C. P. R.*; the original is in the Bibl. Nat., Clairembault 1188, and more likely comes from the seignorial archives of Montfort, of which we have given a brief description in the Introduction. Matthew Paris reports the contents of the patent inaccurately: 'confecit ei cartam suam de custodia per sex annos continuanda; et de thesauro suo decem milia marcarum largitus' (v. 293); the chronicler adds the orders which the king doubtless gave orally: 'supplicavit, persuasit et praecepit ut ipsos [the Gascons] dire et dure tractaret suppeditatos. . . .' The word 'suppeditatos' seems a verbal play on the expression 'sub scabellum pedum tuorum' of Ps. cix. 2, which Paris does not omit to cite. On the same day (1 May), Henry III ordered the barons of the Exchequer to grant Simon respite until the quinzaine of Michaelmas for paying the sums they demanded of him (*C. R. 1247–1251*, 43). On 28 August, he granted Simon that if he were to die in his service, his English revenues and the honour of Leicester should be employed during the eight years after his decease in paying his debts and in executing the clauses of his will (*Royal Letters*, ii. 379; cf. *C. P. R. 1247–1258*, 26).

[2] *Simon de Montfort*, p. 342.

[3] See *C. P. R. 1247–1258*, 2, 9, 31, and *C. R. 1247–1251*, 119, for the acts relating to the summons of the knights. The general embarkation took place at Portsmouth under the direction of Nicholas de Meulles. Military service in Gascony allowed men to compound for certain crimes. Thus on 7 September 1248, the king gave a recognizance that 'Hugo de Tywa' had paid 'in his wardrobe' to Simon de Montfort's credit 100*l*., 'pro fine quam fecit cum rege pro morte Laurentii quondam Archidiaconi Ebor.'; and in connexion with this crime, John, Hugh's brother, declared himself ready to set out for Gascony and to remain there till Easter. Consequently the king ordered the sheriff of Yorkshire to release Hugh and not to molest the pledges provided by him (*C. R. 1247–1251*, 85).

[4] *Layettes*, no. 3713.

and the Colom had just made peace,[1] and at first therefore he took no side, but made representatives of both factions enter his council, although his preference for the Colom did not pass unmarked.[2] He then went off to tour the rest of the province.

From the standpoint of feudal jurisdiction, Gascony was at this time divided into four courts of judicial areas, with their principal centres normally at Bordeaux, Bazas, Saint-Sever, and Dax. It was here that the king's lieutenant had to receive the homage of the vassals, and to swear to govern them 'according to the laws and customs of the country'; here that he dealt out justice in his court 'furnished with nobles, knights, and burgesses'.[3] Simon appeared successively in each of these towns; his military force in attendance made it possible for him to execute then and there his own decisions and the judgments of his court. At Dax appeared the knights of Labour. These petty lords were largely composed of bandits who relieved traveller and merchant of their goods, friend and foe alike. Simon had several of them arrested without trial, made them hand over their fortresses and did not release them until he had imposed heavy ransoms.[4] He expressly forbade forcible exaction of security unless a court had given the order; for this, he said, 'was the beginning of all wars'. He forbade all men to carry arms, or to form companies or 'mesnies', which were frequently no more than bands of highwaymen.[5] Several burgesses of Dax were punished arbitrarily, like the knights of Labour, and when they came to complain of this violation of their privileges, Simon dealt roughly with their illusions: had they not set themselves outside the law by disturbing the public peace? The same summary treatment was meted out to certain knights who were not afraid to present themselves at the court of Saint-Sever, in spite of the complaints brought against them. The most redoubtable, the only one of all these brigands whose

[1] On 30 July 1248, the king ratified the peace concluded between Gaillard Colom and Rostein Delsoler (*C. P. R. 1247–1258*, 23). A seal of William Raymond Colom attached to a charter of May 1251 reads: 'Sig. W. Ramon Colom' (Bibl. Nat., Clairembault 1188, fol. 7v.).

[2] *Simon de Montfort*, pp. 280–6.

[3] See *Revue historique*, iv. 264.

[4] These ransoms, it was reported, reached the figure of 7,000s. (of Morlaas). *Simon de Montfort*, p. 313.

[5] *Études sur Bayonne*, ii. 584.

memory Matthew Paris has preserved, was the vicomte de Gramont;[1] he was arrested and imprisoned in the castle of La Réole. There he remained six years, without being brought to judgment.[2] The vicomte of Soule took note of this example, and was careful not to appear in court at Saint-Sever; and as the attorney to whom he had entrusted the defence of his case did not appear on the day assigned to him, the earl stormed the town and later the castle of Mauléon. The vicomte was made prisoner and had to promise a ransom of 10,000s. (of Morlaas).

The vicomtes of Gramont and Soule would have been deserving of small pity, had they not been the victims of arbitrary action; with the burgesses of Saut it was different. Their account was that when the king came to Gascony, they went to swear fealty to him at Bordeaux; but the king's lieutenants had always come to Saut; it was they who first took the oath to respect the privileges of the town; then, and only then, did the burgesses swear fealty to him. Such was the privilege of Saut and of many another town. But to Leicester it did not matter. He loftily told the burgesses that he would never finish the round if he had to go taking and receiving the customary oaths from town to town, and he compelled them to send deputies to him at Saint-Sever. Two of them, it appears, had already in 1242 refused to do homage to the king.[3] Simon detained them for more than a year; an inquiry into their conduct, which was taken back as far as 1225, when Richard of Cornwall was seneschal of Poitou and Gascony, failed to produce any charge against them; but they were none the less held to ransom. The borough of Saut was assaulted and taken by the earl's men.

[1] *Chron. maj.*, v. 49.

[2] *Études sur Bayonne*, ii. 591; *Royal Letters*, ii. 61; *C. R. 1247–1256*, 387.

[3] Guillaume-Arnaud de Brocas and Guillaume-Arnaud de Naude; they claimed to hold from Marie-Bertrand, the daughter and only child—she was then (in 1242) a minor—of their deceased suzerain; but Amanieu d'Albret, guardian of the young heiress, had transmitted his rights of wardship to the king, and the burgesses of Saut were forced to yield. Later, Gaston de Béarn, in defiance of the king's rights, married the heiress of Saut to Garsie-Arnaud of Navailles, and the burgesses swore that they would aid the couple in the recovery of their rights. Such are the facts of the case, at any rate as they appear in the 'Querele de Saltu' (*Simon de Montfort*, p. 297). The affair was finally settled, but not until 1262, in favour of Prince Edward, Henry III's eldest son. See Bibl. Nat., Manuscrits français, no. 20685, in the Collection of Roger Gaignières, p. 7.

The vicomte of Béarn dared not move. He knew that many people, most of all the burgesses of Dax, had brought complaints against him; but Simon was not looking for war with 'the most important man in the country', who—amongst other things— was uncle of the English queen.[1] He thought that it would be more politic to let him have a truce.[2] He may have been wrong here, but the people of Dax, who demanded justice and rigorous justice, cried out aloud when they saw Simon negotiating with the man who had victimized them so often.[3] But if the earl did not propose to make a frontal attack upon Gaston de Béarn, he did all he could to isolate him. The taking of Mauléon (Soule) and of Gramont began the carrying out of this plan; and Simon followed it up by securing firm support in Bigorre.

For long Gaston de Béarn had been coveting the inheritance of his mother-in-law, the old countess Perronelle, then widowed of her fifth husband.[4] His wife had brought him in dower the vicomté of Marsan and all that might accrue from her father, Boso de Matha, in the Chabanais, at Confolens and in the Limousin. He was anxious to add to these territories the county

---

[1] Gaston's mother, Garsenda, had been married first to Raymond Béranger, count of Provence, father of Queen Eleanor. Gaston was thus uterine brother of the English queen's father. See Marca, *Hist. de Béarn*, p. 588, and Adrien Blanchet, *L'hommage du Béarn à l'Angleterre, XIIIᵉ–XIVᵉ siècles* in *Moyen Âge*, 2ᵉ série, xxvi. 44–62.

[2] *Chron. maj.*, v. 48.

[3] *Études sur Bayonne*, ii. 580. On 28 Dec. 1249, the king wrote to Simon that he had pardoned Gaston de Béarn and his partisans 'omnia damna et homicidia que nobis et hominibus nostris intulerunt'; he desired 'quod ballivi et fideles nostri sint eis familiares et amici sicut prius' (*Royal Letters*, ii. 57, cf. *C. P. R. 1247–1258*, 57). On the same day he notified the earl that he had received on St. Lucia's day (13 December) the submission of one of Gaston's partisans, Arnaud Séguin 'de Hasta'. Matthew Paris (v. 104) reports under 1250 the taking of Fronsac and Gramont, and the amnesty accorded to Gaston de Béarn: 'intercedente regina, cujus se fecit consanguineum, in gratiam regis receptus est.'

[4] She was the daughter of Bernard IV, count of Comminges, and of Sté- phanie, countess of Bigorre. About 1198 she had married Gaston de Béarn IV, who died childless in 1215; the following year she married again, her husband being Nuño Sanchez; but Simon de Montfort, the victor of the Albigensians, had the marriage broken off immediately by the Church, in order to secure the rich inheritance of the countess for his son Guy. Guy de Montfort was killed in the siege of Castelnaudary in 1220, and his widow married in succession Aimar de Rancon (1221), then Boso de Matha, lord of Cognac, who died in 1239. I take these details from P. Meyer, *La Chanson de la Croisade contre les Albigeois*, ii. 290.

of Bigorre, to the prejudice of the daughters and grandchildren of Guy de Montfort.[1] Simon's arrival in Gascony quickly stopped these acquisitive schemes. He got the Countess Perronelle to grant him the guardianship of Bigorre for an annual rent of 7,000s. (of Morlaas). On her death he was to possess it 'until he had secured compensation for the money spent in defending it'.[2] Thus, with Bigorre safe, Simon kept Gaston de Béarn under observation along his eastern frontier in the same way as he already restricted him in the north and the west. And he did more than this; he tried to sever all relations, political and economic, between Béarn and Bigorre,[3] and succeeded so well that Gaston later on uttered bitter complaints of the 'continual vexations' which Simon de Montfort made his subjects endure.

Here we may be allowed to anticipate a little, and sketch the ups and downs of the complicated game of intrigue played between Gaston and Simon for the possession of Bigorre. Boso de Matha, father-in-law of Gaston, died in February 1251. The vicomte of Béarn, in his wife's name, immediately laid claim to the deceased's goods in Chabanais and at Confolens. Alice, daughter of the Countess Perronelle and Guy de Montfort made a counter-claim in the interests of her young son Esquivat; but she in her turn died, and Gaston once more urged his case. The affair was submitted to the court of Chabanais presided over by Simon de Montfort; Gaston did not appear;[4] and after a year judgment was pronounced against him by default and Esquivat

---

[1] *Simon de Montfort*, p. 315.

[2] See the testament of Perronelle in Marca, *Histoire de Béarn*, p. 827.

[3] Mathe de Bigorre, daughter of Perronelle and Guy, had married Gaston de Béarn, to whom she brought Marsan in dower. Simon tried to divert the merchants of Bigorre from following the Gabardan and Marsan routes; he constrained the knights of Marsan to come and plead their suits before Gascon tribunals and prohibited natives of Bigorre from appealing from the court of Bigorre to that of Morlaas. At the same time he established a prévôt to supervise the frontiers of Marsan (*Simon de Montfort*, p. 316).

[4] Gaston pretended later that Simon had refused 'to do right' to him. Simon, on the other hand, alleged that a summons to appear on a definite day had been issued to Gaston, husband of Mathe, and to Ralph of Courtenai, second husband of Alice de Montfort, but the latter alone had been present. The defaulter was in the wrong. The revenue of the lands under dispute amounted annually to 500 marks. In 1253 Esquivat was in peaceful possession. See *Simon de Montfort*, p. 315, and *Études sur Bayonne*, ii. 576.

was put in possession of the whole property. The will of the Countess Perronelle (3 November 1251) finally robbed Gaston of his last hopes: sacrificing the issue of her fifth husband to that of her third, she chose as heir her grandson Esquivat and, failing him, his younger brother, Jourdain; if these two lords happened to die without heirs, the succession was to go to Mathe, Gaston's wife.[1] But it was the earl of Leicester whom she charged with the duty of supervising the defence of the county and of protecting the weakness of her grandson, Esquivat, whom she had preferred as heir. Henceforth, and for more than ten years, Simon was to remain master of Bigorre, the object of Gaston de Béarn's covetous ambition.[2]

Furthermore, Simon had to keep under observation the count of Toulouse and the king of Navarre. Against the former he made an alliance with the vicomte of Lomagne.[3] The illness, later the death, of Raymond VII (27 September 1249),[4] were soon to relieve him of all anxiety from this quarter. The king of Navarre he sought out and met. At an interview on the Spanish frontier (Ainhoa, 30 October 1248)[5] they agreed each to choose two arbiters to regulate their disputes; if the arbiters did not reach agreement, the matter of the king of Navarre and

[1] She then enumerates her credits and debts. Simon was due to pay her 7,000s. of Morlaas in annual rent; at the moment when the will was drawn up he was 15,500s. in arrears. The testatrix humbly prays and requires him, in the name of Our Saviour Jesus Christ, to pay this entire sum to the executors of her will, 'in order that they may be able to execute her last wishes.' This was not the first time that Simon was regarded as a bad debtor, and it was not to be the last.

[2] Simon was at the time supreme in this area, i.e. Armagnac and Fezenzac; that is at any rate the inference to be drawn from the date given in a charter in *Cartulaire de Berdoues*, no. 443, p. 291: 'secunda feria ante festum purificationis B.M.V. anno Domini MCC. quinquagesimo primo (1251 or 1252?) domino Simone de Monteforti in comitatibus Fedenziaci et Armaniaci dominante.'

[3] Arnaud-Otton, vicomte of Lomagne, territory situated in between the lands of Toulouse and Condom, was vassal both of the king of England and of the count of Toulouse. Cf. Vaissette, *Hist. Languedoc*, ed. Privat, viii. 1251; Guillaume de Puylaurens in *Histor. de France*, xx. 772; Potthast, *Regesta*, nos. 13069, 13070; *Registres d'Innocent IV*, nos. 4204, 4205.

[4] On 13 December 1249 the king charged Simon to claim the Agenais from the executors of Count Raymond VII (*C. P. R. 1247-1258*, 56): the district was only restored definitively by the treaty of 1259.

[5] *Simon de Montfort*, p. 265. The agreement was ratified by Henry III on 6 February 1249 (Rymer; *C. P. R., ibid.*, p. 36).

the earl of Leicester was to be taken in the last resort before the King; Henry III was to decide by Candlemas (2 February 1249) at the latest if he approved of their agreement, and his sentence was to be given before St. John Baptist's day (24 June).

Thus without drawing the sword, in a few months (October–December 1248), Simon had chastised the rebels, rallied the king's supporters, and disposed of the danger of international complications. When he arrived at Westminster during the Christmas festivities, he was joyfully received by the king and the whole court;[1] later he returned to Gascony.[2] On 28 June violent dissension broke out in Bordeaux. The immediate causes are not known, but plenty of information about the facts is forthcoming from the chief participants; their testimony, however, is clearly partisan, and the fact makes it difficult to disentangle the intentions of the principal actors.[3] It is evident that the earl was taken by surprise; he was still in bed when he was informed about it. He armed quickly, and with a following of a few knights, dashed into the fight. The partisans of the Colom immediately put themselves under his orders and charged their enemies. But the leader of the enemy faction, old Rostein, ill as he was, knew how to take energetic measures. Acting in co-operation with him, the mayor summoned the jurats and the three hundred burgesses liable for police functions in the municipality, and marched with them to the market-place, now in the occupation of the Colom. He was repulsed and began to beat a retreat, when near the Porte Begueyre he was set upon by armed retainers of the earl, who dispersed his small company. Rostein's house was marked down, and soon there was nothing for it but to capitulate. He had to surrender, and hand over his prisoners taken from the Colom. On the morrow (29 June) the earl demanded twenty hostages from each party, and three houses selected by him with their complete 'armaments'; but, considering that the Rostein were the more compromised, he

[1] *Chron. maj.*, v. 48.

[2] According to Matthew Paris (v. 76), Simon left England during the early days of June: 'mutato vel protelato voto suae peregrinationis, transfretavit,' at the same time as the English contingent for the Crusade, now under the command of William Lungspee (see *D. N. B.*, *s.v.* Longespée).

[3] See the accusations brought by the Gascons before the king's court in 1252 and the earl's refutation of them in *Études sur Bayonne*, ii, and my *Simon de Montfort*, pp. 279–321.

released the leaders of the Colom party, and took in their place their sons, nephews, and cousins, while he had the others carefully guarded.[1] A canon of Saint-Seurin, Gaillard by name, who was undoubtedly a partisan of the Rostein, was severely treated: the earl took possession of his oxen, cows, and other live stock, seized the inheritance of a nephew who had just died, prevented the confirmation by the archbishop of Bordeaux of his election as dean of the chapter, and started a process against him in the Roman Curia, then at Lyons, which he visited twice in order to impugn his conduct. The unfortunate dean, who was a papal chaplain, when enumerating two years later the losses caused him by these confiscations and the long journey to Lyons, estimated them at more than sixteen hundred marks, not reckoning the damage to reputation of which he had been the victim.[2] Several of the insurgents fled to escape these drastic measures of suppression and the reprisals of the 'Colombins', who had pillaged the houses of their enemies after their chiefs had been set at liberty. The earl had it publicly cried throughout the town that those who had fled could return in security, if they undertook to present themselves before the judges. This stipulation mostly frightened them; Simon then seized their property 'because they were defaulters'.[3]

Upon this the Rostein party sent two delegates to the king: Guillaume Bener and a monk, a son of the old Rostein.[4] At first

[1] Rostein and the hostages of his party were first imprisoned in the castle of Bordeaux. Rostein himself was lodged 'en une bele chambre onestemant et honorablemant', where he had servants to look after him and was well treated. The party were later transferred to the castle of Roquer. Then Rostein fell ill and offered to leave his son Gaillard as a hostage until he was better. Simon accepted; but Gaillard was at the time imprisoned in Fronsac with his brother Peter (they were both absent from Bordeaux on 28 June) and several of his friends; he refused to come and replace his father, who died. He died of grief, said Simon, 'kar, se Rosteins fust loiaus homs, plus li deust grever la desloiauté que ses filz fist d'estre contre le roi, et ce qu'il ne le vout ostatger, que autres noveles' (*Simon de Montfort*, pp. 281-3, 287-9). The castle of Roquer or Roqueys is situated in the parish of Tabanac. A few fragments of its walls still survive. On the topography of Bordeaux, see the important work of Leo Drouyn, *Bordeaux vers 1450*.

[2] *Simon de Montfort*, p. 317: 'Querela decani Sancti Severini.' In the text the dean's name is given as 'Guilhardus', doubtless for 'Gaillardus'.

[3] *Ibid.*, pp. 291-2.

[4] *Ibid.*, p. 284: 'miserunt ei (the king) Rostandum monachum, filium quondam domini Rustandi, et Guillelmum Bener. . . .'

Henry III appeared to sympathize with their misfortune; on learning that, as a result of the disturbance, the earl had ordered the seizure of the vineyards and property of Rostein and his friends, he took the advice of his council and ordered (5 September 1249) that their goods should be restored.[1] Then came a change of attitude, doubtless after the arrival in England of Guillaume-Raimond Colom, leader of the victorious faction, who had been mayor of Bordeaux since the day of Revolution (28 June).[2] A royal letter of 30 November [3] contains an official pronouncement worth analysing.

It begins by compliments and thanks to the earl for 'his loyalty and his diligence', for the profit which the king and Gascony itself will reap from his watchfulness and his 'energy'. 'We pray and exhort your wisdom to continue your undertaking and to bring it to a good result; you will receive from us and our heirs the recompense which your efforts deserve.' Then the king gives the earl some news about Gascony: Amaubin de Barès, 'dilectus et fidelis noster,' has come to England. In the king's court[4] he accused the vicomte of Fronsac with conspiring against his suzerain; he offered to prove that he had been present in person at an interview when this traitor had offered the count of Poitiers [Alphonse, brother of Louis IX] to give him Gascony. The court had consequently decided to summon the vicomte to appear before it in England on the morrow of the Purification. Simon was ordered to transmit this summons to the vicomte. As concerning the project Simon had laid before him of exchanging Bourg-sur-Mer for Fronsac,[5] the king gave Simon the

---

[1] *Simon de Montfort*, pp. 279–85: 'Querimonie Gaillardi de Solio': Gaillard made out that the king, 'sicut bonus dominus eis compatiens,' ordered the earl to restore everything he had taken from them, to bring them back to Bordeaux without delay, and to set the prisoners at liberty. The king's letter (5 September 1249) merely says that the earl must restore 'vineas et bona Rustandi de Solar et amicorum suorum' (*C. R. 1247–1251*, 231).

[2] *Ibid.*, p. 291. He was the bearer of letters sealed with the communal seal.

[3] Rymer, *C. R. 1247–1251*, 343–4. This letter close is addressed 'dilecto et fideli meo S. de M., com. Leyc., senescallo meo Wasconie.' This is the sole example of a letter where Simon is termed Seneschal: in no other place is this title given him.

[4] 'In plena curia nostra (one may translate this 'in full', i.e. open, 'parliament') appellavit vicecomitem de Frunziaco de seditione nostra, offerens se probaturum . . . quod interfuit corporaliter ubi predictus vicecomes convencionavit comiti Pictavie quod ei, qui de capitalibus inimicis nostris est, terram nostram Wasconie proderet.'

[5] The hill of Fronsac is extremely well suited for the establishment of a

responsibility of deciding the case himself, and approved in advance the resolution taken with the request to be informed of it as soon as possible.[1] In the meantime (the letter continued) Gaillard Delsoler and Guillaume Arnaud Moneder had arrived in England, accompanied by several 'abettors and accomplices' who, it was said, had taken part in the rising in which the earl's standard-bearer had met his death;[2] and who afterwards had taken refuge in the castle of Fronsac, taking arms against the king and thus retarding the capture of the castle. The king had had them arrested immediately and put in prison. They had thereupon offered to submit to the judgment of the royal court, and had delivered over as hostages one of the sons of Rostein Delsoler and Guillaume Arnaud Moneder himself.[3] The court had decided to send them back for judgment in the country where their misdeed had taken place: consequently the king ordered the seneschal to see that they appeared on the prescribed day. The end of the letter needs literal translation: 'We draw your watchful attention to all these facts; act energetically and unremittingly, see that no excessive indulgence encourage the criminals to begin again, but that the punishment be not greater than the offence, as befits a consistent and just judge. Finally, in order that the hostages shall be secure while the process is pending, we have found them safe-conducts, so do not treat them as suspects, that their judge himself be not suspected.'

These last words are expressive: they contain a discreet, but perfectly clear allusion to the severity of the earl's repressive measures.[4]

In fine, Simon was given a free hand.[5] Did he follow the

powerful fortress, protected by a steep slope which gives no cover to an assailant.

[1] In a letter dated Bordeaux, 29 January 1250, Simon announced that he had received 'in commendam' from Arnaud de Blanquefort the castle of Bourg, for a year from the coming Easter (*Simon de Montfort*, p. 300). See *ibid.*, pp. 307–9, for the complaints of Arnaud de Blanquefort.

[2] In his reply to the complaints of Gaillard Delsoler, Simon said that the insurgents 'navrèrent ii. de ses chevaliers si qu'il morurent, i. de ses escuers oucistrent et plusors autres de sa gent naufrèrent' (*Simon de Montfort*, p. 287).

[3] According to Gaillard Delsoler, the king and his council 'decepti et circumventi per litteras comitis et Willelmi Raymundi Columbi et suorum qui tenebant et adhuc tenent sigillum communie civitatis, eos captos et diu in turri Londonie detentos comiti dicto in adventu reddidit et dimisit, qui eos, scilicet Willelmum Arn. Moneder et Petrum de Soler et Vitalem Comitis, cives Burdegalenses, in ferris turpiter duxit et incarceravit in terram regis Francie' (*ibid.*, p. 284; cf. p. 294).

[4] Cf. Letter CLXI of Adam Marsh, p. 298.

[5] On 27 December 1249 the barons of the Exchequer received an order to

counsels of moderation that were given him ? Was the court of Gascony held on 3 February 1250 ? The documents which have come down to us have left no indication, and it is often difficult to date them with precision when they refer to subsequent events. But they are sufficient to show that the insurrection had far-reaching ramifications, and one gains the impression that it had been long planned: in fact it embraced the whole country.

In the neighbourhood of Bordeaux two towns, La Réole and Bazas, were torn by factions, each equally anxious to ruin the other. After the disturbance of 28 June, the earl seems to have listened to the advice of the new mayor, Guillaume Raimond Colom, and forced La Réole to give him hostages, taken from the family of Piis,[1] whom he kept as prisoners ; he entrusted authority then to the men who had formerly delivered over their town to the king of France. These lost no time in levying so insupportable a tax upon the burgesses that a revolt broke out. Thereupon the mayor and commune of Bordeaux, together with the seneschal and a numerous company, marched against La Réole, to reinstate their friends, devasted the country and killed a good many people.[2] The Piis, loaded with chains, were dragged off to Bordeaux, then to Bourg, afterwards to Fronsac, and even finally deported to the Isle of Oléron. Others, exiled from the town, found refuge at Marmande, or even in Spain.[3] The same thing happened at Bazas, where the earl demanded hostages from the faction especially detested by Guillaume Raimond Colom ;[4] 'but these folk, fearing lest they might be treated as those of Bordeaux had been, that is to say imprisoned, put to ransom or even condemned to death, took refuge in the church

pay Simon de Montfort's steward, Richard de Havering, the sum of 500 marks out of the tallage imposed 'super communitatem Judeorum Anglie', the king intending it 'ad firmandum terram Wasconie' (*C. R. 1247–1251*, 248).—On 5 July 1250 the king ordered Drogo de Barentin and William de Boeles to visit Gascony on the following 15 August so as to render their accounts to Simon de Montfort 'de tempore quo fuerunt senescalli regis Wasconie (*C. R. 1247–1251*, 300).

    [1] The family is extant to-day.   [2] *Simon de Montfort*, p. 310.

    [3] Cf. the letter addressed about 1252 to the king by the mayor, jurats, and the whole 'communitas' of the town (*Royal Letters*, ii. 72). One of the hostages 'burgensis noster, nomine Johannes Gast, de melioribus ville vestre, quod nobis valde grave est, in patria extranea est mortuus et sepultus.' *Ibid.*

    [4] *Simon de Montfort*, p. 310.

and shut themselves up there throughout all the time that Simon was in the town.'[1] Many burgesses were killed and the property of the vanquished pillaged by the conquerors. Whatever may have been Simon de Montfort's own personal share in these events—and the more his enemies needed to justify themselves, the darker were they concerned to depict it —it is certain that he remained master of the situation. Matthew Paris bears witness to this, though he confuses the dates.[2] Direct testimony also is given by the chaplain of Alfonse of Poitiers, Philip, treasurer of the chapter of St. Hilary, in a letter[3] wherein he informs his master, then on crusade, of the situation created in France by the recent death of the count of Toulouse, whose heir he was. Invited by Simon and the countess Eleanor to visit La Réole, Philip came and settled certain matters under litigation. 'And know', he wrote, 'that we spoke to my lord Simon about his passage overseas and heard that he intended to go at the feast of St. John. And know that he holds Gascony in good estate, and all obey him, and dare undertake nought against him; and he has taken the castle of Fronsac from my lord Ernaut de Blanquefort and holds it in his hand.'[4] Then Philip returned to France 'a little before Candlemas'.[5] Simon followed him; he was at Melun about half-way through April, when he secured the prolongation of the truce granted to England for five more years (from 24 June).[6]

[1] *Simon de Montfort*, p. 311: 'ad ecclesiam confugerunt et intus steterunt quamdiu comes fuit in villa; ita quod naturalia inhoneste oportuit eos facere in ipsa ecclesia.'

[2] *Chron. maj.*, v. 104: 'Comes ... studens per omnia patrissare et magnifici patris sui vel sequi vestigia vel transire, aliorum domini regis rebellium apud Burdegalim et in tota Wasconia adeo edomuit insolentiam ut Willelmum de Solariis et Rusteinum et alios superbos et recalcitrantes effugatos exheredaret et extorres condempnaret. Multos etiam patibulis excelsis presentavit.' Let us hope, however, that the earl of Leicester did not treat the Gascons with the same cruelty as his father had done in the suppression of the Albigensian heresy.

[3] Published by Boutaric, *Saint Louis et Alfonse de Poitiers*, pp. 69–77. It is dated at Corbeil, the Wednesday after the three weeks of Easter.

[4] Boutaric, *Saint Louis et Alfonse de Poitiers*, p. 73.

[5] *Ibid.*, 'nos revenimes en France un poi devant le chandeleur, droit a Bealmont ou madame la Roine estoit.'

[6] *Ibid.*, p. 75: 'et fut traictié de trive, et a esté alongnié cele trive de la saint Jehan en cinc anz.' From a deed copied in Register JJ 26, fol. 324 of the Trésor des Chartes, the truce was to run from 21 March to 29 September, and thence to be prolonged for five years. The passage in Philip's letter needs, therefore, slight modification.

His departure was immediately turned to profit by the Gascons. On Easter eve (26 March 1250) Simon found it necessary to communicate some unpleasant news to Henry III:[1] certain knights, he wrote, discontented at not having recovered through Gaston de Béarn's agency lands which the earl 'holds in the king's hand by judgment of his court', had 'planned' to recover them by armed force; 'and I have good evidence that they will begin shortly after Whitsuntide to ride through the land. As I am evilly regarded by the great persons of the land because I defend your rights and the poor people against them, peril and shame would be mine and great loss yours, if I were to return to Gascony without having spoken to you or received your orders'. It was not a question of military operations, since the offenders would merely plunder and burn the country, arresting the inhabitants and holding them to ransom, and riding about by night just like thieves in troops of twenty, thirty or forty marauders. Simon, then, was anxious to find the king, since those who had let him hear 'many sinister things about me', as the earl wrote, would tell Henry that he was the author of all the trouble. 'It is, however, useless to pay heed to them, for the king's castles, his domains and men are well enough looked after for my absence to be still further prolonged. While waiting for the interview, I have sent Vital de Caupenne into Gascony, with orders to aid and counsel our people, and I have announced my coming at Whitsuntide.' Simon did not make haste, for it was only on 3 May, Rogation day, that he disembarked in England.[2] He immediately obtained the subsidies he needed,[3]

---

[1] *Royal Letters*, ii. 52; I have corrected the letter with the aid of the facsimile, printed at the beginning of Shirley's second volume, in *Simon de Montfort*, p. 267. Shirley is wrong in giving the date as 1249; everything points to 1250.

[2] *Chron. maj.*, v. 117.

[3] On 28 May 1250, the king undertook (1) to pay Simon 800*l*. sterling in lieu of the knights that he had to find, for their maintenance for one year in his service; (2) to pay a Florentine merchant called Tholosanus and his associates 1,800 marks, being the amount advanced by them to the earl for putting the castles of Bourg, Fronsac, and Miremont into a state of defence (*C. P. R. 1247–1258, 67*; *Royal Letters*, ii. 382). On 29 May the king informed the earl of the following facts: Arnaud-Guillaume de Gramont had informed him that he would hand over the castle of Gramont, would make amends for all his misdemeanours committed after he had made peace with the king, during the time when Nicholas de Meulles was seneschal, and that he would give as hostage for this two of his nephews apart from the two sons who were already under

and at the end of the month returned to Gascony at the moment he had specified.[1]

The situation there he found less developed than he had at first feared; the 'companies' which he mentioned in his supplication to the king had not taken up arms. Nevertheless precautions had to be taken, and he strengthened his position on all sides. He had already, as we noticed above, forced Arnaud de Blanquefort—the man spoken of by Philip the Treasurer in his letter—to cede him 'in commend' the town and castle of Bourg-sur-Mer,[2] and now he bought the alod of Cubzac and had a fortress built on the site.[3] He thereby occupied the right bank of the Dordogne; his alliance with Amaubin de Barès gave him the left, and established him in the district of Entre-Deux-Mers.[4] By offering a perpetual income of 100 marks a year he secured Arnaud-Otton de Lomagne (28 May), who held in check Géraud d'Armagnac, vainly supported by

the king's surveillance. The letter ends with the following phrase that left the earl's hands untied: 'vos igitur super premissis facietis secundum consilium fidelium nostrorum Wasconie, secundum quod videritis commodo et honori nostro convenire' (C. R. 1247–51, 357).

[1] Simon was still in England at Whitsuntide (15 May). 'Circa eosdem dies,' says Paris (v. 127), the burgesses of London protested against certain privileges granted by the king to the Abbey of Westminster; when the king showed no sign of yielding, 'cives admodum commoti comitem Ricardum et comitem Leycestrie et alios regni magnates . . . adierunt.'

[2] Charter, already cited, of 29 January 1250.

[3] Royal Letters, ii. 383; C. P. R. 1247–1258, 73: the king gives the earl 'potestatem faciendi commutaciones rationabiles de terris nostris in Wasconia pro loco et placia de Cusacio, ad firmandum ibidem castrum ad opus nostrum.' Cubzac is on the right bank of the Dordogne, about 10 km. from Bourg-sur-Mer. The castle was situated on a slight rise commanding the little port and the road which runs from Saint-André-de-Cubzac to Bordeaux by La Grave-d'Ambarès and Lormont. On the 9 September, the king put 1,000l. at the earl's disposal for fortifying Cubzac (C. P. R. 1247–1258, 321; C. R. 1251–1253, 241). This money was forthcoming 'de denariis Judaismi'.

[4] On 13 February 1250, the king undertook to give to his 'amé et féal' Amaubin de Barès (Varreys in the text) the equivalent of the goods, possessions and revenues he owned at Fronsac; Simon de Montfort and Peter of Savoy would assign him in exchange lands in a more favourable neighbourhood; and he would have in addition the wardship of the young heir of Gombaud de Barès, with the right of his marriage (C. P. R. 1247–1258, 60). On 14 February, the king converted the fifty marks of rent formerly assigned to him into 'ten marcates of land' situated in the châtellenie of Montferrand (C. R. 1247–1251, 205). Barès is to-day Ambarès, in Entre-Deux-Mers. Montferrand is in the same region, but on the Gironde.

Amanieu d'Albret.[1] The same day he granted Rudel de Bergerac a rent of 50 marks a year for the guard of the castles of Mouleydier, Castelmoron and Montcuc-sur-Lot.[2] On 8 June Géraud did homage to him for the Armagnac and the Fezenzac areas.[3] The burgesses of Bordeaux, who had been treated so harshly the year before, had to resign themselves to a treaty Simon imposed upon them (27 November).[4] There were four main articles: 1. Certain of those exiled from Bordeaux could return if they provided sufficient security and written promises of submission; others had to give hostages; and the remainder were to remain in exile as long as the earl decided. 2. No man, under penalty of banishment was to bear arms or raise troops against the earl or the mayor and jurats of Bordeaux, to make conventicles (illicit assemblies) or to take part in secret societies. 3. Two hundred burgesses were to swear to these terms; and every year the entire commune was to take the same oath. It was to resist to its uttermost all who were desirous of breaking the peace, 'especially those who, like Gaillard Delsoler and his accomplices, true sons of discord, are set on disobeying the earl, and the justice and rights of Bordeaux.' 4. Finally the earl had the power, if he thought fit, to modify this peace by his own authority, while respecting the rights of the mayor, the jurats, and the Commune.[5]

Bordeaux may have been subdued, but the rest of Gascony was in a fever of excitement. Already on 10 June, Henry III informed his seneschal that the vicomte of Fronsac was trying to stir up trouble, and recommended him to take precautions.[6] On 14 August Amanieu d'Albret made an alliance with Gaston de Béarn, that indefatigable insurgent, and handed over to him the castles of Bazas and Caseneuve,[7] thereby establishing him

[1] C. P. R. 1247–1258, 67.

[2] Ibid., Mouleydier (Dordogne, arr. and c. Bergerac); Castelmoron, on the river Ségur (Gironde, arr. La Réole, c. Monségur); Montcuq (Dordogne. arr. and c. Bergerac, commune of Saint-Laurent-des-Vignes).

[3] Lafforgue, Histoire de la ville d'Auch, i. 61.

[4] Rymer, and Layettes, ii, no. 3909.

[5] On 12 January 1251 the king ordered the vicomte of Fronsac to provide Simon de Montfort, his brother-in-law, with all possible assistance 'in custodia terre nostre Wasconie' (C. R. 1247–1251, 401); the letter, however, is marked as cancelled.

[6] Royal Letters, ii. 68; C. P. R. 1247–1258, 68.

[7] Archives historiques de la Gironde, ii. 303. Caseneuve is on the banks of the

in the lower basin of the Garonne, which Simon on his part was labouring to put in a state of defence. Under these conditions it was no longer possible for Leicester to go on Crusade, and he doubtless made excuses to Innocent IV, still at Lyons. But the rising announced by the king broke out. Simon was taken unprepared, for he had neither men nor money. He left precipitately, crossed France, and arrived all of a sudden in England, on the day of Epiphany (6 January 1251) with a very small attendance, his horses thin and exhausted.[1] He found the king in London and demanded from him troops and money. He could not, he said, 'continue this ruinous war unaided'; in vain had he exhausted the resources of his earldom. 'Sir king,' he added, 'remember what happened to you the first time that you were in Gascony (1242–3): these folk whom you thought loyal have abandoned you. You were on the point of falling into the hands of the French; the queen, who fell sick at La Réole, was brought to bed at Bordeaux. Yet so little troubled were they at your distress that they dissipated your treasure and let your domain and your authority go to rack and ruin.'—'By the head of God, earl,' replied the king, 'you speak true. You have fought bravely for me, and I will not refuse effective help. But there are complaints about you: it is said that persons who come peaceably to you or who have been summoned under guarantee of good faith, have been thrown into prison, put in chains and sent to death.'[2] The earl denied all. 'Sir, their treason is well known to you, you have suffered from it, can you believe them?'[3] Eventually the king ordered the delivery of considerable sums to the seneschal,[4] and at the same time sent

Ciron, in the former parish of Insos and the commune of Préchac (Drouyn, *Guienne militaire*, ii. 266).

[1] *Chron. maj.*, v. 208: 'venit subito, festinus et inglorius, vix tribus armigeris concomitantibus, equis macie confectis et labore.'

[2] This charge occurs throughout the petitions of complaint proferred by the Gascons in 1252. Adam Marsh makes discreet allusion to certain 'rather drastic police measures' taken by Simon de Montfort (Letter clxi, 298). Gaston de Béarn had just sent his chaplain to complain of the earl (*Simon de Montfort*, p. 314). This mission took place just before the sending of the inquisitors, Nicholas de Meulles and Drogo de Barentin.

[3] At this point Paris gives a picturesque description of the castle of Gramont, a true haunt of brigands. In taking it Simon certainly did a service to the humbler folk, whom he had an interest in defending against their lords.

[4] *Chron. maj.*, v. 209: 'comes, . . . licet insurgente proditorum Wasconen-

commissioners of inquiry 'to search out the causes of the dis-
agreements arisen between Simon de Montfort and the king's
subjects, to appease them and deliver an exact report.' [1]

During the same period the Pope must have yielded to the
requests of the crusading leader now detained from service in
Palestine, and tried to intervene between the disputants. He
granted Simon the privilege ('indulget') of not being excommunicated, suspended, or put under interdict by any one in
Gascony, without special mandate from the Apostolic See
(28 January 1251).[2] He gave orders to the archbishops of Auch
and Bordeaux and their suffragans to intervene between the
king's lieutenant and the local nobles; he empowered them to
release any nobles from the oath whereby they had engaged
themselves to fight against Simon, to use all ecclesiastical censure against the 'raptores publicos et predones et eorum recep-
tores', to find out and punish any clerks guilty of having encouraged such seditious persons (31 January).[3] On the same
day he wrote and told Simon to receive 'ilariter et benigne' the
bishop of Agen, commissioned to act in his name in this business, and he authorized the bishop to demand from exempt and
non-exempt churches alike the 'procurations' necessary to support him during his journey, on condition however that they
were moderate in amount.[4] The Pope told the bishop of

sium universitate oppressus fugerit a Vasconia, erectus est in spem alacrem,
receptisque a thesauro tribus marcarum milibus, et a comitatu suo Leyreces-
triae et de terra que fuerat Gileberti de Humphravilla, cujus habuit custodiam,
collecta pecunia non minima, laetus . . . remeavit.' To this first gift of 3,000 *m.*
was shortly added (17 January) a sum of 550 *m.* for the wages due to the
knights and serjeants composing the garrison of Fronsac, Bourg-sur-Mer, and
Miremont (*C. R. 1247–1251*, 401).

[1] *C. P. R. 1247–1258*, 85. A royal charter of 20 November 1250 grants
Peter, barber of Simon de Montfort, rents which had been confiscated at La
Réole as a punishment for the felony of Étienne 'de Pinu' and Forton 'de
Pinu' (clearly members of the Piis family); each year he is to pay the royal
prévôt two cheeses and ten pears of the country (*C. Ch. R.* i. 349). On 22
January 1251, the king authorizes Earl Simon to effect certain exchanges useful
to both parties with the archbishop of Bordeaux (*C. P. R. 1247–1258*, 85).

[2] *Registres d'Innocent IV*, no 3019.

[3] *Ibid.*, no. 5016–5018.

[4] *Ibid.*, no. 5020. Two passages in this bull are to be noted: the Gascons are
represented as people 'quorum sic fervet impatientia in aliorum offensas, sic
excandescit insania circa guerras, seditiones et scandala suscitanda, quod eis
nec bene vivere nec bono quoquam preferri videantur.' The bishop received
the order 'quatinus eidem terre contra hujusmodi pestilentes super premissis

Angoulême what he had learned from the crusader Simon de Montfort, 'the rising of numerous Gascons animated with an insensate longing for wars, seditions and scandals', and he ordered him to take measures to repress this scourge (1 February).[1] Without awaiting the result of these inquiries which he may perhaps have regarded with suspicion, Simon embarked for Gascony at the beginning of March. He raised two hundred mounted infantry and a certain number of Brabançon crossbow-men in order to besiege Castillon; its capture was to make him master of the lower course of the Dordogne.[2] There he received through Nicholas de Meulles and Drogo de Barentin a letter[3] from Gaston, 'by the grace of God vicomte of Béarn,' and from Amanieu d'Albret, speaking in their own names, in the presence of Bernard de Bouville, vicomte of Bézaume (or Bénauge),[4] Raymond, vicomte of Fronsac, Guillaume-Arnaud

precavens presidiis oportunis, eam perturbari vel molestari a talibus non permittas.' Beneath the phrasing of diplomacy we catch a glimpse sometimes of the horror of these wars.

[1] *Registres*, no. 5028. With the exception of the last, all these bulls have been inventoried by Bliss, *Papal Letters*, i. 260, but they are best read in the text edited by Élie Berger. The archbishop of Bordeaux was Géraud de Malemort, who already in 1236 had headed a protest addressed to Henry III against the excesses committed in the country by his officials (*Gallia Christiana*, ii, Instrumenta, cols. 289–93). Elected in 1227 he died in 1260; we shall refer to him later. The bishop of Agen was Guillaume III, one of the executors of the will of Raymond VII, count of Toulouse (*Gallia Christiana*, ii, col. 918); the bishop of Angoulême was Géraud III (*ibid.*, col. 1,008); the archbishop of Auch was Hispanus, 1248–61 (*ibid.*, i, col. 992).

[2] *Chron. maj.*, v. 210: 'Significavit duci Brabantiae et ejus conterminis ut milites et servientes, armis communitos, sibi destinarent applicanti . . .; obtemperans autem dux transmisit ei ducentos ruptarios et aliquot cum eis balistarios . . ., contra quos Wascones sese imperterriti munierunt.' P. 228: 'imminente vernali serenitate, . . . Symon, rediens cum multo comitatu et thesauro in Wasconiam, contra ipsum omnes fere Wasconiae potentes conspiratione communi confoederatos invenit ei rebellare praeparatos.' The words 'conspiratione communi' explain the bull of Innocent IV on the oath taken by the Gascon lords, leagued together against the earl. The duke of Brabant was Henry III, called le Débonnaire (1248–61).

[3] For the correspondence passing in April–May 1251 between Simon and the leaders of the league during the siege of Castillon, see *Simon de Montfort*, pp. 268–72.

[4] See Fr. Bladé, *Notice sur la vicomté de Bézaume, le comté de Bénauge* (1878), p. 27. The comté was formed by the union of the vicomtés of Bézaume and Bénauge. It included the region comprised between Créon, Branne, Sauveterre, Saint-Macaire, and the Gironde. The castle of Bénauge is described by Drouyn, *Guienne militaire*, ii. 244. On 9 September 1243 an agreement was

of Tontoulon and Gaillard Delsoler, espousing the cause of 'the barons, knights, nobles, citizens and burgesses of Bordeaux and La Réole'. They complained of the earl of Leicester. They offered to submit to the arbitration of Nicholas de Meulles and Drogo de Barentin, as representing the king, and of Gerald archbishop of Bordeaux and William archbishop of Agen, as representing the Pope; but the earl refused. They then proposed to submit their case to the judgment of the four courts of Bordeaux, Bazas, Saint-Sever, and Dax (Meilhan, 29 April 1251); but this course led to so much haggling, and so strong was the atmosphere of mutual distrust, that no agreement was possible. Finally, the taking of Castillon[1] and the destruction of Lados[2] by Simon de Montfort decided the League to submit to the victor's terms (25 May 1251). They were as follows: The king's commissaries were to receive from all desirous to abide by the present peace the formal assurance that they would appear in court and submit to the sentence given by the tribunal. 2. The tribunal was to be composed of two commissaries and four judges chosen by them in each of the four courts of Gascony: it was to take cognizance of all disputes that had arisen between the earl and his opponents, since the earl had had charge of the province; it was to judge according to the customs peculiar to each court, and according to the statutes of the cities and the towns. 3. The commissaries were empowered to permit entry and domicile within Gascony, except in the cities of Bordeaux and La Réole, to those who had not ventured to return after

reached between the abbey of St. Croix of Bordeaux on the one hand and the vicomtesse of Bénauge and his son Géraud de Bouville, 'super justitia sanguinis ville Sancti Macharii, per quam dicta justitia remansit abbatie per judicium regis Anglie' (Brit. Mus. MS. Cotton, Julius E. 1; copy in Gaignières Fr. 20685, p. 159). Finally in May 1251 Guillaume-Raimond Colom undertook to deliver to the earl of Leicester the strong point of Saint-Macaire, in the event of Bernard de Bouville, vicomte of Bézaume, making war upon the king or the earl (Clairembault 1188, fol. 7v).

[1] *Chron. maj.*, v. 256. 'Tempore sub eodem (after the bull of absolution in favour of Thomas of Savoy, 22 June, Potthast, no. 14341) comes Legrecestriae Simon in partibus transmarinis de multis domini regis inimicis triumphavit Vasconensibus, et quoddam castellum, quod erat omnibus refugium, Castellium, occupavit.' Cf. Fernand Guignard, *Histoire de Castillon-sur-Dordogne* (1912), p. 33.

[2] Lados (Gironde, arr. Bazas, c. Auros). The castle was situated on rising ground dominating the course of a little stream, the Beuve, and the road leading to Bazas.

banishment following upon the rising of the 28 June;[1] the judges were to decide if prisoners actually in the hands of the earl were to have the benefit of the peace. Finally, the bishops of Agen and Bazas promised to excommunicate all who might violate it.

The documents do not tell us if the tribunal actually sat, but they record some important acts of submission. Amanieu d'Albret was one of the first instances;[2] the king of Navarre, the ally of Gaston de Béarn, retired from the coalition, and was granted a truce;[3] Gaillard Delsoler and his accomplices paid a heavy ransom,[4] promised to remain at peace, and agreed not to re-enter Bordeaux before the earl of Leicester's government reached its term.[5] On these conditions they might return to Gascony. At Dax the mayor, jurats, and commune swore to observe the peace granted to their town after the murder of the mayor, Dominique de Balembits (25 July) ; all contravening the peace would be prosecuted, and their immovables confiscated to the king's use, while one half of their movables would go to the king, the other sold in order to maintain the town walls.[6]

---

[1] *Simon de Montfort*, p. 274.

[2] At the request of Nicholas de Meulles and Drogo de Barentin, Amanieu promised (27 May) to make the knights and burgesses of Meilhan and Castel-jaloux, and his vassals of the Bazadais swear to remain loyal to the king and his lieutenant, and to hand over the strong place of Castelnau until the complete execution of the treaty (Clairembault 1188, fol. 7; Arch. nat. J 1030, no. 2).

[3] *Royal Letters*, ii. 383; *C. P. R. 1247–1258*, 123; Rymer, under 2 January 1252.

[4] 15,000 marks, according to Gaillard; 4,000, according to Simon, and this was small, he said, in comparison with their misdeeds (*Simon de Montfort*, p. 295).

[5] Gaillard further claimed that Simon had made them swear not to complain against him before the king: 'le comte lor fist a force fere lor chartre e promettre par lor serement qe il ne descovereit au roi ses fez, ne qe il ne se pleindreient au roi de lui' (*Simon de Montfort*, p. 296). Henry III in letters close of 16 May 1252 (*C. R. 1251–53*, 218) recalled his allegation which Simon de Montfort's denial was not sufficient to counteract. Simon did not give up all the prisoners of Delsoler's faction: P. Bonefus and B. Vital, arrested by the Colom on 28 June 1249, were maintained in captivity to expiate the murder of Guillaume Gondomer and his son. Another, Pierre Beger (or Viger), who had been delivered over as a hostage, was taken to La Réole and set free on his parole, but escaped and died in exile (*Simon de Montfort*, p. 295).

[6] Bibl. Nat. Clairembault 1188. On 12 September, Simon entrusted to two arbiters, one named by him, the other by Arnaud de Blanquefort and Mabel his wife, the task of fixing the indemnity due to the latter party for the castle of Bourg and its dependencies (*Arch. histor. de la Gironde*, iii. 4). This is the only measure of reparation we can trace; as yet it had no effective result.

Meanwhile the earl's lieutenant, William Pigorel, carried out a military ride in Labour. At Ustaritz a group of bandits had fortified themselves in the house of a noble widow; in spite of her entreaties, her house was set on fire.[1] Simon was then called in by influential citizens of Bayonne and came in person to the capital of Labour, assembled the local populace and, when all were gathered there, had a number arrested and put to ransom. The people who had appealed to him he alienated by protecting a formidable brigand,[2] previously expelled from the country by Nicholas de Meulles, whom he re-established in his rights and possessions.

So once again the operations of 1251, begun so disastrously, ended with such success that upon his arrival the earl seems on his own initiative to have suggested that the king should resume the government of the province,[3] with the sole request to be reimbursed for the expenses incurred 'for setting the land at peace'.

[1] *Simon de Montfort*, p. 306.

[2] Amigot de Garro. Simon compelled the people of Labour to make a truce with the rascal, allowed him to build a fortified house higher than local requirements permitted, and at the same time forbade all other persons in Bayonne to bear arms. This unjust act exasperated the people of Bayonne (complaints of the commune of Bayonne in *Simon de Montfort*, pp. 302, 306). At Bayonne the earl recovered the rights of the crown, now usurped, over the bakehouses and in the wharves and the riverside areas. At these spots rich burgesses had established their warehouses, with free use of certain landing-places; and at points they had even built their houses alongside. These edifices projected into that part of the river-bed which was uncovered at low tide. Simon, perhaps rightly deciding that the ground belonged to the seigniorial domain, ordered a survey to be made along certain alinements, an operation which was to have the result of forcing the majority of the merchants to pay a quit-rent for the usurped ground. A decision along these lines was given on 11 July 1251 in Simon's presence, by the prévôt, Pierre de Rauzed, who acted both as prévôt of the king and mayor of the town (*Études sur Bayonne*, ii. 117). The name of the prévôt (Darroseis in our text) is more correctly given by Giry, *Établissements de Rouen*, i. 110.

About this time there was an irruption of the Pastoureaux into the Bordelais. It was found possible to check it by closing the gates of Bordeaux, and by threatening the insurgents with exemplary punishment, if they did not disperse immediately (*Chron. maj.*, v. 232; *Ann. Burton*, p. 291; cf. Letters of Adam Marsh, p. 109).

[3] *Simon de Montfort*, p. 336. Leaving in Gascony his lieutenant William Pigorel or Pigoreu (*ibid.*, pp. 298, 306), he returned with his wife and the king's third step-brother. He took ship at Wissant, and after weathering a violent storm, they arrived safely at Dover. Paris, who gives these details (v. 263), relates them after the dedication of the church of Hales, on 5 November. Cf. *Chronicle of John of Oxenedes*, p. 186.

The king on the other hand made out that these were for the earl to bear.[1] This was in flat contradiction with the terms of the act investing the earl with the government of Gascony. The queen had to intervene to make Henry III give way on this point.[2] It is not known whether she succeeded in dispelling the atmosphere of coldness with which the king received Simon's return, reserving all his demonstrations of pleasure for Guy de Lusignan whom the count brought back with him.[3] All the same Simon was taken to York, where on 26 December 1251, the marriage of Henry III's daughter, Margaret, to Alexander III of Scotland was celebrated with great pomp.[4]

This, it seems, was the moment when violent protests against the king's representative arrived from Gascony, denouncing him as a traitor, a brutal and faithless tyrant.[5] News also came that a league had been formed to oppose him. Foreseeing new

[1] *Simon de Montfort*, p. 336: 'li rois . . . volet qe le conte li gardat les chastiaus qu'il ot pris, a son coust, qui estoent hors de la convenance qui estet entre eus.' It is to this period that letter xxii of Adam Marsh refers.

[2] *Ibid.*, p. 336: 'madame la reine li pria ententivement qu'il tenist ces chastieus et nes ostast mie de sa mein. . . .'

[3] *Chron. maj.*, v. 263. A little later, the chronicler sums up the result of the operations: 'comes . . . de multis domini regis inimicis triumphavit Vasconibus, et quoddam castellum, quod erat omnibus refugium, scilicet Castellium, occupavit.' These are practically Simon's own words: 'il ot de luer plus forz chastiaus en quoi il avoent luer recez' (*Simon de Montfort*, p. 336).

[4] *Chron. maj.*, v. 266–70. *Simon de Montfort*, p. 342: 'Quant le conte out mise la terre en bon état et fu revenuz en Angleterre, li rois le mena aveque soi a Everwik; e la vindrent noveles au conte ke les genz de Gascogne s'estoient aliancés. . . .'

[5] *Chron. maj.*, v. 276: 'significantes domino regi quod comes memoratus fuit proditor nequissimus, . . . ipsum graviter accusantes quod nobiles Wasconiae vocavit ad suum consilium pacifice, qui regi fuerant subjecti fidelissimi, et convocatos in dolo retinuit, incarceravit et nequiter fame interemit; unde regi nimis suspectum talibus sibilis comitem reddiderunt.' This, on the contrary, was the way the facts were presented on the king's behalf in 1262: 'li rois dit ke le conte de Leycestre vint a li a Everwik quand il maria sa file au roi d'Escoce et li dit ke une grant partie des barons de Gascogne estoent ja levé contre li par guerre . . .; k'em li avet fet entendre ke ce estet par les tortz que le conte et ses suz-baillifs lor avoent fet . . . [Then] le conte li pria qu'il envoiast en Gascogne et mandast a tuz ceus qui pleindre se voleent, k'a certein jour fussent a Londre devant le roi a monstrer leur grefs . . . [It was also] par [le] lous et par le conseil le conte [that the king] envoya le mestre du Temple qui donc fu, et sire Henri de Wengham, qui ore est evesque de Londre. . . .' (*Simon de Montfort*, pp. 339–40.) It is very improbable that the initiative for sending these inquisitors came from the earl. Henry de Wengham was consecrated bishop of London on 15 February 1259 (*D. N. B.*).

complications, Simon was anxious to return;[1] but the king held him back, saying that he first wanted to hear his accusers. With the earl's consent he nominated (4 January 1252) a commission consisting of practically all the members of the royal family, in order to determine the cost of the Gascon operations to date.[2] Then suddenly, it appears, after two days of hesitation,[3] he sent (6 January) a circular saying that he was ready to do his subjects 'full justice'; he consequently called upon them either to come in person, or to send delegates furnished with full powers and protected by a safe-conduct coming and going. He announced that he was sending his clerk Henry de Wengham (or Wingham) and Rocelin de Fos, the Master of the Templars, with mandate to inform them of his intentions.[4] The earl was greatly roused by this *volte-face* which portended him no good; he lost his temper and addressed the king with some heat. 'What, do you lend your ear and open your heart to traitors? You know what they are like at bottom; they have been shown it, realize it too, and yet you believe them more than myself, who have always remained loyal to you! It is on my conduct that you are ordering this inquiry.' But, replied the king, with a malicious thrust, 'if your innocence is so evident, why fear an inquiry? It will only have the effect of making your glory brighter still.'[5] Nevertheless, they ended in agreement: a convention arrived at on 23 March 1252 regulated the question of defended places, several of which were to be handed over to the king, and the matter of the earl's expenses, which were now to

---

[1] *Simon de Montfort*, p. 342.

[2] *Chron. maj.*, v. 276; *Royal Letters*, ii. 68. Shirley dates this letter from Thorp instead of York (*C. P. R. 1247–1258*, 124).

[3] *Chron. maj.*, v. 277: 'Rex . . . fluctuans sub incertitudine, in Wasconiam clam et subito Henricum de Wengham, clericum suum, . . . ad inquisitionem diligenter faciendum super premissis destinavit.'

[4] *C. R. 1251–53*, 207. This circular is addressed to the mayors, jurats, and communes of Bordeaux, La Réole, Bazas; to the townships (villatae) of Saint-Sever, Dax, Bayonne, and Saint-Émilion; to the archbishop of Bordeaux and the bishop of Bayonne, to the prior of Mas d'Agenais; to the deans of the chapters of Saint-André and St. Seurin in Bordeaux; to Pierre Caillau, Gaillard Delsoler, Gaston de Béarn, Amanieu d'Albret, Bernard de Bouville, vicomte de Bénauge (Shirley prints 'vicecomiti de Bennag'), Guillaume Seguin of Rions, Élie Rudel the younger of Bergerac, Geoffrey Rudel lord of Blaye, Ayquem Guillaume of Lesparre: a very instructive list, doubtless giving the names of the heads of the league opposed to Simon de Montfort.

[5] *Chron. maj.*, v. 277.

be fixed by arbitration; the earl was to be assigned a sum of two thousand marks, which he was to receive at the Exchequer a fortnight after Easter. This agreement [1] explains much. First and foremost it throws light upon the purpose of Simon's mission: it was to tame the Gascons; the burgesses, who struggled for power within the towns; the insubordinate vassals; a lord (Gaston de Béarn) who considered himself exempt from all ties of vassalage towards the duke of Guyenne, the king of England, whom he affected to recognize only as his cousin. It was thus a military operation of long duration, undertaken with the clearly warranted design of destroying the castles of the rebels (e. g. that of Lados) and of occupying their fortresses and turning them against their former masters. Look on the map at the commanding positions occupied by Castillon, Fronsac, Cubzac, Bourg-sur-Mer, which line the right bank of the Dordogne, or by La Réole, St. Macaire, Gironde on the Garonne; this will be to grasp the political importance of their occupation by Simon de Montfort as well as the interest which urged the king to secure their delivery to him, in order to extract from them all the advantages, even the economic advantages, of their immediate posesssion. In the second place, an equitable regulation of the financial problem helped to terminate or at least to quieten the dispute between the king and his representative. [2] The earl who had already received authority to leave, [3] crossed the sea in all

[1] *C. R. 1251–53*, 207. The principal conditions were these: the castles of Fronsac, Castillon, Gurson, and Puynormand were to be placed in the king's hands at Easter. If the earl was indemnified before this date for his expenses in fortifying Cubzac, this castle was to remain his till All Saints' Day. The earl was to surrender to the king the castle of Bourg-sur-Mer, but at the formal order of Arnaud de Blanquefort, 'without which nothing can be done'.

[2] To the sum of 2,000 marks, to be paid at an early date, other concessions were added: On 19 March, the king granted a like sum, but to be collected from the king's debtors 'in partibus transmarinis' (*Royal Letters*, ii. 386; cf. *C. P. R. 1247–1258*, 132). On 20 March, letters close were issued for that purpose, but the sum was to be charged to the royal wardrobe (*C. R. 1251–53*, 207). On 25 March the king requested Pierre Caillau and Raimond Makayn, burgesses of Bordeaux, to lend him 24*l.* for the garrison of the castle of Roquefort [in Marsan?], of Marsan [Mont de Marsan?] and of Castelnau de Cernès (*C. P. R. 1247–1258*, 132). Paris (v. 277) seems rather to imply that these sums were given to Simon on loan: 'accomodavit pecuniae partem non modicam supplicanti.'

[3] Letters of protection granted to the earl on departing for Gascony, 22 February 1252 (*C. P. R. 1247–1258*, 129).

haste, profoundly disturbed at heart, but resolved to take vengeance upon his accusers.[1]

But events had moved fast   We are informed about them in a letter [2] of the two commissioners addressed to the king on 6 March, which had probably not yet arrived by the 16th. After leaving the queen of France,[3] at Tours they had met Geoffrey de Lusignan ready to start for Gascony with a great number of knights at the urgent request of William Pigorel, Leicester's lieutenant, for the castle of La Réole had to be rescued from the burgesses of the town who had taken up their quarters in the priory church.[4]   At Bourg they found the whole country under arms: Pigorel had already summoned to Gironde [5] practically the whole of his forces and the communal militias:

'Then Messer Geoffrey, your brother, left Bourg to find the seneschal (Pigorel) while he counselled us to apply to the archbishop of Bordeaux and show him your letter. The prelate received the letter with great reverence and promised to obey your orders; but, he said, he would himself go to the army with us, to confer with the other magnates of the country upon the causes of the war. He had been, however, at La Réole, and for three weeks he had laboured to make peace or at least conclude a truce; but two truces had been almost as soon abandoned by the parties as made.[6] On reaching the army, we found all the grandees and the mayors of the towns to which you addressed your letters. We showed them (the letters of January) in the presence of your brother and transmitted your orders to them orally. After taking counsel, they replied to us in your brother's presence that they neither could nor would retire, nor come over to

---

[1] *Chron. maj.*, v. 277: 'Conflans . . . copiosum exercitum de Francorum militibus et servientibus stipendiariis, regem Navarriae et comitem Bigorriae et multos alios, in exterminium adversariorum suorum se ipsum insuperabiliter roboravit.' The chronicler who perhaps exaggerates the number of these leaders, adds that Simon subdued the pride of the Gascons to such a point that if they had not had such economic need of England for their wine sales, they would have transferred their fealty to another lord.

[2] *Royal Letters*, ii. 76.

[3] Blanche of Castile, regent of the kingdom.   Margaret of Provence had accompanied her husband the king on crusade.

[4] See in *Annales du Midi*, xxxi (1919) the article on La Réole, town and castle.

[5] Town on the Drot, below La Réole (Gironde, arr. and c. La Réole). 'Dominus Willelmus Pigorel jam adunaverat fere totum exercitum suum et communitates villarum apud Gyrundiam juxta Regulam' (*Royal Letters*, ii. 77).

[6] *Ibid.*, p. 77: 'Formatae fuerunt duae treugae, et statim ruptae ex utraque parte.'

England, during the present troubled state of the country, unless a peace or truce was first made, saying that if they absented themselves they ran the risk of losing their castles, liberties, lands, and goods. Then the prelates, and all the barons and the mayors of townships,[1] in agreement with your brother, agreed with the archbishop, the bishop of Bazas, and Pierre Caillau to enter La Réole and make the contents of your letter known. We found there messer Gaston de Béarn with more than a hundred men-at-arms, a great part of the barons of the Agenais, the mayor of Bazas[2] with his posse, the greater part of the people of Sainte-Bazeille[3] who were besieging your castle of La Réole by night as well as by day. The garrison of the castle were defending themselves with two mangonels and other engines of war.[4] We then exhibited your letter, in the presence of the archbishop and bishops to messer Gaston, to the Prior of Mas d'Agenais, to the mayor of Bazas, the commune of La Réole, and we reproached messer Gaston especially for having entered a town to besiege a castle belonging to you. After reading your letter, they made the same reply as the others, but they neither would nor dared come over to England without peace or truce. As far as concerns La Réole, they declared unanimously that they would undertake nothing against your lordship, and this is how they explained the facts: the factions of the town, in insurrection the one against the other, had begun to attack each other, and then one of them, with the authority of your constable,[5] had made its way into your castle and there had attacked the other, which had remained in the town. The attacked replied in like manner. The seneschal [Pigorel] who ought to have rendered equal justice to all, far from expelling the new-comers from the castle, inflamed them against their enemies. It was to protest against this unjust treatment, declared Gaston de Béarn, that the magnates had taken up arms, not to damage the king's rights. These were

[1] *Ibid.*, p. 78: 'barones omnes et majores villatarum'.

[2] *Ibid.*: Shirley, whose transcripts are not always impeccable, printed here 'et majores Vasatenses cum posse suo', an impossible reading. Mr. Charles Johnson sends us the correct version, from the letter in *Ancient Correspondence*, 'et majorem Vasatensem', which we translate accordingly.

[3] *Ibid.*, maximam partem hominum de Sancta Basilia'. Sainte-Bazeille, Lot-et-Garonne, arr. etc. Marmande. The Abbé R. Alix in his *Histoire de la ville et de la baronnie de Ste-Bazeille* (1892), p. 50, takes account of this letter translated here, but is completely confused.

[4] *Royal Letters*, ii. 78, 'et ipsi (ipso in Shirley's text) de castro insimul et e converso cum duabus blidis et aliis ingeniis'. Cf. Ducange, 'Blida, machina bellica' and the citation is given of a passage from Richard of San Germano under 1239, alluding to 'ingenia que biddae, dominae et mangonelli fiunt'. To translate 'blide' as 'mangonels' is not far out.

[5] *Ibid.*, 'de permissione constabularii vestri'.

feeble excuses, and knowing, as we did, better about the situation
we judged them insufficient.[1] When we had reported their reply, the
archbishop, the bishop of Bazas and the barons present, foreseeing
the ills to come if war continued in La Réole and Bazas, counselled
your brother, ourselves and others your faithful subjects to make a
truce, since without your authority a peace was impracticable. The
truce was then concluded, to last till St. John's day. . . . They
further demanded that messer the earl of Leicester should be present
before you in England, when they arrived, during the month after
Easter;[2] for it is in his presence that they will set forth the facts.
If he is now returning to Gascony, they ask that he be recalled immediately; unless this is done, they will in no wise come. All those
who have been summoned by letter promised to be present on the
day assigned, except messer Gaston de Béarn, who will be represented by a knight and a clerk.'[3]

It is likely that Wingham did not delay his return. The report
which the commissioners of inquiry made to the king[4] recognized
that the earl had obviously treated certain people with a lack
of humanity, but that their crimes nevertheless called for
punishment. Without taking this reservation into account, or
else in order to gain a better insight into a matter arousing the
fiercest passions, Henry III ordered his representative to return
(23 March);[5] he desired, he said, to have him at hand during
the Easter festival; then on 1 April,[6] he sent the vicomtes of
Fronsac and Castillon a safe-conduct to come, dwell and return

---

[1] *Royal Letters*, ii. 79, 'quas excusationes debiles tenemus et quoad hoc
insufficientes'.

[2] *Ibid.*, p. 80: 'Petunt quod dominus comes Leycestriae presens sit in Anglia
in eorum adventu coram vobis a die Paschae in unum mensem, in cujus praesen-
tia vobis statum terrae intimare proponunt.' In 1252 Easter was on 31 March.

[3] The date when this important letter was sent is given expressly at the
close: 'the bearer of these present letters (p. 81) left us at Bordeaux Wednesday
before the feast of St. Gregory the Great (6 March). As far as we are concerned,
we are awaiting the day when the condition of the truce to be concluded between you and the king of France shall be determined, the day fixed by the
queen for Passion Sunday (18 March). Before this date, if it can be arranged,
Henry de Wingham will return to inform you of the situation in Gascony and
about the truce.' Queen Blanche's stay at Pleneselve (Gironde, arr. Blaye, c.
Saint-Ciers-la-Lande), to which the letter alludes, is not noted by Élie Berger,
Blanche de Castille, pp. 403, 413, where it should have found a mention.

[4] *Chron. maj.*, v. 289: 'exploratores, cum rediissent, domino regi inti-
marunt. . . .'   [5] *Royal Letters*, ii. 81.

[6] *C.R. 1251–53*, 208: 'Nos etiam,' run the letters close, 'injurias et damna vobis per ballivos nostros Wasconie illata faciemus secundum justitiam ad plenum

'with their retainers, horses, and baggage'. The royal mandate certainly did not reach the earl, who was en route for Bordeaux. There he found many of the burgesses leagued together to make fresh trouble for him. The chronciler Matthew Paris gives us to understand that this conspiracy was secret;[1] but from his own account we can infer that everything went on above board: the Gascons, he says,[2] had met and announced their intention of sending a solemn embassy to England, bearing written proof of their accusations against 'the violent invader of castles and towns, the fierce exterminator of men'.[3] Obviously Paris himself invented these expressions, so resonant with the exaggeration with which Northerners were fond of taunting the Gascons and folk of the Bordelais. At the head of the deputation was the archbishop of Bordeaux, who, together with the deputies of La Réole and other towns, took ship for London and arrived a few days before Whitsun.[4] They had by this means avoided running into the earl, for Simon, knowing that he had been traduced in the king's courts and that numerous witnesses were being produced against him, was returning in all speed to make his reply.[5] He was very coldly received by the king[6] and asked

emendari.' Shirley printed, under the same date and after this entry, another safe-conduct addressed, 'prelatis, baronibus, magnatibus, civibus et aliis de terra sua Wasconiae' (ibid., p. 83). There we read, 'dedimus etiam in mandatis Simoni de Monteforti quod ad diem statutum, scilicet a die Paschae (31 March) in unum mensem (30 April) intersit convocationi vestrae Londoniis; et idem comes nobis rescripsit quod ad prefatum diem ibidem vobis occurret et hoc nullo modo omittet'. Cf. C.R. 1251–1253, 208. Another letter (p. 218) prorogued the truce until the Assumption.

[1] Chron. maj., v. 284: 'Simon de M., plures sustinens tribulationes, cum pervenisset Burdegalim, invenit multos de civitate ex civibus contra eum, facta occulte conspiratione, . . . novas parare insidias ac redivivas.'

[2] Ibid., p. 287: 'Decretum est communi Wasconiensium assensu ad dominum eorum regem (the king, not the earl, they recognize as their master, whom they ought to obey) sollempniter nuntios destinare. . . . Provisum igitur communi decreto ut maximus de tota eorum regione et dignissimus, scilicet archiepiscopus Burdegalensis, cum aliis quibusdam magnatibus famosis . . . in Angliam sub omni festinatione dirigeretur.'

[3] Ibid., p. 287.

[4] Ibid., p. 288: 'Circa Pentecosten, paucis ante diebus, venerunt de Wasconia archiepiscopus Burdegalensis, et de Regula et aliis civitatibus Wasconia magnates (here the 'magnates' are the burgesses), venientes in Angliam navigando usque Londonias, invenerunt ibidem regem.'

[5] Chron. maj., v. 287, 289.

[6] Ibid., p. 294: 'comes, cum de Wasconia propere venisset et regem Londoniis invenisset, non est ab ipso salutatus, vel, prout decuit, honorifice receptus'.

to be heard.[1] On 9 May the trial that was to last for five weeks opened in the refectory of Westminster Abbey.[2]

The public debates that followed took place before the king's court and often in the king's presence. Should we say the 'king's court' or 'parliament'? In contemporary documents the term 'curia regis' is almost exclusively used,[3] although *parliamentum* had already made its appearance. To-day we should feel inclined to give these two expressions a different interpretation: *curia* suggests the idea of a court of justice, *parliamentum* that of a political assembly. Nothing could be more inaccurate than such an interpretation for the time when the earl of Leicester's process was at Westminster, for parliament in its profoundest origin is, and has never ceased to be, a court of justice;[4] in the thirteenth century the members composing it could scarcely be distinguished from the functionaries of the King's Court. Nevertheless, the modern idea of a parliament, with its observances and customs, would not be entirely inapposite when applied to the assembly of May–June, 1252; for at any rate the procedure of justice was singularly disturbed and upset by rowdy scenes, fierce and passionate altercations, and even by episodes of violence, vividly portrayed for us by the pen of Adam Marsh, who was present at the debates. He acted as an intermediary between the earl and his opponents,[5] working to appease the angry tempers and upholding the dignified and moderate attitude of the great lord he loved and ad-

[1] *Chron. maj.*, v. 289.
[2] The date is given by letter 30 of Adam Marsh: 'circa festum Ascensionis Domini . . .'; the length of the trial, 'fere usque ad festum beati Barnabae'; and the place, by Simon himself (*Simon de Montfort*, p. 342): 'Et il en vint plusours qui monsterent plusours grefs envers le conte a Westmostier en refeitor.' The place of the refectory is marked by the word *frater* in the plan of the abbey at the end of the volume *Westminster Abbey*, published by the Historical Monuments Commission in 1924. The Abbey was built to receive, along with the prior, about 50 monks (Pearce, *The Monks of Westminster*, 1916, p. x).
[3] Letter 30 of Adam Marsh: 'processum habitum in curia domini regis'.
[4] Such at any rate is the opinion of Mr. McIlwain (High Court of Parliament, 1910) and Professor Pollard (Evolution of Parliament, 1920); but Professor Tout (*Chapters in Mediaeval Administrative History*, iii. 62 n.) well demonstrates the difference between *curia* and *parliamentum*.
[5] 'Me ipso nonnullos de majoribus alloquente.'

mired. We may note that the letter he addressed to the bishop of Lincoln a few days after the end of the trial gives the impression of absolute sincerity. The character of the two men is a sure guarantee of this. Matthew Paris is comparable with neither, for he is a chronicler who loves a good story. Although he is here simply reporting what he has witnessed and takes no long-sighted view, he none the less had a first-hand knowledge of events. He may even have been acquainted with the written complaints submitted during the course of the trial by the earl of Leicester's enemies,[1] and the biographer of Simon will not fail to remark the striking resemblances to be discovered between Paris's account and Adam's letter. We may therefore follow these two guides, whose assertions can be critically checked and supplemented by the depositions of the chief actors.[2]

About Ascensiontide,[3] writes the wise and gentle Franciscan,[4] a great number of Gascons, clerks, and laymen, presented themselves before the king, the prelates, and barons; they launched a vehement and slanderous attack upon the earl, accusing him of misgovernment, fraud, and generally oppressive conduct. They had a favourable hearing, both in public and in private sessions, to the great astonishment of all lovers of justice and equity. The king himself employed abusive and reproachful

---

[1] At any rate he knew of their existence, since he alluded (v. 287) to 'scripta communarum (*variant*: communiarum) civitatum Wasconiae, magnatum, castellanorum et ballivorum'.

[2] We must distinguish between the depositions put in for the trial of 1252 and the defence which, ten years later, the earl of Leicester was obliged to make once more, when he was, so to speak, maligned by Henry III before Louis IX. The depositions ('Querimoniae'), which have come down to us, at any rate the examples which I found and published in my thesis (pp. 279–310), emanate from Gaillard Delsoler, Arnaud de Blanquefort, Guillaume Ayquem (not Ayquelin) of Lesparre, for the Bordeaux region; from Bazas, Dax, Gosse, and Saint-Sever for the district of the Landes; from Bayonne and Guillaume d'Armandarits for Labour; from the vicomtes of Soule, Béarn, and Sault-de-Navailles for the Pyrenean region. To these should be added the 'querimoniae vicecomitis de Sule' printed in *Royal Letters*, ii. 74–6; those of the 'pauperes homines regis' of Marsac in *C.R. 1251–53*, 224; and the group recently brought to light in the Chancery Miscellanea of the P.R.O., but in a barely legible condition. In an Appendix I have printed fragments of four of these documents, which the officials of the Public Record Office kindly pointed out and had photographed for me.

[3] 9 May in 1252.

[4] Letters of Adam Marsh, xxx, p. 123.

language to the earl, shouted, and lost his temper. Matthew Paris adds some details: that day, he says, Simon had brought into court earl Richard (rejoicing to see the Gascons, who had caused him such vexation, now in adversity), the earl of Gloucester, for once favourable to the earl,[1] and many important persons who would not have tolerated Simon being condemned to a traitor's penalty. The earl having said enough to prove his innocence, the king began an altercation that led to outbursts of temper and disorderliness. 'Sir king,' Simon said, 'keep to your engagements, observe the gist of your letter investing me with the government of Gascony for seven years;[2] restore me all the money I have spent in your service out of my own resources.' To which the king made the astonishing reply: 'No, I will not keep my promises, they have no value, since you have yourself betrayed me!' Overcome with rage, the earl rose up and told the king to his face that he lied, saying that it was a shame that such a word should have issued from the king's mouth, seeing that he did not intend to preserve even a semblance of royal dignity.[3] The king would have had him arrested immediately, had he not known that the magnates would not have allowed it on any account. The earl queried: 'Are you a Christian? Have you ever confessed?'—'Certainly,' the king replied.—'What is the good of a confession if it is not followed by penance or reparation?'—'Never,' replied the king in exasperation, 'never have I repented anything so much as the day when I allowed you to enter England and possess lands and honour here.'[4] Adam Marsh is certainly too indulgent towards the earl when he writes: 'he ever observed towards his sovereign and his adversaries the law of mercy with the mature wisdom of a great-hearted soul.'[5]

Matthew Paris gives what we may call the bill of accusation in these terms:

'Sir king and you, sir earl Richard, and all you great men of the kingdom present here, these are the letters of credit which we bring

---

[1] *Chron. maj.*, v. 259: 'in hoc casu comiti S. favorabilis'. We shall encounter him later.

[2] Paris repeats the error which he earlier made: 'cartam suam de obtinenda terrae custodia sex annis confecerat'.

[3] Paris, *ibid.*: 'mala hora ipsum tale verbum a faucibus ejus emisisse'.

[4] *Chron. maj.*, v. 290–1.   [5] p. 123.

you on behalf of the Gascon nobles, faithful subjects of the king, the knights, burgesses, governors of fortresses, and peasants, who have come hither to expose their grievances. We are all unanimous in complaining of the earl of Leicester, who, charged with governing the country, brings it to ruin and expels its inhabitants with ferocity. The men to whom earl Richard heretofore accorded life and immunity, the men whom the seneschal Henry de Turbervill, and later Waleran the German,[1] treated as friends, this fellow—and as they said this they looked at him with eyes glittering with passion[2]—seizes and ruins. He quashes judgments long determined, breaks engagements entered upon by his illustrious predecessors, and sends the Gascon nobles, your faithful subjects, prisoners into France,[3] where several have died of starvation and under the weight of chains. He extorts from them infinite sums, of which the king knows nought; or else he gets them to his side by peaceful words, under the pretext of having conversations with them, and then has them arrested so as to put them to death. He asks for delivery of the castles necessary to the king, and then guards them as if they were his own.[4]

The earl replied by recalling all he had done since his arrival in the country, his moderation in war as in peace, the care and trouble he had taken on behalf of the king's dignity and majesty, and the safety of clergy and people.[5] He too produced letters patent of the commune of Bordeaux,[6] and his witnesses were the knights and burgesses who had bravely served the king and the earl; they were present to prove in eloquent words[7] the zeal, wisdom, just moderation, and long-suffering with which the earl had governed the country, restored the courage of his devoted servants, chastised the rebels, in spite of the dangers, the heavy expenses, the cruel embarrassments which he had to undergo.[8] These written proofs and reiterated testimonials should have sufficed to give the earl and his party the victory;

---

[1] 'Walerandus Theuto', elsewhere called Le Teys (*C. P. R.*, index).

[2] 'Qui fascinanti (oculo) comitem intuentes'.

[3] This certainly happened to two members of the Piis family of La Réole, retained in the castle of Mehun-sur-Yèvre (*Rôles gascons*, no. 4317).

[4] *Chron. maj.*, v. 295. Cf. Adam Marsh, p. 125.

[5] *Ibid.*, p. 124.

[6] *Ibid.*, p. 124: 'communitatis Burdegalensis in qua quasi totum robur Wasconiae ad distringendum hostiles et fideles protegendum consistere dinoscitur'.

[7] 'Per sermones discretos manifeste monstrarunt.'

[8] Adam Marsh, pp. 124–5.

none the less his side went so far as to propose recourse to the judicial battle or to any other procedure ordered by the court; they offered to appear before any tribunal in England or before judges sent by the king into Gascony, promising to respect any judgment, even if it went against them, and to renounce the safe-conduct, if their enemies insisted upon it.[1] But the opposing party repulsed all these offers in the single determination to demand the earl's removal from office.[2]

This passage in Adam's letter is confirmed by a reading of the complaints as we have them. While certain plaintiffs assessed the moral and material damages they had suffered in pounds or in marks, others openly called for the deprivation of the earl. 'We supplicate your majesty,' said the deputies of Bazas, 'to banish him from Gascony, to forbid him ever entering it, and to send there as soon as you can, if you cannot come yourself, your son Edward, who will find us all at peace.'[3] Bayonne said the same: 'In the name of the fealty we owe you, we counsel you not to send the earl back to Gascony, for this would be for you and for your province a course of great loss and danger; but we beseech you to come in person, or to give Gascony to your eldest son, that he may keep it for your honour and profit.'[4] The grievances of Béarn ended with a threat: 'These,' said Gaston's proctors, 'these are the facts about which our master makes personal complaint. He humbly asks justice of the king, for he neither will nor can bear such horrible treatment any longer.'[5]

In the end the king was convinced by Simon, and publicly recognized that the earl's party had established the falsity of their opponents' assertions. This opinion was approved with unanimous acclamation (Adam is speaking here)[6] by earl Richard, the prelates, magnates, and counsellors of the king. All that apparently remained was to compensate truth and punish perjury. But after the night had passed, 'the bonds of equity and justice due to the earl were broken, once more recourse was had to threats, to bitter and fierce recrimination, and indecent railing. The king's anger burst out, and the deceitful guile of the

---

[1] Adam Marsh, p. 125.
[2] *Ibid.*, p. 126.
[3] *Simon de Montfort*, p. 312.
[4] *Ibid.*, p 307.
[5] *Ibid.*, p. 317.
[6] p. 127.

wicked made its shrill noise to be heard. From that time, during day and night, the torment of an unbearable crisis did not cease to grow.'

Simon found it difficult to witness his own work being demolished stone by stone through his sovereign's clemency.[1] He had gained his suit before the court, but lost it before the king. He suggested that Henry should first impose silence on either party; then he asked for authority to return to Gascony, in order to govern no longer by rigorous methods (as he had been commanded to govern at the beginning), but by justice and mercy. If the obstinacy of his opponents made peace impossible, he offered to lead a military expedition which should bring the rebels to reason. If in the end the king rejected both of his proposals, the earl preferred himself ready to renounce the government, 'if the prelates, magnates and counsellors gave their consent', merely demanding to be indemnified for his excessive expenses, to be cleared of all stain of guilt, guaranteed against all reprisals, he and, above all, those devoted to his service. The king would hear none of this; in his own headstrong way, without consulting any one,[2] he took advantage of the inertia of his mute sycophants, and dictated his conditions

---

[1] On 15 May the king extended to the Assumption (15 August) the safe-conducts granted to the nobles and burgesses whom he had cited to appear before him, as well as the truce concluded at La Réole between William Pigorel, Simon's lieutenant, and Gaston de Béarn, Amanieu d'Albret, Bazas, La Réole, and their partisans (*C. P. R. 1247–1258*, 139). On 16 May he censured Gaillard Delsoler and his friends for having promised never to bring complaint against Simon, and cited them before his court (*Royal Letters*, ii. 388; *C. R. 1251–1253*, 218); on 21 May he ordered Pigorel, the mayor and jurats of Bordeaux, and the bishop of Bazas to observe the truce (*Royal Letters*, ii. 389; *C. R. 1251–1253*, 210); on 14 May he granted letters of protection to the people of Uza, with prohibition to any to violate the liberties granted to them by the kings his predecessors (*C. R. 1251–1253*, 92, cf. *Royal Letters*, ii. 57–8). On 6 June he ordered Arnaud Guillaume de Gramont to be set at liberty. Trusting in Arnaud's promise to surrender his castle to Nicholas de Meulles or to any other of his faithful servants, except the earl of Leicester, the king authorized the delivery of this castle to Peter of Bordeaux, Arnaud's cousin and friend (*Royal Letters*, ii. 86–8, cf. *C. P. R. 1247–1258*, 157). That same day he ordered the mayor, jurats, and commune of Bayonne to look after the goods of the bishop of Bayonne, whom he had summoned to England; and similar letters were sent to the mayor, jurats, and commune of Bordeaux in favour of three burgesses likewise summoned before him (*Royal Letters*, ii. 89, cf. *C. P. R. 1247–1258*, 142).

[2] Adam Marsh, p. 128: 'pro suae voluntatis arbitrio ... ordinationes quasdam proprio motu conceptas redigi fecit in scripta suo sigillo signata'.

which he sealed with his privy seal. A truce was to be imposed upon the two parties and scrupulously observed till next Candlemas. Then he would go himself or send his eldest son so as to bring to an end all matters of litigation and private war. In the interval a bailiff and no more was to handle current administration;[1] certain castles were to be handed back to their owners; prisoners in the earl's custody were to be set at liberty under safeguards. The king, adds Adam Marsh with some justice, had succeeded in undermining his inheritance, weakening his kingdom, and fomenting disorder in the country.

In letters patent of 13 June the clerks of the royal chancery put the same facts into official shape.[2] The king, having heard the explanations given by the archbishop of Bordeaux, by several nobles, by clerks and laity of Gascony, has determined [3] to visit Gascony, either in person or through his eldest son next Candlemas or later, so as to make fit disposal of the affairs of the province. In the meantime, for the maintenance of peace, he orders the earl of Leicester and his bailiffs, as well as all faithful subjects of the king, to observe the following conditions: first, the truce imposed on the two sides, which, to last till the Assumption, was to be prolonged till the Purification. Then follows a long list of particular instructions concerning Bourg-sur-Mer, the castles of Fronsac, Castillon, Gurson de Puynormand, Sault-de-Navailles, and the condition of prisoners; the prisoners of the Piis family taken at Bordeaux on 28 June, were to be sent to the king, to stand their trial: those of La Réole who were detained in Oleron as hostages were to be set at liberty under safeguards.[4]

---

[1] Adam Marsh, p. 128: 'praemittendo bajulum in Wasconia'.

[2] Rymer, under this date.

[3] 'De consilio nostro sic duximus providendum.' This does not mean that the king consulted his Council, but that, in accordance with Adam Marsh's letter, he took *counsel* with himself.

[4] To the same date belong various acts which complete and give greater clarity to the instructions contained in the patent of 13 June. In virtue of an arrangement undertaken towards the prior of Mas d'Agenais, the king determined that Raimond and Doat de Piis, the brothers of the prior, and Arnaud and Poitevin de Piis, his uncles, captured at Bordeaux by the earl on the famous 28 June should be set at liberty immediately under safeguards. On 16 June, he orders the mayor, jurats, and commune of Bordeaux to hinder the

It was now 13 June, and consequently the settlement was postponed to a pretty advanced date, a point which Simon could use to his advantage. He seems to have had a last wrangle with his brother-in-law, the king. Paris translates, or rather travesties it, under the heading 'Return to Gascony': *The king—* 'You love war and rejoice in arousing it. You will find in Gascony opportunities to your taste and the advantages you deserve, as did your father.' *The earl—*'Yes, I will go to Gascony with pleasure, and never, I hope, return before I have laid the rebels at your feet. . . .' Paris sarcastically observes that for such a remark the king deserved the favour of the Gascons present;[1] they would scarcely have forgotten how Simon the elder had treated the Albigensian rebels, or the confiscation which had made him a rich man. But we perfectly well understand why Simon, as Adam writes, could take leave of the king in a friendly spirit and with a smiling countenance,[2] and without receiving any formal instructions, a point which gave him the opportunity to act according to his own lights. He crossed on 16 June [3] with his eldest son Henry, the 'dear pupil' of Robert Grosseteste.[4] At midday he disembarked at Boulogne, ready to start for Gascony, if need be.[5] Adam Marsh ends his letter by announcing the departure of the Gascons,

rivalries of the Colom and the Solers; he promises to come and settle this matter in person. On the same day, he nominates the master of the Temple, Rocelin de Fos, and Nicholas de Meulles, keepers of the truce which he has imposed upon Simon de Montfort on the one hand and Gaston de Béarn, Amanieu d'Albret, Bazas, and La Réole on the other (*C. P. R. 1247–1258*, 159). On 16 June, he grants his protection until his or his son's arrival, to Gaillard Delsoler, Guillaume Arnaud Moneder, Brun In Chausat and other friends of Gaillard; they can go freely about Gascony, but he forbids them to enter Bordeaux (*ibid.*, p. 142). On 16 June, also, he gives Guillaume d'Armandarits authority to reconstruct and enclose his house, destroyed by order of the earl of Leicester (*ibid.*).

[1] *Chron. maj.*, v. 313: 'in quo verbo aculeato rex Wasconensium, qui praesentes erant, meruit gratiam et favorem'.

[2] Adam Marsh, p. 129: 'sospes et hilaris'.

[3] *Ibid., loc. cit.*: 'sub obscura dimissus licencia'.

[4] *Ibid., loc. cit.*: 'cum Henrico, primogenito suo, acceptissimo vestrae sanctitatis alumno'.

[5] Did the countess accompany her husband on this occasion also? In the text printed by Shirley we read: 'et cum amabili comitissae suae frequentia', but with a variant 'comitivae' for 'comitissae'. In any case, the epithet 'amabili' is very strange. Should one not rather read: 'cum innumerabili comitive frequentia'? In a letter of Adam written about the same time (no.

discontented with the nobility of the kingdom and the advice they had received, and dreading the return of the earl to their country.

Adam's letter, lengthy as it is, deserves careful examination. It casts a somewhat startling light on the king's character and policy, and throws into relief the earl's personal situation and relations with the nobility of the kingdom, perhaps we may even say with the persons composing the Parliament. On Adam Marsh's testimony, the only really cordial and loyal support Simon found was with the bishop of Worcester, always one of his warmest partisans, Peter of Savoy, the queen's uncle, and Peter de Montfort.[1] The others take a purely political line.[2] Their maintenance of the earl is prompted by distrust and dislike of the king's fantastic and arbitrary conduct, by hatred for the aliens who doubtless were working underhand against the earl, possibly during that famous night when Henry III changed everything by his tactical *coup*. As for Simon, perhaps we may not share the somewhat mystical admiration of Adam Marsh; but we may forgive him if these weeks of suffering engraved upon his mind bitter feelings of resentment against the sovereign and his counsellors.

If we are now asked which party was in the right in this trial, our first answer would be that we by no means possess the full facts and pleadings on either side. Had Simon behaved in a violent and cruel manner? He had been sent into a seditious province with orders to bring it back to peaceful ways; he may have thought that in such a case a mild policy would be weakness, and that hard blows would mean an early ending to the disorders. *L'emploi de la force a ses raisons que la raison ne*

188, p. 332) we read: 'scripsi etiam dominae comitissae Leycestriae per cursorem suum . . . quod, si fieri poterit opportune, accelerabo Boloniam accedere, secundum comitis Leycestriae et ejusdem comitissae anxias petitiones, non videns quid ei signare (*sic*: *corr.* significare?) conveniet de hoc in presentiarum'.

[1] Adam Marsh, p. 123: 'paucissimis praeter dominum Wygorniensem, dominum P. de Sabaudia, et dominum P. de Monteforti, inter tanta fastidia et discrimina, praesidium fidele ferentibus'.

[2] A passage in *Chron. maj.*, v. 289, should be noted here. The nobles feared, says Paris, 'ne rex per impetum festinum, quia tam alienigenis propitius esse probatur, comitem virum nobilem et naturalem juberet capi et retineri'. With the aliens (*alienigenis*) the chronicler brings into clear contrast the earl, now, so to speak, virtually an Englishman (*naturalem*).

connaît pas. The Gascons, on their side, were defending a cause to all appearances unexceptionable, one to which the active participation of the archbishop Géraud Malemort lent dignity and justification. But who would venture to pass considered judgment on the conduct of people in a revolt of twenty-five years' standing or longer against the king?[1] We had better admit that the question of responsibility is insoluble, and return to Simon de Montfort.

Once abroad, he used the subsidies given him by his relations and friends to raise a large and powerful army of mercenaries, attracted by the promise of rich booty.[2] In Gascony he took steps to put the country in a good state of defence, and established himself in a strong position to await the return of the Gascon deputies. These immediately upon reaching the county spread the rumour that their new master, prince Edward,[3] was shortly to arrive together with his father. To attack Simon de Montfort whom they now regarded more as a public enemy than as the king's lieutenant, they raised the largest army they had put in the field for five years, and marched out to assail Simon's forces. They discovered an ambush which he had prepared for them, routed his troops, and took one of his knights. The earl was warned in time, and hurling himself upon his enemies cut his way by sheer force to the prisoners and set them free; then, surrounded by a horde of enemies thirsting for his blood, he fought singly and unaided for several moments: thrown from his horse he was about to perish, overborne by sheer numbers, when the prisoners he had released made a

---

[1] *Chron. maj.*, v. 291.

[2] *Ibid.*, 313: 'promittens eis ut de acquirendis manubiis sibi condigna praemia praepararent'.

[3] It has been noted above (p. 110) that Henry III had already thought of giving Gascony to his eldest son. On 27 April 1252 he renewed the donation for ever, and added to it the Island of Oléron. 'Ista carta missa fuit Petro de Sabaudia ad mandatum Johannis Mansel per manum Artaldi de Sancto Romano, qui eam predicto Petro detulit' (*C. Ch. R.* i. 386). On the next day the king granted his brother Guy de Lusignan that part of Oléron which had belonged to the deceased count of Angoulême, the lord of Cognac, without prejudice to the conditions agreed upon between the king and the earl of Leicester (*ibid.*). Finally, on 28 April, Guy de Lusignan 'recognized' that he had received his donation and declared that he would hold these lands until the king's eldest son was put in possession of Gascony, and he repeated the reservation made in regard to the earl of Leicester's rights (*C. P. R. 1247–1258*, 136).

desperate charge, and got him away. He was mounted once more and the battle began with new fury. After half a day's fighting the Gascons were defeated, and many killed. Their leaders, a Rostein among them, were captured and sent to the king. 'Never', says Matthew Paris, 'did the earl run so great a danger; but his triumph was complete and his enemies henceforth dared no more murmur against him.'[1] Evidently the chronicler did not know that shortly afterwards Simon found himself blockaded in the castle of Montauban,[2] a powerful stronghold, but one that had neither garrison nor supplies. Simon was only saved by the devotion of some of his own troops, and in order to deliver the others, was forced to give up to the besiegers a number of the prisoners taken in the earlier action.[3] He took his revenge by marching to deliver his supporters besieged in the castle of La Réole, and punished his enemies by ravaging their lands.[4]

He was still at La Réole after bringing supplies into the castle,[5] when the Master of the Templars and Nicholas de Meulles arrived to bring him the order to observe the truce. He refused to obey, saying that it was impossible for him to lay down arms when confronted by an armed force.[6] The royal commissioners then showed him the letters patent depriving him of his command,[7] and prohibiting the Gascons from obeying him any longer. Simon made out that the charter of 1 May 1248 could not be thus set aside, that the royal command had been given 'more by caprice than by reason, and maintained that he would

[1] *Chron. maj.*, v. 315.

[2] A castle in the commune of Casseuil (Gironde).

[3] *Ibid.*, v. 334. On 7 August the vicomte of Tartas promised Simon help and assistance to the end of his command. The mayor, jurats, and commune of Saint-Émilion renewed their oath of fealty to him. Bibl. Nat. Clairembault 1188, p. 20; *Archives historiques de la Gironde*, i. 3.

[4] *Simon de Montfort*, p. 343: 'et si damages i [at La Réole] fu feiz de vignes couper ou d'autres choses, ce fu pur lor tort, qui avoent la triwe brisée, ne mie par le tort le conte'.

[5] *Ibid.*, p. 343: 'il li covint qu'il alat garnir le chastel de viandes et de genz qu'il ne se perdit; a laquel chose fere cil de la vile de La Réole le destorberent quant qu'il poerent'.

[6] *Ibid.*: 'il dist qu'il ne lor poet ne devet triwe tenir quant il le guerroent'.

[7] On 27 August 1252, the king ordered the barons and men of Gascony to give assistance to all wishing to take advantage of the truce; if the earl showed opposition, they were not to obey him or to consider him as seneschal; they should preserve their loyalty to the king alone (*C. P. R. 1247–1258*, 161).

remain at the head of his army until the king had observed his obligations towards himself'. He then went off to besiege Rions. In England, the barons continued to support him. In the October parliament [1] the king made a great fuss about the check which Simon had experienced at Montauban; he was told in reply that the news was not certain; that in any case the Gascons deserved to be treated with the greatest rigour, and that it was right to let the earl of Leicester reach the end of his seven years' governorship. 'These remarks displeased the king: he had in fact thought to carry the dispute with Simon to the last extremity; he was anxious to have him declared a traitor and to deprive him of his inheritance.' Far away as he was, the earl knew of these plans. To those who brought him this information of them he replied: 'I know what he wants: it is to enrich some Provençal or Poitevin from my confiscated possessions.'

The intrigue had failed [2]; violence was no longer possible. Henry III resigned himself to proposing acceptable terms to the earl. He could not deprive him of the government of Gascony, he would buy it from him. He promised to pay him 7,000 marks and to shoulder all his debts; [3] Simon on his side undertook to surrender to prince Edward the castles held by him from the king and all those he had acquired or conquered. With regard to prisoners, those taken outside Gascony should remain in the earl's hands; the others were to be set at liberty for a ransom. Finally, the Pope, who had on several occasions given a

---

[1] *Chron. maj.*, v. 327: 'Convocatis dominus rex optimatibus suis qui . . . suo impetui primi restiterunt, convenit eos de negotio Wasconiae quid agendum.' We may note this frequently recurring expression of the chronicler's: the king acts impulsively, takes sudden resolutions without asking advice. Then the magnates who are his 'natural' counsellors show their indignation.

[2] *Ibid.*, v. 338: 'Solutum est igitur concilium, rege hinc inde tam contra magnates quam contra praelatos ira succenso vehementi.' The king then conceived the idea of applying to the legate to authorize him to constrain the clergy to give him the subsidies he needed.

[3] *Simon de Montfort*, p. 337: 'et li rois vout . . . que le conte se partist du païs et parla as amis le conte qui lors estoent en Engleterre qu'il preist .vij. mile mars pour ses despans . . . Quant le conte vit que le roy son seignur s'estet afermé en ceste volanté, il ne se vout metre encontre; quar a souffrir li covenet la volonté son seignur, et prist les vij.m. mars de ce dont, de part le roy, li avoent, avant qu'il partit en Engleterre, esté offert .xiij. mile mars . . .'

friendly reception to Simon's requests on behalf of his family, took up the earl's cause.[1]

It was all very well to victimize Leicester; but some one had to replace him. Henry III doubtless thought that to obtain peace it would be sufficient to enjoin it upon the Gascons, and —the most infallible way of all—to get rid of the man whom they had incriminated. He was mistaken. Simon had never ceased to aver that he would obey his liege lord, and, as a matter of fact, he 'resigned the charter of his government' and left the country. No sooner did this happen than Alfonso of Castile, once more in pursuance of ancient, if continually disputed, rights over Gascony, summoned Gaston de Béarn and other powerful persons to his court.[2] Many Gascon lords abandoned the king of England and transferred their allegiance to the Castilian; and there was a danger of numerous defections among the merchants who had grown rich on the sale of wines in England, but had often been seized by the king, or had their cargoes confiscated, without reason or restraint. The clergy itself took part in the movement; Gerald de Malemort, archbishop of Bordeaux, the very man who had led and doubtless inspired the noisy Gascon deputation acting under his direction, did not scruple to fulminate excommunication against Simon, with complete disregard of the earlier papal indult. The earl of Leicester made such lively protests at the Roman Curia that Pope Innocent IV ordered an inquiry to be made. This was put in the hands of the bishop of Clermont, a suffragan of Bourges, who was probably a more impartial person than had been the bishop of Agen, a Bordeaux suffragan, two years earlier. If the earl had known anything about the bulls drawn up on that occasion by the papal chancery, he could have found some satisfaction in passages like this: 'the earl has complained to the Pope about the barons, knights, burgesses and other people of Gascony, who after swearing to obey him faithfully, have gone into revolt; but the archbishop appears to have encouraged them to conspire against him and to violate their oath, and he has done the earl grave acts of injustice.' While awaiting the result of the inquiry, Simon secured the immediate

---

[1] *Registres d'Innocent IV*, nos. 2791, 3475, 5159.
[2] *Chron. maj.*, v. 365.

raising of the excommunication, a penalty which could not be inflicted on him without the Holy Father's assent.[1] But the rebels upon whom Henry had naïvely tried to impose the will to peace, would have to be brought to that mind by brute force. Who was to be called in to do it? Henry III's eldest son, already endowed with the duchy of Gascony in appanage, was still in his 'teens.[2] Richard of Cornwall held moodily aloof: he had been granted the duchy once, and had taken it bitterly to heart when the heir presumptive to the throne was invested with the fair province, and he saw himself supplanted after Leicester's disgrace.[3]

Was Simon to be recalled? The king, it seems, showed regret at having sent him into disgrace;[4] but Simon had deliberately broken the bridges behind him. He had retired into France; there, brilliant offers were made him by the great nobles of the country, who were disconsolate at the recent death of Blanche of Castile (27 November 1252) and the prolonged absence of

[1] These facts are set forth in detail in four bulls of Innocent IV published by Élie Berger under the dates 27 March, 2 and 3 April 1253. (i) 2 March: the earl has complained of his excommunication 'sine causa rationabili' (no. 6504). (ii) 2 April (no. 6502): he had been excommunicated 'contra indultum ut per aliquem de Wasconia non posset in personam ipsius per biennium absque speciali mandato nostro excommunicationis sententia promulgari. . . .' The indult having been granted, as we saw above, on 29 January 1251, the delay of two years had expired on 27 March 1253. We must therefore suppose that the sentence affecting Simon was earlier than this 29 January; otherwise the Pope had not been consulted. Nos. 3 and 4 Bull of 3 April (no. 6500): the archbishop of Bordeaux had accused the earl of the arrest, 'non sine injectione manuum violenta'; and (no. 6501): the earl had complained of the archbishop because the 'barones, milites, burgenses et alii homines de Wasconia' had been encouraged by him to make conspiracy, in spite of the oath they had sworn 'sibi tanquam domino fideliter intendere et obedire . . . propter quod idem Symon incurrit dampna gravia et expensas; idem quoque archiepiscopus sibi in hiis et aliis graves injurias irrogavit'. Consequently the Pope ordered the bishop of Clermont (Guy de la Tour, 1250–86) to hold an inquiry quickly, 'de plano, sine judiciorum strepitu '; he was to summon the archbishop to attend, and if the accusations were not justified, he was to release Simon from the sentence of excommunication. If the sentence had not been pronounced under legal form, it was to be quashed, provided that the earl afterwards accomplished the acts of reparation enjoined by the bishop (no. 6504). Two of these bulls had been already published by Hauréau after the copies of La Porte du Theil, in a short article in *Notices et Extraits des Manuscrits*, xxiv. 2, pp. 238–40, on the subject of Géraud de Malemort.

[2] Born 17–18 June 1239, Edward was in his fourteenth year.

[3] *Chron. maj.*, v. 366: 'quia de Wasconia supplantabatur'.

[4] *Ibid.*: 'Doluit et poenituit ipsum.'

Louis IX. Matthew Paris says that it was proposed to make him seneschal in France, the office he already held in England. Simon refused, preferring to remain loyal to his oath of allegiance and not to incur the charge of treachery by serving two masters simultaneously.[1]

The Gascons, however, took advantage of the lack of all local vigilance and authority; on 19 April 1253, internal struggles began again with their inevitable train of pillaging, violent disseisin, arson, and murder. That wildest exponent of disorder, Gaston de Béarn, ravaged the country; he nearly reduced the very town of Bordeaux to starvation, and Bordeaux normally supplied the whole of Gascony with provisions.[2] In this he was particularly encouraged by his alliance with the king of Castile. It was only at the end of May that Henry III ordered the assembly of troops and vessels necessary for a new campaign which he hoped would be decisive. After a delay caused by contrary winds, he embarked at Portsmouth on 6 August,[3] and put into Bordeaux about the 20th.[4]

The military situation was not unfavourable. There was

[1] *Chron. maj.*, v. 366: 'Comes ne precibus pulsaretur ut rediret, cessit in Franciam ubi magnates regni Franciae libenter ipsum retinuissent, proponentes . . . ut esset eis pro senescallo'; cf. p. 415. The chronicler evidently did not know that the title of seneschal did not have the same meaning in France as in England: to recreate the functions of the seneschal, in abeyance since the time of Philip Augustus, would have been to act against the traditional policy of the French monarchy. A little further on Paris uses different language; 'postulabant ipsum ut . . . unus foret custodum corone'; for they knew that Simon, like his father 'qui pro ecclesia contra Albigenses dimicaverat', loved France, 'nec est a sanguine Francorum alienus' (p. 372). Simon refused, 'ne videretur proditor extitisse' (pp. 366 and 415).

[2] *Ibid.*, p. 368: 'Eodem tempore, videlicet quadragesimali, increbuerunt diversi rumores . . . quod Regula in Wasconia cum Sancto Milione et multa alia castra capta sunt et amissa, et strages hominum facta est non minima.' In 1253 Lent began on 2 March, Easter being on 20 April. P. 370: 'circa festum sancti Aelphegi (19 April) proditores regis de Wasconia . . . coeperunt ad invicem sese corrodere . . . Ex quibus praecipuus Gasto . . . ita ut Burdegalis, quae toti Wasconiae victualia consuevit ministrare, coepit egere.'

[3] *Chron. maj.*, v. 381: 'circa kal. Junii rex . . . milites sibi servitium militare debentes . . . fecit edicto regio submoneri . . . ut apud Portesmeue in Octabis Trinitatis (22 June) promti essent ad transfretandum'.

[4] Paris exaggerates when he speaks of a delay of three months. The king (p. 383) left on the 8th of the ides of August (6 August) he was 'apud Cumineys' (a place unidentified, on the Breton coast) on 12 August, and on the 20th at Bordeaux (*Rôles Gascons*, nos. 2636 and 2637). *Chron. maj.*, v. 388: Circa Assumptionem beate Mariae'. *Oxenedes* (p. 178): 'in crastino Assumptionis'.

nothing immediately to be feared in the valley of the Dordogne, where the strongholds conquered and equipped by Simon, Fronsac,[1] Cubzac, Bourg,[2] commanded the course of the stream. The centre of resistance was on the Garonne, La Réole itself, the haunt of the king's enemies;[3] on the other hand the mayor's palace of Bordeaux had been held by the earl's partisans since 29 May 1249, and consequently was on the king's side. It was a valuable tactical point from which it was easy to go upstream towards the rebel town by following the right bank; along this route the king was able to find billets for himself and his troops at Rions, Loupiac-de-Cadillac, Saint-Macaire, and Gironde, which lies practically at the gates of La Réole. The king did not delay long at Bordeaux;[4] he was at Gironde on 4 September, and before La Réole on the 7th. There he ordered war to be made by all possible means on Gaston de Béarn.[5] Then from his camp near Bénauge he summoned Simon de Montfort (4 October).[6] His letter was both a mandate and an entreaty. 'We command and request you to come to Gascony and discuss matters with us; if you think that it befits neither our honour nor yours to remain with us, you can withdraw when you please, without incurring our indignation. Knowing that the roads are

---

[1] *R. G.*, no. 2640: order to Nicholas 'de Bolevilla', constable of the castle of Fronsac (20 August) to send to the king at Bordeaux two of the three machines of war ('ingenia') which he has there for the defence of the castle; he may keep the third, the strongest, for himself.

[2] *Ibid.*, no. 2644: 'in castris apud Girondam' (4 September): mandate to the mayor of Bourg to sell the provision of wine belonging to the king, the proceeds to be employed in victualling the castle.

[3] *Chron. maj.*, v. 388: 'ubi quam plurimi hostium suorum Guasconensium latitabant'.

[4] *R. G.*, no. 2642. Bordeaux, 27 August. Mandate to send to Blaye those burgesses of Bordeaux who are under garrison at Rions; at the same time the earls of Norfolk and Warwick, accompanied by the seneschal John de Grey are to go and take possession of the castle and town of St. Macaire. On 11 September, 'in castris ante Regulam' the seneschal received the order to reinforce the castle of Rions in all haste (no. 2657).

[5] *R. G.*, nos. 2641, 2644, 2647.

[6] *Ibid.*, no. 2111: 'et si nobiscum moram faciatis morando, de malivolis vestris vos defendemus secure.' Cf. *C. P. R. 1247–1258*, 244. Before leaving England Henry III had commanded Leicester (from Portsmouth, 10 July): 'quod festinanter occurrat regi usque Burd., sciens quod honori suo non expediret quin ad presens esset ibidem ad innocentiam suam declarandam, plures enim possent in absencia sua ei imponi que, ipso presente, penitus omitterentur' *C. R. 1251–1253*, 489).

dangerous for you, we desire that the earls of Norfolk and Hereford, Guy de Lusignan, John de Balliol, William de Cantilupe
and Stephen Lungspee shall conduct you to a safe place.
Throughout the time you remain with us, you shall have nothing
to fear from those who wish you ill.'

Simon was not untouched by the spirit of charity that bids
men render good for evil, and remembering, perhaps, the advice
given some years ago by his close friend Robert Grosseteste,[1]
the bishop of Lincoln, he forgot his resentment and returned,
escorted by a large bodyguard of picked men which he had
raised at his own expense.[2] The king was moved by his mag-
nanimous conduct, and welcomed him with joy;[3] took numerous reparatory measures in his favour,[4] had recourse to his
arbitration in a suit with Amanieu d'Albret,[5] kept him constantly by his side at Saint-Macaire (November) and at Bazas
(December and doubtless January also).[6] From the beginning
of 6 February 1254 [7] the earl's name does not figure among the

[1] He died on 9 October 1253 (*Chron. maj.*, v. 407).

[2] *Ibid.*, p. 415.

[3] *Ibid.*, p. 416: 'ipsum cum maxima suscepit exultatione'.

[4] *R. G.*, no. 2076, 11 September 1253: mandate to Arnaud Caillau, R.
Moneder, R. Makayn, burgesses of Bordeaux, to pay without delay to Walter,
clerk of the earl of Leicester, 200 marks out of the 500*l.* which the king had put
at their disposal for striking the new coinage of Bordeaux (nos. 2076, 2658,
cf. *C. P. R. 1247–1258*, 242). The king also allowed the same clerk to bring a
vessel laden with wine into harbour without paying the tariff (*R. G.*, no. 2677).
8 October at the camp before Bénauge, mandate to the queen and Richard of
Cornwall, regents of England, to have a writ of 'liberate' issued to the earl for
the money he owed him at last Michaelmas (no. 2729). On 9 November at
Saint-Macaire, the king allowed the earl 500*l.* on the Exchequer to indemnify
him for his losses and expenses in the king's service (*Ibid.*, no. 2153, *C. P. R.
1247–1258*, 249); and in addition rent of 600 marks until it could be translated
into land (*R. G.*, nos. 2154–2157; cf. *C. P. R. 1247–1258*, 249–50). On the same
day the king granted the earl and his wife the castles of Odiham and Kenilworth for the duration of their lives (*R. G.*, no. 2160). On 18 November, Simon
was given authority to draw a sum of money deposited in the house of the
Mathurins in Paris (no. 2815). On 10 December, mandate to John de Sawerk,
king's clerk, to oblige all the earl's debtors at Bordeaux and Bazas to pay their
debts to him, as it had been to the king himself (*C. P. R. 1247–1258*, 258).

[5] *R. G.*, nos. 2204, 2105, 2210. Cf. *C. P. R. 1247–1258*, 254–5.

[6] *R. G.*, no. 2129, 22 October, in camp before Bénauge (cf. *C. P. R. 1247–
1258*, 246); no. 2131, 23 October (*C. P. R. ibid.*); 8 November (no. 2186);
cf. *C. P. R., ibid.*, p. 252; no. 2195 (Bazas, 28 November).

[7] *R. G.*, no. 2325: the earl is designated by the king to contract a loan in his
name with certain merchants. This is the last mention of the earl in the
Rôles Gascons.

witnesses of royal acts, in all likelihood because he had left Gascony never to return. We find him in London during April.

Towards the end of 1253 the king sent the earl marshal Roger Bigod and Gilbert de Segrave to the queen and Richard of Cornwall, the regents during his absence. Before the parliament[1] where sat the great nobles of the kingdom and the majority of the bishops, the king's speaker[2] described the position in Gascony: stubborn enemies, he said, had been destroyed; but there were others resisting still. The king of Castile, whose friendship was counted upon because of his relationship with the royal family of England, had revealed himself a bitter enemy; the Gascons inclined towards this alien sovereign more than to their natural lord. In the present need, the king asked that the nobles of the kingdom should be called together for the morrow of St. Hilary (14 January 1254).[3] The general assembly could not take take place till fifteen days later.[4] The reply[5] came that the earls and barons would assemble three weeks after Easter, ready to embark at Portsmouth to fight the king of Castile, if this king were in fact to invade

[1] *Chron. maj.*, v. 423: 'ad parliamentum venientes'. This is one of the earliest examples of the use of the word.

[2] *Ibid.*: 'prolocutor domini regis'. This is the term later used for the speaker. This speaker was doubtless Segrave, a noble, rich and of good character (*ibid.*, 263), who had already exercised judicial functions (*D. N. B.*, s.v. Segrave, Gilbert de).

[3] Hilary (13 January) was one of the four annual 'terms' of session for the principal courts of justice, it normally ran from 11 January to the end of the month.

[4] Matthew Paris gives the precise date: *Chron. maj.*, v. 423: 'Sexto Kalendas Februarii, die videlicet sancti Juliani' (27 January).

[5] This reply made by the queen and Richard of Cornwall, has come down to us in two versions which show basic identity. The former was copied by Matthew Paris in his Additamenta (vi. 283) and from that source found its way into Rymer's *Foedera*; it is undated, but certainly later than 27 January. The letter appears in Shirley's *Royal Letters*, ii. 101, dated Windsor, 14 February. The second text is corrupt (the king of Castile is constantly called 'rex Castellionis') or else Shirley has copied it inaccurately. If the date 14 February is right, the letter must have been sent three days after the writ of 11 February which has been reprinted in the 9th edition of *Select Charters*, p. 365. This writ is of considerable interest for the history of parliament, since it instructs each sheriff to see that two knights of his county are elected to be present at the next parliament so as to declare 'quale auxilium nobis in tanta necessitate impendere voluerint'. This is the first time that representatives of the smaller nobility of the shires were summoned to Parliament.

Gascony.[1] All the others made the same promise, and added the same reservation. At the end, the earl of Cornwall announced that he also would go with the queen, accompanied by her son Edward and her daughter Beatrice, 'if the king summoned them to go to him'.[2] When parliament met for the second time that year, on the prescribed day (about the middle of May) the nobles promised to provide the sovereign with the military aid he was requesting; but Simon, who had just arrived,[3] informed them that the king of Castile had not yet carried out his threat. Convinced that an attempt had been made to deceive them,[4] they retired 'amid gloom and indignation'.

In reality, though the war was to continue and much[5] was to be spent on it, negotiations were none the less prosecuted with Castile. On 8 February 1254 Henry III announced that he had sent Peter d'Aigueblanche, bishop of Hereford, and John Mansel, provost of Beverley, to the court of king Alfonso to discuss a treaty of peace and amity.[6] These two plenipotentiaries were closely attached to the king's personal service. Peter,[7] who belonged to the lords of Briançon and 'vicomtes' of Tarentaise, began by being clerk to William of Savoy, bishop

[1] Paris (*Chron. maj.*, v. 424) insists upon this restrictive condition, which he regards as essential.

[2] *Additamenta*, vi. 233.

[3] *Chron. maj.*, v. 440: 'per comitem S. qui tunc de partibus rediit transmarinis, qui veritatem super hoc nuntiavit'.

[4] Paris is convinced that it was intended to hoodwink the nobles through a false report. He was acquainted with the writ of convocation of 11 February 1254, since on p. 445 he reproduces a passage and gives its gist in his *Additamenta*, vi. 286; but he declares it 'falsum et deceptorium'. Cf. what he relates on p. 424: the earl of Gloucester having declared that he promised his aid 'secundum posse suum', added, 'si ipsum (Henry III) Castellae rex hostiliter impeteret'. Richard of Cornwall made the same promise with a like reservation, 'si vera sunt quae dicuntur'. The assembly had the impression that it was being hoaxed. 'Why', it was asked, 'does the king ask for the queen and his eldest son? Is it to fight the powerful king of Castile? Is there not talk of a marriage contemplated by the two kings? All this is in contradiction with what we have just been told.' The chronicler faithfully echoes these recriminations, when he adds: 'et sic incredibilem se prebuit [the king] universitati'. At the end of the writ of convocation, Paris reproduces, on p. 287, a writ of 25 February relating to Gascon affairs, preceding it with the remark: 'Item mandatum regis de Wasconia, sed super fraudem fundatum et falsificatum.'

[5] *Chron. maj.*, v. 484: 'Debita ejus (Henry III) ad plusquam trecenta milia marcarum dicuntur ascendisse.' Add the account which he estimates on p. 450.

[6] Rymer.   [7] *D.N.B.*, *s.v.* Peter of Aigueblanche.

elect of Valence in Dauphiné, and he had come over for the first time to England with his chief at the time of Henry III's marriage with Eleanor of Provence. Keeper of the royal wardrobe, he was elected bishop of Hereford in 1240 at the king's express recommendation, but he resided but little in his diocese and was constantly employed in all sorts of more or less confidential missions.[1] John Mansel[2] had entered the Exchequer while quite young—he appears to have obtained the office of chancellor; in 1238 he accompanied Henry de Turbervill who was taking a troop to assist the emperor in Italy, and in 1242 he was by the side of the king at the battle of Saintes, when he unhorsed the seneschal of the count of Boulogne. The next year he was severely wounded at the siege of the castle of Vérines. This fighting clerk was also a diplomat: after a mission to Scotland (1251) with the purpose of negotiating a marriage between king Alexander III and Margaret, Henry III's daughter, he was sent into Spain on business connected with the projected union between prince Edward and the step-sister of Alphonso X of Castile; along with this he had to discuss with Alfonso a treaty of peace and alliance between the two countries, now at variance over the question of Gascony.[3] Keeper of the privy seal,[4] king's secretary,[5] he was employed on the most confidential side of the king's policy, the side that normally escaped the suspicious curiosity of the magnates. He

[1] On 11 February the king remitted the bishop of Hereford 300l. which he had lent him, wishing thus to compensate him for the expense and labours undertaken on his (king's) behalf 'proficiscendo gratuita voluntate pro nobis in Hispaniam ad regem Castelle' (R. G., no. 2351).

[2] Mansel was illegitimate, and, as Miss Neilson (The Cartulary of Bilsington, p. 56 n.) remarks, had no heir.

[3] Chron. maj., v. 396: The document of the treaty, sealed with a golden bull weighing a mark of silver is preserved in the P.R.O. (Rymer, under 15 May 1253.)

[4] R. G., no. 97: 22 September 1242 : 'Hic recepit Johannes Maunsell sigillum regis.' The great seal is not in question here, as Luard seemed to imply (see Index, p. 397). In the passage to which Luard refers (iv. 601) Paris remarks that John Mansel was in 1247 named chancellor of St. Pauls in London by the imperious will of the king: 'custodiam sigilli regii suscepit, cancellarii vices acturus et officium'.

[5] In letter patent of 15 May 1253: 'Johannem Maunsell, cancellarium London' ac prepositum Beverlacensem, secretarium nostrum.' So also in letters patent of 22 August 1254 (Rymer, under this date, cf. R. G., no. 3947): 'Johannem Maunselli, secretarium nostrum et fidelem.' The expression should be remembered for the history of the secretaries of state.

was now associated with Peter d'Aigueblanche in the dual
negotiation of the preceding year, for strengthening family ties
between two rival houses and in guaranteeing the security of
Gascony from both sides of the Pyrenees. If this was an act of
Henry's own personal devising, he should receive the credit for
it. And while in London parliament was beating the air and
working itself into indignation against the king and his counsellors, a treaty was concluded (1 April 1254), which was soon to
have its full effect.[1] In the matter of the marriage, the queen,
summoned by her husband,[2] embarked on 29 May with her two
sons Edward and Edmund (the latter was already the accepted
candidate for the Sicilian crown),[3] and under the escort of her
uncle Boniface, archbishop of Canterbury,[4] reached Bordeaux
on 12 June. Prince Edward, who was at Burgos on 5 August,
married Eleanor of Castile and was knighted at the end of
October. John Mansel returned, bearing with him the charter
by which Alfonso gave up all pretensions over Gascony.
Henry III made haste to transfer to Edward the possession and
government of the duchy, now that it had been freed from all
external menace.[5] Thus we find in Rymer, in the *Rôles Gascons*,
and in the patent and close rolls, decision after decision in favour
of the earl of Leicester's victims. A practically complete
amnesty was proclaimed, the inevitable and necessary course,
whatever Matthew Paris may say.[6] The king had originally
commissioned the earl to chastise and bring the rebels to their
knees: he now had the task of pacifying the country. The
question of the earl's financial position and the payment of his
debts was obviously settled on the basis of the understanding
of 1252 [7] between him and the king's eldest son.[8]

[1] Rymer, under this date.

[2] How is one to explain what Paris writes on p. 447: 'mandatum regis priori
contrarium et urgens praeceptum nunciatur ne regina transfretaret'?

[3] *Chron. maj.*, v. 457.

[4] *Ibid.*, p. 447. On the end of Henry III's stay in Gascony and the beginning
of Edward's government, see the preface to vol. i of the *Rôles Gascons*, supplément, pp. xxii f., lxxxiv f.

[5] *Chron. maj.*, v. 450. The original of this charter is in the P.R.O. Museum.
See *Catalogue* of the Museum, 12th ed. (ed. Maxwell-Lyte, 1926), p. 67.

[6] See his lamentations on p. 450.

[7] *Simon de Montfort*, pp. 321–4.

[8] *R. G.*, no. 4062. On 13 September 1254 the king told Simon that the

Henry III was still at Bordeaux, where, on 25 August 1254, he sent Simon with Gilbert de Segrave to the young king Alexander III with a commission to communicate to him 'certain secrets which greatly exercised him'.[1] It may have been a question of the highly difficult matter of the county and 'honour' of Huntingdon which several members of the royal family of Scotland claimed.[2] We do not know what was the outcome of this embassy; and besides, it was towards France, above everything else, that the earl's activity was directed. We shall treat of this further on in the chapter devoted to the negotiations and the conclusion of the Treaty of Paris in 1259. He also found himself dragged directly or indirectly into the business of the Sicilian succession, which had been in train for several years and was to terminate first in a miserable check,

---

Treasurer, Peter Chaceporc, had received 100 marks of the debts contracted by the earl in Gascony. As for the rest, the king had presented them to his son Edward; and he consequently ordered the earl to deliver over to the prince 1,900 marks 'de debitis vestris Wasconie quemadmodum vobiscum convenimus'. Cf. *C. P. R. 1247–1258*, 331.

[1] Rymer, under this date. *Rôles Gascons*, no. 3955. Alexander, b. 1241, was not yet fourteen. He had succeeded his father Alexander II, on 8 July 1249. On 26 December, at York, he married Margaret, eldest daughter of Henry III, then fifteen, and was knighted by his father-in-law (Archibald H. Dunbar, *Scottish Kings*, 1899, pp. 94–5).

[2] The 'honour' of Huntingdon had entered the possession of the royal family of Scotland by the marriage of David, brother of Alexander I (1106–24) with Matilda, grand-niece of the Conqueror and widow of Simon de Senlis, earl of Northampton (d. 1109). The son of this Simon, Simon II, married a daughter of Roger de Beaumont, earl of Leicester, whose relationship with Simon de Montfort we know. David succeeded his father Alexander in 1124 and did homage for his earldom to Henry I, to Stephen and to the empress Matilda. The 'honour' was given by William II the Lion (1165–1214) to his brother David, who took the title of earl and died childless in 1237; the honour was then divided between two of his nieces, one of whom married John de Balliol (d. 1269) father of John I, king of Scotland. A table of the fiefs constituting this honour has been made by Margaret F. Moore, *The Lands of the Scottish Kings in England* (1915), p. 122, a work to which I owe the details of this present note. Now on 16 August 1256, Henry III restored to the king of Scotland, 'dilecto filio et fideli nostro' the honour of Huntingdon, 'ut jus suum, cum omni sua integritate . . . adeo libere et integre sicut antecessores sui eum melius et liberius habuerunt'. The witnesses were Richard of Cornwall, Richard de Clare, earl of Gloucester and Hertford, Roger de Quincy, earl of Winchester, Simon de Montfort, earl of Leicester, Humphrey de Bohun, earl of Hereford, &c. (*Royal Letters*, ii. 120). See also W. Farrer, *Honors and Knights' Fees*, ii. 294–416, where the fiefs of the honour of Huntingdon are exhaustively treated.

and then, fatal consequence, in the rising of the barons against
the ruinous ambitions of the king in collusion with the Pope.

Supplementary Note: The Question of Bigorre

We may here attempt to clear up the tangled question of Bigorre.
Its complications were destined to increase. We saw above that the
death of the countess Perronelle (1251), while bringing Esquivat de
Chabanais into the succession to the county, in reality left Simon in
the position of master. In the early stages he looked after it until
1254, giving his nephews and nieces in marriage,[1] and putting strong
places in a state of defence. But his situation was none the less very
embarrassing. If, as we saw above, he owed considerable sums for
succeeding to the old countess,[2] he could only pay by bringing
energetic pressure to bear upon the heir. A solemn act, delivered in
the great hall of the castle of Chabanais (3 June, 1253) gave him as
security the Perigord lands of the Chabanais, Confolens, and Loubert:
Simon was to enjoy their revenues until they equalled the sums owed
him by his small nephew. In return he would give up to Esquivat
Bigorre, Armagnac, and Fezensac. While he commanded in Gascony,
the possession of these counties allowed him to hold the vicomte of
Béarn in check. When he had left Gascony, Henry III was obliged to
continue his policy and Bigorre was what he wished to secure against

---

[1] In 1249 Simon decided on the future marriage of Esquivat with Maskarose,
daughter of Otho de Lomagne, and heir of Armagnac and Fezensac, through his
mother. It was the earl who advanced the dower in the sums stipulated in the
contract (charter of 3 June 1263 in *Simon de Montfort*, p. 371). About the same
time, he married Perronelle, younger daughter of the old countess, to a Norman
seigneur, Raoul de Taisson; the dower, paid in money and not in lands, was
levied on the revenues of Bigorre. He was probably influential in determining
the marriage in 1249 of Esquivat's mother, Alice de Montfort, with Raoul
de Courtenai.

[2] The testament of Perronelle, analysed by Davezac-Macaya (*Esquisses
historiques sur le Bigorre*, i. 280) was composed immediately after the death of
the countess, 13 November 1251. There is a copy in Bibl. Nat. MSS. Collection
Dupuy, vol. 823, cols. 251–3. The article concerning Simon de Montfort is
drawn up in these terms: 'Item dominus S. de M. comes Liuc[estrie], tenetur
dicte domine comitisse, singulis annis ex quo suscepit terram Bigorre, dare .vii.
milia solid. Morl.; de quibus pro .m. solidis concessit eidem comitisse villam
de Bays (*sic*) et redditus pertinentes ad eandem. Quos redditus unius anni
semel tantummodo percepit. Preterea persolvat comes Simon de residuis .vj.
milibus solidis quos annuatim debebat dare dictus comes prefate comitisse
m.m.m.m.d. sol. tantum solvit.' She therefore humbly begs the earl to pay the
said sum to her heirs.

Gaston, when he concluded the agreement of November 1253 with the bishop of Le Puy.[1]

[From the eleventh century the county had been under the suzerainty of the bishop and the chapter of Notre-Dame du Puy-en-Velay; a relief of 60s. *Morlaas* was the mark of this vassalage.[2] Bishop Bernard III of Montaigut le Blanc, shortly before his death (1255) sold Henry III his rights of suzerainty for 3,000l. once and for all.[3] Henceforth Esquivat was vassal of the English king, served him in Gascony 'with nine other knights';[4] accompanied him to England,[5] and took every possible step to interest Henry III in maintaining him in his legitimate possessions.[6] But Gaston de Béarn was too

[1] *Simon de Montfort*, p. 370.

[2] Ch. Rocher, *Les rapports de l'église du Puy avec la ville de Gérone en Espagne et le comté de Bigorre*, p. 120.

[3] *Recognitiones Feodorum*, no. 409.

[4] *R. G.*, no. 3615. On 16 June 1254, Henry III promised not to demand from Esquivat, his vassal, any other services and customs than those regularly rendered by his ancestors or himself to the bishop and chapter of Le Puy, his former suzerains (*ibid.*, no. 3791). In t. 1 of the *Rôles Gascons*, for the erroneous ' de speciali mandato et assensu episcopi et capituli Auxicensis' read *Anniciensis* (Le Puy).

[5] On 20 February 1255, Henry III declared that he could not permit 'quod eidem comiti propter adventum suum ad regem in Angliam aliquid juris depereat quoad debita que ecclesia Aniciensis ei debebat' (*C. P. R. 1247-1258*, 399). I copied these words, which could not be reproduced in the Calendar, from the original roll. The Index of the Calendar has mistakenly interpreted ' Aniciensis' as an altered form of ' Ambianensis', and the reference to p. 399 is accordingly found under ' Amiens'.

[6] On 4 June 1254 Esquivat pledged three of his castles, Auch, Laverdun in Armagnac, and Espas in Fezensac to Henry III at the price of 1,500 marks, 500 of which were paid on the spot (*R. G.*, no. 4274). Here also Francisque Michel miswrote the latin name of Le Puy under the form ' Auniciensis' (cf. *ibid.*, no. 4276, under 5 August). On 1 December, the king paid Esquivat 80l. (of Tours) out of the money due to prince Edward from the town of Bayonne. On 19 February 1255 he 'recognized' that he owed him 1,000 marks for the three castles just mentioned, 'et pro vadiis suis dum fuit in servitio regis in Wasconia'. The same day Esquivat transferred this credit to Simon de Montfort; ' et idem comes assignavit S. de M. et A., uxorem ejus, ad pecuniam illam recipiendam pro debitis in quibus idem comes dicto comiti Leycestrie tenebatur' (*C. P. R. 1247-1258*, 398). On 7 March, Henry III granted Esquivat an annual rent of 200 marks, and Esquivat transferred it, as the other, to his uncle (*ibid.*, p. 403). On 8 July, Eleanor provided the king with part of the promised sum: ' cum teneamur', the charter says, ' A. comitisse L., in magna pecunia tum pro comitatu Bigorre, cui pro nobis se obligavit in mille marcis et nos inde acquietavit' (Rot. Claus.). On 3 August, 1256 ('Vᵃ feria post festum sancti Petri in Vincula') the bishop of Tarbes, Arnaud III de Coarrase, Esquivat and his brother Jourdain, the ' very humble nephews' of the earl of Leicester, the court of Bigorre and the burgesses of Tarbes, informed Simon of the horrible persecutions they were suffering at the hands of Gaston de Béarn, who never

near, and Henry III too far away. So Esquivat had recourse once again to his Montfort uncle. On 6 June 1256, in agreement with his younger brother Jourdain, he ceded him the whole county with its dependencies, because he preferred, he said 'to see it in his hands rather than in the hands of a foreigner'.[1] What foreigner? Gaston, who declared himself vicomte of Béarn by the grace of God, or the king? As a pledge of faith, Simon gave up the castle of Lourdes, the watch-tower planted where the Gave de Pau emerges from its gorge, and that of Mauvesin, which the counts of Foix were to convert into a redoubtable fortress a century later.

ceased to persecute them with a deadly hatred. Allied to the son of the king of Aragon, to Giraud d'Armagnac, to certain barons of the English crown and to the count of Foix, Gaston had been oppressing them to such an extent that they did not dare to emerge from a defended town or a strong castle which they had succeeded in entering. In vain they had proposed to him that their disputes should be communicated to the court of Bigorre, or to the seneschal of Guyenne, or the king of England, or even the king of France, or the count of Champagne (Thibaud, king of Navarre). He had rejected all their proposals. They therefore prayed earl Simon to succour them ('nobis qui vestre semper sumus creature'); otherwise, 'in brevi nos totam Vasconiam relinquere oportebit.' With regard to the considerable expenses likely to be involved, Esquivat declared 'vobis terram Bigorrie, de consilio et assensu venerabilis patris et domini episcopi Bigorre et Jordani fratris nostri, ac etiam curie Bigorre, tradimus, vel terram de Cabenasio (Chabanais), si forsitan malueritis, possidendam quousque vobis de omnibus expensis premissis ad vestram satisfaceremus voluntatem . . .' (Archives Nat., Cartulaire de Champagne, *Liber ecclesiasticorum*, 1ère partie,' KK 1065, fols. 255–6).

[1] *Layettes*, no. 4279. This act, dated at Tarbes, was confirmed at Paris in 1258, 22 November: 'quia malo quod dictus Symon et heredes sui vel assignati habeant dictum comitatum quam aliqui alii' (no. 4453). On the same day Esquivat adds to the country of Bigorre, 'Sanctum Chanzanum et Montem de Marchan et vicecomitatum de Marchan' (no. 4454); i.e. the Marsan and perhaps the Tursan (Sanctum 'Chanzanum' is certainly a word altered by the copyist). On 23 November Esquivat engaged (no. 4455) to deliver over to his uncle, as soon as he asked for them, the castles of Lourdes (Hautes Pyrénées, arr. Bagnères de Bigorre) and Mauvezin (c. Lannemezan). Blaauw knew and published these documents, (*Barons' War*, pp. 362–3), but with many inaccuracies.

V

HENRY III'S FOREIGN POLICY FAILS OVER THE AFFAIR OF SICILY. OPPOSITION OF THE BARONS WHO IMPOSE A NEW CONSTITUTION ON THE KING. THE PROVISIONS OF OXFORD AND THE PROVISIONS OF WESTMINSTER (1254-9).

THE death of the emperor Frederick II, king of Sicily and Apulia (1250), gave Henry III's ever-restless ambition an opportunity to interfere in Italy and in Germany. Innocent IV who had excommunicated the deceased sovereign and declared him deprived of the Sicilian crown, held by him as a fee of the Holy See, offered it in 1254 to Henry's brother, Richard of Cornwall. Richard first laid down his terms. He did not want it to be said of him: 'I sell or give you the moon, go up and take it.'[1] Rebuffed here, the Pope made direct overtures to the simple-minded monarch,[2] with the assurance that he would provide 'all the help he could dispose of'[3] for the conquest of the kingdom. In spite of the equivocal nature of such vague terms, Henry made haste to accept on behalf of Edmund, his younger son, the noble prize that seemed already in his grasp,[4] and sent off to the Pope all the money he could extort,[5] to

[1] *Chron. maj.*, v. 457. It was the papal envoy, Master Albert, who told the chronicler Richard's remark: 'vendo vel do tibi lunam; ascende et apprehende eam'.

[2] *Ibid.*, p. 458: 'ut simplicitatem ejus circumveniret'.

[3] *Ibid.*: 'ad hoc acquirendum, juvamen prestaret tale quale poterat sine aliquo gravamine'.

[4] *Ibid.*: 'adeo dilatatum est cor suum inani gaudio quod . . . filium suum Edmundum regem Siciliae palam vocaret, credens profecto se jam de ipso regno subarratum.' See *D. N. B.*, s.v. Lancaster, Edmund earl of, and particularly E. Jordan, *Les Origines de la Domination angevine en Italie*, pt. ii, ch. v; for the abandonment of the English project by Urban IV and the offer of Sicily to Charles of Anjou, see pp. 370-410. Cf. Berger, *Innocent IV*, t. ii, p. cclxxxv.

[5] *Chron. maj.*, v. 458: 'Rex igitur quicquid de thesauro suo, quicquid de scaccario, quicquid mutuo potuit a fratre suo Ricardo recipere, quicquid poterat a Judeis abradere, quicquid de rapinis justiciariorum itinerantium valuit extorquere, misit papae.' The list is worth remembering (cf. *ibid.*, p. 588). Another source of revenue came from grants and confirmations of municipal charters, very numerous during the years 1256-7 (Tait, *British Borough Charters*, ii. xvii). Among these charters the one in favour of Leicester should be noted (30 May 1257) delivered 'ad instanciam dilecti et fidelis nostri Simonis de Monteforti' (*ibid.*, p. 330; cf. Bateson, i. 53, who misdates).

assist him in the struggle against Conrad IV, Frederick's son and successor; in exchange, he won for himself release from his several times repeated vow to go on crusade. The possession of Sicily and Apulia [1] would serve nicely to compensate for the abandonment—it had already been agreed upon in principle— of the French provinces lost ever since the condemnation of John Lackland. And finally, a firm position at Messina and in Naples would mean the partial resumption (in another form) of Henry II's plans, of the dream to reconstitute for his own advantage the work of the Norman kings in the centre of the Mediterranean. Then came Conrad IV's death (21 May 1254), leaving an infant in the cradle, Conradin, to succeed. The Pope turned so favourable an occasion to profit by claiming the tutelage of the minor and invading the kingdom. He made a triumphant entry into Naples; but Manfred, prince of Tarente, Frederick II's bastard son,[2] took up arms in the name of his nephew, and the rapid successes that he won dragged Henry III into a war which was to be ruinous and indecisive.

Henry III had indeed carried out a stroke of personal policy. Doubtless he had taken the advice of his council; but who were his councillors? A memorandum of 30 November 1255 [3] tells us that all the privileges enumerated under the king's seal in the business of Apulia, were sealed by his order in his castle of Windsor by the counsel of persons whose names follow: Peter d'Aigueblanche, bishop of Hereford; the king's three half-

---

[1] The concession of Sicily ('regnum Siciliae et totam terram quae est citra Pharum usque ad confinia terrarum Ecclesiae') was made on 6 March 1254 (Rymer). The deed, delivered by Master Albert, papal notary, is dated: 'A.D. millesimo ducentesimo quinquagesimo tertio (old style), pridie nonas Martii (6 March), pontificatus domini Innocentii papae IV undecimo.'

[2] *Chron. maj.*, v. 572.

[3] Rymer, p. 332, following letters patent authorizing prince Edward to contract by oath to fulfil all conditions imposed upon his brother Edmund in the business of Sicily: this letter or memorandum is dated Windsor, 1255, 13th indiction, the eve of the kalends of December, in Henry's 40th year. (Cf. *C. P. R. 1247–1258*, 451). I do not know why Hardy in his *Syllabus* gave the date as 19 November, or proposes to date the *Memorandum* 11 November. On the patent roll the *memorandum* ends with words that Rymer does not reproduce: 'et transcripta omnium privilegiorum sigillata sunt sigillo . . . venerabilis patris . . . Bononiensis episcopi et commissa in garderoba nostra salvo custodienda. Teste R. apud Windes'. The bishop of Bologna was James Buoncambio, Innocent IV's Vice-Chancellor, nominated to that post in 1244 (*Reg. Innocent IV*, no. 720–41).

brothers, Aimar bishop-elect of Winchester, William de Valence, and Geoffrey de Lusignan; two earls, Richard of Gloucester and John de Warenne; John Mansel, provost of Beverley,[1] Philip Lovel, Treasurer of the Exchequer,[2] Ralph FitzNicholas;[3] five judges, Roger de Thurkelby,[4] Henry de Bath,[5] Henry de la Mare,[6] Henry de 'Bretton',[7] Nicholas de la Tour,[8] and 'others of the royal council'. The 'others' unnamed were doubtless inferior officials, who had to accept the king's intentions as commands. It was a kind of secret council assembled behind closed doors to settle business which was to involve the revenues of the crown for years and to throw the kingdom into confusion.

In Germany the premature death of Conrad IV opened an era of troubles which ended in an embittered crisis. William of Holland the king-elect having died (28 January 1256) in an obscure fight among his subjects in revolt, who was to succeed him? Two foreign competitors stepped in: Richard of Cornwall, who was elected 14 January 1257,[9] and Alfonso X the Wise, king of Castile and Leon, elected the following 1 April.[10] Richard, the candidate preferred by the Pope, was crowned on 17 May at Aix-la-Chapelle.[11] His coming was a menace to Manfred, but it was too far away to stop the course of his success. So great was

[1] John Mansel had been nominated provost of Beverley in 1247. He became treasurer of York in 1256 (*D. N. B.*).

[2] Philip Lovel was nominated treasurer, at John Mansel's advice, on 27 August 1252 (*D. N. B.*).

[3] Ralph FitzNicholas, steward of the king's household, was disgraced in 1236, and came back into favour in 1242 (*Chron. maj.*, iii. 363, and iv. 191). He took the cross in 1250 (*ibid.*, v. 101), and died in 1257 (p. 616).

[4] Roger de Thurkelby, justice of the Bench, frequently employed on Assize (cf. Dugdale, *Origines Juridicales*, p. 17 and Foss, *Judges of England*, ii. 484) is termed by Paris 'miles et literatus' (*Chron. maj.*, v. 317). Paris relates a bitter remark of his about the Poitevins (*ibid.*).

[5] Henry de Bath, itinerant justice, 'miles et literatus, legum terrae peritissimus, domini regis justiciarius et consiliarius specialis' (*Chron. maj.*, v. 213). Attacked with violence by Henry III in the London parliament of 1251, he was successfully defended by John Mansel, the bishop of London and Richard of Cornwall (p. 223).

[6] Justice itinerant in 1254 (Paris, *ibid.*, 443). He died in 1256 on the course of a mission to the Pope (*ibid.*, p. 618).

[7] The famous jurist Henry de Bracton, d. 1268 (*D. N. B.*).

[8] Justice itinerant in 1257 (*Chron. maj.*, vi. 330), and in 1261 and 1262 (Jacob, *Oxford Studies*, pp. 102–3).

[9] *Chron. maj.*, v. 601–4. Cf. *D. N. B.* (important art. by Prof. Tout).

[10] *Ibid.*, 624, 649.　　　　　[11] *Ibid.*, 640.

this that in 1258 the bastard son crowned himself with his father's crown. The Pope, who now had to admit the defeat inflicted upon his forces, never ceased to solicit money, soldiers, and a competent general to command them.[1] To continue the war, he had made considerable loans to the aspirant of his choice, advances that in 1257 reached the figure of 150,000*l.*,[2] and he became more and more insistent in his claims to be refunded the money.[3] The English prelates in the end granted him only 52,000 marks.[4] In return, the clergy demanded the confirmation of their liberties, and on this occasion there was drawn up a sort of constitution in fifty articles 'like those for which Thomas Becket had fought'.[5] This was the prelude to the imminent revolution. It was the clergy who, so to speak, showed the nobles the pathway to resistance.

The earl of Leicester may well have approved of this important manifesto; but it is very difficult to follow him through the confused incidents of 1257. Matthew Paris relates a violent altercation of his with the king's half-brother, William de Valence, on the subject of the robberies committed on Simon's lands. The earl's steward having rescued the captured property, William made a slanderous attack on Simon, calling him traitor, 'the worst offence that can be done to a knight'; Simon would have killed him, if the king had not intervened in time between the two brothers-in-law; 'from that time forth the poison of enmity never ceased to alienate the one from the other.'[6] We shall find them later in opposite camps.

For the time being it was essential to meet the obligations contracted in the affair of Sicily, which in view of the successes

---

[1] Bulls of 14 Kal. October, 1 Alexander IV, or 18 September 1255 (Rymer; cf. Potthast, no. 16018), and the 5th of the kalends of October, 2 Alexander IV (Rymer; cf. Potthast, no. 16556).

[2] *Chron. maj.*, v. 533. [3] *Ibid.*, p. 581.

[4] *Ibid.*, p. 637. In the text the figure of 42,000*m.* is given, and in the rubric that of 52,000, which has already appeared before, p. 624.

[5] *Ibid.*, p. 632. The bishops of London (Fulk Basset) and of Worcester (Walter de Cantilupe) had already declared their firm intention of following in the footsteps of the holy martyr, 'qui pro libertate ecclesiae se permisit excerebrari' (p. 525). These two prelates were then friendly to Simon de Montfort, but Walter alone remained faithful. The Cantilupes took their name from Chanteloup, arr. Coutances, c. Bréhal (cf. *Société historique et archéologique de l'Orne*, xlv, Bulletin de janvier 1926, pp. 101–7).

[6] *Chron. maj.*, v. 634.

won by Manfred [1] was now taking an increasingly disquieting turn. The king made a great effort. On 26 June 1257, his son Edmund sent the Pope Alexander IV an embassy consisting of the archbishop of Tarentaise (Raoul le Gros I of Chastelar), the earl of Leicester, Peter of Savoy, and John Mansel. They were commissioned to find the Pope and secure from him an amelioration of the terms imposed by Innocent IV. On the same day, the king gave his full powers to these negotiators and provided them with detailed instructions,[2] which Artaud of Saint-Romain had the duty of conveying to Simon de Montfort and Peter of Savoy, then at Paris. Most probably these two refused to go to Rome, and on 8 July the king had to content himself with sending one of his clerks, Nicholas de Plumpton, also a papal chaplain,[3] instead. Alexander IV's reply was a little time in coming, but peremptory when it came. On 4 October [4] he commanded the clergy, under pain of excommunication and privation of all offices and benefices, to pay the tenth of ecclesiastical revenues and all the sums conceded to the king for the fulfilment of his promises, 'taking no account of the protests of bishops or of any other persons in England, and without possible recourse to the Apostolic See'. This bull merely inflamed already excited tempers. The kingdom was at the moment passing through one of those powerful crises which occur in the life of peoples as much as in that of individuals. The season had been bad, abundant rain had destroyed the harvest and rotted the crops: there had been serious mortality, bread was dear and there was a lack of coin, drained off by the needs of Richard of Cornwall in Germany and of Edmund in Sicily: all these misfortunes fell at one and the same time on the unhappy country.[5] The Welsh, after being temporarily repulsed into their mountains, now trooped down to ravage the plains, their supplies of corn and salt exhausted.[6] Finally there was a risk of having to fight the

[1] *Chron. maj.*, v. 511.

[2] Six papal bulls, or royal letters (from king Henry III and his son) are analysed in *C. P. R.* 1247–58, p. 567 and f. 68, with the dates 26 and 28 June. See Rymer at those dates.

[3] Rymer 28 June.

[4] *Reg. Alexander IV*, no. 2238. Cf. Rymer, 5 and 8 July. On the levying of this tax, see W. E. Lunt, *The Valuation of Norwich*, 192 f.

[5] *Chron. maj.*, v. 660–1; Oxenedes, 195.

[6] *Chron. maj.*, v. 639, 645, 648. 'Victores effecti' (the Welsh), p. 677,

insurgent Scotch barons, and even the bishop of Durham himself, who in proud reliance upon his palatine privileges had contemptuously refused every summons to the king's court.[1] To confront his enemies, Henry called out the feudal host; but the knights complained of being summoned too frequently and unprofitably.[2] It was during this low ebb of social and economic life, in the middle of the discord between king and people, that the parliament which was to give the realm a new constitution opened at London on 2 April 1258.[3]

Before going further, we need to make a brief sketch of the governmental machine, to show how it worked and the forces actuating it.

The main principles followed out by Henry III in his government were by no means new. They were part of the inheritance which had come to him from his father John Lackland, his uncle Richard the Lion Heart and his grandfather, the great Henry II. These are names of sovereigns living in the period of autocracy. They had circumstances at their command. Throughout the course of the twelfth century the power of the central government had suffered no serious check in its effort to expand and improve its administrative methods; but in the thirteenth, starting from John Lackland, it had met with organized resistance.

In England, as in other continental monarchies, kingship had a double character: it was sacred and it was feudal. It rested upon the clergy and the nobility, two foundations deeply rooted in the national soil. But the victory of William at Hastings had given it a wholly peculiar position. The Conqueror had subjected an entire people with its native life and institutions to a comparatively small number of alien adventurers. For some time there was a risk that his companions would follow the lot of the Danes, who after winning numerous victories over the Anglo-Saxons, had ended by being eliminated or absorbed by the former possessors of the land. Such a danger could only be avoided after 1066 by the close union of the

---

sese frumento, sale et aliis sibi necessariis, quibus antea indiguerant, prudentes instaurarunt.'

[1] *Chron. maj.*, v. 657.   [2] *Ibid.*, v. 675, 677.

[3] *Ibid.*, p. 676.

victorious leader and his helpers in the conquest. William I's chief merit was that he retained in his service and employed in his government both the nobility, now permanently established on the conquered soil, and the clergy with its new personnel and its leaders who, imbued with Roman maxims, brought with them powerful elements of moral and political reconstruction. William received unction at his consecration, and the clergy strove to secure a popular triumph for the ideas of submission to authority, of respect and reverence for the lay representative of God upon earth. Moreover, all, clergy and nobility alike, were bound to the prince by oaths of homage and fealty varying in their application. Later the monarchy made a bid for absolutism. Then the clergy and nobles, together or separately, spontaneously or by common consent, vindicated each the rights of its own order, and after struggles which are matters of common knowledge succeeded in winning recognition and solemn confirmation of their privileges. The Charter of Ecclesiastical Liberties and the Great Charter (1215) set up the barrier of law against the establishment of an absolutist régime. It was a precarious victory, and one that never ceased to be challenged: but let us hear the opinion of the jurists, Ranulf de Glanvill, one of Henry II's most valued officials, and Henry de Bracton, the prolific commentator on English law and custom, for they wrote some strong words on the matter. 'The royal majesty,' says Glanvill,[1] should rest not only upon force of arms, whereby subjects in rebellion and nations in revolt are brought low, but upon the laws. The laws of England are not written; but it is not unreasonable to call them laws, law being the 'will of the prince which has the force of law. I am here speaking of laws which in doubtful cases have been discussed and drafted in council, that is by the magnates of the kingdom on the initiative of the king.' Half a century later Bracton, the pupil of the famous Italian jurist Azo of Bologna, gave voice to

---

[1] *De legibus Angliae*, Prologus, ed. Phillips, i. 237: 'Regiam majestatem non solum armis contra rebelles et gentes sibi regnoque insurgentes oportet esse decoratam, sed et legibus. . . . Leges namque Anglicanas, licet non scriptas, leges appellari non videtur absurdum, cum hoc ipsum lex sit *quod principi placet et legis habet vigorem,* eas scilicet quas super dubiis in consilio definiendis procerum quidem consilio et principis accedente auctoritate constat esse promulgatas.' The words in italics are from the Codex of Justinian.

similar ideas in almost mystical language: 'There is no one in
the kingdom', he writes, 'who is the equal of the king, nor, *a
fortiori*, his superior.' 'Just as Jesus and the Virgin submitted to
the Law, so the king must be submissive to it also. His power
cannot be entirely without check'; 'No one in the kingdom can
be greater than he. If justice is asked for against him, it cannot
be granted in the ordinary ways. He must be asked to correct
and amend what he has done. If he refuses, he will be punished
by God.'[1]   Yet his authority must not be arbitrary; 'since he
is the minister of God upon earth, he may only do what is just,
and the Roman maxim *quod principi placuit legis habet vigorem*
cannot be applied here. . . . King when he does good, he is a
tyrant when he oppresses his people and dominates them by
violence.'[2] Bracton adds to this passage of rather incoherent
rhetoric certain observations which reveal the professional
lawyer, with the technique and terminology of a civilian:
Neither judges nor individuals may discuss the king's charters[3]
or his deeds; even if there are obscurities in a charter, such
persons cannot interpret them. The king alone can; but he must
do it according to right, and must amend injustice, lest in their
turn the king and the judges may themselves be judged by the
living God. The king has a superior over him, who is God; and
over him too is the law that has made him and his court, that is,
the earls and barons of his kingdom. The word *comes* means

[1] Bracton, ed. Twiss, i. 38: 'Parem autem habere non debet in regno
suo, quia sic amitteret praeceptum, cum par in parem non habeat imperium.
Item nec multo fortius superiorem, nec potentiorem habere debet. . . . Et quod
sub lege esse debeat, cum sit Dei vicarius, evidenter apparet ad similitudinem
Jesu Christi, cujus vicem gerit in terris, quia . . . esse voluit sub lege ut eos qui
sub lege erant redimeret. . . . Sic ergo rex, ne potestas sua maneat effrenata,
igitur non debet esse major eo in regno suo in exhibitione juris . . . Si . . . ab eo
petatur . . . locus erit supplicationi quod factum suum corrigat et emendet;
quod quidem si non fecerit, satis sufficit ei ad poenam quod Dominum expectet
ultorem.' Cf. ii. 272; v. 402; v. 250.

[2] *Ibid.*, ii. 172: 'Nihil enim aliud rex potest in terris, cum sit Dei minister et
vicarius, nisi id solum quod de jure potest; nec obstat quod dicitur quod principi placet legis habet vigorem. P. 174: 'Dicitur enim rex *a bene regendo* et
non a *regnando*, quia rex est dum bene regit, tyrannus dum populum sibi
creditum violenta opprimit dominatione.'

[3] *Ibid.*, i. 268: 'De chartis vero regiis et factis regum non debent nec
possunt justiciarii nec privatae personae disputare; nec etiam, si in illa dubi-
tatio oriatur, possunt eam interpretari et in dubiis et obscuris . . . domini regis
erit expectanda interpretatio et voluntas.'

king's companion; and these companions are there to teach justice. In this sense the word companion means master, that is, teacher.' [1] Here is a strange medley of words and ideas, with streaks of illumination here and there that light up the period studied in the present work; for Bracton wrote his treatise not far from 1240, when Simon de Montfort's political life was just beginning. We must now observe how the supreme authority of the king functioned in actual practice.

Originally the seat of government was the court of King's Household, the *domus regia* or *curia regis*, two equivalent expressions. Their initial designation was the place dwelt in by the king and his family; there he lived in the midst of attendants ministering to his person (*domestici, ministri*). These *domestici* shared amongst themselves a certain number of offices. Some of them both originally, and later on served in an entirely private capacity; others, in charge of administrative functions, fulfilled the *ministeria* destined later to become public services, and later still ministries in the full sense. Three of the latter, without ceasing to belong to the Household, early assumed a similar importance: the Chamber, the Wardrobe, and the Chancery.

The Chamber, as the name signifies, was the solidly constructed room (*camera*) where the king rested and slept: the Wardrobe (*vestiarium, garderoba*) the apartment where he had his clothes, as well as his ornaments, jewelry, the locked coffers containing his money, in safe keeping. The chief officer of the Chamber is the Grand Chamberlain (*magister camerarius*, later Master Chamberlain) who followed the king in all his wanderings. The coffers for the coined money, termed the Privy Purse, that is the financial department of the Household, were under the charge of the Treasurer (*thesaurarius*),[2] originally quite an inferior official, who never ceased to grow in importance to the

---

[1] Bracton, ed. Twiss, i. 268: 'Rex autem habet superiorem, Deum; item legem per quam factus est rex; item curiam suam, videlicet comites, barones, quia comites dicuntur quasi socii regis; et qui habet socium habet magistrum. Et ideo, si rex fuerit sine fraeno, id est sine lege, debent ei fraenum imponere, nisi ipsimet fuerint cum rege sine fraeno.' Bracton's theory, a curious blend, it seems, of traditional and Germanic ideas, is the subject of important discussions by Dr. Holdsworth, *Hist. Eng. Law*, 3rd ed., ii. 252–4, and by R. W. and A. J. Carlyle, *A History of Medieval Political Theory in the West*, iii. 52–75 and v. See also the new edition of Bracton by G. E. Woodbine, esp. i. 331–3.

[2] Tout, *Chapters in Med. Admin. History*, i. 83–6, 102–15.

T

detriment of the Grand Chamberlain. It was the Treasurer, for
instance, who during Henry III's first expedition to France
(1230) had to find and expend the money for the army;[1] for
money was the sinew of war. Thus there gradually formed a
veritable ministerial department operating under the direct
exclusive control of the king. After Henry III's marriage, the
queen had also her Wardrobe, and later their son Edward
had his.[2]

These two offices, Chamber and Treasury, at once separate
and interwined, normally had the same personnel, whose cease-
less activity was given written form, by way of record or war-
rant, in the Chancellor's *scriptorium*. This official, who became
in the end one of the chief personages in the state, was at first
simply the keeper of the royal seal. Under Henry I, when the
bureaucracy was in process of organization, he drew up or made
his scribes draw up the documents giving effect to the royal
will. Thomas Becket was originally a simple clerk in the Chancery. From the twelfth century onwards the Chancery tended
to become a real Secretariat of State. During Henry III's
minority the Chancellor has become a great personage; he is
chosen from among the bishops; he purchases his office, a fact
that confers upon him a sort of security of tenure; and then, as
often in history, there appears a counterpoise, and his position
is diminished by the creation of the Small Seal, reserved for the
private needs of the Chamber, while the Great Seal is applied to
the deeds drawn up under solemn formulae, like *cartae*, letters
patent, &c.

From the three great offices of the Household specialist
departments in time detached themselves. They too were the
children of the *curia regis*, and took their parent's title. The
Court of Exchequer was the first to separate from the Chamber
and the private Treasury. Its officials, who from Henry II's
time onwards were called 'barons of the Exchequer', were by
origin just officials of the Chamber. The Treasurer and the
Great Chamberlain, while continuing their service to the king's

---

[1] Tout, *Chapters*, p. 198. See *The Great Roll of the Pipe for the fourteenth
Year of the Reign of Henry III, Michaelmas 1230*, ed. by Chalfant Robinson,
1927.
[2] Tout, *Chapters*, pp. 252-7.

person, became the heads of this new body as well;[1] but before the end of the twelfth century the Exchequer had become established at London or Westminster, while the Treasury remained confined to Winchester. This was the first separation, and a second was soon to follow. The Chancellor, who was always attached to the king's person by reason of the Great Seal in his keeping, was replaced at the Exchequer by a clerk who became in turn independent of his former patron, and instead of being nominated by him, was selected by the king. Here then we have a second chancery wherein the Small Seal was also exclusively employed. Round the Exchequer table sat other officials of the Household, the Marshal, Steward, and Constable, clear evidence of the type of bond that in earliest times united the members of this numerous *personnel*.

The Exchequer was the department of account: not that it had to verify, whether in receipts or expenditure, all the sums passing in and out of the Treasury, since the king never failed to keep a particular treasury of his own, maintained out of his special resources; it had rather to scrutinize the moneys that went through the hands of the sheriffs. Twice a year, at Easter and at Michaelmas, these officials, the heads of their shires nominated by the king and empowered to act on his behalf, were bound to render account to the barons of the Exchequer and to bring the nett product of their receipts or to show cause for the deficit in cases where such occurred, and they were not rare.[2] These receipts came from three chief sources: the farm of the counties, the proceeds of justice, and the feudal revenues. Sheriffs and king were equally concerned to increase the

---

[1] So minutely described in the *Dialogus de Scaccario*, drawn up in its original form about 1179; for the date see H. G. Richardson, 'Richard FitzNeal and the Dialogus de Scaccario,' *E. H. R.* April–July 1928, pp. 161 and 336 f.

[2] These transactions took place in two offices: one above (*scaccarium superius*) where the statements of accountants were audited, the other below (*scaccarium inferius*) where the money paid in was counted out, weighed, and tested. The final result was entered upon parchment rolls in duplicate: one for the Treasurer, the other for the Chancellor. The former of these rolls was officially known by the unique name of the *Magnus Rotulus Pipae*. The bulk of these rolls grew rapidly, as can be seen from comparing the Great Rolls of the twelfth century published by the Pipe Roll Society with one of 14 Hen. III (1230) edited by Chalfant Robinson (see before, p. xxxviii, and one of 26 Hen. III (1241–2) edited by N. H. L. Cannon, which by reason of its date is of such interest for our period. Cf. Giuseppi, *Guide*, i. 132–6.

receipts, whence grave abuses resulted. The sheriff who, at his own risk and hazard, undertook to farm the royal domains, had no hesitation in bringing pressure to bear upon the people under his administration so as to clear his farm, and after that to enrich himself, since any surplus belonged to him. On the other hand amercements, which were generally severe and arbitrary in amount, reliefs, wardships of minors and the marriages of rich heiresses, three sources of profit belonging to the king, were some of the means more or less arbitrarily employed to fill the Treasury. Several articles of the Great Charter aimed at repressing the more crying abuses committed by irresponsible officials to the detriment of the nobles, small or great, and of the burgesses in certain towns, like London, specially exploited on account of their wealth.[1] The clergy were hard hit by the abuse of the right of the *regale*, a privilege that proved most profitable to the crown: at the death of a bishop or an abbot the king laid hands upon his goods and confiscated the revenues as long as the see was vacant, that is to say, at the king's pleasure, since his authorization was necessary before a new election could be proceeded with. Henry III frequently had recourse to this legitimate, but none the less arbitrary procedure. Complaints against this sort of spoliation were generally ineffective, but on several occasions the clergy can be seen joining with the barons in a concerted struggle against royal 'tyranny'.

The administration of justice gave rise to abuses of a different kind, though none the less painful to bear. The common stock of the *Curia regis* had thrown off two higher tribunals, whose duty it was to do justice and punish in the name and often in the presence of the king, considered as the source of all justice. The first to become differentiated was the Common Bench, which heard the *Placita de banco*, that is cases between subject and subject. Article 17 of the Great Charter of 1215 ordained [2] that such pleas should no longer follow the king on his journeyings, but should be heard 'in a fixed and determined place'. This

[1] Art. 2 dealing with the relief of a barony; art. 4 protecting the goods of minors; art. 6 forbidding the disparagement of minors; art. 13 confirming the City of London in its ancient liberties and customs, by land and by sea, &c.

[2] 'Communia placita non sequantur curiam nostram, sed teneantur in aliquo loco certo.'

place was Westminster, close by the Exchequer.[1] Difficult cases, reserved for the special consideration of the sovereign (*placita coram rege*) were at first, as their nature demanded, submitted to the king wherever he might be found: later, in the course of the thirteenth century, they came to be examined out of his presence by a small number of judges constituting a separate tribunal in a fixed place called King's Bench. From these superior tribunals, and against their decisions, recourse could always be had to the king or his Parliament. The justice meted out there was rigid and severe; the costs which it involved and the amercements it inflicted constituted an important source of revenue to the fisc.

More interesting to us here than the composition or competence of these tribunals is the institution of the commissions of inquiry or itinerant justices (*justiciarii itinerantes*, Justices in Eyre). This feature went back to the reign of Henry I, who used it to control his fiscal agents. Under Henry II's reorganization the commissioners received the most extensive powers in matters of justice and police. In 1179 with the object of suppressing abuses of all sorts committed by royal or seignorial officials, Henry sent throughout the country clerks, 'wise men'[2] who knew the law, to do speedy justice without appeal. Practically abandoned by John Lackland,[3] this redoubtable institution became regular under Henry III.[4] Once a year at least the king nominated commissions of justices with the duty of making circuits in a given number of countries.[5] Their competence varied: some of them were designated 'justiciarii ad omnia placita', others could only take cognizance of special cases,

---

[1] Tout, *Chapters*, i. 178. Cf. Giuseppi, *Guide*, i. 219.

[2] 'Viros sapientes de regno' says the anonymous author known as Benedict of Peterborough (i. 238). Cf. Ralph de Diceto, i. 434.

[3] 'Much curtailed' would perhaps be more accurate, for cf. *The earliest Lincolnshire Assize Rolls*, ed. (Mrs.) Doris Stenton (Lincoln Record Society, vol. xxii).

[4] Art. 18 of the Great Charter of 1215 ordained that two judges should be sent four times a year into each county to inquire into cases 'de nova disseisin, 'de morte antecessoris et de ultima presentatione'; according to the Charter of 1217 the circuit was to take place once a year (art. 13). Bracton mentions circuits for all the years between 1219 and 1239.

[5] In 1240 Henry III assigned Southern England to William of York, provost of the collegiate church of Beverley, and Northern England to Robert de Lexinton (*Chron. maj.*, iv. 34).

e. g. infractions of the forest laws. These inquisitors had the task of examining the judgments given, deferred or sold by sheriffs, bailiffs, by officials of the forest whom an inhuman code of legislation armed with a dangerous degree of authority, even by the seignorial officers themselves. They had among other things to review the armed force of the shire, to see that the 'king's peace'[1] was respected, by punishing outrages committed against the lives and property of individuals. Equipped with discretionary powers, they could amerce counties and hundreds contravening police regulations, obstructing the work of local courts or neglecting military service and castle guard. They punished pleaders for non-appearance or negligence, since their default (by diminishing the number of judicial actions) prejudiced the Treasury. They were accused of too great zeal in the acquisition of money for the king.[2] In 1242 there were complaints that ever since the levy of the thirtieth for the marriage of the king's sister Isabella (1235), that is for five years, 'the itinerant justices had not ceased their circuits in all parts of the kingdom, so much so that the counties, hundreds, cities and boroughs, and almost all townships have been afflicted with heavy penalties.[3]

Their method of procedure deserves attention. When they started out, the justices received orders to summon before them, in accordance with legal form,[4] all archbishops, bishops, abbots and priors, earls, barons, knights, and freeholders of the county, twelve 'loyal burgesses' from every city or borough, and four 'loyal men' and the reeve from each township: together with 'all those who normally came or were bound to come before the

---

[1] In 1249 Henry de Mara was sent to suppress robbery in the Winchester area (*Chron. maj.*, v. 56–7 and 466).

[2] *Chron. maj.*, iv. 34: 'sub praetextu justitiae, infinitam pecuniam ad opus regis omnia dispergentis collegerunt.'

[3] *Ibid.*, iv. 186. See *Book of Fees* (*Testa de Nevill*) i. 405 f.

[4] 'Per bonos summonitores.' The term 'summonere' is fully technical; it is found in all the summonses to Parliament. This is not a simple invitation, but a bidding, a service commanded. To come to Parliament was a feudal obligation, not a right. Here it may not be irrelevant to mention a curious fact: when Henry III on his return from Gascony in 1243 arrived at Winchester, he gave orders for his own reception with the highest honours, and had heralds proclaim 'ut ex qualibet civitate vel burgo quatuor cives vel burgenses honorabiliores obviam ei procederent in vestibus preciosis et equis desiderabilibus' (*Chron. maj.*, iv. 255).

justices as members of the court or as pleaders'.[1] Before this assembly, exact replica of future parliaments, the sheriffs who had administered the county since the last Eyre were due to appear, to give account for their term of office. Such an organization seemed to hold out serious promises that justice would be equitably administered. Why then were there so many complaints against it? It was surely because the arbitrary government of a sovereign like Henry III had it in its power to travesty the most protective of institutions; bad kings make bad judges. The study of local administration, where the action of the sheriffs is the predominant factor, would lead to similar conclusions; abuses of all kinds could be discovered here, complaints of an equally lively nature on the part of the smaller folk to the effect that these royal agents were normally drawn from the nobility of the counties, that they bought their offices and were frequently changing. Those among them whose hands were not soiled were not the less to be feared, for a meticulous type of justice is sometimes as hard to bear as a less rigid brand, and against it there is no recourse.

Two vital organs of centralized government remain to be considered: council and parliament, which together with the king made up what is frequently termed the Crown. The council was composed of persons whom the king chose to summon. He consulted them on every occasion when he had need of an opinion on the conduct of internal or foreign affairs. The nobles naturally had a place on it, but this was by no means an invariable necessity; they came when the prince had need of their counsel or services, or when they wished to communicate their intentions and their requests, or even to impose their will upon him. Out of this council, afforced, grew parliament. Their common origin is the explanation why parliament could long be considered an auxiliary of the sovereign, an instrument of governance; only by slow stages did it become, at first as the colleague of the sovereign, then later in conflict with him, a means of permanent intervention in the government or a weapon of opposition. In Simon de Montfort's time this stage had not yet been reached. Power lay in the hands of a single individual, the king; his omnipotence could only be confronted

[1] Bracton, ed. Twiss, iii. 188.

by two legitimate barriers, that is to say, the oath he took on his coronation day, and the Great Charter, an imposition which he endured with some impatience.

In the oath taken in 1100 Henry I undertook a threefold engagement towards 'the Christian people subject to him': to devote his will, to strive to the uttermost 'that the Church of God and the Christian people might ever enjoy true peace'; that 'rapine and iniquity be forbidden to every degree' (in all classes of society), and that judgments should be given in a spirit of equity and mercy.[1]   It was a formula of venerable antiquity, since it had been employed at Ethelred's coronation in 978, and in those of William I and II.[2]   After John's death Henry III, then only nine years old, had to recite it (28 October 1216) before putting on the crown; it was only on the morrow of this that the bishops, earls, and 'others' then came to do homage and swear fealty.[3]   From this moment a sort of mystical contract had been formed between the king and his people: but a contract formulated in such general terms that it could be no practical rule of action, even to the most scrupulous of sovereigns.

The Great Charter, on the other hand, introduces us into the world of fact. In 1215 for the first time the united leaders of clergy and baronage found means of imposing upon the king their wishes, substantiated in an official act. Naturally the treaty to which John Lackland had to submit at Runnymede contains many marks of incoherence, and, needless to say, of limited intelligence so far as the real interests of the nation were concerned. It was hastily drawn up by privileged persons determined to seize the opportunity to strengthen what they termed their 'liberties'. Yet without any desire to play on the words, it may be stated that in certain important directions it is the foundation of English liberties. One article, the last (61), framed wholly in the interest of the conquerors, had a patently revolutionary attraction: it instituted a committee of twenty-five members chosen by the barons with the purpose of compelling the king, if necessary by force, to amend 'within the

---

[1] *S. C.*, 9th ed., p. 116; cf. *E. H. R.*, xli, July 1926.

[2] L. G. Wickham Legg, *English Coronation Records* (1901), p. xxviii.

[3] Roger of Wendover, ii. 197, followed by Matthew Paris, *Chron. maj.*, iii. 1–2.

forty days' all 'acts of injustice committed by him and his officials'. Naturally this was a salutary precaution to take against a cruel and faithless king, but it could not survive the circumstances that called it into existence. In the definitive version of the charter (1225, 9 Hen. III) granted 'freely and graciously' on that occasion. From that day the document of Runnymede ceased to be a weapon directed against the king. If its spirit was faithfully observed, it was capable of being an instrument of pacification, and so it was as long as the minority of Henry III lasted. When he was competent to exercise his full royal authority, he disregarded the obligations upon which he had been forced to enter. He filled his council and his household with favourites, and deliberately with gusto organized a system of autocracy. Still, the charter had become the constitutional law of England, and more than once Henry had to promise to obey its articles. The frequent summons of parliament then presented the heads of the feudal party with the opportunity and means of imposing their will anew.

Parliament, we earlier observed, issued forth from the council, itself a branch of the *curia regis*. The impersonal expression *the Crown in Council* denotes the close bond that originally united these institutions; the nature of this tie was later to be defined in a more developed formula; the *Crown in Council in Parliament*. In the Great Charter the parliamentary organism, scarcely yet differentiated from the parent stock, is designated as *Commune consilium*; between 1230 and 1240 the word *parliamentum* enters summarily into use.[1] Two articles of the Charter of 1215 describe its composition, the manner of summons and—up to a point—its competence: (No. 12) 'No scutage[2] nor aid[3] shall be levied in our realm without the assent of the Common Council,[4] except for an *auxilium* in three cases;'[5] Art. 14

---

[1] A. F. Pollard, *Evolution of Parliament*, p. 261.

[2] Scutage is the contribution of 20s. per knight's fee (scutum).

[3] An aid is an extraordinary contribution in money, the knights being theoretically bound to contribute no more than personal service. Cf. J. H. Round, 'Barons and Knights in the Great Charter', *Magna Carta Commemoration Essays*, p. 46.

[4] In what sense should the words 'commmune consilium' be interpreted? Cf. A. B. White, 'Was there a Common Council before Parliament?' *American Historical Review*, xxv.

[5] 'Nisi ad corpus nostrum redimendum (a case had arisen when Richard

stated 'in order to establish the Common Council summoned to grant the aid due outside these three cases, we shall cause to be summoned the archbishops, bishops, abbots, greater barons (*majores barones*) individually by letters issued from our Chancery;[1] and we shall further have a general summons issued to all our other immediate vassals through our sheriffs and bailiffs, at least forty days in advance, the place and reason being indicated.'[2] Thus two categories of persons are summoned to respond to the king's invitation: on the one hand, the leaders of the clergy and of the 'greater barons', a vague title on which there has been much discussion (personally we think that it certainly included the earls, and that in the case of other nobles the choice probably rested with the king or his chancellor who had the duty of sending out the summonses); on the other, the generality, due to be summoned by the sheriffs and bailiffs, are described in the very maladroit and almost enigmatic drafting of the Charter as 'all tenants-in-chief of the crown', which is inconsistent with the earlier category. This article is only comprehensible by imagining that what actually took place later was intended in 1215, i. e. that the sheriff assembled these tenants-in-chief not in order to come to parliament, but in order to send representatives to it.

We need not ask whether the practice of representation is directly derived from the usages of the county court or from the methods used in certain ecclesiastical assemblies like those of the Dominicans;[3] the fact of representation still remains and we must insist upon it. On 11 February 1254 queen Eleanor and

Cœur-de-Lion had had to be delivered, and people would remember the fact very sorely), et primogenitum filium nostrum militem faciendum et ad filiam nostram primogenitam semel maritandam (earlier we noticed the case of Isabella, Henry III's sister, married in 1235). The amount of this 'auxilium' was not fixed like that of the 'scutagium', but it had to be 'rationabile'. The City of London owed the aid under the same conditions.

[1] The words 'by letters . . . Chancery' are my own addition.

[2] 'Et preterea faciemus summoneri in generali per vicecomites et ballivos nostros *omnes illos* qui de nobis tenent in capite ad diem certum. . . .' The interval of forty days was the regular custom of the county courts. Parliament, the supreme court of justice, naturally had to adopt this rule.

[3] See D. Pasquet, *An Essay on the Origin of the House of Commons*, tr. R. G. D. Laffan (1925), p. 20. This translation, the text of which has been brought up to date, is preferable to that of the author's original thesis, published in 1914.

the earl of Cornwall, regents of the country, summoned two loyal and discreet knights from each county to be present at the parliament due to meet in the *quinzaine* of Easter.[1] The writ of summons that was sent out then is the first of its kind so far discovered. The fact is doubly interesting, both because it has a direct bearing on the origin of the House of Commons, which is a chamber of representatives, as well as because Simon de Montfort was present, as we have seen, at this memorable parliament. We ought to add that, if there was any innovation in procedure made there of a kind that historians ought immediately to notice and emphasize, contemporaries at any rate do not seem to have noticed it. To read the chroniclers alone, one would not have an inkling that here is the beginning of a transformation destined to become of capital importance in English political institutions; and Simon himself was doubtless far from suspecting that he was going to make any contribution thereto.[2]

We know how the April parliament of 1254 came to an end. Enlightened by what Leicester told them about a pretended Castilian invasion, its members broke up in high indignation and disgust, yet happy to have 'escaped the traps of the king who was fattening the aliens on the goods of an endangered England.'[3] It may well be that the Poitevins gave Henry III

---

[1] *S. C.* 9th ed., p. 365.

[2] It is not known whether Leicester was present at the parliaments of April and October 1255, also notable in constitutional history. These were the circumstances: Henry III on his return from Gascony (see his itinerary for 1254 in *Rôles Gascons* i (suppl.) pp. xvii–xxxii), overwhelmed with debt, asked his parliament for subsidies. He was answered with grievances and petitions. Complaint was made of numerous violations of the Great Charter, and the members of parliament claimed the right to elect the Chancellor, Justiciar, and Treasurer, the three great figures of public administration; in future, it was asked, these high officials should not be turned out of office 'nisi clarescentibus culpis'. This demand, which was really an excessive one, but very significant of the state of mind governing the enemies of the king's personal authority, was rejected in April; then parliament postponed to its next meeting the decision on the question of subsidies, if in the interval the king did not reform and observe the Great Charter (*Chron. maj.*, v. 493). The king gave way (*ibid.*, p. 500). Parliament assembled on 13 October at Westminster, but refused to consent to any aid, 'because it had not been summoned in accordance with the rules laid down in the Charter;' there was a month's fruitless dispute, and Parliament broke up without voting any subsidy (p. 520).

[3] *Chron. maj.*, v. 440: 'magnates edocti muscipulas regis praecaverant, qui ex bonis Angliae periclitantis alienigenas saginavit. Hoc autem subdolum consilium ex sulphureo fonte Pictavensium dicitur emanasse.' The embarrass-

(as Paris accuses them of giving) the idea of obtaining a new
subsidy from parliament by the help of false reports; always
remembering that the St. Albans chronicler cannot invariably
be taken at his word, as he is ready to attribute the worst
motives to people, and makes no bones about his dislikes. But
on the other hand it is certain that the striking confidence
enjoyed by the king's half brothers at the court had made them
numerous enemies; but side by side with these favourites, well
known to everybody, there were others, of a more or less obscure
character, who had achieved their influence in subordinate posts
of the household.[1]

Their prosperity had already begun under John Lackland, the
husband of Isabella of Angoulême. One clerk advanced to pre-
ferment by that monarch was a Poitevin, Peter des Roches.[2]
Elected bishop of Winchester in 1205, he had remained faithful
to his sovereign even during the Interdict. Henry III had an
affection for him, and out of recognition for his services lavished
his protection upon one of the bishop's nephews (some said his
illegitimate son) Peter ' de Rivaux' (Rivallis).[3] As the magnates
had imposed Hubert de Burgh upon him to govern at any rate
during his minority, he seems to have taken a delight in making
his favourite's fortune. From 1218 to about 1258 he constantly
employed Peter in his Household as Clerk of the Wardrobe,
and Treasurer of the Chamber; [4] he even placed him at the head
of these offices simultaneously, and finally nominated him
Treasurer of the Exchequer, with implied permission never to
render account of his administration.[5] He gave him custody of
the Small Seal, named him sheriff for life of more than twenty
counties, governor of his most important strongholds, chief
justice of the royal forests, and sequestrator of all wardships and

ment of the Treasury was only too real, and it is difficult to believe that the
money collected was bestowed upon the 'Poitevins'. Paris is here merely
retailing a rumour.

[1] In what follows here I have done no more than summarize the facts collected and co-ordinated in so precise and well-informed a manner by T. F.
Tout, *Chapters in Mediaeval Administrative History*, vol. i.

[2] On Peter, see T. F. Tout, *op. cit., passim,* and *D. N. B., s.v.* 'Peter des
Roches'.

[3] Professor Tout is the first to trace his history and the important part
played by him.

[4] Tout, *op. cit.,* i. 200.   [5] *Ibid.,* 217.

escheats.[1] Peter was closely in league with his uncle, the bishop of Winchester. Henry III later confessed that he had been 'constrained' by Peter des Roches and Peter de Rivaux to seal certain letters the tenor of which was concealed from him [2] and which had cost the earl Marshal in Ireland his life.[3] And then, without a tremor, the king abandoned his favourite to the vengeance of the nobility; charged with prevarication, Peter was brought to justice and even forced to render account, despite the royal promise. Roger of Wendover accuses uncle and nephew of dismissing, 'out of hatred for the English nation', the English servants in the king's household, embezzling the military resources of the country by getting possession of the royal castles, of subjecting the Exchequer to their influence (1233).[4] After he had come of age, Henry III made no change in this system of favouritism and arbitrary government. In 1236 he tried to relieve the bishop of Chichester, the chancellor, Ralph de Neville, of the Great Seal. Ralph stoutly declared that 'he owed his office to the Common Council of the kingdom,[5] and could not resign it without the assent of this Council';[6] none the less the king drove him from his Council and Court (1238) and gave the keepership to two subordinates.[7] In the

---

[1] Tout, i. 219.

[2] Wendover's accounts, in Tout, p. 224 n. 4.

[3] D. N. B., s.v. Marshal, Richard, third earl of Pembroke. See also G. H. Orpen, Ireland under the Normans, iii. 67–70. Richard died on 16 April 1234.

[4] Wendover, iii. 47; Chron. maj., iii. 240, and cf. Miss Mabel H. Mills, 'Experiments in Exchequer procedure 1200–1232' (Trans. Roy. Hist. Soc., viii. 166–9).

[5] On this point see the long note in Tout, op. cit., i. 183–4.

[6] Chron. maj., iii. 364: 'dixit se nulla ratione hoc facere posse, cum illud communi consilio regni suscepisset.'

[7] Ibid., p. 491: 'rex a consilio suo et a curia postulatum irreverenter, sublato ab eodem sigillo quod per consilio praedicto cancellario commissum fuit totius regni, amovit;' further on p. 495: 'sigillum suum quod idem episcopus per universitatem regni receperat custodiendum rex violenter abstulit, et fratri Galfrido Templario et Johanni de Lexintuna commissit bajulandum.' Cf. p. 530. Neville died in 1244: 'vir per omnia laudabilis et immota columpna in regni negotiis fidelitatis' (Chron. maj., iv. 287; Cf. Miss Dibben, 'Chancellor and Keeper of the Seal under Henry III', E. H. R., xxvii. 39–51). Paris eulogizes John de Lexinton (d. 1257) thus: 'miles elegans et facundus et literatus, qui quandoque regii sigilli propter sui peritiam bajulus extitit et domini regis consiliarius specialis' (v. 610). It is interesting to note the king's determination to do without a chancellor: in 1239, he expelled from court Master Simon le Norman, 'qui diu antea non tantum regni regiique sigilli magister

wake of queen Eleanor arrived the Provençals, and to the new-comers,[1] as to the Poitevins before, the king gave the preference in the control and guidance of his household. From 1240 to 1258 nearly a score of them are to be found, three in the service of the Wardrobe: Peter d'Aigueblanche, Peter Chaceporc, and Artaud de St. Romain. The two former are familiar figures. Artaud,[2] who came from Provence or Burgundy, succeeded Chaceporc as keeper of the Wardrobe in 1255 and received the deanery of St. Martin-the-Great in London, a post regularly conferred on a clerk of the department. When Artaud died in 1257, Henry appointed as his successor our friend Peter of Rivaux whom the barons had got expelled in 1233. This was certainly an insult to the nobles who, at this very moment, having at last discovered a leader, were provoking an immediate contest, not indeed with the king 'who could do no wrong', but with his 'evil counsellors'.

If this was a challenge, it was soon taken up, and Simon de Montfort was the man. One can only conjecture what his motives were. Unquestionably he continued to feel acute re-sentment against his brother-in-law for the acts of injustice with which he still saw fit to reproach him; and it is not unreasonable to suppose that in the end he adopted as his aim the higher interests of the class that was his by birth and inheritance, ranging himself with the party hostile to Henry III's fantastic and un-English government. But it is well to remember that in his relations with men of lofty nature and wide culture like Adam de Marsh and Robert Grosseteste, he had come to form generous ideas about morality and politics, to acquire convic-tions that outstripped the mere desire to renew the personnel

fuit, immo et regis et aulicorum rector fuerat et dispositor', and gave the seal to Richard, abbot of Evesham (*Chron. maj.*, iii. 629). In 1247 John Mansel received 'custodiam sigilli regii, cancellarii vices acturus et officium (iv. 601). In 1250 the Seal 'quod clavis regni esse comprobatur' was given to Master William de Kilkenny 'viro bene literato, in jure canonico et civili perito' (*ibid.*, v. 130). After his election to be bishop of Ely in 1255, William was replaced by Henry de Wengham 'qui clericus ejus (Henry III) et consiliarius extiterat specialis' (*ibid.*, p. 485). It is often difficult in these passages to distinguish the Great from the Small Seal; but it is worth remembering that the Great Seal was often entrusted to a bishop.

[1] The complicated question of the aliens is studied by Kingsford in his notes to the *Song of Lewes*, pp. 22–77.

[2] See the details of his career in Tout, *op. cit.*, i. 277–80 and *passim*.

of government by more judicious selection. Proud, headstrong, and dogmatic, with a limited outlook and a tempestuous heart, capable of inspiring mortal hatred and undying affection, a great character rather than a great man, Simon had all the qualities necessary to a party leader; he was one of those who venerate the cause in which they sacrifice themselves. His contemporaries gave him unrestrainedly their hostility or their gratitude.

The conflict between the king in the full flush of his power and the brother-in-law convinced of the need of restraining that arbitrary authority, broke out at the London Parliament. The king demanded money to satisfy the papal envoy, Arlotus, and to repel the Welsh. The discussion on the latter topic revealed the sort of feelings that animated the chief members of that assembly. William de Valence, earl of Pembroke,[1] forgot himself to the extent of saying that the Welsh had powerful accomplices in England, and he did not scruple to insinuate that Gloucester and Leicester had an understanding with them; then, addressing himself to Simon, he heaped abuse on his head, calling him once more a liar and inveterate traitor. It was a repetition of the scene enacted the year previously; it likewise ended in the opportune intervention of the king.[2] The session

---

[1] He had taken the title of earl of Pembroke because he administered the county in the name of his wife, a distant inheritor from the first earl, William Marshal. See *D. N. B. s.v.* William de Valence.

[2] Paris, *op. cit.*, p. 677. We may note here several details of interest, for the earl's biography but difficult to fit into the general history of this time. On 7 January 1258 the king commissioned the bishop of Worcester, the elect of Winchester, and Simon de Montfort to make reparation of trespasses done to persons landing in England, on condition that the king of France and the countess of Boulogne did the same for the passengers arriving by the port of Wissant and other ports on the French coast (*C. P. R. 1241–1258*, 610). On the same day the king, with the assent of William de Valence and Simon, granted Peter de Montfort authority to acquire the manor of Moulton, co. Suffolk, which had been sequestrated. On 8 March Simon witnesses a charter regulating the respective rights of the abbot of St. Albans and of his monks (*Chron. maj.*, v. 668). The chronicler John Oxenedes, after mentioning the consecration of a new bishop of Norwich (10 March, 1258), notes the arrival of a writing sent to Leicester called 'de vita et moribus Tartarorum' (p. 197); he adds that the document is to be found 'apud Sanctum Albanum in libro Additamentorum'. Matthew Paris alludes to it when he speaks (*Chron. maj.*, v. 611) of the 400,000*l.* constituting the resources of the king of the Tartars, quoram vitam spurcissimam apud S. Albanum poterit indagator sedulus reperire'. This can in fact be read in *Additamenta*, vi. 75 under the form of a

was, however, continued on the morrow (9 April) and following days. For measures against the Welsh it was decided that all owing military service should assemble on 17 June at Chester.[1] Near the festival of the martyr St. Vitalis (28 April) [2] Henry III put forward, on behalf of the Pope, the demand of a 'burdensome, unheard-of, terrible' tax of a third of all movables and immovables, to fall upon everybody, free and unfree alike. The nobles obtained a delay (*inducias*) of three days for consideration, and the meeting broke up

The clergy, however, did not dare proceed to extremities. 'So as not to excite the choler and indignation of the king' the bishops decided to withdraw and were authorized to return home.[3] The nobles remained, more than ever decided on resistance, because they were now organized. On 12 April a comprehensive oath of mutual assistance against all and every one 'droit feisant et prenant, sans meiffeire' was sworn on the gospels by Gloucester, Roger Bigod, earl of Norfolk and marshal of England since the death of the last Pembroke, by Leicester, by Peter of Savoy, whom close relations with the royal family did not restrain from following a moderate policy of opposition, and by two personal friends of Simon, John fitz Geoffrey and Peter de Montfort.[4] From this formidable alliance sprang the revolution: its members may not have foreseen the gravity of the step they were taking.

The discussions between Henry and the nobles continued until the Sunday following Ascensiontide (5 May) [5]; every day new complaints arose against the king's arbitrary conduct: he failed to carry out any of his promises, it was said; he violated the Great Charter; he favoured his step-brothers, as if they truly belonged to the kingdom, and forbade the Chancery to send out any writ contrary to their interests. William de

letter sent by a Hungarian bishop to the bishop of Paris; but Oxenedes exaggerates when he speaks of a writing 'quod tantum continet litterae quantum continet unum psalterium'.

[1] *Chron. maj.*, v. 677.
[2] Tewkesbury, p. 163.　　　　　[3] *Ibid.*, p. 163.
[4] *Simon de Montfort*, p. 327. Paris knew of the existence of this league to recover liberties: he says (v. 689): 'interim optimates Angliae, utpote Glovernie, Legrecestrie et Herefordie comites, comesque Marescallus, et alii praeclari viri, sibi praecaventes et providentes, confederati sunt.'
[5] *Chron. maj.*, v. 688–9.

Valence, they complained, surpassed them all in effrontery, and Leicester, addressing the assembly, demanded from it the reparation due.[1] Others urged that the king was ruining the country by contemptuous plundering of his own subjects; special measures must therefore be taken against him.[2] Henry bowed before the storm, swore on the altar and on the relics of St. Edward that he would reform and would henceforward listen with friendly ear to his own subjects. On 2 May he promised to give effect before next Christmas to the reform advised by 'the honest and faithful people of his realm', as well as by the papal legate, if he came for the Sicilian business.[3] By another act of the same date[4] he swore to hand over the deliberation upon the reforms to a committee of twenty-four members, half to be nominated by his Council, half by the nobles, who were to meet at Oxford a month after Whitsun.[5] But as no one knew 'with what knot to hold Proteus fast', the nobles adjourned till 11 June.[6] It was then that the league came in arms, protected by numerous retainers.

At this point an eye-witness shall speak.[7] 'On the day agreed upon, as the third hour (9 a.m.) approached, the noble and brave men, the earls, barons, and knights came to Court, that is to Westminster, in great array, their swords by their sides. At the entrance of the royal chamber they laid down their weapons,

---

[1] *Chron. maj.*, v. 689: 'comes praecipue Legrecestriae non tamen regi sed universitati praecordialiter est conquestus.' It seems that shortly afterwards Simon 'feist peis a monseignur W. de Valance de contanz qui estoent antre eus avant que la purveance d'Angleterre fust fete, et ne mie de choses que a la comune porveance apartenist, si cum il apiert por un escrit qui fu fet de cele peis, ou seus de prodes homes pandent' (*Simon de Montfort*, p. 350). By the comune porveance' we should understand the Provisions of Westminster, with which we shall deal later.

[2] *Chron. maj.*, v. 689: 'excessus regis tractatus exigit speciales.'

[3] Rymer, patent dated 2 May 1258, reprinted in *S. C.* p. 371. Witnesses: prince Edward, Geoffrey de Lusignan, and William de Valence, Peter of Savoy, John, earl of Warwick, John Mansel, treasurer of York, Henry de Wengham, dean of St. Martin-the-Great in London, Peter 'de Rivallis', Guy de Rocheford, Robert Walerand 'et multis aliis comitibus, baronibus regni nostri.' On Robert Walerand, an early bearer of the title 'secretarius regis', cf. E. F. Jacob in *Trans. Roy. Hist. Soc.*, 1927, p. 24, and *C. P. R. 1247–1258*, 626.

[4] Rymer, *ibid.*

[5] Rymer, *ibid.*, and *S. C.*, p. 372. The delay was of about six weeks, in agreement with the time specified in art. 14 of the Great Charter for the summons of the 'commune consilium'.

[6] *Chron. maj.*, v. 689.   [7] Tewkesbury, p. 164.

and when they appeared before the king, saluted him with the reverence that was due to him. At the threatening aspect of the barons in their complete suits of mail, the king was seized with sudden terror: "What is this, sirs?" he said. "Am I you prisoner?"—"No, sir," replied Roger Bigod, "no; but the miserable, insufferable Poitevins, as well as all aliens, must be banished from your presence and ours. This is our secret: we reveal it to you for the dignity, honour and profit of your lordship and of the kingdom. Swear to follow our counsels in their entirety: it is the best remedy and the best comfort that you could find."—"And how see you that I shall follow your counsels?" The barons replied: "Swear, with hand on holy gospels, you and your son and heir Edward, that you will do nought without the advice of the twenty-four good men, the elected bishops, earls and barons;[1] that you will in no wise think to burden your subjects with a yoke unheard-of till these times and contrary to the rights of your kingdom: that you will without delay hand the Great Seal to a loyal person selected by the twenty-four.'" Contemporaries were struck by the firm attitude of the earl of Leicester. 'As of old Simon Maccabaeus had risen in arms for his father Judah,' one wrote,[2] 'so Simon rose to defend to death the liberties and rights of England'.

Under the compulsion to yield to such threats, the king's humiliation was profound. It was his brother-in-law whom he held primarily responsible. His resentment comes out clearly in an anecdote related by Matthew Paris.[3] One day in July during the extreme heat of that summer (1258) the king left Westminster and embarked on the Thames to have dinner out of doors. Suddenly the sky became overcast, thunder growled and torrents of rain fell amid flashes of lightning. The king, alarmed by the violence of the storm, ordered his servants to put in to shore. The boat was discovered to be in front of the bishop of Durham's palace[4] where Leicester was lodging.

---

[1] Tewkesbury, p. 164: 'absque consilio virorum prudentium Angliae scilicet episcoporum, comitum, baronum electorum.'

[2] William de Hemingburgh, p. 304.

[3] *Chron. maj.*, v. 706.

[4] The palace was situated where Charing Cross is now; the little street called Durham House Street indicates the position (Wilberforce Jenkinson, *The royal and bishops' palaces in Old London*, 1921, p. 51).

Simon at once appeared, with smiling face, and saluting the king, deferentially asked: 'What are you afraid of? The storm has already passed.' The king answered in a mortified tone: 'I am extremely afraid of the thunder and the flashes, but by God's head I am more afraid of you than of all the thunder and lightning in the whole world.'—'Sir,' replied the earl, 'it is not myself, your constant friend, the faithful servant of king and country, that you should fear, but your enemies who live on pillage and falsehood.'

The royalists had five weeks' grace. By intrigue Henry III tried to undermine the work of the reformers. It should cause no surprise to find Aymer de Valence among the leaders of the reaction. The nobles, however, increased their vigilance: under colour of an expedition against the Welsh, they had their vassals armed, and with an impressive military parade there opened on 11 June 1258 in the Dominican convent at Oxford the famous assembly often called by the disdainful and otherwise misleading name of the Mad Parliament.[1]

In the Middle Ages parliament never had what we to-day call the initiative in legislation. It was a court of justice to which suitors addressed themselves by way of request. As in the case of the Great Charter of 1215, the barons in 1258 began by framing a petition.[2] They demanded reforms in civil legislation (marriage, right of succession, the ward and guardianship

---

[1] This expression is borrowed from the author of the *Chronica majorum et vicecomitum Londoniarum* in the *Liber de antiquis legibus* edited by J. T. Stapleton (1846) p. 37: 'Hoc anno fuit illud insane parlamentum apud Oxoniam.' Mr. Jacob has observed (*History*, 1924, p. 189, n. 3) that the word *insane* has been written by a copyist over an erased word, of which only a slight interlineal trace has survived, and he proposes to read *infame*. Study of the facsimile published in the *Bulletin of the Institute of Historical Research*, iii, no. 8, November 1925, reveals over the *a* an abbreviation-mark which Dr. Poole and Mr. Little have interpreted as being the accent over an *i*; they suppose that the erased word is *insigne* (*E. H. R.* xl (1925), 402). I should most readily like to adopt their opinion, but all that is clear to me is that *insane* has been written over some other word, which leads one to query the intention of the author or the copyist. On the other hand the *Annales Radingenses 1134–1264*, ed. C. W. Previté-Orton (*E. H. R.* xxxvii. 1922) note under 1258 'Magnum parlamentum baronum apud Oxoniam' (p. 403). Matthew Paris simply remarks (p. 695): 'De parlamento apud Oxoniam et de fratribus regis; his continuator, the anonymous author of the *Flores historiarum*, for long termed Matthew of Westminster, writes 'colloquium generale' (ii. 417).

[2] Reprinted in *S. C.*, pp. 373–8 after the *Annals of Burton* (pp. 439–43).

of minors, rights of relief and escheat), in criminal law, in the
administration of justice, now irregularly dispensed by the
courts of county and hundred, in the custody of castles, &c.
The constitutional reforms were the special work of the Twenty-
four.[1] The committee's plan seems to have been to make no
change in the form of government, but to reorganize the administrative personnel so as to withdraw it from sole and entire
control of the king, to limit the competence of the great officials
of the Crown, and to purify the household by expelling the
aliens. For the future the Council was to consist of fifteen
members,[2] chosen by two electors on behalf of the opposing
parties, the royal and the baronial, but selected by the side to
which they did not belong; for example, the earl Marshal and
Hugh Bigod were picked by the king's partisans to serve in the
interests of the 'commun', while the earl of Warwick and John
Mansel were named by the 'commun' to serve in the interests
of the king.[3] Once made, the choice was to be submitted to the
Twenty-four, who would decide by a majority of votes. The

[1] The list of the Twenty-four given in the *Annals of Burton* has been reprinted in *S. C.*, p. 379. It should include a group of twelve members 'electi ex
parte domini regis', but Burton only gives eleven, to wit, the bishop of London,
the bishop (elect) of Winchester (Aymer de Valence), Henry son of Richard of
Cornwall, king of Germany, the earl of Warrenne, Guy de Lusignan and his
brother William de Valence, the earl of Warwick, John Mansel, brother John
de Darlington, the abbot of Westminster, Henry de Hengham (*sic*). John de
Darlington was a Dominican summoned by the king in 1256 'ad familiare consilium suum'; Paris says of him (v. 549): 'literatura pollebat excellenter et
consilio'. The abbot of Westminster was Richard de Croxley, the intimate
friend of John Mansel (Paris, *ibid.*, p. 304). Henry de Hengham is an error for
Henry de Wengham or Wingham (Ramsay, *Dawn*, p. 170). The twelve members 'electi ex parte comitum et baronum' were the bishop of Worcester
(Walter de Cantilupe), the earl of Leicester, Richard earl of Gloucester, Humphrey earl of Hereford, Roger the Marshal, Roger de Mortimer, John fitz
Geoffrey, Hugh le Bigod (son of the 4th earl of Norfolk and brother of the earl
Marshal, 'qui officium justiciariae strenue peragens nullatenus permittat jus
regni vacillare, says Paris, p. 698). The others were Richard de Grey (cf.
D. N. B. s.v. Grey, Richard de), William Bardolf (*ibid.*), Peter de Montfort
(of the family of the lords of Beaudesert), and Hugh Despenser (cf. *D. N. B.*).

[2] The fifteen 'jurez del conseil le rei' were Boniface of Savoy, archbishop of
Canterbury, the bishop of Worcester, the earls of Leicester and Gloucester, the
earl Marshal, Peter of Savoy, the earls of Aumale, Warwick, and Hereford,
John Mansel, John fitz Geoffrey, Peter de Montfort, Richard de Grey, Roger
Mortimer, James de Audley. The last was a lord of the Welsh March who the
previous year had conducted a campaign of bloodthirsty reprisals against the
Welsh (*Chron. maj.*, v. 656, cf. *D. N. B.*).   [3] *S. C.*, p. 381.

Fifteen 'shall have the power to give honest counsel to the king for the government of the kingdom, so as to amend and redress all that they shall see to need amendment and redress, even in matters concerning the Justiciar and the other officials.' [1] Parliament was to be summoned at least thrice a year, on the Octave of Michaelmas (5 October), on the second day of Candlemas (3 February), and three weeks after St. John's day (3 June). The members of the Council had the right to come, even if they were not summoned; at any other period than these three they would be summoned by royal mandate; [2] but, as the meetings of parliament imposed heavy obligations on those summoned to them, a sort of permanent commission of twelve members was to have the duty of deliberating on 'the needs of king and kingdom'. [3] The 'commun' (the full assembly) was to pay the greatest attention to their opinion. [4] A committee of twenty-four members fairly chosen half from the royal, half from the baronial party; a council of fifteen nominated in the last resort by this committee and empowered to hold its sessions in parliament, and a permanent commission of twelve members charged with preparing the business submitted to parliament: this in brief was the new constitution designed by the united leaders of the aristocracy to place the king under tutelage. It was known as the Provisions of Oxford. A fine façade, ingenious and intricate like most ideal political constructions of the Middle Ages, behind which the primitive organisms lasted on, though change might take place in the *personnel*.

We should note here that Simon de Montfort was one of the Twenty-four elected by the party of the earls and barons, a member of the Committee of Fifteen and of another Twenty-four whose duty was 'to treat of an aid for the king'. He did not occupy a position of undisputed leadership.

[1] *S. C.*, p. 383: 'E averunt poer del rei conseiller en bone foi del governement del reaume et de totes choses ke al rei u al realme pertenent, e pur amender et adreser totes les choses ke il verrunt ke facent a adresser et amender; e sur la haute justice et sur totes autres genz.'

[2] *Ibid.*, p. 383. [3] 'E ceo serra fet pur esparnier le cust del commun.'

[4] 'E le commun tendra pur estable ceo ke ces xii front.' The twelve were the bishop of London, the earls of Winchester and Hereford, Philip Basset, John de Balliol, John de Verdun, John de Grey, Roger de Sumery, Roger de Mold (or Monte alto) steward of Chester, Hugh Despenser, Thomas de Greslei, Giles 'de Argentein.'

The system which the reformers were out to destroy
rested essentially, we said above, on the household and its
numerous public and private services, which were closely
interconnected and more or less fused. The barons began by
restoring to their ancient dignity the three great offices of the
crown: those of Justiciar or Chief Justice, of Treasurer, and of
Chancellor; but out of very natural feelings of jealousy[1] they
took care to limit their independence. The Justiciarship (*la
haute justice*, as the Provisions called it) vacant since 1234, was
put in the hands of a new officer who was to bear the title
Justitiarius Angliae, like the Steward and the Marshal 'of
England'. The point of this was to show that they were ministers of state and no longer inferior officials of the household; on
the other hand, the office could be filled by two persons simultaneously.[2] The Treasurer received an annual salary of 1,000
marks, fixed at that figure to banish any temptation to enrich
himself out of commission fees, which most people winked at;
but he was bound to render an annual account of his administration, and he did not hold office for long: in seven years there
were three treasurers, all of them baronial. The Treasurer of
the Exchequer, who also usurped the title 'Treasurer of England' was treated in the same way. There were at least five
between 1258 and 1265. To turn to methods, it was ordered
that all the revenue should be paid in to the Exchequer, a
measure evidently taken against the clerks of the Wardrobe,
who had frequently delved into the State treasury to fill the
king's coffers. The Chancery had not raised the same complaints
nor aroused the same jealousies as the judicial and fiscal offices,
and in consequence we find baronial chancellors alternating
with royal. But the Chancellor was no longer nominated for
life; he did not pocket the takings of his post, he was forbidden
to receive any gratuity; in return he received a fixed salary of
4,000 marks. He might be allotted a 'colleague' according as
the Council decided.[3]

Ministers and councillors were alike bound to take the most

---

[1] Professor Tout has made this point fully clear (*Chapters*, i. 295).

[2] *Ibid.*, p. 296. Philip Basset filled the office along with Hugh Bigod: he
only took the title after Hugh had left in 1262 (p. 299, n. 4).

[3] *S. C.*, p. 300; cf. Tout, *Chapters*, i. 297.

solemn oaths: the 'Commun de Engleterre',[1] that is to say, the nobles, met in parliament, swore on the gospels to assist each other, 'doing right to every one and take nought from any man', under penalty of being counted 'mortal enemies'. The Twenty-four swore to enter upon an understanding with the nobles 'to reform and amend the estate of the realm', without letting themselves be diverted 'by gift or promise, love or hate'. The Justiciar promised to give equal justice to all according to the arrangements made or to be made by the Twenty-four and in conformity with the counsels of the king and the nobles; the Chancellor swore to seal no writ 'without the consent of the king and his Council'.[2] With regard to the king's and queen's households, it was thought sufficient for the time being[3] to expel certain undesirables and here and there to introduce other aliens in their places. For example, Artaud de St. Romain was not disturbed: but side by side with him we meet Giles de Argentein and Imbert de Pugeys, who were no more English than he.

Local government naturally remained in the hands of the sheriffs, but they were henceforward selected from among the 'loyal and good men'[4] owning possessions in the county itself. It is important to lay stress upon this point, because it shows the tendency on the part of the baronial side to rely upon the smaller country gentry. In this class Simon seems to have sought and found his most devoted helpers. The sheriff was to be nominated for one year only, a restriction permitting a greater number of local knights to be initiated into local affairs. Neither he nor his bailiffs were to receive 'rewards',[5] but the king would give him a suitable pittance. To county court four 'discreet and loyal' knights were to be summoned, 'to hear all complaints of trespasses committed by the king's agents and to appoint such persons to appear before the itinerant justices.'

[1] S. C., p. 379.   [2] Ibid., p. 380.
[3] Ibid., p. 383: 'A remembrer fet del hostel le rei et la regine amender.'
[4] This had been done frequently before; henceforth it tends to become the rule. On the nomination of the new sheriffs and the oath they had to take, see Jacob, pp. 51–2.
[5] S. C., p. 382; cf. Paris, Chron. maj., v. 720, and Dunstable, p. 210. Should we see in the prohibition to receive any 'reward' an allusion to the 'sheriff's aid', which raised so much grumbling in Thomas Becket's time? Had it continued to be levied?

The Provisions of Oxford do not appear to have been drawn up in any official form;[1] they have not been copied upon any of the rolls of the Chancery.[2] The king who on 26 June had commanded the four electors to proceed without delay to the election of the Council, declared in a patent of 4 August[3] that he would deem 'firm and stable' all that was decided in that body, and he made his eldest son Edward take the oath to observe it as he had done.[4] It took no less than fifteen months to consummate the work that was merely outlined at Oxford.[5] During this long interval, it was the Council of Fifteen with the Parliamentary Committee of the Twelve that formed the centre and actual basis of government. As Professor Powicke rightly remarks, 'it controlled the employment of the Great Seal, acted in collaboration with the Justiciar and the judges, dominated the Exchequer.' It made no change in the constitution, but supervised all the machinery.

It is probable that the king, certain that his eldest son, acted in a spirit of unwilling resignation; their immediate entourage, however, was resolutely hostile to the new constitution. Henry, son of the king of Germany, refused to take the oath without his father's permission: he was told in reply that if the king's own younger brother Richard refused to obey the baronage, even he would not have an inch of land in the country.[6] Richard

---

[1] Information on the work accomplished at Oxford is given us in a 'littera cujusdam de Curia regis', copied in the Annals of Burton. Professor Powicke analyses it in his study 'Some Observations on the Baronial Council and the Provisions of Westminster, 1258–1260' in *Essays in Medieval History presented to T. F. Tout*, pp. 121–2.

[2] Powicke, *ibid.*, p. 120.

[3] The letter is in French. See Rymer, and *Royal Letters*, ii. 129; *C. P. R. 1247–1258*, 645. Simultaneously, for the seventh time, Henry III swore to observe the Charters of Liberties and dispatched into the counties writs *de intendendo* on behalf of the commissioners nominated at Oxford (*Chron. maj.*, v. 696).

[4] 'Et ce meismes jurra Edward nostre fiez einzné, e de ce dona ses lettres overtes'; but listen to Paris (p. 697): 'licet dominus rex et Edwardus filius ejus primogenitus juraverint, verumtamen, prout potuit, coepit Edwardus renuere, simul et Johannes, comes Warennae.'

[5] The story of these fifteen months is narrated in Professor Powicke's article, cited above. From another angle Mr. Jacob, drawing upon unpublished material, has shown how the work at Oxford was moulded and completed so as to receive its final and definitive form in what were called the Provisions of Westminster (*History*, ix. 188–200 and *Studies*, pp. 72–3).

[6] *Chron. maj.*, v. 697.

having at the end of the year expressed a lively wish to go and see once more 'his parents and friends, the property that belonged to him, the land of his birth',[1] a deputation was sent to meet him, and ascertain from him the real reason for his journey, and what he intended doing during his stay in England; he had to swear 'to bring no disturbance into the kingdom and in no respect to oppose the Provisions of Oxford'. Only then did the distrustful barons authorize this unlooked-for visit.[2] Then the hunt was turned upon the Poitevins, whom it was intended to make disgorge. 'Calling to witness the wounds and death of Christ,' they declared that as long as they lived they would give up nothing that the king had given them, neither castles, rents, or wardships. 'Very well,' cried Leicester, violently interrupting William de Valence, 'know that you shall restore the castles you hold of the king, or you will lose your life!'[3] The strongholds were entrusted to English keepers,[4] who had to swear to guard them loyally and faithfully for the king: and the latter, before granting any lease of them, had to seek the opinion of the 'good men of the land elected to his Council'.[5] Without any claim for compensation Simon gave back Odiham and Kenilworth, the free gifts from the crown and the source of heavy expenses to him;[6] but he got the king and council to grant him Winchester castle.[7] Thus he satisfied the

---

[1] *Chron. maj.*, p. 729.   [2] *Ibid.*, p. 732; cf. Wykes, p. 122.
[3] *Ibid.*, v. 697.

[4] Burton, p. 443: 'postea commissa fuerunt omnia castra domini regis certis personis anglicis, que fere omnia erant in manibus alienigenarum.' The appointments are in *C. P. R. 1247–1258*, 637–8, under 12 and 13 June, and 17 July. In the lists given by the Burton annalist (cf. *S. C.*, p. 384) a notable feature is the care taken by the barons to put their followers into the fortresses commanding the roads to London. Thus the Tower was given to Hugh Bigod, Dover to Richard de Grey, Rochester and Canterbury to Nicholas de Meulles, Bridgwater to Peter de Montfort. All these people were friends of Leicester. On 6 July, Richard de Clare, earl of Hertford and Gloucester, was appointed keeper of the Isle of Portland with the towns and ports of Weymouth and Wight; the witnesses to this act being Leicester, the earl Marshal, the Justiciar Hugh Bigod, John fitz Geoffrey, John Mansel, &c. (*C. P. R. 1247–1258*, 640). On 4 August Roger Bigod, earl Marshal, was appointed keeper of the littoral of Norfolk and Suffolk (*ibid.*, p. 649).   [5] *S. C.*, p. 380.
[6] *Chron. maj.*, v. 697; *Song of Lewes*, pp. 79, 94.
[7] *C. P. R. 1247–1258*, 638. On 26 October 1258 Henry III authorized the earl, so long as he had Winchester castle in keeping, to cut firewood from the ancient oaks and undergrowth in the royal forest of Bere (co. Southampton), *ibid.*, p. 654.

claims of legality. And now it was the turn of the king's half-
brothers. They could not resist, since 'all the people, especially
the common people' would have flocked to besiege them in
their castles and they would have been taken or starved to
death. So they fled in haste, and, without sparing their horses
flanks, made for Winchester before Leicester had taken possession. The barons, after nominating Hugh Bigod Justiciar
followed hard with their retainers on the tracks of the fugitives.
To preserve the lives and liberty of his brothers the king had no
other course than to give his official consent to their exile.
They left England on 19 July: they were protected by a safe-
conduct as far as Dover, where they took ship. Having reached
Boulogne, their way was obstructed by Simon's eldest son
Henry de Montfort had succeeded in rallying the people to his
side by his tales of the atrocious charges William de Valence had
made against his father to his very face, and had found no
difficulty in recruiting mercenaries among them.

There remained the much more thorny question of Aymer de
Valence. None of the Poitevins was more detested by the
barons. We have a letter of theirs to Pope Alexander IV begging him to forbid the bishop to return to his diocese. No other
evidence that we possess testifies with such vivacity to the
extreme irritation of the English nobility, and no document
portrays more strikingly the grave events of the preceding
months: it may help if we give a translation here:

'To the very holy father and lord Alexander, by divine providence
sovereign pontiff of the Universal Church, the community of earls

---

[1] *Chron. maj.*, v. 710. This account is confirmed by Tewkesbury (p. 164),
Dunstable (p. 209), Worcester (p. 449), Winchester (p. 100), Waverley (p. 350).
In Wykes we read: 'dominum Hugonem Bigot constituerunt totius Angliae
justiciarium, abbatem de Burgo qui fuit Normannus [John de Caux] thesaura-
rium scaccarii, magistrum Nicolaum de Hely cancellarium.'

[2] *Chron. maj.*, v. 701–3. The treasure of the Poitevins was seized at Dover by
Richard de Grey; and seizure was even made of the vast sums they had
deposited at the Tower of London in the hands of the Hospitallers (*ibid.*, pp.
704, 713). Geoffrey de Lusignan had been nominated seneschal of Gascony by
prince Edward; his commission was revoked on 12 July (Rymer), by special
mandate of the king and council. The steward of William de Valence was
thrown into the Tower to atone for the crimes he had committed (*Chron. maj.*
v. 720). On 4 November 1258 prince Edward revoked the donation of the
Island of Oléron, which he had made 'by negligence' to his uncle Guy de
Lusignan.

nobles and others of the realm of England, humble submission which is his due.

As you know, on several occasions you have notified us whether by letter or through the venerable Arlotus, sub-deacon, your notary, and requested us to aid our lord, the illustrious king of England, in securing the kingdom of Sicily by providing him with subsidies. Although our lord the king undertook the business without consulting us, without our assent, indeed in spite of our aversion and complaints, yet in order to prove our reverence towards the apostolic see and to you, we made answer to the king that if he was prepared to reform the kingdom upon the advice of his nobles, and if you, on your part, were to consent to lighten the burdensome terms specified in your privilege (terms that we are incapable of fulfilling), we should make all possible sacrifices to aid the king in bringing to a happy completion the matter he had started without our approval. We may tell you that the aforesaid king, our lord, feeling himself powerless to support the burden of this enterprise, and seeing the lamentable condition of his realm, has expressly charged the nobles and the barons to accomplish the reforms asked for; to carry them out, a special commission of twenty-four members, twelve chosen by the king and twelve others by the community of the nobles, was to be nominated and invested with full powers. . . .

'But among the twelve members chosen on behalf of the king's party were nominated the elect of Winchester and his brothers. The said bishop, oblivious of his eternal salvation and entirely set on disturbing the kingdom, encouraged the king by all manner of means to resist, and promised him enormous sums, exhausting the resources of the church of Winchester, to induce him to perjure himself and revoke the Provisions, to the great prejudice and irreparable detriment of his kingdom; then, having failed in this effort, he turned to prince Edward and several of the highest of the baronage, and brought upon them all the pressure he could bring, to overturn the kingdom, like one who conspires to compass the irreparable ruin of the state; and it might be said of him: "Est vir qui turbavit terram et concussit regnum";[1] but he and his brothers were unable to do more than retard the work of the commissioners; to prevent it they could not. The more obstacles they raised, the more fervently did the others apply themselves to their work of reform, and showed that union gives strength. But the excesses committed by the said elect and his brothers were so serious and heavy, that the complaints of

---

[1] Isa. xiv. 16: 'Numquid iste est vir qui conturbavit terram, qui concussit regna?'

the poor resounded to heaven; for their agents and officials—
assassins and bandits they should rather be called—fleeced the poor,
laid traps in the way of the simple, sustained the wicked, oppressed
the innocent, rejoiced in public misfortunes, delighted to behold the
tears of the poor, the nakedness of orphans, the oppression of the
people; their fury was so far uncaged that their subordinates could
not live beneath them, their equals remain with them, their superiors
maintain themselves above them.

'Consequently, considering that the state is a body nurtured by
the benefit of divine providence, animated by the grace of sovran
justice and governed by reason, and that there must be harmony
between the different parts of the same body, we have several times,
and after taking much counsel, bidden the said bishop and his
brothers to appear before us, as disturbers of the quiet and tranquillity of the kingdom, and have had them summoned by the king
to stand their trial and reply to all the accusations made against
them, in accordance with the law and custom of the country; and it
was decided that two of them (of their own choosing) should leave
the land, that two others should give security if they wanted to
remain, or that they should all go, if they thought it preferable. But,
fearing the chastisement which was awaiting their crimes, they all
preferred to leave the kingdom. If the elect of Winchester, whom
we hold responsible for all, these troubles, were today to return to
England, his presence might well destroy everything that our care
has built up by dint of infinite labour and watchings. Thus it is the
ardent desire of each and the will of all that this author of division,
this man of discord and scandal, should not again be found among us.

'The said elect and his brothers had so much perverted the mind
of the king and Edward our lord, that not only their faults remain
unpunished, but also—and this cannot be said without shame or
heard without alarm—if a pleader brought one of them to justice,
the king, bound as he was to punish the guilty and correct the wrong,
encouraged him in his misdeeds, grew wroth with the complainant,
and instead of being a compassionate judge, espoused the interests
and enmities of the wrong-doer. Supported thus by royal power and
royal favour, they oppressed whom they would, violated the cor-
porate rights and liberties of churches, wounded clerks, threw people
into prison, to the prejudice of the Crown which alone possesses this
right, and giving full reign to their licentiousness, admitted no other
rule than their own passion. If the said elect (please God that it may
not be!) were to return to England, we should have to fear evils
worse than before; thus we beseech Your Holiness, with all the
affection of which we are capable, to deprive the said elect of the

administration of the church of Winchester, which he owes to the munificence of the Holy See. It is better that this should be done without scandal and with your full assent, and that we your faithful servants, should not be drawn into courses which we are loath to adopt. Further it would be ruinous for the realm and its people if he were to draw the revenues of his diocese, with which, as well-informed persons tell us, he is preparing to trouble the kingdom. The matter can certainly be arranged without scandal, Holy Father, since he has not yet been consecrated bishop. On all matters we beg you to pay your fullest attention to our measures and to give our requests a favourable reception.'[1]

This overbearing statement of their requests was to be borne to Rome by an embassy composed of four knights.[2] They were to explain to the Pope, as succinctly as possible, the cause of the English barons, and then to return as soon as they could. As a matter of fact, they were not going to open negotiations, but far rather to bring an ultimatum. At this time occurred the death of Master Bernard de Ninfa; by birth a Campanian, he was a clerk of Richard of Cornwall, given the task of selling commutations of crusading vows at very expensive rates, and while on this remarkable mission had employed an ingenious amount of rapacity ('extortor nummorum argumentosus'). Upon his death, it was said, a box was found full of blank bulls dated in advance; they were immediately confiscated, and the ambassadors received orders to take them along with them to be shown to the Pope. To defray expenses on the journey they received a distribution of a thousand marks belonging to the bishop of Winchester, but discovered and confiscated by

[1] This letter, which is undated, but most probably belongs to July 1258, is only known to us through the chroniclers, Tewkesbury, Burton, and Matthew Paris. The latter copied it in his *Additamenta* (vi. 400). Rymer took the version in his *Foedera* from the chroniclers. It is attested by Richard de Clare, earl of Hertford and Gloucester, Simon, earl of Leicester, Roger Bigod, Marshal of England, Humphrey de Bohun, earl of Hereford and Essex, William of Aumale, John de Plessis, earl of Warwick, Hugh Bigod, Justiciar, Peter of Savoy, John fitz Geoffrey, James de Audley, Peter de Montfort, 'vice totius communitatis'.

[2] *Chron. maj.*, v. 716 and vi (*Additamenta*) 405. The chronicler only names Peter Branche, who died in Paris at the outset of the journey. In his reply to the barons the Pope speaks of Rustand, his chaplain, and three others, introduced by the archbishops of Embrun and Tarentaise (not Tarante as Luard says in his n. to p. 410).

Richard de Grey, the vigilant keeper of Dover Castle, one of the Fifteen.[1] The ambassadors were preceded by a letter addressed by Henry III to the Pope, which had certainly been drafted by the barons (1 August) 1258.[2] It ran thus:

'The best ordered city, it is written, is the one wherein each forgets his own personal interests. This saying receives today striking confirmation in the reform and reorganisation of our kingdom, for our barons, neglecting their own affairs for ours, are working with all their power upon our business and the business of our kingdom. Today we have a constitution prepared by them, one most profitable to us and our heirs. Thus we beg your Serenity, with all the affection we can, to bestow upon it the favour of the Holy Apostolic See, and to give it the support of your authority and consent.'[3]

The Pope replied to the barons[4] in a tone of apparent conciliation. Of the reform, he wrote: 'if, as is hoped, it has been made and directed for the glory of God, the exaltation of the Church, the honour and interest of the king, the profit and tranquillity of the kingdom, we rejoice greatly thereat: it is the firm intention of the holy mother, the Church of Rome, to favour and support it.' In the affair of Sicily, the Pope had taken the advice of 'all his brothers', and they had unanimously declared that as the king of England had fulfilled none of the conditions on which that kingdom had been given to his son, the Roman Curia was under no obligation towards him, and had the right to negotiate

---

[1] *Chron. maj.*, v. 713.

[2] Rymer. A memorandum attaching to this letter declares that all letters, close or patent, written concerning the affair of the Court of Rome, had been drawn up by Master Rustand; 'and that all this was done by the advice of Simon, earl of Leicester, Peter of Savoy, John, earl of Warwick, John Mansel, treasurer of York, John fitz Geoffrey, Peter de Montfort and others of the King's Council.'

[3] 'Scriptum esse audivimus quod illa civitas ordinatissima dicitur, in qua quisque proprios nescit affectus. Hoc hodie in reformatione et ordinacione regni nostri apertissime comprobatur. Nam nostri proceres et magnates, sua postponentes negocia propter nostra, suis spretis negociis, nostris et regni nostri invigilant toto posse. Unde, cum ordinacionem ipsorum nobis et heredibus nostris plurimum fructuosum habeamus gratam non immerito et acceptam, serenitati vestre cum omni affectione qua possumus supplicamus quatinus favorem sedis apostolice hujusmodi ordinacioni dignemini impertiri, fulcientes eandem vestre auctoritatis robore et consensu' (Close, 42 Hen. III, m. 4d.).

[4] Undated letter in the *Additamenta* of Paris (vi. 410): it is addressed 'Nobilibus viris consiliariis carissimi in Christo filii nostri illustris regis Anglie et ceteris proceribus et magnatibus regni Anglie.'

with other persons who would offer better terms. This it had not yet done, but would certainly do, if the king did not keep his engagements, and above all did not pay 'in their entirety' his debts towards the Church. Finally 'on the matter which the English representatives have set forth in our presence and in the presence of the cardinals against the bishop of Winchester, if it is true, we are greatly troubled and disquieted, for it is our wish that all Christ's faithful, and especially high ecclesiastical dignitaries should turn towards God and walk in the path of his commandments; but as no lawful advocate for the defence has been found to plead the cause of the elect before the Holy See, it has not been possible to take legal proceedings in all these matters.' The letter ended by appealing to the sentiment of loyalty and respect which should inspire the barons in their treatment of the king, the 'most devout and most Christian prince', and of his family.[1]

In reality the Pope granted nothing, promised nothing. It should be noted that the letter of the barons could not have arrived in Rome at a worse moment, when Manfred after his success was in the act of assuming the royal crown at Palermo with great pomp and magnificence (10 August 1258).[2] Moreover the Pope, who held the English responsible for the check he had just received, so far from wishing to sacrifice Aymer de Valence was endeavouring with Henry's full connivance to secure his recall to England,[3] and ended by consecrating him with his own

[1] Two other points were dealt with in this letter. The barons had requested the Pope to send a legate to discuss peace with France and the reform of England. The Pope replied that he ardently desired peace of England both within and without, but that 'as there are for the moment but few cardinals here, and since above all he wishes to be better informed on the situation in England, he thought it best to defer the sending of a legate.'

[2] *Chron. maj.*, v. 722.

[3] The intrigue over this, begun between the king and the Pope, has been related by Dr. R. F. Treharne (*E. H. R.* xl, 1925, 403–4). On 29 January 1259, the Pope sent to England one Velascus, his chaplain and penitentiar, in order to persuade the king and the nobles to allow Aymer to return. The Council, however, (8 June) gave orders that no important person should be allowed to enter or leave the kingdom without special authority. A month later, in the absence of the chancellor Henry de Wengham, the Great Seal was entrusted to a subordinate, Walter de Merton (6 or 7 July). On 28 July a letter close requested Velascus to be at Wissant on 16 August, and a patent, dispatched without having been submitted for the Council's approval (29 July), commanded Richard de Grey, constable of Dover, to receive Velascus and facilitate

hands at Rome. But Aymer died shortly after, to the great joy of the reformers.

The barons, after satisfying their feelings of bitterness by driving out their enemies and relieving them of their goods, had no intention of stopping there. To consolidate their victory, they were anxious to make certain of the support of London. The city which in 1215 had sustained the barons against John Lackland lent its co-operation in their efforts against Henry III. On 22 July 1258 [1] the Steward and the Marshal of England, John fitz Geoffrey and several others, deputed by their colleagues, summoned the citizens to the Guildhall,[2] and presenting the charter whereby the king and his eldest son swore to observe the Provisions, asked them to approve it also. After taking counsel, the citizens consented, and the seal of the commune was attached to the bottom of the act of agreement.[3] Several further meetings took place, at the New Temple and elsewhere, in which the barons discussed with the citizens the reforms that needed to be introduced into the kingdom.[4] Finally on 13 October in a proclamation drawn up or published in French and English,[5] Henry III solemnly declared that he

his arrival at the court. This was done. Velascus, however, was met with a categorical refusal, and was obliged to cross back again (11 September). A letter of the king's to the Pope explains the whole affair, and it is difficult not to scent collusion between them. Was Henry then merely weak or deceitful? In any case his ambiguous conduct authorizes the latter suspicion. Matthew Paris did not know the details of the intrigue; he simply observed (p. 713) that the Papal clerk 'seeing the kingdom in a tumult', prudently and tacitly returned from England when the Assumption drew near, awaiting better days for his return. The anonymous author of the *Flores historiarum* (ii. 434) believes that Richard de Grey was disgraced for having allowed a certain brother Velascus to enter England; he did not know that the king himself had given the order. Aymer de Valence, consecrated 16 May 1260, died a little afterwards, 4 December. During the whole of this time the diocese of Winchester was in fact vacant. The monks forming the chapter elected Henry de Wengham, the Chancellor, who refused to act, alleging his ignorance in matters of theology, but really because he knew that the king would never abandon his brother (*Chron. maj.*, v. 731).

[1] The day of the quarrel between Simon and William de Valence, related above.

[2] *Chron. maj.*, v. 704: 'convocaverunt totius civitatis cives quos barones vocant.'

[3] *Ibid.*: 'Quod cum gratuiter (*corr.* gratanter?) omnes concessissent, confecerunt super hoc eis cartam suam de communi consilio civitatis signatam.'

[4] *Ibid.* Cf. *Chron. maj. et vic. Lond.*, p. 39.

[5] The French version was added to the *Foedera* in the Royal Commission's

vould maintain all the decisions taken by his councillors 'for he honour of God, the king's service and the good of the ountry'; an excellent formula, but easy to falsify through nsincere interpretation of its real intention. He bade all his ubjects swear to, and defend, the statutes drafted by his coun-illors, and treat as enemies of the public all daring to infringe hem. 'This famous decree may be regarded as the first public atification of the Revolution, giving it the character of a national enterprise. In the first parliament of the new order, on he eve of a new regnal year, the king took his people into partnership in the adhesion which he had promised in his letters patent of May 2 and August 4.'[1] The scholar whose words I borrow adds: 'the word employed to designate the acts of the ouncil is significant; instead of provisions we read the "etab-isemenz ke sont fez", "sunt à fere",' and to this last expression he attributes,[2] perhaps with a slight touch of exaggeration, a juridical value greater than ordinarily attached to decisions hat were provisional and not guaranteed by legal sanctions.

A year was still to pass before the work of the reformers was accomplished. Theirs was certainly an uneasy task; it may well have been obstructed by the discord that was beginning to manifest itself among the barons, particularly between Leicester and Gloucester. It has left behind a body of evidence which Mr. Jacob has collected and discussed with remarkable industry, races of activities that find their official expression in the act of 3 October 1259, known under the name of the *Provisions of Westminster*.[3] At the end of this document, at any rate in the

dition (i. 377). There is a copy in the Archives Nationales (J 918, no. 8); how did it come into the Trésor des Chartes de France? Did it get there from the e Montfort archives? The English draft has the considerable interest of being the earliest known specimen of a royal charter drawn in English since the time f the Confessor. See the facsimile in *New Palaeographical Society's Transac-ions*, 1905, 2nd part, no 73. Sir Henry Ellis published it in 1868, and W. W. Skeat devoted a special study to it in the *Academy*, 13 May 1882. Cf. *S. C.*, p. 387–8, and Ramsay, *Dawn*, p. 186. The date is thus given: 'a Londres le isotime jor de Octobre, l'an de nostre regne quarant second.' The 42nd year f Henry III having begun on 23 October 1257, it belongs to the last days of his regnal year. Among the witnesses Leicester comes immediately after he archbishop of Canterbury and the bishop of Worcester, at the head of the aity.

[1] Powicke, *op. cit.*, p. 124.   [2] *Ibid.*, p. 126.
[3] *Studies in the Period of Baronial Reform and Rebellion, 1258–1267.* In

French version, are found the words: 'Ce sont les purveance et les establissimenz fetz a Westmoster al parlament a la sain Michel par le roi et son Conseil et les XII pour le Commun Conseil esluz par devant la communance de Engleterre ke dunk fu a Westminster le an del regne Henry le fiz le roi Johan quarantime terz.' Here we can see what parliament hat become; it was in fact composed solely of the king, the Counci of Fifteen, and that of the Twelve. The 'communance' [1] signi fies the assembly of barons who normally came in great number. to be present at the festival of St. Edward's day (13 October) always celebrated by the devout Henry III with peculia splendour. Their presence gave particular strength to the roya ordinance.

How was the new constitution administered? What part dic Leicester take? Upon the first of these points, where the chronicles provide only sparse and vague indications, the works of Professor Tout and Mr. Jacob, based upon a systematic exploration of judicial and financial records, have thrown strik ing light.[2] An extensive inquiry ordered to be held into 'the oppression of the weak by the strong' was apparently conductec

Chapter III Mr. Jacob compiles a table of the different drafts, which in their totality form a homogeneous and coherent whole, and constitute what ar commonly called the Provisions of Oxford and Westminster. These drafts are 1. the *Provisio facta apud Oxoniam*, 22–3 June 1258 (after the Annals of Burton) 2. A *Nova Provisio magnatum Anglie publicata apud Novum Templum*, Marc 1259 (inserted by Paris in his *Additamenta*, p. 4967; 3. The *Ordinaciones facte pe magnates de Consilio regis*, 28 March 1259 (copied in the Patent Roll, ca *C. P. R. 1258–1266*, 19); 4. the *Provisiones baronum* of 13 October 1259; th Latin text, copied on the Close Roll, and confirmed by the king in 1263, whe still in agreement or in apparent agreement with his barons, and again in 126 when he was their prisoner, was incorporated in 1267 in the Statute of Marl borough, and consequently figures in the official edition of the *Statutes of th Realm*, i. 2–11; cf. *S. C.* pp. 389–94. The Annals of Burton contain a hybrid version, half Latin and half French; cf. Powicke, p. 128, n. 4.

[1] It would be much better to read 'communauté', writing of both word being identical in contemporary script.

[2] Professor Tout (*Chapters*, i. 295–312) has proved that if changes were mad in the personnel of the administration (cf. *Chron. maj.*, v. 719), the mechanism was not changed. Mr. Jacob shows the importance of the work carried out by the new personnel; he emphasizes the preponderating part played by th Justiciar Hugh Bigod, a distinguished jurist (*Chron. maj.*, v. 698), though one who had not yet exercised any judicial function. Thanks to Jacob, we can follow this great magistrate, stage by stage, throughout the circuits he performed from June 1258 to January 1260.

with scrupulous impartiality.[1] In the only original record of the proceedings that has come down to us, that of a hundred in the county of Suffolk,[2] all the royal agents are seen appearing, even the officers of seignorial 'liberties',[3] even municipal officials of London in spite of the City privileges.[4] The sheriffs chosen by the four knights representing the nobility of the county and probably drawn from its ranks[5] were made, after they had taken a new oath at the Exchequer, to carry away with them the famous English proclamation of 13 October and to read it several times in public.

What part did Simon take in this much discussed work, in all its chequered career? In 1258, during the whole of May, he was in France, negotiating the Treaty of Paris. He contrived to be at Oxford from the time parliament opened; the first ordinances constructing the new constitution are of 22 June, and his place on the committees has been noticed. A month later (22 July) he was present at the meeting with the citizens of

[1] *Chron. maj.*, v. 714 and *Additamenta*, p. 396.

[2] Loes, co. Suffolk. The fragment was discovered by Miss Cam, *Oxford Studies in Social and Legal History*, vi. 109–10. It is printed and commented on at length by Jacob, pp. 23 f.

[3] Jacob, p. 56.

[4] *Ibid.*, pp. 56–7, cf. *Chron maj. et vic. Lond.*, p. 40.

[5] These knights were themselves under supervision: thus Peter de Montfort had three out of four changed in Shropshire because they were inefficient (Jacob, p. 23). Over and beyond the knights properly so called, this *petite noblesse* comprised vassals of subordinate status called by the term 'vavassores' (p. 93), 'valetti' (p. 117, n. 2) and 'bachelarii'. A protest against the Provisions of Westminster was forthcoming from the 'communitas bachelerie Anglie', a much canvassed phrase, to which Mr. Jacob devotes a long discussion (pp. 126–42); he sees in it something like the clients of an important magnate, people always ready to sustain their patron's cause. In time of peace, the bachelors had plenty of opportunity to deal with administrative affairs, e. g. in the courts of hundred and county. They were thus in a position to provide their lords with some constructive ideas. In spite of its ingenuity, Mr. Jacob's theory is still an hypothesis. But see his article 'The Complaints of Henry III against the baronial Council in 1261' (*E. H. R.*, xli (1926), pp. 559–71), and Professor Powicke 'Some observations on the baronial Council 1258–60 and the Provisions of Westminster' (*Essays in Medieval History presented to T. F. Tout*, p. 127, 137 &c.). For the term bachelor, cf. 'The Commune of Bury St. Edmunds 1264', by H. W. C. Davis in *E. H. R.*, xxiv (1909): 'memorandum quod ante bellum de Lewes quedam multitudo de villa Sancto Edmundi CCC vel plus in numero, qui se bachelarii vocari fecerunt, per conspirationem mutuam quandam gildam levaverunt quam gildam juvenum vocaverunt,' p. 316; cf. p. 317, of 1264: 'quidam juniores et minus discretiores . . . suscitarunt, quam gildam [juvenum] sub colore appellari fecerunt.'

London at the Guildhall and there threatened William de Valence with death. It is unlikely that he was not present at the consultations of the barons nor collaborated with them in their decisions; but we are in complete ignorance of what he said, and what he might have said remains a problem. During the rest of 1258 and the greater part of the following year he was often absent. In November 1258 he went off with the bishops of Lincoln and Worcester and the earl marshal to be present at a 'great and secret parliament' held at Cambrai to discuss the affairs of France, Germany, and England.[1] At this time he made his will; the original, written by his eldest son (1 January 1259) has survived.[2] It is an interesting document, psychologically because it reflects certain hitherto unobserved traits in his character: sincere charity, deep piety. Regret, perhaps rather indignation, was felt when he failed to be present at the unexpected and unauthorized return of the king of Germany to England (January 1259).[3] He attended, however, when parliament met in London on the Octave of the Purification (9 February).[4] In an interval during its session a violent quarrel broke out between him and Gloucester.[5] They accused each

[1] *Chron. maj.*, v. 720. This parliament did not take place, because the barons stopped Henry III from going.

[2] By a royal act of 20 February Simon had been authorized to dispose by will of all his goods and revenues (*Royal Letters*, ii. 392). See the text of the will in *Simon de Montfort*, 328, printed at the end of the present volume, Appendix A.

[3] *Chron. maj.*, p. 732. Richard was not allowed to reside in England (he landed 27 January) until he had sworn not to oppose the work of reform. This oath he took in the Chapter at Canterbury (p. 735).

[4] *Ibid.*, p. 737.

[5] *Ibid.*, p. 744. Mr. Jacob deals at length with the quarrel between the earls (pp. 84–6). He analyses a letter in French from Richard de Clare, promising to aid and counsel prince Edward and his allies. This letter is dated London 'le quatorzime jur de marz, l'an del regne le roi Henri, le fils le rei Johan, quarante treiz (14 March 1259); it was published by the Hist. MSS. Comm., in the *Report on the MSS. of Lord Middleton preserved at Wollaton Hall* (1911, pp. 67–8). It is probably to this quarrel that reference is made in the passages where John de Oxenedes recounts the overtures and inducements made to Simon by 'many Englishmen', begging him 'to persuade Henry III not to waste his treasure to no purpose, but to expel the aliens from England, to love native-born Englishmen, to extirpate evil customs, to confirm the liberties and the laws of the past'. Simon, it seems, hesitated, saying that the English could not be relied upon: 'after having put people into a hole, they left them there, like cowards.' 'Cowards,' 'cowering Englishmen' were terms of abuse with which Frenchmen took pleasure in taunting their rivals across the Channel

other of betraying the good cause.[1] Simon was saddened by the
ill-treatment he suffered. One of their colleagues wavered in his
loyalty between the king and the barons. 'I dislike,' said the
earl, 'living among people so fickle, so deceitful. We have all
sworn to carry out the business in hand, and you, sir earl of
Gloucester, the more you excel in dignity and position, the more
strictly you ought to observe the salutary laws we have given
the country.' Then he left England without delay, but doubtless also on a diplomatic errand.[2] His friends importuned
Richard de Clare so strongly that he granted all the satisfactions
demanded. In June, in August as well, Simon was in France,
but we know that he returned to be present in parliament at
St. Edward's festival (13 October). Two days later, in London
(15 October) prince Edward swore to give him and his heirs aid
and counsel, against all men, saving their fealty due to the king.
More, he promised to uphold the barons' enterprise 'al cuor de
Dieu et au profit du roy et de ses heiers et du royaume', and not
to make war upon any involved in the coalition.[3] It is evident
that the earl wished to guard against new attacks from an even
higher quarter still. And now he returned once more to France [4]
to be present at the final conclusion of the treaty which he had
been constantly engaged in negotiating, the treaty that affected

---

(*Revue historique*, lii. 309). The Lanercost Chronicle also speaks of Simon's
hesitation.

[1] On 10 March 1259 Henry III sent over to France Leicester, Gloucester
(were they reconciled ?), Peter of Savoy, John Mansel, John de Balliol, Robert
Walerand, to settle matters of dispute between the two kings (*C. P. R. 1258–
1266*, 18).

[2] On 17 June Louis IX gave notice that a marriage had been arranged
between his nephew, Robert of Artois, and Amicia, daughter of the late Peter
de Courtenai. The friends who had planned and organized this match were, on
Amicia's side, Robert de Courtenai, bishop of Orléans, Ralph, John, and William
de Courtenai, her uncles; Simon de Montfort and the young lady's mother
Perronelle, wife of Henry de Sulli (Delisle, *Cartulaire Normand*, no. 618). The
Register of Eudes Rigaud, bishop of Rouen, tells us that on 19 August Simon
dined at the castle of Neaufles-Saint-Martin with this prelate. To this period
belong several considerable donations made by the king to his sister Eleanor,
Simon's wife (*C. Ch. R.*, ii. 20, under 27 July; *C. P. R. 1258–1266*, 34–5).

[3] Clairembault, 1188, p. 13. Together with his seal the prince attached those
of his dear freinds, 'mon segnur Henry, fiuz le roy d'Alemagne, et mon segnur
Jehan conte de Warenn., et mon segnur Rogier de Leyborne.'

[4] Already on 19 October Simon was present at the consecration of the
bishop of Évreux, Ralph Grosparmi de Périers (*Histor. de France*, xxiii. 467;
Cartulaire Normand, no. 617).

his personal interests because of the clauses touching the inheritance of his wife, John Lackland's daughter.

The king too was about to leave England—but under what conditions! He had been forced to ask permission! Was he then no longer his own master? If, as was natural, he was vexed at this loss of liberty, he doubtless consoled himself with the thought that although the treaty imposed a certain amount of sacrifice, it was also going to furnish him with the means of regaining the ground lost in his quarrel with the barons.

VI

THE TREATY OF PARIS, 1258–1259

IN spite of the check suffered by his second expedition into Western France in 1242–3, Henry III had never given up hope of recovering the provinces lost since 1204. For a brief while it occurred to him to take advantage of Louis IX's absence in distant Palestine to make a third attack upon the kingless kingdom: but a formal prohibition from the Pope compelled him to abandon the sacrilegious project, and he had to resign himself to the *status quo*. Hence the truce of five years concluded in 1243 came to be several times renewed. When Louis IX returned, Henry III no doubt found him well disposed in favour of a lasting peace. He was too well acquainted with the court of France to be unaware of the saintly king's scruples on the subject of John Lackland's condemnation by the peers of the French court in 1202, which Louis IX considered unexceptionable in law [1] but too extreme in the matter of its execution, pursued remorselessly and in a manner out of all proportion to the offence. Since the time when they had married two sisters and their children had become first cousins.[2] Henry had appreciated Louis IX's tokens of friendship. He thought that an amicable agreement with his French brother would allow him more scope both to secure the triumph of his personal policy as well as to aid the Pope's design and further the interests of his younger son in the Sicilian enterprise. Negotiations were therefore indicated; but the preliminaries lasted a long time, primarily of course owing to the feelings of distrust and rancour persisting on both sides of the Channel, but also on account of the sacrifices which both parties had to agree to. Five years were absorbed in this delicate matter (1254–9), and no surprise will be felt at seeing the name of Simon de Montfort frequently appear; for he too had interests to defend, not only on behalf of himself but on behalf of his wife. In 1248 and 1249, as we

---

[1] On this point see the dissertation of M. Ch. Petit-Dutaillis in *Revue historique*, t. cxlvii and cxlviii.

[2] Joinville's testimony on this matter has been often quoted. For further details, see Ch.-V. Langlois in Lavisse's *Histoire de France*, iii. 2e partie, 92–4, and especially Gavrilovitch, *Étude sur le traité de Paris de 1259*.

noticed above, the earl secured a prolongation of the truce made in 1243, and the same happened in 1255.[1] A further mission to renew it was sent in 1257,[2] but its progress was disturbed by a new fact: Richard of Cornwall had just been summoned by part of the German electors to wear the imperial crown (14 January 1257), an event well calculated to make Louis IX and his counsellors stand on their guard. The victory won at the parliament of London (April–May 1258) by the English barons in league against the king's favourites brought about a decisive change of attitude; on 8 May, Henry III entrusted full powers to the earls of Leicester and Norfolk, to Peter of Savoy and Geoffrey and Guy de Lusignan to treat with the king of France, and, in the meantime, to prolong the truce for a year or two further as might be needed.[3] As a matter of fact, peace was concluded for the first time at the Temple in Paris on 28 May 1258, in the presence of the king of France, and was sworn to by the English

[1] On 10 May 1255, the king ordered Peter of Savoy to depart without delay for France, so as to secure the truce strongly desired by the king of Castile; there he would meet the earl of Leicester 'qui pro quibusdam suis negociis ad partes Francie se jam transtulit' at the same time one of the king's secretaries (' aliquem de nostris secretariis ') would be sent out to transmit the royal instructions and to report his replies (*Royal Letters*, ii. 107). On 20 May the king granted Simon de Montfort and Peter of Savoy full powers to conclude, confirm, and prorogue the three years truce (*C. P. R. 1247–1258*, 411) ; the truce, concluded actually in June, was to have effect from St. Rémi's day, 1 October (*Layettes*, no. 4178). On 20 January 1256, the king dispatched Peter de Montfort to regulate the numerous cases of broken truce already submitted to the examination of the French by Simon de Montfort and Peter of Savoy (Rymer; cf. *C. P. R. 1247–1258*, 458), and on 24 January full powers were entrusted to John Mansel, provost of Beverley and to Bertram de Crioyl to conclude a truce of three years (Rymer; cf. *C. P. R. 1247–1258*, 460, under 25 January).

[2] On 20 February 1257, two patents contain (1) the announcement by Henry III to the French king of the arrival of Simon de Montfort and Robert Walerand, steward of his household, 'ad tractandum de pace inter vos et nos '; (2) information to the effect that, if the king of France is prepared to restore to Simon what was his by inheritance, whether whole or in part, Henry III authorized him (the earl) to receive it (*Royal Letters*, ii. 121 ; cf. *C. P. R. 1247–1258*, 542). On 22 June, full powers to treat were given to Walter Cantilupe, bishop of Worcester, Hugh Bigod and—this deserves notice—Adam de Marsh, who are to take the decision after having received the advice and consent of Simon de Montfort and Peter of Savoy (Rymer; cf. *C. P. R. 1247–1258*, 594).

[3] Rymer. On 18 December 1258 Simon is noted as present at the reading of the marriage contract between a daughter of the earl of Gloucester with the marquis of Montferrat, which took place in the queen's chamber at Westminster (*C. Ch. R.* ii. 3).

king's representatives.[1] Certain points of detail delayed the final conclusion for more than a year, to October 1259:[2] the matter of the Agenais and the county of Bigorre on the one hand, and on the other the attitude of the countess of Leicester who refused to renounce her rights over the lands ceded to France by her brother Henry III, before the eternal question of her dower had been settled.[3]

[1] *Layettes*, nos. 4416, 4417. Henry III later reproached his brother-in-law for the part he had taken in the Treaty of Paris: 'Nostre seigneur le roi dit que le comte de Leycestre fu de son Conseil et que il li conseilla qu'il treitast de pais au roi de France des terres de là.' The earl replied that in fact 'il fu au Conseil et li conseilla aveques autres prodes hommes de son Conseil et de sa terre' (*Simon de Montfort*, p. 343). An echo of what passed in the council has been preserved by a rhymester who, in bad French, relates a dispute on the subject between Simon, Roger Bigod and the king. Henry, it seems, had proposed to go to war instead of to treat. At this Simon grew angry.

> A dit a roi anglais: 'Par le cors saint Anel
> Lessiez or cesti chos; François n'est mi anel.'
> (Wright, *Political Songs*, 1839, p. 66.)

Tr. 'by the body of the Paschal Lamb, the Frenchman is no lamb.'

[2] It is not irrelevant to recall here the testimony of Matthew Paris about this particular date, because he made a note of it in his chronicle after the departure of the English negotiators in April 1259, and had ceased to write (he was in all probability dead) before the definitive conclusion of the Treaty (October). About the Kalends of April, he says (v. 741) 'ex praecepto et consilio domini regis Henrici et totius barnagii', the earls de Clare and Leicester, John Mansel, Peter of Savoy and Robert Walerand crossed over to France, 'sed, quia de eorundem nuntiorum dispersione quid super hoc actum est in publico non profertur, nulla exinde certitudo scripturae adhuc commendatur.' Then at the moment when it was thought that peace was going to be concluded, the countess of Leicester refused (p. 745) to give up that part of Normandy over which she had claims. The earl of Gloucester abused Simon in opprobrious terms for this ('verbo inhonesto'), and Simon replied with pointed sarcasm ('aculeatis verbis verba retundebat'); friends had to intervene to keep them from blows. They therefore returned to England empty-handed amid the laughter of the French ('cachinnantibus Francis'). Thomas Wykes attributes to the earl a far-reaching and ambitious vision, yet one that could not be termed a mere hallucination—for the future evades every man's grasp: 'comes L.,' he says, huic paci opposuit, proponens quod processu temporis contingere posset quod eedem terre simul cum regno Angliae ad filios suos vel heredes jure hereditario descendere possent' (p. 123).

[3] Henry III later complained (*Simon de Montfort*, pp. 344–5) that Simon had refused to implement the renunciations imposed by the Treaty, because the king had not yet carried out the agreements accepted by him in July 1259, viz. 'que les quatre cenz livres qu'il (Simon and his wife) prennent du don le roi et de sa chartre, lor seient otriées en terre.' *C. P. R. 1258–1266* brings to notice a whole series of letters concerning the claim of the earl and countess: on 9 March 1259 a memorandum relates that the proctorial powers given to the

The terms laid down in the Treaty of Paris [1] are well known. They can be reduced to five principal headings: 1. The king of England renounced, on behalf of himself, his heirs and successors, Normandy,[2] Anjou, Touraine, Maine, and Poitou. 2. The king of France ceded him the rights 'quil avoit et tenoit en ces trois éveschiés et ces citez, c'est à dire de Limoges,[3] de Cahors et de Pierregort, en fiez et en demaines.' 3. The Agenais, claimed by the king of England as part of the inheritance of Henry II's daughter, was to remain French until the question of legal right was determined; but Henry III was to receive the annual value of its revenues in the form of a money rent. Article 6 touching the homage of the counties of Bigorre, Armagnac, and Fezensac referred the matter in similar fashion to the decision of a tribunal of arbitration. 4. All that Louis IX abandoned in favour

earls of Leicester and Gloucester, to John Mansel, John de Balliol, and Robert Walerand starting for France during Lent (which in 1259 began on 2 March) had been put in the hands of John Mansel (p. 14). Three pairs of letters, i. e. three patents, sealed at Windsor Sunday before St. Gregory's day (9 March), had also been committed to him (pp. 14, 15). On 12 March the king announced that he had given Hugh de Dive, marshal of his Household, orders to pay 100 gold marks to the ambassadors (Leicester and Gloucester, Peter of Savoy, John Mansel, Robert Walerand), for their expenses (p. 15). On 20 May the king informed Louis IX that in the presence of numerous prelates and magnates assembled at Westminster he had besought his sister to accept the sentence of arbitration recently given at St. Germain-en-Laye in the king's name by the earl of Gloucester, Peter of Savoy, John Mansel, John de Balliol, and Robert Walerand (p. 25). On the same day he promised Louis IX to indemnify him if the countess of Leicester and her children did not meet his demands in full (p. 27). On 24 May the king wrote again informing Louis IX that Wednesday after St. John *ante portam latinam* (14 May) he had made the exchequer assign to the claimants the money owing to the earl and his wife, whether for the dowry of Eleanor or for any and every other reason (p. 26).

[1] The text should be read in *Foedera* (Rec. ed.), i. 390; cf. *Layettes*, no. 4554. Auguste Longnon, *La formation de l'unité française* (1922), pp. 140–1 speaks only of the treaty concluded in May 1258 and ratified by Henry III on 5 September 1259.

[2] The treaty merely determines the political relations between the two kings, suzerain and vassal; the periodical effects of the confiscations taking place after the conquest of Normandy by Philip Augustus in 1204 in their bearing upon individual tenants naturally remained in force. This is the explanation of the following passage in a letter by which Henry III grants John Mansel, Treasurer of York, on 12 May 1263, a hundred acres of land, with this reservation: Et si contingat quod terra nostra Anglie et terre normannorum sint communes ... non disseisiemus ... predictum Johannem ... aut heredes ... de terra predicta, priusquam eis pro terra illa escambium fecerimus rationabile (N. Neilson, *The Cartulary and Terrier of the Priory of Bilsington, Kent*, p. 82).

[3] See Ch.-V. Langlois, *Le règne de Phillipe III le Hardi*, p. 420.

of Henry III, i. e. his fiefs and domains in the Limousin, Quercy, and Périgord, and all that remained to England of the ancient duchy of Guyenne, i.e. Gascony with Bordeaux and Bayonne, was to be held by the king of England as an hereditary fee, in conformity with feudal custom: which meant that he had to take the oath of fealty and liege homage to his suzerain, the king of France, 'come per de France et duc de Aquitaine'. 5. The French king promised to pay the English king, in six instalments spread over two years, the sum necessary to maintain five hundred knights during this period; the English monarch could only employ this money for the service of God, the Church, or the welfare of England: in the latter case, however, the expenditure was to have the authorization of the 'good men of the land'.

This is no place to inquire whether the saintly king was deserving of blame for having granted the English advantages considered by his entourage to be exorbitant. Looked at from the English point of view, these advantages were real: if Henry II's inheritance was severely reduced, the remnants at any rate were protected for the future by feudal law and the sacred authority of the oath. It would be more interesting to know what subtle influence had succeeded in introducing into the Treaty the article on the maintenance of the five hundred knights. Nothing is more natural than that Louis IX should have thought of them as going to fight in the Holy Land; but that he could have admitted the idea that the money promised to this end could also be applied to the political needs of England, passes understanding.[1] Did he not suspect its possible

---

[1] The fact is worth establishing. Proof is to be found in two letters of Henry III to Louis IX, dated 13 May 1264, the very eve of the battle of Lewes. The first is entitled 'de sustentatione militum in terra sancta', and can be summarized thus: Louis IX has promised Henry III to pay him the charges of maintaining five hundred knights for two years. On the strength of this Henry III has decided to raise in advance 2000*l.* (of Tours) for the work of the crusade, and has charged John de Valentin, knight of the king of France, to convey this money to Palestine and expend it there upon God's service. This sum was doubtless only a fraction of the account, for in another letter copied on the roll after the previous one (14 May), Henry III gives Louis IX complete discharge of the total sum, amounting to 132,000*l.* (of Tours). In the same deed Henry III recognized that he had already spent *the greater part* of this sum 'in utilitatem regni Anglie', and promises to expend *the rest* 'in servicium Dei aut ecclesie, vel in utilitatem predicti regni Anglie.' Thus 132,000 pounds of French money

employment by the king against his barons, or by the 'good men of the land' against their sovereign? As a matter of fact Henry III alone was to benefit by this perilous liberality; it gave him the needful reinforcements for reconquering from the coalition of his enemies the ground he had been forced to yield to them during the first year of the civil war, as will shortly be seen.

The solemn ratification of the Treaty took place at Paris on 4 December 1259.[1] On that day Henry III attended by the highest nobility of England and France, and in the presence of an innumerable assembly swore to observe the conditions. Kneeling at the feet of the king of France, he made him the oath of fealty and liege homage to which Louis IX with every reason attached the highest importance.[2] That same day the Treaty was confirmed by the earl and countess of Leicester. Eleanor surrendered her claims to the heritage of her father, King John; Simon gave up all claims bequeathed to him by his father and

went to subsidize the civil war. The second of these deeds is attested 'per ipsum Regem, regem Alemannie, Edwardum filium regis, Henricum filium regis Alemannie, Rogerum de Leyburn, et alios de consilio regis. Et sciendum quod magister Arnulphus, cancellarius regis Alemannie, dictavit et scripsit manibus propriis litteram supradictam, sine consilio et assensu alicujus clerici de cancellaria, et consignata fuit coram consilio domini Regis apud Lewes die supradicto.' Rymer under 14 May 1259; cf. *C. P. R. 1258–1265*, 317. See further a confirmation of the promises already made in a letter written in the name of Queen Eleanor, Peter of Savoy, and John Mansel, dated Paris, Sunday after the Ascension (1 June), 1264 in Blaauw, *Barons' War*, 358–9 (from the National Archives, J 630; the original sealed).

[1] On the day before (3 December, Wednesday after St. Andrew) at St. Germain des Prés Louis IX had promised to pay Henry III a certain sum; but he declares that he intends to keep 15,000 marks, until Henry III had finished his dispute with the earl and countess. The balance will be paid to the king in the two following months; the dispute must be settled in the course of the two years following next St. Nicholas (6 December). The text of this letter is in *Layettes*, no. 4564. Analysis in *C. P. R. 1258–1266*, 106, with a series of others on the same subject, dated 11 January 1261 (p. 136), 14 March (p. 145), 5 July (p. 162), 20 July (p. 169). From this day, 4 December 1259, the English chancery suppressed in royal acts the titles of duke of Normandy and count of Anjou, that still figured in the royal proclamations of 18 October (the English text) and 20 October (the French text).

[2] Here again we must invoke Joinville. The mention of liege homage has been preserved, under the guise of an authentic copy, in a *vidimus* of 1320 (*Layettes*, no. 4566). The witnesses are the archbishop of Tarentaise, the bishops of Lincoln and Norwich, the bishop-elect of London, Peter of Savoy, John de Balliol, Peter de Montfort, John Mansel, treasurer of York.

his brother over the county of Toulouse, the vicomté of Béziers, the Albigeois, the town and county of Évreux.[1] Splendid festivities were held in celebration of this important event, which put a happy ending to half a century of latent or declared animosity.

While he was in Paris engaged in the negotiations for the Treaty, Simon sent his clerk Raymond Bodin of Aurillac to England to treat with the council, 'quant que apendoit a l'afere de Bigore.'[2] At first sight there seemed a chance of definite settlement: on 25 July 1259, the English barons, prince Edward and his brother Edmund,[3] gave their approval to a convention which can be summarized in two points: 1. The earl of Leicester delivered Bigorre to King Henry for seven years: in return the king was to pay him 1,000l. at the following Easter drawn on his account at the Temple at Paris. 2. If instead the king wished to pay in territory, the arrangement was to be submitted to two arbitrators; at the end of the seven years the king was to restore the land free of all charge to the earl and his heirs.[4]

It is impossible not to feel some astonishment at the sequel: the spectacle of Esquivat de Chabanais allied to the count of Foix and even seconded for the time being by his eternal enemy,

---

[1] Vaissète, *Histoire générale de Languedoc*, iii, preuves, 451.

[2] *Simon de Montfort*, p. 346.

[3] *Layettes*, nos. 4500, 4501.

[4] The convention is dated London, 26 July, after a copy in the Bibliothèque Nationale, MSS. fonds Moreau. t. 688, p. 119, and approved by the bishop of Winchester and 'plusor grant baron'. It runs thus, in the very inaccurate copy found in the Cartulary of Champagne already cited: 'Saschés que nos les couvenances faites entre seignor le roy d'Angleterre, d'une part, et Simon de Montfort, conte de Leicestre, d'autre part, d'androit la conté de Bigorre, que li devant dits contes a baillé au devant dit roi selonc la forme qui est contenue en l'escrit qui an a esté fait entre aus parties par cirographe, loons et conseillons et avons promis en bonne foi que nous les tanrons et ferons tenir et acomplir quant a nos an apartient.' The names of the witnesses have been badly mutilated: they should read, Walter bishop of Winchester (*Ulcester*), Richard de Clare earl of Gloucester and Hertford (*Erfort*), Roger Bigod earl of Norfolk (*Mouffort*), Humphrey de Bohun earl of Hereford and Essex, William de Fors earl of Aumale, Hugh Bigod 'Justiciar of England', Peter of Savoy, John Mansel treasurer of York (*Ehurvic*); Roger Mortimer, Philip Basset (*Blaset*), Richard de Grey, and Peter de Montfort. On 6 August at Windsor the king gave the custody of the county during the seven years to Amaubin de Barès, with the promise to restore it to Simon if, previously, the king had not paid his debt to the earl (*C. P. R. 1258-1266*, 38).

the vicomte of Béarn,[1] entering his county by armed force, disputing it with Gaston, his friend of yesterday, and then throwing himself once more into his uncle's arms and submitting to his decisions (6 August 1261).[2] But the point that cannot easily be explained is the reason why Simon de Montfort abandoned the suzerainty of the English king and reverted to that of the bishop of le Puy. On 20 July 1262 he gave orders to his lieutenant, Raymond Bodin of Aurillac, to lay upon the high altar of the church of Le Puy the sixty shillings (Morlaas) which each new possessor of the county of Bigorre had to pay as relief.[3] If, as Gaston de Béarn claimed,[4] the first donation made by Esquivat to his uncle was simply in the nature of a commission or a deposit, 'comenda', there is at any rate no mistaking the character of these sixty shillings; what Esquivat was sealing was his abdication, and to Simon Bigorre was henceforth to belong.

How are we to explain these new complications? Were Esquivat's debts to Simon de Montfort so pressing that to acquit them he had to cede the inheritance of his mother and grandmother to his uncle? Was he so nervous of Gaston de Béarn, or was he simply a pawn in Simon de Montfort's hands? Was it due to his powerlessness or his double-dealing? On the other hand, why did Simon shut his eyes to Henry III's suzerainty and renew the feudal pact attaching the county of Bigorre to the cathedral church of Le Puy? Had the king of France raised difficulties over the substitution of the powerful English king for the feeble prelate of the Auvergne? Did Simon recognize the suzerainty of Henry III before he had quarrelled with him, then repudiate it on the day when he became the leader of the barons leagued together against the king? All these explanations may be offered one after the other, but none is satisfactory. We have only the deeds, but they are full of contradictions, and there is no historian, no chronicler to give us the key to their solution. But we know quite clearly the result of all these obscure events, whether they were the outcome of

[1] This is explained in a letter of Gaston de Béarn to Simon on 23 May 1260 (*Simon de Montfort*, p. 371).

[2] *Bibliothèque de l'École des Chartes*, 1857, p. 317.

[3] Vaissète, *Histoire générale de Languedoc*, ed. Dulaurier.

[4] See the letter of 23 May, cited above.

chance or of intrigue; and for the future, the act of 20 July 1262 laid in store one of the most complicated processes ever to be decided by the Parlement of Paris: before the end of the century it was to bring the kings of England and France to hostilities; but it was the king of France, quite definitely, who was to remain the heir of the earl of Leicester.[1]

[1] When Simon died (1265) the countess his widow, a refugee in France, gave Thibaut, count of Champagne and king of Navarre, the rights she possessed over Bigorre, 'par ochoison de nostre seigneur Monsieur Symon de Montfort, comte de Lyncestre, qui eut la dite comté de Monsieur Eschivat de Chabanès, avant lui comte de Bigorre' (October 1265). On his side, the young Simon ceded Thibaut 'le chastel de Lourde et ses appartenances, et o tout le droit que nous avons et pouvons avoir en la conté de Bigorre' (*Bibl. de l'École des Chartes*, 1857, p. 317). The Cartulary of Champagne contains a letter addressed by the bishop and chapter of Le Puy to Thibaut (29 March 1266), where the expression occurs: 'quod, quando constiterit et declaratum fuerit nos habere et habere debere dominium feudi et feudum castri de Laurda (*sic*) et comitatus Bigorre per sententiam vel compositionem, dictum regem Navarre, heredes et successores ejusdem venientes ad hommagium et fidelitatem episcopi et capituli ecclesie Aniciensis predicte, ratione castri et comitatus predictorum, recipiemus sine difficultate qualibet.' He promises him 'quod negotium comitatus et castri [of Lourdes] predictorum, quod movemus vel movere intendimus contra illustres viros regem Anglie, dominum Edouardum ejus primogenitum, et nobilem virum Eschivardum de Chabanesia (*sic*), militem, bona fide prosequemur, dicti domini et regis expensis, usque ad finem, secundum quod dicto regi Navarre et nobis expedire videbitur et ipsius negotii natura requiret' (Arch. Nat. KK 1065, fol. 250; cf. Blaauw, *Barons' War*, p. 362). In reality Esquivat went back to his county and lived a troublous existence there till his death (1283). As he left no direct descendants, his inheritance was disputed by the king of England in virtue of the act of November 1253, by Joan of Navarre, queen of France, and by the collaterals of Jourdain de Chabanais. For the whole of this suit see the works of Marca, Davezac, Merlet, and Rocher, already cited.

VII

THE ROYALIST REACTION AND THE 'AWARD OF AMIENS'

WE now arrive at a turning-point in the biography of the earl of Leicester, and, by a more distant extension, in the history of English institutions. This is the definite rupture between the king and the earl, the formation of an opposition party resolved to impose upon the king, even by force, respect for the pledge given by him to observe the reforms of 1258–9. Until the end of 1259 it is difficult to characterize with any clarity the feelings which the brothers-in-law entertained towards each other. Minor storms and reconciliations, these are indeed apparent; but from the beginning of 1260 their more or less latent animosity changed to manifest hostility. Why was this? It is possible that the five months that Henry III passed in the intimacy of the French court [1] may have exercised a decisive influence on his impulsive and capricious nature: that his indignation against Simon grew as he came to think of him as the leader of the forces of disturbance, as the persecutor of the Poitevins; that he now viewed in a more unfavourable light the measures dictated at Oxford and at Westminster to limit the exercise of the royal power. The problem must be stated, if we are to realize the gravity of a situation that ended in civil war.

The periodical assembling of parliament was one of the most efficacious guarantees of support obtained by the barons. The king had solemnly promised to convene it thrice a year; at Candlemas, in June, and in October. Now in February 1260 he was still in France, detained there by the marriage of his daughter Beatrice to the young count of Brittany, John II, and later by the obsequies of Louis IX's eldest son.[2] Should the

---

[1] Henry III left for France 'circa festum sancti Martini', 1259 (*Flores Historiarum*, ii. 437), and returned, as will be seen, on 20 April 1260.

[2] *Ibid.*, 441–2. On 26 January 1260, Henry III wrote to his Council from Luzarches saying that he had intended to cross the Channel after Christmas. The king and queen of France had wished to be present at the marriage of Beatrice, which was to take place at Compiègne three weeks after that festival; but on that day (14 or 15 January) had occurred the burial of the

prolonged absence of Henry III prevent parliament from meeting? It was a serious question, on which depended the future of the reforms. If parliament was to remain what it had been before, a feudal council assembled when the king willed, the victory of the barons would be unfruitful; if on the other hand its business was to take complete account of all matters of internal or external policy at certain fixed dates, then it must be able, not only to meet, but also to deliberate in the king's absence. The latter was Simon's opinion, and he gave utterance to it in the proceedings in which several months later he was involved.[1] But the king did not cease to oppose the meeting of parliament which might, he said, in his absence make 'innovations'; and he further added that instead of having parliament meeting, justice could always be administered by Hugh Bigod under the supervision of the Council[2]—a group of twenty now already thinned by defections! But why did Henry III delay his return? The reason, he told his counsellors, was to clear up certain difficult points adjourned by the Treaty of Paris for later solution—for example, the question of the Agenais, the pecuniary value of which remained to be fixed, as well as of the five hundred knights to be sent on crusade with French money.[3] Taking advantage of an absence which threatened to be further protracted, Simon left Paris without taking leave of the king, and, accompanied by his wife whom he had rejoined in Normandy, took ship at Wissant and came straight to London at the head of an armed escort.[4] Other

---

eldest son of the French king, also called Louis, and in consequence the marriage had been postponed till the 22nd and celebrated then at St. Denis. Close, 44, Hen. III, m. 3.

[1] *Simon de Montfort*, p. 351: 'le conte dit que, en la commune porweance, fete par le roi et son Conseil, est porveu que trois parlemanz soient tenuz par an. . . . Et le conte, pour sauver son serment i vint . . .' As the king reproached him for coming 'a chevaus e a armes', which was forbidden by parliamentary police regulations, the earl replied that he had acted 'en la manière qu'il est costumiers d'aler aval le païs.' When charged with the alliances he had made, he replied that he had done nothing 'encontre la foy de roy ne autrement, fors por la commune emprise.'

[2] Letter of 19 February, 1260 in *Royal Letters*, ii. 158.

[3] Letter of 20 January 1260 (Close [in France], 44 Hen. III, m. 3d.).

[4] On St. Scholastica's day (10 February) Simon was at St. Albans, where he passed the night and made the monastery the gift of a valuable silk to adorn the martyr's tomb (*Flor. Hist.*, ii. 443).

members of the Council who were in England came with similar retinues.

At the request of the Justiciar, the barons waited three weeks for the king's return, then decided to enter into session. The earl of Leicester showed—and boasted of it later—great activity on behalf of the 'common undertaking'.[1] Once more the aliens were attacked. The king's relations, the Poitevins, had been expelled in 1258; in 1260 it was the turn of the queen's relatives. Until that time, Peter of Savoy had lived on terms of friendly understanding with Simon. He had sworn to the Provisions, as he represented therein the moderate party; but none the less he was now obliged to leave the Council.[2] His disgrace distressed the queen, who was fond of her uncles. She had several times intervened with the king in favour of Simon: henceforward she was to throw all her influence on to the side of his enemies. The earl understood the position and made preparations for an immediate struggle. He surrounded himself with retainers from overseas, looked for new helpers [3] and succeeded in gaining for a while the support of his nephew Edward, the heir presumptive to the crown.[4] When Henry III demanded a pecuniary aid of the Council, Simon inveighed against those who appeared willing to concede it, and threatened to make the Justiciar, who was one of them, 'give up the money that he was for sending to the king.' [5]

During this time Henry III was in a considerable state of agitation. From St. Omer he announced (1 March 1260) [6] that he had not yet received any reply on the subject of the money equivalent of the 500 knights given him by the Treaty, nor upon that of the value of the Agenais; in consequence he was compelled to continue his already very expensive visit to France.[7]

---

[1] *Simon de Montfort*, p. 351.   [2] *Ibid.*

[3] The king charged him with this. The earl replied (*ibid.*) that he secured no one's help nor 'fist alliances encontre la foy le roy ne autrement fors por la comune emprise'. Here again too subtle a distinction.

[4] Dunstable, pp. 214-15. In this short moment of friendship between Simon and Edward two of Simon's sons were armed knights by the heir to the throne (*Flor. Hist.*, ii. 156). Wykes (p. 124) has reported the rumour that Edward was thinking of deposing his father and ruling in his stead.

[5] *Simon de Montfort*, p. 353.

[6] Close [in France], 44 Hen. III, m. 2d.

[7] On 12 February, from Thérouanne the king informed the exchequer that

A month later he told Richard de Clare, whom he knew to be on bad terms with Simon, that the king and queen of France were reproaching him for remaining absent so long, which was 'great danger and great disgrace' for him, and so he had resolved to return.[1] In the end he had the pleasure of seeing the affair nearest to his heart settled: Louis IX granted him payment of 12,500*l.* (of Tours). 'After God,' he wrote to the French king (18 April), 'you are my salvation.'[2] Then he departed, but only leisurely. On 20 April he told Louis IX that he had arrived at Wissant on the 7th of the month, with his wife and children, and was waiting for a favourable breeze to cross the Channel, taking with him, he said, 'a few knights' and adding, to save his face, that Simon had already transported horsemen and arms by the same route, a manifest proof of his hostility.[3] Finally, on 30 April he arrived at London and occupied the bishop's palace, after having had the gate of the city closed and guarded night and day by armed men. Prince Edward and Simon were lodged outside the walls, and their troops were billeted in the houses built between the city and Westminster.[4]

The news of his arrival aggravated in the highest degree the Council's defiance and Simon's rage. Oblivious of the fact that several weeks earlier he had done the very thing he was complaining of so bitterly now, Simon was anxious to make an example of the foreigners brought over by the king. He took it ill that the king 'se fiast plus en genz estranges que en genz de

---

he had borrowed from the Temple at Paris 1,000 marks to be repaid a month after Easter; on 15 March, from St. Omer, that he had pledged his jewels for 1,200*l.* (of Paris), at a quarterly interest of 60*l.* (*ibid.*).

[1] *Ibid.* At the end of the letter, the king said that he was returning 'ad supportandum vobiscum onus illud, ut alter alterius onera valeat supportare', and he asked Richard as well as Hugh Bigod and Philip Basset for their advice.

[2] *Ibid.*

[3] Rymer, but under the wrong date, 28 April. The 20th is the reading given in the Close Roll [French section]; further, the Chronicle of the Mayors and Sheriffs of London states expressly that the king disembarked two days before St. Mark's Day (23 April) and arrived in London the fifth day of the festival (30 April). In *Flor. Hist.*, ii. 447, we read that the king arrived on the vigil of the Apostles Philip and James, which falls on 1 May.

[4] *Chron. maj. et vic. Lond.*, p. 45; *Flor. Hist.*, ii. 446: 'assumptis ad minus trecentis militibus cum innumeris sequacibus, circa festum Sancti Marci Evangeliste apud Doveram applicuit intrepidus.' The magnates who came to meet him received him 'honorifice cum gaudio'; but to some of them (and to his son) 'nec verba pacis et oscula praebuit, nec ab eis admisit.'

sa terre.'[1] This counsel was not listened to. The king gave a
gracious reception to the earl of Gloucester, but would not see
Simon or Edward.[2] The prince, however, did not persist in his
rebellious attitude, and refusing to appear before the court of
the barons,[3] declared himself ready to abide by the discretion
of the two kings, his father and his uncle. This 'defection' gave
the king courage to resist; in the April parliament he was not
afraid to set forth the motives hindering him from obeying the
Provisions,[4] and had no hesitation in accusing his brother-in-law
before the Council of perjury and *lèse-majesté*.[5] The earl declared that he was ready to hear the complaints of all his accusers except five, whom he did not name.[6] Gloucester and his
friends then moved to adjourn the case till July. The magnates
demanded that an inquest should be made by upright and loyal
(*probes et loyaux*) jurors in the presence of the archbishop of
Canterbury, and the bishops of London, Lincoln, Worcester,
Norwich, and Exeter: the result to be reported to the Council,
whose business it would be to examine the imputations directed
against the king by the earl: if any security had to be taken, the
inquest would be afforced by judges of rank equal to the ac-
cuser's.[7] In this process we only know the complaints set forth
in the king's name and Leicester's replies.[8] It is probable that
the affair merely ended in an interchange of acrid replies, since

[1] *Simon de Montfort*, p. 352.

[2] Dunstable has preserved (p. 215) a characteristic example of a father's love
when he puts into Henry's mouth the words: 'coram me non appareat filius
meus Edwardus, quia, si eum videro, quin ipsum osculer non me cohibebo.'

[3] *Flor. Hist.*, ii. 448: 'dicens omnes alios barones et comites sibi de jure non
esse pares.'

[4] Wykes, p. 125; cf. Jacob, p. 73.

[5] *Flor. Hist.*, ii. 449; Dunstable, p. 215. In a chronicle of Evesham of which
Stapleton has published a fragment (*Rot. magni scaccarii Normanniae*, ii. p.
ccviii), we read that the archbishop of Rouen, Eudes Rigaud, and John
Harcourt helped the earl in these circumstances.

[6] *Flor. Hist.*, ii. 449: 'exceptis quinque tantum inimicis, tam suae quam
Edwardi discordiae seminatoribus.' The detailed charges were numerous, says
the chronicler, but so unbelievable that he refused to copy them in, so as not
to help disseminate falsehood. We know them at greater length than the
chronicler himself, since we have a long list of the king's points of complaint
and the earl's replies. It is printed in *Simon de Montfort*, pp. 339–53.

[7] *Ibid.*

[8] Their contents are analysed in *Simon de Montfort*, pp. 219–327. The most
recent facts to be found there would appear to belong to 1260, after the king's
return to England. It is impossible to date them more closely.

on the following 1 August, Leicester was nominated commander-in-chief of an expedition summoned to fight the Welsh.[1]

If he could do nothing against the man, Henry III was more successful against the ideas he represented. Here again we have the good fortune to know, from direct testimony, the grievances of the king, not indeed against a single leader of the barons, but against the constitution imposed upon him.[2] Although the document in question was written, it seems, in March or April 1261,[3] we may take account of it now because it conveniently gathers up the motives animating the monarchy in its struggle against the aristocracy. What in fact does the king complain of? Of being condemned to powerlessness, of being placed under tutelage.[4] The counsellors, he says, forget that they have taken the oath of fealty to the king at the same time as they did homage.[5] Before all this happened, the props of monarchy were the Common Law, the Exchequer and the offices of the Great Seal of the Chancery,[6] administered by wise and good persons.

---

[1] Rymer, under this date. Cf. *Flor. Hist.*, where it is said that Simon was chosen 'tanquam prudentior bellator Angliae, Anglorum exercitus dux et gubernator' (p. 454). On 13 October 1260, Simon got himself replaced by his nephew, Henry of Germany, in order to carry out the duties of his steward's office, 'a servir pour li a l'avant dite feste [St. Edward], si com il apend au service de la seneschaucie.' The patent delivered him on this occasion was, as an exception, drawn up in French, after being read and approved by Edward, the king's eldest son, Henry of Germany, the earls of Gloucester and Oxford, Hugh Bigod, Justiciar, John Mansel and Robert Walerand (Maxwell-Lyte, *Historical Notes on the Use of the Great Seal of England*, p. 180).

[2] Published by E. F. Jacob in *E. H. R.* xli (1926), 561–71, from a Cottonian MS., Tiberius B. IV. The document is divided into twenty-nine articles; it begins with the heading: 'Cez sount les grevancez dont le Roy se pleynt de son Conseil, que luy devoit avoir conseil (i. e. which ought to give him counsel) al honour de Dieu et de le Roi et au profit de son reaume.' This memorandum was drawn up in French, like the one that figures in the process against the earl in 1260, because it was to be utilized in the discussions of the magnates. Before a court of ordinary justice, it would doubtless have been drawn up in Latin.

[3] See Powicke, *art. cit.*, p. 133.

[4] Art. 4. The king says he cannot tolerate that 'ceux du Conseil' should say: nous volons qe issy soit,' and 'autre resoun ne mettent'. Art. 5. When the king, 'se mit en lour conseil, il se se myt en garde.'

[5] Art. 24: 'Com touz ceux de Conseil eient fet homage au Roy et féauté uré en terrene honour a luy garder . . ., si come eux doivent quant le Roy se obligea a eux.'

[6] Art. 28: 'Le regne ad esté gyé (guided, ruled) avant ces heures par treis choses especialement, c'est a savoir par la ley de la terre [Mr. Jacob rightly adds here the 'Great Seal'] et par l'eschekere;' but the new functionaries are

Now everything is different: the organs of government ar
corrupted; the 'three sovereigns' put at their head are in th
hands of servile officials, who are disciples instead of masters
The king is no longer master of his seal; [1] he is stripped of hi
judicial power. [2] The sheriffs and bailiffs that have been nomi
nated are actually infringing the king's rights and ruining th
country, while their incompetent administration impoverishe
the king. [3] The affairs of Sicily, Wales, and the Agenais hav
been mishandled, and no one knows what may come of them
so too the mutual exchanges prescribed by the peace Treaty
which have been continually retarded. [4] The barons on th
contrary deny that they have put the king under tutelage; the
have never ceased to look upon him as their sovereign. He i
and ought to be listened to and obeyed 'when he speaks well'.
If the counsellors assemble, debate, and discuss the affairs of th
king and the kingdom away from the royal presence, it is t
enable them to deliberate in greater quiet. When the discus
sions are over, they ask the king's assent, as is befitting, bu
they take no action without his orders. They obey their king a
their lord and they have no intention of diminishing his dignit
or his power. [6] Finally, if acts of injustice have been committed
if the nominations to official posts have been unfortunate
inquiries should be made and the wrong remedied, as is onl
right. Here there are the two opposing theses confronting eac

'disciples la au il dussent estre mestres'. The text of this article is in othe
respects very corrupt.
   [1] Art. 9: 'le Roy a nul poer de son seal, mes ceux fount lour volontée saun
le sey (*corr.* seu) le Roy.'
   [2] Art. 10: 'Come touz plaiez somons devant le Roy deyvent et soloien
devant luy estre pledez, et ces pleez soient pledez aillours loyns du Roy, si qu
par défaute de justice [I have made a slight change in the order of the words
nul pleignant droiture puit avoir pres du Roy.' Art. 2: 'droigture est fay
mey[n]s qe ne soleit, et le regne est enpoveri pluis qe avant.'
   [3] 'les droitures du règne deperisont au meyns de malvais bailifs qu
conselerers ount mys. . .'
   [4] Arts. 20–3, and 25.
   [5] Art. 5. They deny 'que lour seigneur soit en nule garde, ne ils ne veu
dreyount pas qil fuist . . ., et dient qil est droit et resoun que, par tut la o
dirra bien, qil soit oïe et entendu cum cil qest seigneur de eux touz.'
   [6] Art. 7: 'ils tretont meynte foith en lieus ou il cuident [MS. cruident] qi
soient pluis en pees et hors de noyse, pur myeus entendre as besoignes le Roy
et puys, quant ils ount tretez, si maundent de Roy son assent et sa volun
come au seignor et a chief, mais il ne fount rien pur [*corr.* contre?] soun dit

ther, and it was impossible to see which would prevail. There ould be no concession nor compromise; the battle was for the leverer or the stronger.

In face of an opposition weakened by internal disagreement, Henry III proved the cleverer or the better served. First he was anxious, as his father had been after Runnymede, to secure from he Pope release from the oath imposed on him by the barons. He solicited and obtained without difficulty from Alexander IV an indult quashing the statutes and ordinances of Oxford and Westminster (29 April 1261); [1] a little afterwards (7 May) [2] the Pope addressed bulls of the same tenor to the queen, the prelates, nobles, and others who had sworn to observe the Provisions. Thus re-established in the fulness of his personal authority, Henry recalled the aliens, pardoned William de Valence and restored to him Hereford Castle (on the Welsh frontier) with its deeds and treasure (30 April); [3] he restored his familiars to the principal offices of his Household and person. [4] Soon he could inform the Pope that he had resumed the castle of Dover from Hugh Bigod's keeping, had secured the City and the Tower of London, and was in peaceful occupation of practically all the other fortresses. Only a few discontented people remained to be dealt with; but 'he soon hoped to reduce them'. [5] When he was

[1] Rymer, dated Rome '3 Cal. Maii'; cf. Potthast, no. 18096, and *Flor. Hist.*, ii. 466.

[2] Rymer, dated Viterbo 'nonas Maii'; cf. Potthast, no. 18098. Alexander died in this town a few days afterwards, 25 May.

[3] *C.P.R. 1258–1266*, 150.

[4] This is the moment when the Justiciar Hugh Despenser, Hugh Bigod's successor, was himself replaced by Philip Basset (Tout, *Chapters*, i. 296, 299); the Great Seal was taken away from master Nicholas, archdeacon of Ely, and entrusted to Walter de Merton, an official of the king's household and a supporter of the king (*ibid.*, p. 299, n. 4 and n. 6). Finally we see Peter de Rivaux back in the king's service again, but in a subordinate position, which he was prevented by death from holding long (*ibid.*, pp. 283, 299). Cf. Wykes, p. 129.

[5] Close [in France], 45 Hen. III, m. 11, schedule. This schedule is attached to the roll in respect of the acts of the end of May; this enables us to date approximately the undated letter of the king to the Pope. This letter begins by disavowing a measure taken by the archbishop of Canterbury, who, after convoking the clergy of his province so as to preach the crusade against the Tartars, had decreed numerous measures 'ad immutationem status nostri, corone et dignitatis nostre, et ad subversionem juris nostri et regni legis, libertatis et consuetudinis, que omnia tam nos quam nostri progenitores hactenus habuimus illibata et illesa.' These measures evidently concerned the

requested to remove several of his intimate counsellors he refused to do so, and barricaded himself with them behind the protecting walls of the Tower.

This new act of defiance provoked an immediate reply. Simon was reconciled to Richard de Clare,[1] and began to hire mercenaries.[2] On 18 July, the barons under the leadership of Walter de Cantilupe, bishop of Worcester, and Simon, supplicated the king of France to appoint arbitrators to whom all the complaints made against them might be submitted.[3] It seems that Louis made no reply to this request, which emanated from a party of whose opinions he could not approve; he contented himself with advising Henry III to enter into negotiations with his opponents. But Henry would not listen, and on 16 August made a clean breach with the reformers and declared that he would no longer stand by and see his authority diminished; that in all time past the selection of his counsellors, the commanders of his castles and of his judges had been one of the prerogatives of his crown; and that he was in consequence fully within his rights in recalling the aliens, admitting them to his counsels and entrusting to his friends the custody of his strongholds. He ended by warning his subjects 'not to listen to the calumnies spread abroad against himself.'[4]

This flagrant violation of the Provisions, this outrage upon public feeling which was setting against the aliens, was boldly countered by three members of the Council elected in 1258: the bishop of Worcester, the earls of Leicester and Gloucester, with the co-operation of other magnates. They summoned three knights from each county south of Trent for the purpose of deliberation.[5] Here was a small revolution that was to make it

rights of the king over the Church. On this point the king could cede nothing even to the queen's uncle; and the barons would not have opposed him.

[1] *Flor. Hist.*, ii. 467.   [2] *C. P. R. 1258–1266*, 185 (18 May 1261)
[3] On 18 July (first letter), the bishop of Worcester, the earls of Leicester, Norfolk, Gloucester, Warenne and Hugh 'dictus Vigod' ask Louis IX to settle their dispute with the king. In a second letter, they ask him to constitute a tribunal of four arbitrators chosen by the two parties, reinforced by Hugh duke of Burgundy and Pierre le Chambrier (Bibl. Nat. Clairembault 1188, fo 20). See in Rymer, under 20 July, three letters of Henry III to Louis IX; in one of them he informs him: 'consilii vestri beneplacitis inherentes, nos super facto baronum nostrorum sumus in tractatu cum eisdem.'
[4] *Foedera* (1816) i. 408.
[5] The fact of this assembly, the date of which is not given, is known by th

way silently into the constitution of 1258. On this occasion there is no thought of a parliament composed of the king and his elected councils; the Twelve had already disappeared,[1] and now came a sagacious return to the traditional form of the *curia regis*, only enlarged by the admission of elected representatives. The king cunningly forestalled the danger: turning against the barons the weapons that menaced him, he summoned the knights to assemble, not at St. Albans with the barons, but with him and his faithful servants at Windsor, in order to discuss the terms of an equitable peace. 'They will clearly realise', he said at the end, 'that I seek but one thing, the honour and common profit of the kingdom' (11 September 1261).[2] Did this assembly meet? There is nothing to tell us. We only know that about this time a lively quarrel broke out between the barons and Henry III, whom they accused of desiring to annul the Provisions.[3] Had not this already taken place since the Papal bull? A new change of front on the part of the earl of Gloucester came once more, by throwing confusion among his opponents, to embolden Henry III, who in the end consented (21 November) to submit the Provisions to the examination of six arbiters, three chosen by the king and three others by the barons.[4] Their findings were to be announced before Whitsuntide (28 May 1262). So long a delay would allow much to be settled out of court. In order to put a better appearance on his attitude, the king granted his pardon 'to the earls, barons and others who, in deed, in word, or in assistance given, had done ought against him'; express mention by name was made of the earl Marshal, the earls of Leicester and Warenne, Roger Mortimer and Hugh Despenser (7 December).[5]

But Simon was no longer in England. In indignation at what

royal charter of 11 September, printed in *S. C.*, p. 394. The deputies were to meet at St. Albans on St. Matthew's day (21 September).

[1] Powicke, *art. cit.*, p. 132.   [2] *S. C.*, p. 394.   [3] Oseney, p. 129.
[4] The arbitrators were: for the king, Giles Bridport, bishop of Salisbury, Peter d'Aigueblanche, bishop of Hereford, and John Mansel; for the barons, master Robert Marsh, dean of Lincoln (brother of Adam?), Roger Bigod, and Peter de Montfort. If they could not agree, they had powers to coopt the king of Germany or the king of France (*ibid.*). See in *Royal Letters*, ii. 193, a letter of the king of Germany to his brother Henry III, 23 October 1261.
[5] *C. P. R. 1258–1266*, 195. On 16 December these barons were invited to add their seals to those of the barons who had already accepted the compromise of 21 November (*Royal Letters*, ii. 196).

one chronicler calls the 'apostasy'[1] of Richard de Clare, he had
declared that he would prefer death to perjury, and with the
baronial assent[2] had retired to the continent, saying that he
wished to go to Palestine. On 2 September Henry III told
Louis IX of Simon's departure; the reason, he said, was unknown to him, but 'it was not for nothing'. At the same time
he besought his royal brother-in-law not to believe any reports
that reached him, before he had received direct information
about the real state of things in England.[3]

Having won over to his side one of the leaders of the revolution and compelled the other to go into exile, Henry III drove
his advantages home. Perhaps in alarm lest Simon might employ force and attempt an attack with an army recruited
abroad, he made great defensive preparations:[4] he reorganized
the internal administration by resuming his right to nominate
the sheriffs and other officials;[5] he ordered new eyres to be
undertaken by the justices itinerant, and demanded the presence, as in the past and doubtless under similar penalties, of
archbishops, bishops, abbots, and priors, the earls, barons,
knights, and freeholders, four men and the reeve from each vill
and twelve burgesses from each borough (22 February 1262);[6]

[1] Dunstable, p. 217 'Inter haec, comes Gloverniae quasi apostatavit.'

[2] Wykes, p. 131.

[3] Mrs. Green (*Lives of the Princesses*, ii. 121) says that this letter, preserved
among the Miscellaneous Documents of the Exchequer, is dated 25 September
1261.

[4] The Close Rolls for October and November 1261 are full of orders that
relate to the raising of troops abroad. From Flanders the king first summoned
50 knights, then 27, then the Count of St. Pol with more than 120 knights.
One of them, Thibaut, count of Bar, was to bring as many good crossbowmen as
he could raise. All were to meet in Dover at All Saints' Day, or the morrow of
that festival. From Gascony he summoned Gaston de Béarn with 9 knights
and as many crossbowmen as possible, his Poitevin brothers, each with 9
knights, Gaillard Delsoler, and Bertrand de Ladils, with good crossbowmen.
From Burgundy he sent for Richard de Montbéliard, &c. In England he
summoned 150 barons to meet at London on 29 October, and ordered 36
abbots to send their contingents (Close, 45 Hen. III m. 4, m. 3d.).

[5] See the award pronounced by the king of Germany in Rymer, under
29 January 1262; the barons merely asked that the sheriffs should be nominated by the king on the advice of his Council, and drawn from among the
knights of their counties. Richard decided that the king must not be hampered
in his liberty of choice. From next Michaelmas he was to choose whom he
liked. Cf. Jacob, p. 74.

[6] 'Commune iter justiciariorum regis ad communia placita in comitatibus

he secured from the new Pope, Urban IV, release from his oaths, just as he had from Alexander IV (25 February); [1] finally he threw off the mask, and published in all the counties (2 May 1262) a circular formally annulling the Provisions which, he said, their authors had themselves violated, and which had twice been condemned by the Holy See. He made a solemn promise of equal justice for great and small, and undertook to observe the Great Charter and the Forest Charter.[2]

Thus the royal counter-offensive had attained its end. No other course lay open to the barons but to begin the struggle over again or to submit. They decided on the latter course. Towards Whitsun (28 May) they made peace with the king; [3] at one stroke they renounced the Provisions of Oxford and of Westminster.

This peace marks a halting-point in the troubles of this country. In the last four years there had been a double revolution. In 1258 and 1259 the king, overwhelmed by the flood of reform, had been continually giving way; he had, in fact, been placed in tutelage by the barons. Then, relieved of the useless burden of the Sicilian war and enriched by St. Louis's exaggerated sympathy, he had slowly made his way against the current, and finally dammed it altogether. The opposition was broken.

It could then be seen what a considerable place Simon the exile held in England. He refused to accept the treaty of May,[4] and his refusal left everything in suspense. A third period was now opening: it was to end by the triumph of the earl at the battle of Lewes.

While Simon remained undefeated, Henry III's victory could

supradictis . . .' (Close, 46 Hen. III, m 16d.). At this time the Justiciar was Philip Basset, one of the king's former counsellors. Rymer, 29 January, 1262.

[1] Rymer. On 20 March, the king accredited at the Curia William de Aette (Ayot), knight, to discuss the business of the Crusade from which he had been greatly diverted, 'praesertim cum varia nobis impedimenta paraverint regni nostri turbacio dudum suborta, et nostrorum rebellio subditorum, quos nobis, ut speramus, jam virtus divina reddidit humiliatos' (Close, 46 Hen. III, m. 14d.; cf. *Flor. Hist.*, ii. 475).

[2] Close, 46 Hen. III, m 11d. Prothero attributes to 1261–2 a Latin poem giving expression to the lively emotion aroused when the Provisions were annulled. Wright, who printed it in his *Political Songs* sees in it an allusion to the events of 1264–5.

[3] Oseney and Wykes, p. 130.

[4] Wykes, p. 131.

not be complete. The earl had retired to France,[1] so Henry
followed him.[2] Then in 1262, before the court of Louis IX, he
tried to accomplish what he had vainly attempted before his
own court in 1260; he utilized the interminable suit that was
pending between himself and the earl and countess of Leicester.[3]

[1] We have a charter of his dated Pacy-sur-Eure, 4 January 1262 (Bibl. Nat.
Clairembault 1188, fol. 19).

[2] He crossed over to France 'circa translationem beati Thome martyris'
(7 July). *Flor. Hist.*, ii. 475.

[3] The essentials of this matter I have already indicated above, p. 177 n. 3. I
need only analyse here the relevant deeds of 1260–2. 5 February 1260, Henry III
orders Simon de Montfort to deliver to Hugh Bigod and Philip Basset the
king's letters promising to submit to the decision of three arbiters (Hugh
Bigod, Ph. Basset and Humphrey de Bohun) the claims deposed by the earl
and countess of Leicester 'ratione dotis prefate comitisse in Hybernia et alibi';
he further declares that at his request Louis IX was retaining to the advantage
of the earl and countess 15,000 marks out of the money he was bound to pay
the English king in virtue of the Treaty of Paris. *Royal Letters*, ii. 393.—11
January 1261, Henry submits to the arbitration of Louis IX 'super omnibus
quaestionibus et controversiis inter S. et A. et regem motis'; he has granted
'Ebuloni de Montibus et Willelmo le Latymer' power to confirm by oath in
his name, 'in animam suam', the French king's decisions (*C. P. R. 1258–1266*,
136).—14 March, Henry gives notice that Simon de Montfort, his wife Eleanor
and himself have submitted to the arbitration of the king of France, or, if
he refuses, of the queen and Pierre le Chambellan (*ibid.*, p. 145).—14 March,
the same letter in French. If the queen of France and Pierre refuse the part of
arbiters, matters are to remain where they are. The arbiters have till Michaelmas (29 September) to pronounce sentence; the king of France may, if he
thinks fit, prolong the period till St. Andrew's day (*Royal Letters*, ii. 168). The
text of this deed in the Clairembault MS. is dated 6 March.—27 March, Henry
III confirms the preceding charter. He desires that the verdict be given on
1 July (*Royal Letters*, ii. 171).—5 July, the king announces that in all the
disputes ('exactionibus, quaestionibus et querelis') that have broken out between
him, his brother-in-law and his sister up to the present, he submits to the
arbitration of Philip Basset and of John Mansel (chosen by him), and of Walter,
bishop of Worcester, and Peter de Montfort (chosen by the earl); the two
parties have further agreed to take as mediators the duke of Burgundy and
Pierre le Chambellan (*ibid.*, ii. 175).—20 July, as these have refused, the king
announces that he submits to the arbitration of the queen of France. (Rymer).—
4 January 1262, Pacy-sur-Eure. The earl and countess of Leicester accept this
arbitration, adding that the queen may consult the duke of Burgundy and
Pierre le Chambellan or any other noble person she wishes; they ask her to give
her verdict before St. John Baptist's day (Clairembault 1188 fol. 19). Next
after this deed, we should certainly place another undated one, wherein the
queen announces her acceptance of the rôle of arbiter. Cf. *Lettres de rois et
reines* i. 136 and *Royal Letters*, ii. 173.—22 April, Henry III asks the queen of
France to name place and day when and where he can consult with her on the
disputes between himself and the earl of Leicester (Close, 46 Hen. III, m. 12d.).
—27 April, Henry grants Imbert de Montferrand full powers to prolong the

in an effort to incriminate his brother-in-law.[1] He cited before
the court of France special witnesses of highly inimical temper
against Simon de Montfort, and again disinterred all the grievances he had against him; he spoke of kindnesses he had
showered upon him, of the ingratitude with which he had been
recompensed. He recalled how he had restored a legitimately
confiscated inheritance to a younger son without land or property, and had given him his own sister in marriage. He
reproached him with the unjust severity of his treatment of the
Gascons, the obstacles he had raised against the conclusion of
the Paris Treaty, the disturbances he had fermented in England,
his contempt for the king's authority and even for his own
person. But, just as in 1260, Simon did not let himself be un-
nerved by these recriminations. He replied that Henry III had
done an act of simple justice in restoring the earldom of Leicester to the legitimate heir; Eleanor had been given to him without a dowry; he had been sent into Gascony on a mission to
suppress the revolted province by force of arms; the circumstances had clearly indicated to him a policy of repression, and
he had never overstepped the bounds of legality; he had sworn
to observe and defend the Statutes of Oxford which the king
himself had accepted, and all his actions had been in conformity
with justice.

What are we to think of these charges and of Simon's apolo-
gia ? His whole history is an answer to the question. It is true
that he owed Henry III a debt of gratitude: the king had let him
have the two sources of his fortune, his earldom, and his wife.
This Simon was too ready to forget. If an excuse in his favour
may be sought in the king's fickle and equivocal conduct towards
him, this does not absolve him from the charge of ingratitude.
But if we take an exclusively impersonal and political point of
view, the king does not come out well. To resist all, even

---

date when the queen's decision has to be given (*ibid*). The queen then assigns
the parties the date of Whitsun (12 June) to appear before her in person or by
attorney (*Lettres de rois et reines*, i. 136; cf. *Royal Letters*, ii. 173). Henry III
left London with his wife on 3 July. He arrived about the 8th (Dunstable,
p. 219). He was at Amiens on 22 July, and on 16 August at St. Germain-des-
Prés. (Rymer).

[1] For the proceedings of 1262 see *Simon de Montfort*, App., nos. XXXV–
XXXVII, *Revue historique*, iv. 276. These documents doubtless come from the
Montfort archives.

legitimate, reforms, to revoke all his oaths, even when taken under no constraints, to claim to govern without obligation or restraint, even to the extent of compromising the kingdom by unpopular favouritism and by ruinous ambition: these were the distinguishing traits of Henry III's policy. That policy was indeed founded upon a tradition already more than a century old, yet one which inevitably drove the barons, forty years after the Great Charter, to resistance, and provoked them to aggression. From this point of view right certainly lay on the side of Simon de Montfort.

But St. Louis was not merely being asked to pronounce between two political systems; on this point his opinion was already made up, and he was to demonstrate it on the day when the dispute, clear of all personal considerations, was submitted to him for decision at Amiens. He had also to conciliate two pleaders possibly in sincere desire for agreement, but totally unable to agree. For this reason it is probable that he shrank from the task. It is possible that the serious illness that endangered Henry III's life [1] prevented the debates from following their normal course; or it may be that the claims of the parties were too high for each other to accept. It is at any rate certain that no sentence was pronounced. When Henry III was cured, the negotiations began again; [2] they were not finished when he returned to England (20 December).[3] While his representatives were importuning the French queen,[4] he was continually re-

[1] He fell ill about the time of the Feast of our Lady in September. *Chron. maj. et vic. Lond.*, p. 51. Cf. Rymer, under 30 September.

[2] In a letter of 18 January 1263, Henry III reminded Louis IX of their conversation at Compiègne 'super pace comitis Leicestrie'; *Royal Letters*, ii. 234, cf. *C. P. R. 1258–1266*, 240–1. We know that St. Louis was at Chauni in December 1262; and it is undoubtedly about this time that the interview took place. On 22 January 1263, John de Chishull, archdeacon of London, and Imbert de Montferrand, knight, were nominated Henry III's proctors to treat with Louis IX (*C. P. R. 1258–1266*, 240). These letters were given back to the king and cancelled on Thursday before Palms (12 March), and on the same day John de Chishull and Imbert de Montferrand handed to John Mansel, treasurer of York, a box containing a charter of the French king relating to 15,000 marks which he had promised to pay after the settlement of Henry's dispute with the earl of Leicester (*ibid.*).

[3] Dunstable, p. 219.

[4] See the letter of 15 February 1263, when John de Chishull and Imbert de Montferrand inform Henry III of the result of their manœuvres concerning Simon and Queen Margaret, in *Royal Letters*, ii. 242, and in Rymer. They relate

minding Louis of Simon's dangerous movements.[1] Only resort to arms could solve so complicated a situation.

The English barons however utilized Henry III's long visit to the continent, in which to reorganize their forces. When the weather became favourable for military operations, they took the field. Their first care was to recall Simon, who returned towards the end of April 1263 and immediately resumed the leadership of his party.[2] On 20 May 1263, while a meeting of the Dominican Chapter-General was being held in London, a great number of the barons assembled there also.[3] Among them Simon de Montfort and many others 'murmured' against the king, the queen and Prince Edward, saying 'that they would be perjured, if they did not observe the Provisions of Oxford'; [4] they announced that they would regard as mortal enemies all who declared themselves against the enactments, and revived the alliances which already on a previous occasion had given them victory. In 1260 they had been able to secure the temporary support of Prince Edward: so now in 1263 they succeeded in attaching Henry, the son of the king of Germany, to their party, while Richard of Cornwall at the head of an army attempted to arrange an agreement between them and the royalists. A good number of young lords took up Simon de Montfort's cause; [5] the most important of these recruits was the new earl of Gloucester. Following his father's example (earl Richard had recently died) Gilbert de Clare was at first to be one of the warmest partisans of Simon de Montfort, then later to abandon him and by this abandonment hurl him to

what Louis IX had told them of an interview he had had with the earl of Leicester. Simon recognized the king's good intentions; but he charged certain members of the Council with preventing any sort of peace, and asked the king not to concentrate on anything further for the moment.

[1] See Henry III's letter to St. Louis, 18 January 1263: '. . . praesertim cum idem comes nos et regnum nostrum adeo turbaverit, quod idem regnum diu sustinuit et adhuc sustinet non modicum detrimentum ' (*Royal Letters*, ii. 234).

[2] Dunstable, p. 221; Wykes, p. 133 'comes Leycestrie, accersitus a baronibus, clanculo de Gallia rediit in Angliam'; and *Flor. Hist.*, ii. 431 'Barones, accepto secum comite predicto in ducem . . .' Cf. *Royal Letters*, ii. 242.

[3] Was this coincidence fortuitous or not? It is impossible to say.

[4] Wykes, p. 133. The Annals of Dunstable say (p. 122), evidently wrongly, that this 'Parliament' took place at Oxford. They even make King Richard appear there by the side of Simon de Montfort and Gilbert de Clare.

[5] Dunstable, p. 222.

destruction.[1] Throughout the majority of the towns strong Montfortian parties came into being, the mayoral authority was disregarded and the lower classes declared for the barons.[2] Having reorganized his party, Simon directed it vigorously against the royalists. Bishop Peter d'Aigueblanche of Hereford was captured in his church, thrown into prison, and his goods confiscated: his crime was that he was 'of Burgundian origin'.[3] Then the force marched against Gloucester, which capitulated at the end of four days; the captain of the castle, Mathias de Besille was also an alien;[4] so he was sent to join the bishop of Hereford in jail. Worcester and Salisbury were occupied without resistance; the Island of Ely, one of England's chief fortresses, fell into the conqueror's hands.[5] Simon then descended upon the south. The king of Germany, encamped at Isleworth, tried to check him by negotiations (29–30 June),[6] but failed,

[1] *D. N. B.*, *s.v.* Clare.

[2] Wykes, p. 138 'Per universum regnum Angliae consuetudo detestabilis inolevit quod in omnibus pene civitatibus et burgis fieret conjuratio ribaldorum qui se bachilarios publice reclamabant, et majores urbium et burgorum violentis ausis opprimebant.' On the meaning of the word *bachilarios* see Jacob, pp. 133–7. In London FitzThomas the mayor put himself at the head of a veritable rising of the people, and urged the City democracy to organize themselves into a commune. He took no step without a direct appeal to the people, saying to them 'Is it your pleasure that this be done?' When the citizens replied 'Ya! Ya!' done it was. He scarcely condescended to consult the aldermen or greater burgesses, 'quasi non essent' (*Chron. maj. et vic.* p. 55, cited by Jacob, p. 134). In the margin we read 'qualiter minutus populus habuit dominationem ultra magnates civitatis.' P. 58 'Hoc anno (1263) iterum electus est major Thomas, filius Thome, per populum, aldermannis autem de magnatibus civitatis parum super hoc consultis.' At Oxford the students who had risen in February 1263, had been dispersed by royal command; they return about June 24 'suffulti presidio domini Simonis de Monteforti' (Oseney, p. 140). Mr. Jacob rightly emphasizes the intensity of the social movement in favour of Leicester's action (p. 143).

[3] See the bull of 21 February 1264, in Bliss, i. 411; *Flor. Hist.*, ii. 479–80. The chronicler also speaks (p. 481) of the rough handling given to all who did not speak English (cf. Rishanger, *Chronica*, p. 17, who calls Simon 'baronum capitaneus').

[4] Rishanger, *ibid.* 'Mathiam de Besille, alienigenam, sed profecto strenuum militem et audacem.'

[5] Rishanger, *ibid.* At the same time, Rishanger tells us (p. 18), Henry of Germany 'qui favit parti comitis et baronum' fell into the hands of the royalists.

[6] *Royal Letters*, ii. 247; *Chron. de maj. et vic.*, p. 61. The London populace, led by a constable and a marshal elected by themselves, went out to burn the king of Germany's manor at Isleworth. 'Et hoc fuit initium dolorum.'

and Simon appeared before Dover,[1] where he was able to sever direct communications with the continent. Six weeks were all that he required for this successful expedition.

Henry III, securely entrenched behind the great moat and thick walls of the Tower, had fallen into his usual apathy. It was his wife who was for action. She tried one day to leave the fortress, where she felt herself to be useless, to join her son who was in command at Windsor; but when she attempted to row up the Thames, the citizens of London made a noisy demonstration, abused her, and forced her to return.[2] The king, now at the end of his resources, consented to negotiate. In the name of the barons Leicester stated his terms: Dover and the other occupied castles were to be placed in their hands, the foreign mercenaries expelled, the Statutes of Oxford to be observed.[3] Henry III yielded. About the middle of July Simon came to London,[4] where he received an enthusiastic welcome, and interviewed the king, who promised to commit to arbitrators the task of revising the statutes in the interest of the king and kingdom.[5] Finally, in order to gain general assent for this provisional agreement, Henry III summoned Parliament for 9 September, at St. Paul's in London.[6] This Parliament only lasted two or three days, long enough however to obtain a royal charter confirming the Oxford statutes.[7] The assembly broke

---

[1] Wykes, p. 137 'Castrum Dovoriae quod non immerito clavis dicitur.

[2] Dunstable, p. 224; *Flor. Hist.*, ii. 482; Wykes, p. 136.

[3] Dunstable, p. 224. On 16 June 1263, the king delivered the earl, the countess, and their children, a safe conduct for their persons, goods, and house, to last till the Sunday after St. Peter and St. Paul (1 July) with authority to come and dwell near the court, but without arms.

[4] On 5 July, he was present with other notables at the ceremony of the handing over of the Great Seal to master Nicolas of Ely (*ibid.*, p. 27 ; see above, p. 191 n. 4, and cf. *Flor. Hist.*, ii. 457). On 20 July the army summoned (25 May) by the king to march against the Welsh was sent against the aliens who had invaded the country and were occupying Windsor Castle (Close, 47 Hen. III, m.). Order was given on 22 July to the bailiffs and barons of the Cinque Ports to observe the decisions taken by the king and the barons on the custody of these places (*C. P. R. 1258–1266*, 272). Cf. Rymer, under 22 August.

[5] *Flor. Hist.*, ii. 483.

[6] Dunstable, p. 214; Rishanger, *Chronica*, p. 15; Wykes, p. 137. La Fontenelle de Vaudoré published in *La Revue anglo-française*, i. 403, a very faulty text of an agreement between the barons and Prince Edward, dated 18 August.

[7] Rishanger, p. 15; Dunstable, p. 224. Mr. Jacob mentions the 'Nove con-

up amid quarrels fomented, it seems, by a tactful distribution of *largesse* by king and prince.[1] Simon de Montfort and Gilbert de Clare had already fallen out![2] Next, the king, Simon and many of their partisans travelled to Boulogne, where Louis tried in vain to bring them to a reconciliation. They all returned to England for St. Edward's day.[3] The queen had stayed behind in France to try to influence Louis IX or Alfonse of Poitiers to come and aid Henry III.[4] At one moment there was fear of a French invasion as in 1216;[5] but Alfonse was too shrewd, and his brother the king too honest, to risk such an adventure, and Eleanor, for all the support she gained from her sister Margaret, could only obtain empty promises.

The festivities of St. Edward's-tide were celebrated at London (13 October) with unusual splendour, and attended by many barons, London burgesses and armed 'Welsh'.[6] In such an assembly the king, now encouraged by the energetic behaviour of his eldest son, found numerous allies. The negotiations with

stitutiones regie' of January or February 1263 and another text published the following 12 June 'de mera et libera potestate ipsius domini regis . . . interveniente consilio fidelium.' He has collected from *C. P. R. 1258–1266* a number of pardons granted for non-observance of the Provisions; cf. p. 140. According to the *Chron. maj. et vic. Lond.*, p. 58, the king desired 'ut illi qui debent esse de familia domus sue fuissent per ipsum electi et in officio positi.'

[1] *Flor. Hist.*, ii. 484, marginal note: 'Rex et Edwardus multas baronibus possessiones dederunt, unde et barones dividuntur.' It may be to this London Parliament that a curious passage on *primogeniture* in the *Grandes chroniques de France* (ed. P. Paris, iv. 380) relates. This custom, strictly applied in England, made it obligatory for younger sons to seek their fortune elsewhere; thus a good number repaired to France, where they found life more pleasant. A knight asked Parliament if partition of goods among sons might be authorized, 'as in France.' The king showed himself favourable to this request, and so too, apparently, did Simon. Cf. P. Viollet, *Précis de l'histoire du droit français*, i. 225, and esp. Pollock and Maitland, *H. E. L.*, ii. 272.

[2] *Chron. maj. et vic. Lond.*, p. 59. The annals of Wykes (p. 131) here accuse Simon of pride and 'improbitas'.

[3] Wykes, p. 137. Dunstable, p. 225; Rishanger, p. 15. Cf. Rymer, under 16 August, 15 and 16 September 1263.

[4] See the very curious correspondence of the queen partly published by E. Boutaric, *Saint Louis et Alfonse de Poitiers*, pp. 104–5.

[5] Tewkesbury, p. 179.

[6] Dunstable, p. 225. Were these Welsh lords of the Welsh marches or independent chiefs? Professor Tout (*Wales and the March during the Barons' War*, 1907) lays stress upon the desertion of Simon's cause by the Marcher barons at Prince Edward's instigation in 1263; cf. J. E. Lloyd, *A History of Wales*, ii. 789, and Jacob, *Studies*, p. 222.

Simon over the revision of the statutes were doomed to failure.[1] Edward retired to Windsor with his father and his partisans; then, suddenly taking the offensive, the royalists made a forced march on Dover; they found the place too well guarded to be taken by assault, and returned towards London. Simon anticipated them, and re-entered the city, after some difficulty, with the help of the 'ribaldi';[2] the barons thus retained their position. But now again desertion began to make itself felt in their ranks. For some little while, the young earl of Gloucester had been on bad terms with Simon de Montfort, his own and his father's host. Leicester was accused, not unreasonably, of having profited by recent events to enrich himself. Had he not secured a large part of the booty captured from the Jews of London? Had he not allotted his son part of the lands confiscated after John Mansel's flight?[3] Was he not protecting

[1] According to the Annals of Worcester (p. 449), Simon and the barons demanded insistently 'quod novae provisiones et constitutiones apud Oxoniam edite per regnum Angliae essent divulgatae et in singulis comitatibus recitatae.' That is what took place in 1259 with the king's assent; but in 1263 the king and his supporters indignantly refused, 'unde lamentabilis et miserabilis orta est discordia.'

[2] At this point Rishanger (*Chronica*, p. 22) gives some valuable information, if the text is rightly understood. After the check before Dover, he says, the king returned to Westminster; thence he sent the citizens of London a confidential order to shut their gates on Simon, who was on the other bank of the Thames, at Southwark. The earl ran the risk of being sighted by the royalist army, if the order had been carried out; but he was warned in time by the shouts of the citizens, and with their help succeeded in escaping. An inquiry succeeded in discovering four citizens who had passed on this treasonable information to the earl. On the other hand, the Dunstable chronicle remarks (p. 226) that Simon re-entered the place with the help of the 'ribalds'. A distinction is thus made between 'ribalds' and 'citizens'. The citizens are the dignitaries of the City, treated with such contemptuous and revolutionary scorn by FitzThomas, the people Wykes calls (p. 140) the 'seniores nobis et sapientes', by contrast with the populace, 'innumera multitudo ribaldorum quos bachilarios vocitabant.' The 'ribalds' are the smaller folk, the lower orders exploited by FitzThomas in his mayoral functions. This is fresh evidence of the popularity acquired by Simon among the lower ranks of the population. We must not however see in him either a democrat or a demagogue. The popular party was maintaining the declared enemy of the autocratic régime. Rishanger remarks that the earl 'pietate plenus' was content to exact from the traitors a ransom employed to strengthen the city chains.

[3] In 1267 the king ordered the judges in Essex to make diligent inquiry 'de transgressionibus factis Johanni Maunsel . . . occasione dicte turbacionis' (Jacob, *Studies*, p. 191, n. 2). By this time Mansel was dead (20 January 1265). The author of the *Flores* says of him (p. 481): 'multarum in Anglia rector

certain aliens, while pursuing and despoiling others? Henry of
Germany, son of Richard of Cornwall, was one of the first to
abandon him. He sought out his uncle Simon de Montfort: 'I
can no longer fight against my father, against my uncle, against
all my relations. That is why, sir earl, I shall leave you, if you
will allow me, but I shall never bear arms against you.'—
'Messer Henry,' replied the earl, 'it is not the loss of your arms
which I deplore, but your inconstancy. Go then, return against
me with your arms. I fear them not.' A great number of barons
'blinded by the gifts' made to them, followed the example of
Henry of Germany; and all was once again in the melting-pot.[1]

The barons then tried to repeat their manœuvre of 1261.
While Henry attempted to hoodwink the country over his acts
and his intentions,[2] they sent into every country orders for
raising extraordinary taxes, with the object of equipping four
or five armed men from every township (*villata*).[3] In this they
were acting as sovereigns, substituting their own authority for
the king's; but was it a sign of strength or a mark of exhaus-
tion? Did they count upon popular favour or feel themselves
at the end of their resources? The latter is the more likely
hypothesis. Their recent successes had been entirely negative.
Thus after a double reverse at Dover and in London, Henry III
had been forced to retreat to Oxford; but he had not been

ecclesiarum, seu potius incubator, reddituumque, quorum non erat numerus,
possessor magnificus.' Cf. Tewkesbury, p. 179.

[1] Rishanger, *Chronica*, p. 12. There is a Latin poem on Henry of Germany's
secession, printed by Wright in *Political Songs and Poems*, entitled 'Plange,
plorans Anglia'. Some of the lines run

> Comes S. de Muntford, vir potens et fortis,
> Pugna nunc pro patria, sisque dux cohortis!
> Non te mine terreant, neque timor mortis;
> Rem defende publicam! . . .

As C. L. Kingsford remarked (*Song of Lewes*, p. 7) 'all the surviving poems of
the Barons' War are in favour of the constitutional cause.'

[2] On 8 December 1263 in a letter close addressed to the burgesses and commune of London, he stated that, contrary to the slanderous rumours spread
abroad by his enemies, he had never conceived the idea of calling in aliens, 'ad
subversionem status ejusdem regni nostri et fidelium nostrorum'; he had even
marched to London out of the intention to forbid them entry into the kingdom.
Confident in the loyalty of the burgesses he commanded them immediately to
banish the earl of Leicester and his troops (*Royal Letters*, ii. 250). The letter is
attested by the king of Germany and other members of the council.

[3] *Flor. Hist.*, ii. 485.

beaten. The strength of the two armies was pretty evenly balanced, and they were equally weary. This indecisive position could only end in a compromise. Once more recourse was had to arbitration, that arm of the weak; once more the king of France was urged to pronounce between the barons and their sovereign. Simon and his allies consented (13 December) to promise under oath *bona fide* observance of everything decided by the French king.[1] This was a singularly imprudent undertaking, if made in all sincerity; it was certainly a discreditable one, if the barons, when they gave their word, had the tacit intention of going back upon it in the event of unfavourable circumstances.

The opportunity to gain upon the barons, one which they themselves had given, was too obvious for the king not to utilize. The verdict was due to be pronounced before Whitsun; Henry made immediate preparations to cross over to France. Before starting he issued (20 December) a clever circular,[2] which can be summarized thus: the king is astonished and surprised to hear the rumours current against him: he is accused of wishing to disinherit the barons, of planning to introduce aliens into the country; nothing is more misleading. Extraordinary imposts,

[1] Rymer. The charter of the barons, dated London, 13 December, is reproduced in the *Award of Amiens* of 23 January. It is drawn up in the name of the bishops of London and Worcester, Simon de Montfort, earl of Leicester and Steward, Hugh le Despenser, Justiciar, the earl's two sons, Henry and Simon, &c. The royal charter, dated Windsor, 16 December, is reproduced *ibidem*; it gives the names of Edward, the king's eldest son, Henry of Germany, the earls of Norfolk and Warenne, Hereford and Essex, William de Valence, &c. On 31 December proctorial powers were granted by the barons to Humphrey de Bohun, Henry de Montfort (the earl's son), Peter de Montfort, Adam 'de Novo Mercato' (Newmarket), William Marshal, William Le Blund, and three clerks, to request and approve everything needful to the present business, with special mandate to give the French king full power to explain ambiguities, and clear up any obscurities contained in his award, once or more times, until next All Saints' Day. Witnesses: the bishops of London and Worcester, the Justiciar and Richard de Grey. Box J 630 of the Archives Nationales contains the charters of 16 and 31 December. No. 20 in the same box is an original sealed with twenty-two seals, among them the earl of Leicester's. The charter of 16 December is in *Royal Letters*, ii. 251; cf. *C. P. R. 1258–1266*, 357.

[2] *C. P. R. 1258–1266.* This patent was sent 'per singulos comitatus Anglie', and every sheriff received a mandate 'quod predictas litteras in plenis comitatibus suis, hundredis et singulis bonis villis comitatuum predictorum legi, et firmam pacem regis proclamari et teneri faciat.' On 26 December the king ordered all sheriffs to proclaim in all hundreds and markets the imminent visit of the itinerant judges, who had been unable to come the session before because of disturbances (Close, 48 Hen. III, m 9d.).

to which the king has never consented, have recently been levied to equip a force against the aliens, but what was the need of them? With the help of the barons who had remained in great part loyal to him, he could repel these. No one therefore was to pay these levies, nor to take up arms. The king was resolved to observe the oath he had sworn at Oxford, and to respect the liberty of his subjects.

Could there be any doubt about the expected award? Louis IX's respect for justice was obviously strong enough to keep him from yielding to the tender friendship he felt for Henry III or to the persuasions of the two queens, who for long had been labouring ardently for the triumph of the royal cause. The point at issue however rose high above personal considerations; it raised the question of two forms of government. The English king was vindicating the full exercise of his authority, while the barons in league against him claimed to limit it to their own advantage by law, by an irrevocable statute. Could the grandson of Philip Augustus, the grandfather of Philip the Fair, even conceive of a *régime* when the highest officials would be nominated by a council almost independent of the monarchy? Beside these considerations should be set the influence of the Roman *Curia*, which was openly working in Henry III's interest. The new Pope, Urban IV, had in fact just sent a legate, Guy Foucod or the Fat, to England. This eminent person, later Clement IV, reported on 22 November 1263, that 'dissent reigns in the kingdom of England; prelates have been despoiled and imprisoned; ecclesiastical liberties violated, crimes of all sorts committed.' Another letter (18 November) was addressed to Leicester, considered as being 'at the head of the disturbers'. Consequently the legate received full powers 'to preach the crusade' against the rebels, nobles, and prelates alike, to 'compel, if necessary by ecclesiastical censure, the Friars Preachers and Minors to obey him'.[1] This last sentence deserves careful note. It proves the sympathy for Leicester and his cause felt by the religious orders most closely associated with the people. Respectful servant of the Church, Louis IX could not but

---

[1] *Registres d'Urbain IV*, nos. 581–7, and no. 2838 (undated). Cf. Bliss, *Papal Letters*, i. 396–8 and 410–11. Bliss's inventory contains no less than 52 deeds relating to the legation of Guy in December 1263 and January 1264.

condemn principles founded upon hatred of the foreigner and defiance of the Holy See's warning.

In the famous award given at Amiens on 24 January 1264, Louis IX declared as null the Provisions of Oxford already condemned by two Popes. He decided that the strongholds given over to the barons should be restored to the king; that in future the posts of Justiciar, Chancellor, and Treasurer should go by the sovereign's nomination. The king was to appoint to all offices of counsellor, justice, or sheriff; and lastly, that the aliens could return to England. In a word, all the guarantees obtained by the aristocracy in 1258 and 1259 were swept away; but the privileges, charters, liberties, and statutes anterior to the Provisions were to be maintained in their full integrity.[1]

The triumph of the king was complete. His opponents gained not a single point to their satisfaction. The result of five years of struggling was annihilated. The barons were not merely to lose the status given them by the constitution of 1258, but were to see it assumed by the imported aliens, a class ill-disposed, it was thought and feared with some reason, to use their victory with moderation. It is unnecessary to ask whether this sentence was just; it was, to say the least, unwise, for it placed the barons in the cruel dilemma of having either to endorse their own political abdication or to break their oaths by refusing to carry out the award. There is normally no appeal against an arbitrator's sentence.[2] The loser has only force to resort to. Instead of

---

[1] Rymer, under this date; S. C., p. 395. Cf. Wykes, p. 139. On 21 February 1264 (10 Kal. Mart.) the Pope ordered the archbishop of Canterbury to declare null and void the oath forcibly imposed upon Peter d'Aigueblanche, bishop of Hereford, and to publish the sentence of excommunication uttered against the earl of Leicester, his two sons &c. who had persecuted the bishop. This sentence could be prolonged till full satisfaction was given; otherwise, their lands were to be placed under interdict (Bliss, i, no. 411). Also on 21 February at the request of the archbishop of Canterbury, the Pope ordered the bishop of Paris to publish the sentence of excommunication against all who did violence to the liberties of his church, notably against those bringing into England apostolic letters (Bliss, i, no. 410). It must be remembered that the archbishop was then in flight; on 18 February the Pope had granted him an indulgence, hindered as he was by the disturbance from returning to England (Bliss, no. 410). Reg. d'Urbain IV, nos. 1322, 1358, 1360–1, 1376–8. No. 1454 is noteworthy. On 14 March Urban IV congratulated Louis on re-establishing peace between Henry and his barons (Bibl. Éc. des Chartes, liv, 411).

[2] The barons none the less appealed (Worcester, p. 448).

bringing the troubles of England to an end, the Award of Amiens gave the signal for renewed civil strife.[1]

[1] Right up to the last minute there were more or less sincere attempts at conciliation. On 13 March 1264, the king appointed proctors, 'ad requirendum S. de M. comitem L. et alios barones sibi adherentes, in presentia Johannis de Valent. militis et nuncii regis Francie, super quibusdam articulis et negociis . . .' (Rymer. Cf. *C. P. R. 1258–1266*, 307). It was decided on 18 March that a conference was to take place at Brackley; the king granted a safe-conduct to those partisans of the earl who wished to come and make peace (Rymer; cf. *C. P. R. 1258–1266*, 308). On 20 March the king gave full powers to his delegates to treat with the barons (Rymer). As a guarantee that the 'form' of the peace was 'pourvue en bonefaye', four arbiters were nominated: the archbishop of Rouen and Pierre Le Chambellan on the one side, and the bishop of London and Hugh Despenser on the other; and if a casting vote were needed, the legate might be approached (*C. P. R. 1258–1266*, 347). About the same time a deputation of bishops went to beg the king 'quod saltem unicum et solum remittat articulum, videlicet quod alienigenis ab Anglia remotis, per indigenas gubernetur'; on these terms, the barons would accept the Award of Amiens. The king refused to make the least concession (*Annales Londinienses*, p. 61).

VIII

THE CIVIL WAR. SIMON CONQUERS AT LEWES. HIS PROTECTORATE. HIS DEFEAT AND DEATH AT EVESHAM. THE BREAK-UP OF HIS PARTY

SIMON was not present at the conference of Amiens. When starting out for France from Kenilworth he had fallen from his horse at Catesby and had fractured a bone in his leg.[1] But he had a representative there to learn the French king's reply. He may have thought that the negotiations would be more protracted than they actually were, and have been surprised at the rapidity of the award; but he was always prepared and ready, never letting himself be discouraged by defections from his cause. 'If all leave me,' he said 'I shall remain with my four sons loyal to the true cause which I have sworn to defend for the honour of the Church and the good of the kingdom;' and he repeated with bitterness the reproach of inconstancy that he had already made against Englishmen: 'I have seen many peoples and countries, Christian and pagan, but never yet have I seen a nation so fickle and forsworn as the people of England.'[2] Profiting by Henry III's absence, he took the field (January 1264).[3] His army he divided into three; he sent his eldest son in pursuit of Roger de Mortimer and Roger de Leyburn, who had just abandoned him: his younger son Simon he dispatched to the north. He himself remained in the south, awaiting, in readiness for action, the result of his sons' expeditions. The royalists on their side did not remain inactive. Prince Edward was sent to confront Henry de Montfort; and Henry III, after some fruitless conferences at Brackley, had all upholders of the

[1] Dunstable, p. 227. (Catesby, co. Northampton).

[2] *Chronicon de bellis*, p. 17. This observation recalls to a remarkable degree the judgment related above (p. 172 n. 4) where reference is made to the cowering English. The oath, which the Chronicler alludes to here, may have been taken before the Charter, dated London, 16 December. In this case Simon could not be accused of perjury.

[3] For the military operations, see Sir Charles Oman, *History of the Art of War in the Middle Ages*, 2nd ed., ii. 415; Kingsford, *The Song of Lewes*, pp. 3–5; Ramsay, *Dawn*, pp. 219–24; Salzman, *V. C. H., Sussex*, i. 475 f. See in *Hist. MSS. Com. 5th Report*, p. 454, the analysis of six documents relating to the Barons' War.

Oxford statutes excommunicated,[1] called his vassals to arms,[2] and marched north to meet the younger Simon.

Events falsified Leicester's expectations of his children. Henry de Montfort, who marched in advance of Llewelyn of Wales, suffered a check in front of Worcester, and was unable to force the castle there; after coming within sighting distance of Prince Edward's little army beneath the walls of Gloucester, he made the signal error not merely of granting a truce at his cousin's request, but, worse still, of retiring in peaceful order to Kenilworth castle.[3] Edward turned the concession to immediate advantage; he broke the truce, re-took Gloucester where he made a great number of prisoners, and returned to his father at Oxford, leaving William de Valence[4] to ravage the country. Henry de Montfort thus found himself cut off from his Welsh allies by a victorious army, and reduced to inactivity. His younger brother was more unlucky still. He had just entered Northampton, driving in front of him the robber bands commanded by Roger de Mortimer.[5] The royal army left Oxford on 3 April, and arrived before the town the next evening. It attacked immediately and was repulsed; but on the morning of

[1] See in Rymer the bulls of 16, 17, 21, 23, and 24 March, and *Registres d'Urbain IV*, nos. 768, 770, 776.

[2] The Close Roll mentions the summons to more than 130 barons, to the ecclesiastical contingents and to the militia (6 March); their destination is against the Welsh. On the same day various northern lords were invited to come to the king with the greatest possible speed and with the greatest available number of auxiliaries, 'in negociis regni arduissimis que rex eis exponet.' On 18 March another summons was addressed to about 110 barons: 'cum jam in regno nostro gravissima turbacio sit suborta, ex qua periculum regni et corone (quod absit!) de facili possit imminere . . .' (Close, 48 Hen. III, m. 7 d.). On 20 March knights and freeholders of the counties were called up (*C. P. R. 1258–1266*, 358).

[3] Worcester, p. 448; Dunstable, p. 228, adds that on hearing this news the earl 'multum confusus erubuit et Henricum filium suum super hoc acriter increpavit.'

[4] On 29 February 1264, writing from Longpont, Alfonse of Poitiers directed his seneschals of Poitou and Saintonge not to oppose the passage of William de Valence, knight, and the Earl Warenne to England, Ireland, or Wales, with men at arms and horses. In doing this he was simply carrying out the order recently sent him by his brother, the French king. Bibl. Nat. *Dupuy* 805, fol. 95.

[5] Who had secured the excommunication of all who held for the statutes of Oxford and expelled the clerks from the city, i. e. in all probability the University students. Rishanger, *Chronica*, p. 20. The same chronicle gives a list of the principal chiefs of the royal army. Cf. *Flor. Hist.*, ii. 488.

the 5th, the besieging troops, guided by the prior of St. Andrew, climbed the walls *via* the Priory, and took the place after a violent struggle.[1] In spite of prodigies of valour, the young Simon was captured;[2] on Sunday, 6 April, the castle capitulated and delivered a new contingent of prisoners to the conquerors.[3] The royal army could then proceed to ravage the lands of the earl of Leicester[4] and his friends, and in passing recruit a good number of fighting men, attracted by the successes just won.[5]

Leicester had thought for a moment of rushing to help his younger son, and had moved as far as St. Albans; but he was recalled to London by the news of a conspiracy set in train by certain citizens who wanted to deliver the place over to Prince Edward,[6] and seeing the king further occupied in the north, he marched towards Rochester, whose castle commanded the London–Canterbury and Dover road. A lucky individual

[1] See the plan of this part of Northampton in *Journal of the Brit. Arch. Association*, viii. 67.

[2] Having repelled the enemy, Simon the younger dashed out through the breach in pursuit; but his horse was brought down under him. It was then that he was taken; but Prince Edward prevented his being killed (Wykes, pp. 144–5). One Henry de Isham made recognizance (9 April) that he owed 40 marks for his ransom to the crossbowmen of the king and prince who had taken him 'in insultu facto ibidem per dominum regem et suos magnates' (Close, 48 Hen. III, m. 7 d.).

[3] *Chronicon de bellis*, p. 24; Dunstable, p. 229; Wykes, p. 144. Cf. the extracts from unpublished chronicles given by Halliwell in the notes to his edition of the *Chronicon de bellis*, p. 124. The elder Simon had left London to go to his son's assistance; at St. Albans he learned what had happened. 'This,' he said, 'is an accident of war;' but to Hugh Despenser he spoke differently: 'they are rejoicing too early; before the end of the month they will be in confusion' (*Chronicon de bellis*, p. 24). The prophecy was evidently attributed to him after the event.

[4] The king had no scruples in entering the town of Leicester, thereby setting at nought an ancient custom by which a king had formerly never dared even to come within sight of it (Wykes, p. 146; *Chronicon de bellis*, p. 26).

[5] The details collected by Mr. Jacob (*Studies*, pp. 222–3) are characteristic of these military operations. It was real guerilla warfare, in which priests took part; a chaplain of Hemington was accused 'quod pupplice predicavit de Simone, comite Leicestrie, contra dominum regem' (p. 229, n. 2).

[6] Dunstable, p. 230. In London the people or (if it is preferred) the *plebs* had altogether declared against Henry III by imprisoning the judges of the King's Bench and the barons of the Exchequer. Rishanger (*Chronica*, p. 21) says that the king entered Northampton on 6 April, Passion Sunday, by a breach in the defences ('fracto muro'). Thence Henry marched towards Nottingham, burning on his way the manors of the barons (*ibid.*).

exploit [1] made him master of the town, which was given up to plunder in order to punish the bishop, Laurence of St. Martin, Henry III's former chaplain.[2] The cathedral was desecrated, stripped of its ornaments, and turned into a stable; many of the monks were killed. To crown its misfortunes, the town had to billet and feed the invaders besieging the castle.[3] This diversion brought the king quickly southwards. Fearing to be caught between the royalists of the castle and the relieving force, Simon returned to London (4 May); there he had numerous conversations with his friends the bishops of Winchester and London, clergy and burgesses, with the object of ascertaining whether any agreement with the king was possible.[4] But Henry III had just taken Tunbridge and Winchelsea, and had made peace with the confederation of the Cinque Ports. Meanwhile Queen Eleanor had been concentrating vessels and troops at Damme.[5] The arrival of these reinforcements had to be prevented at all costs. On 6 May Simon left London with several thousand men,[6] and on the 12th encountered the royal army not far from Lewes, the little county town of no great importance save for its abbey and its castle, modest sentinel guarding the valley of the gentle river Ouse.

Before they committed themselves to the hazard of battle, the barons wrote a letter to the king. 'Experience has shown that several of your counsellors have misrepresented our action to you. Know however that we are sincerely desirous to remain loyal to your person; we only intend to fight your enemies, who are also the enemies of the State.' [7] The missive was sealed with the seals of the earls of Leicester and Gloucester. The

---

[1] *Flor. Hist.*, ii. 490. Wykes, p. 146.

[2] *Monasticon Anglicanum*, i. 156.

[3] Dunstable, p. 130; Rishanger, *Chronicon de bellis*, p. 25; *Chron. maj. et vic. Lond.*, p. 62; Halliwell, *loc. cit.*, p. 126. Rishanger (p. 25) loudly extols Simon's military talent: 'vir in omnibus circumspectus . . . exemplum relinquens Anglicis qualiter circa castrorum assultationem agendum sit, qui penitus hujusmodi diebus illis fuerant ignari.'

[4] *Chronicon de bellis*, pp. 20-4.

[5] Wykes, p. 155; Worcester, p. 453; cf. Boutaric, *Saint Louis et Alfonse de Poitiers*, p. 108.

[6] The *Chronicon de bellis* boldly gives the figure at 15,000. The chronicle of Battle (*Simon de Montfort*, p. 376) allows us to trace in some detail the march of the royal army from Winchelsea to Lewes.

[7] *Chronicon de bellis*, p. 27.

r cum mille anni consūma
ti fuerint soluetur sathana⁵
de carcere suo ꝛseducet gentes q̄ sūt
super quatuoꝛ angulos terre. Gog
er magog: ꝛcongregabit eos inpꝛe
lium quorum numerus est sicut a

ꝛos seducet nisi que spiritaliter gog ꝙmagog ue
cantur. Gog namq̄; interpretatur tectum. ꝙ̄agog
deteco. Per gog igitur qui interpretatur tectum
hu designantur qui maliciam suam in corde tegēr
ꝛs. usq̄ ab homimbꝰ uidebuntur cum sintui sint
mente reprobi. Ꝛ̄agog uero quod interpretatur
deteco eos designat. qui deterio cordis sui in ap[er]
tas miserias prorumpentes omnibꝰ semetipos ef[er]
tri demonstrabunt. Tales itaq̄; diabolus ꝑ anti
xp̄m̄ finale deuiper
er cetera. ꝛ cetera.   Ꝛ congregabit e

SATAN GATHERS HIS ARMY

A Canterbury artist's impression of preliminaries to a battle.
Douce Apocalypse, MS. Bodl. 180, fol. 56

counsellors alluded to replied in the king's name: The flame of war kindled throughout the country, the burnings, the acts of pillage directed against the king's servants proved on the contrary that Simon, Gilbert de Clare, and their accomplices were the worst enemies of the crown. And, as if to underline this statement, the king of Germany and Prince Edward the next day (13 May) sent formal challenges to Simon de Montfort and Gilbert de Clare. The bishops of Worcester and London tried to intervene, but they themselves were too deeply implicated in the baronial interest to be listened to.[1]

On the morning of 14 May the two armies were drawn up in battle order.[2] The forces were more or less equal. If the royalists were more numerous, they were also more fatigued; they had been continually harassed by the Welsh archers distributed throughout the irregular country lying between the sea, the Thames, Rochester, and Lewes; and they had suffered greatly from hunger. The baronial force on the other hand had been reconstituted with the help of fresh troops in London, and had arrived in perfect order; and Leicester's clever tactical arrangements did much to give the victory to the fresher army. In the centre, on top of a hill dominating the rest of the plain, Simon planted his standards so as to make the enemy think he was occupying the position with the bulk of his army; in actual fact he placed in reserve[3] there the London militia, on whose steadiness he could scarcely count. His knights he divided into two corps, forming wings whose duty was to fall upon the enemy in the event of his attacking—as was hoped—Simon's centre and driving it back. This is what actually happened. Edward, entrusted with the principal attack, dashed furiously at the unmounted infantry: at the first shock he sent them running, and then, letting his ardour outstrip his discretion, pursued the flying foe too far. Simon seized his chance, and fell unexpectedly on the second line of the royalists, enveloped it, and in a flash

---

[1] *Ibid.*, p. 29; Waverley, p. 357. On the sympathy of the bishop of London for Simon de Montfort's cause, see *Rotuli Ricardi Gravesend*, p. ix.

[2] Several chronicles, that of Battle among them (*Simon de Montfort*, p. 376) relate that Simon and his party prepared for battle by devotions. Before the fight Simon armed Gilbert de Clare knight (*ibid.*).

[3] Sir Charles Oman (*Social England*, ii. 38, and *Art of War*) says that this is the earliest known example of the use of reserves in feudal armies.

took prisoner Henry III, his brother Richard and Henry of
Germany. In the midst of the confusion Edward returned. His
knights seeing the battle lost, abandoned him; in the pursuit
that followed many were cut down and drowned.[1]

The victory, more complete than Simon had ever dared to
hope, allowed him to dictate his terms. Conversations were held
the night following the battle. The king swore to observe the
Great Charter and the Charter of the Forest, as well as the
Provisions of Oxford, which were to be modified at the pronouncement of arbitrators; he had to promise to cut down his
expenses and to be content with the revenue of his domains.
Finally, a full and complete amnesty was accorded to Leicester
and Gloucester. As security for his promise, Henry delivered
up his eldest son as a hostage, who passed into Simon's keeping
on 6 May, and his nephew Henry of Germany, already a
prisoner. They were to be set at liberty as soon as a definitive
peace was concluded, and provided they swore acceptance.[2]
What the chroniclers and a number of official acts call the *Mise
of Lewes* [3] was in fact no more than a provisional agreement.[4]
Thus by an unexpected stroke of fortune, due perhaps to

[1] *Chronicon de bellis*, pp. 32 and 136 (notes); Dunstable, p. 232; Wykes,
p. 150. The king returned Gilbert de Clare his sword, but not to Simon,
'quoniam dominus Simon de Montforti ejus animo displicuit'; the other
prisoners ('quique excellentiores') gave themselves up to him (Waverley,
p. 357). There was a second, and very lively engagement in the town of Lewes,
where Hugh Bigod and the earl of Warenne had taken refuge (*Simon de Montfort*, p. 377). Richard of Cornwall had escaped at the end of the action to a mill
which in the seventeenth century was still called King Harry's Mill (Halliwell,
loc. cit., p. 135). On the number of barons and knights who fought at Lewes,
see *History*, iii (1918), p. 30; on the number of the dead, see *Song of Lewes*, p. 56.
Cf. also the fragment dealing with the battle of Lewes published by J. P. Gilson
in *E. H. R.* 1896 (July). Diagrams of the battle are to be found in the works
cited above by Oman, Ramsay, Salzman, &c.

[2] *Chron. maj. et vic. Lond.*, p. 53; *Chronicon de bellis*, p. 37; *Flor. Hist.*
ii. 496.

[3] One of the charters inaugurating the new régime (Rymer, 'mense Junio')
mentions 'Misa apud Lewes facta'. Cf. Wykes, p. 152: 'statutum quoddam
quod quidam Misam Lewensem inusitato nomine nuncupabant.' Along with
the members of the royal family mentioned by the chroniclers we should doubtless reckon the younger son of Henry III. The Archives of Lord Middleton at
Wollaton Hall contain an order (undated) given by Leicester to the Justiciar
Hugh Despenser to conduct Edmund to a safe place (*Hist. MSS. Comm. 18th
Rep.* 1911, p. 71).

[4] The 'compromissio pacis post bellum' is known to us through the *Chronicon
de bellis*, p. 37.

Simon's tactical ability,[1] the ground lost during the last three years was won back in a few hours by the barons. But the success had to be exploited with haste: on 15 May the king (or more probably the conqueror)[2] ordered the garrisons of castles to abstain henceforth from all offensive action.[3] The prisoners taken at Northampton were given up,[4] and those captured at Lewes conducted under sufficient escort to various strongholds.[5] Simon reserved the more particularly confidential posts for his sons: Henry, the eldest, became governor of Dover and the Cinque Ports,[6] and treasurer of Sandwich; the third, Guy, received the custody of Devon and Cornwall, with the fortresses and revenues of the king of Germany; the lands and castles of the county of Norfolk were handed over to the junior, Simon the Younger.[7] Once master of the south coast, Simon returned with his prisoners (28 May) to London, the day after the agreement putting an official end to hostilities had been publicly proclaimed.[8] On 4 June order was given[9] for the appointment in each county of a guardian or conservator of the peace (*custos pacis*), charged with preventing violence against persons and their property, with the duty of arresting any one bearing arms

[1] Kingsford, *Song of Lewes*, p. 84.

[2] The king being a prisoner, all acts emanating from him (*Teste me ipso*) were imposed upon him by force. Later, mention occurs on the rolls that the acts had been issued 'Rege captivo'.

[3] *C. P. R. 1258–1266*, 318.

[4] Rymer, 17 May and 4 June.

[5] Rymer, 4 June.

[6] The Cinque Ports had taken advantage of the disturbance to renew an old quarrel against their rival Yarmouth (Jacob, *Studies*, p. 236).

[7] Rymer, 28 May. On 30 June, the morrow of SS. Peter and Paul, judgement was pronounced by the earl's son, Henry de Montfort, Hugh Despenser, and Henry de Hastings against William 'de Breuse' (Briouze) on the subject of the losses which this lord and his followers had inflicted upon certain domains of the younger Simon and his men (*Bibl. Nat. MS. Clairembault*, 1188, fol. 25 b).

[8] *Chron. maj. et vic. Lond.*, p. 65.

[9] Rymer. Stubbs (*C. H.* ii.) sees in these 'custodes pacis' the origin of the Justices of the Peace. Cf. C. A. Beard, *The Office of Justice of the Peace*, 1906, p. 20. At the end of the list of keepers reproduced in the *Foedera* appears the name of Henry de Montfort, with the title of sheriff of Kent: this, however, is not the son of the earl of Leicester, for the sheriffs were drawn almost exclusively from the ranks of the lesser nobility, but another person of the same name, who is often mentioned in the *Rotuli finium* after 4 August, 1265, the day on which Simon's eldest son was killed alongside of his father (cf. *Excerpta e rotulis finium*, ii. 446, 489, 585, &c).

without authority,[1] and of pursuing criminals: and orders were given for the election in each county of four deputies drawn from among the most 'lawful and discreet' of the knights. These deputies were to come to London on 22 June or later, to deliberate with the prelates, magnates, and other faithful subjects upon the interests of the kingdom. In this Parliament we can see the elected representatives of the lesser nobility of the shires making their appearance for the second time; but whereas while ten years before they had been convened solely, it seems, to consent to an aid, now in 1264 they are summoned to give their advice on the re-organization of the governmental system.[2] The resolutions made in this assembly, that were compulsory for the king, are of the highest significance.

'For the reform of the kingdom,' we read in the act,[3] three 'discreet and faithful' persons called 'electores', 'nominatores' are to receive from the king the right and the power to select nine councillors [4] to act on their behalf. At least three must be present in rotation at court, and according to the advice of the

[1] On 18 July the king ordered several of his vassals to be at London on 3 August with horses and arms, prepared to repel an invasion of aliens (*Royal Letters*, ii. 259, 269). On 16 July Simon had been authorized to come too, with horses and arms, and in spite of a contrary decision taken by the Council; the reason being that he was bringing hostages and prisoners with him (*C. P. R. 1258–1266*, 337).

[2] It should be observed that the writ of summons was issued at the request of Leicester and Gloucester (*C. P. R. 1258–1266*, 359).

[3] The date is given in the preamble: 'quedam ordinatio facta in parliamento Londoniis habito circa festum Nativitatis beati Johannis Baptiste; cf. Rymer, under 23 June; *C. P. R. 1258–1266*, and *S. C.*, p. 401. The witnesses are the bishops of Lincoln and Ely, the earl of Norfolk, Marshal of England, Robert de Vere, earl of Oxford, Humphrey de Bohun (son of the earl of Hereford and Essex), William de Montchesny and the mayor of London.

[4] Mr. J. P. Gilson has printed in *E. H. R.* xvi. 1901, p. 500, from a volume of miscellanea coming from Ramsey Abbey, a letter which is a sort of confirmation of this ordinance. It is dated 25 June and drawn up in the name of the prelates and the magnates of the kingdom, the clergy and people. They declare themselves ready to ratify the measures taken in the name, and with the assent of the king by Simon de Montfort, Gilbert de Clare, and the bishop of Chichester, bidden by the king to select 'novem de fidelioribus et utilioribus regni . . . de quorum consilio negotia regni sui secundum leges et consuetudines regni sui regere possent.' At the end, Mr. Gilson published a circular addressed by the king (27 July) to all the English bishops and prelates as well as to all faithful Christians; he protests against the depredations committed to the detriment of certain churches by marauding bands (*cursores*); he declares that he will take

Nine the king must dispose matters concerning the custody of castles and all other business, must nominate the Justiciar, Chancellor, Treasurer, and all other officials, major or minor, whose business it is to govern the court and the country. The Three and the Nine shall take an oath to fulfil their duties conscientiously, for the honour of God and the Church, without receiving any other compensation than the meat and drink normally served at table. If an act of embezzlement or any other possible offence of peculation is committed by the councillors or by one of them, the guilty are to be dismissed, and their successors chosen by the king upon the advice of the Three electors. Officials of a subordinate type are to be replaced without delay by the king upon the advice of the Nine. Decisions in the Council shall be valid if taken by a two-thirds majority, provided it include a prelate when ecclesiastical matters are under consideration ; and if a majority cannot be had, the issue is to be settled by the Three. 'All these measures shall be taken by the Council of Nine: and the present ordinance (*ordinatio*) shall remain in force until the agreement (*misa*) drawn up at Lewes is completed or modified by common agreement.'[1] This peace treaty was thus purely provisional, dependent upon the good understanding of the two opposing parties and, in consequence, singularly precarious. In the interim, special measures were decreed: the state of the Church was to be reformed 'as was befitting'. The Three and the Nine, the keepers of castles, and all the royal bailiffs were to be drawn exclusively from persons of English nationality. Aliens were allowed to come, reside, and return without molestation ; so too merchants and traders, on condition that they bore no arms nor brought a baggage train of a suspicious nature, and provided that none of them was employed in any public service, or in the service of

all legal steps to compel them to restore the stolen goods ; and in order to prevent any effort to place a sentence of interdict or excommunication against the country, he declared that he appealed forthwith to Rome, placing himself and his kingdom under the protection of the Holy Trinity and of the holy Apostles Peter and Paul.

[1] The whole passage runs: 'omnia autem predicta faciat dominus rex . . . presenti ordinatione duratura donec Misa apud Lewes facta . . . fuerit conc orditer consummata, vel alia provisa quam partes concorditer duxerint approbandam.' If agreement could not be reached, force would have to be used. Cf. Prothero, p. 287 and Ramsay, *Dawn*, p. 230.

the king's Household. All the ancient privileges granted by the
king were to be confirmed: charters of liberties, statutes recently
promulgated concerning abuses in the administration of justice,
national customs long in vogue. A complete amnesty was to be
accorded by the king and his son. The civil war had caused
grave injury to churchmen and church property: bishops had
been driven from their sees and forced into exile, property
pillaged or confiscated. Provision against these disorders was
made by a proclamation, the result of consultations in the
October parliament.[1] By the common assent of the king, prelates, earls, and barons, three bishops were to be appointed with
power 'd'establir des amendes résonnables pour les forfez qu'ont
esté feit contre seint Iglise'; to 'porvaier les choses qi besoin-
gnables (*necessary*) sont a plein reformement de l'estat de seinte
Iglise, a l'oneur Dieu e a la foi nostre seignor le roi e au profit du
reaume'; the recalcitrants were to be punished 'par sentence
de sainte Iglise', and if necessary 'par laie force'. For this
purpose the Justiciar was to have a hundred knights or paid
serjeants under his orders 'eluz a destreindre les meffesseurs'.
Benefices possessed by aliens or others 'qi ont esté contre
la terre' were to be confiscated, and 'sauvement gardez par
les mains des prelaz'. The present provision was to last for
one year or two, until a peaceful settlement had been reached
(29 October 1264).[2]

Such were the arrangements made by the victors of Lewes:
executive power placed in baronial hands, aliens expelled from
the government, satisfaction granted to the Church, which preserves its property and its independence in regard to Rome.
This is Simon de Montfort's own achievement. If it is desired to
form some idea of this 'governance of souls and bodies' so

---

[1] *Foedera* (Rec. ed. 1816) under 29 October 1264. Cf. *Simon de Montfort*,
p. 355.

[2] Wykes (p. 154) adds a very interesting comment: the prelates promulgated
statutes 'in elusionem potestatis apostolicae, quod eis processu temporis non
mediocriter cessit in damnum'. Here is a discreet allusion to difficulties constantly recurring between the English Church and Rome through the intervention of the Papacy in nominations to benefices and in the contributions imposed by the Holy See. Robert Grosseteste's protest at the Council of Lyons in
1245 had given characteristic expression to this latent hostility. We shall notice
below the reprisals carried out by the Papacy against the prelates favourable
to the reforming cause.

frequently discussed with Adam Marsh and Robert Grosseteste, it is here that it must be looked for, granting always the modifications which practical necessity makes, by way of addition or diminution, in the form of the idea as originally conceived.[1]

The constitution as reformed in 1264 was an extensive modification of the 1258–9 type. The committee of the Twenty-four was replaced by a Triumvirate. The royal Council counted no more than nine members chosen by the Triumvirate; but it was the Nine, like the earlier Fifteen, that governed. There is no mention of parliament; but as the decisions taken at Oxford and Westminster were confirmed, it was due to be summoned in accordance with the forms there decreed. Satisfied at having secured its regular assembly, the barons made no change in its composition. The principle of representation, which was regularly applied in synods of the secular clergy and of certain monastic orders, as it always had been in County Courts, only made a timid appearance in 1264. On the other hand the Provisions of Oxford had, in a certain sense, restrained the action of parliament by giving the Fifteen power to advise the king 'de totes choses ke al rei u al reaume pertenent'. At bottom, the government was always carried on by the king and his Council;

---

[1] This is indicated in a long Latin poem published in the *Political Songs*.— In places we can discover Bracton's idea about law.

> 'Ista lex sic loquitur: "per me regnant reges;
> per me jus ostenditur hiis qui condunt leges . . ."
> Dicitur vulgariter: "ut rex vult, lex vadit;"
> Veritas vult aliter; nam lex stat, rex cadit . . .
> Ergo regi libeat omne quod est bonum,
> Sed malum non audeat . . .
> Qui regem custodiunt ne peccet temptatus
> Ipsi regem serviunt.'

The king must choose his counsellors from among the people of his own country and not among foreigners, who come and supplant the others:

> '. . . Magnatibus incumbit videre
> Que regni conveniant gubernationi,
> Et pacis expediant conservationi.
> . . . Rex indigenas sibi laterales
> Habeat, non advenas, neque speciales
> Vel consiliarios vel regni majores,
> Qui supplantant alios . . .'

Cf. Prothero, pp. 178, 319, 375.

but, as in 1258, a new *personnel* was instituted [1] and should have brought with it a new *ethos*.

The Triumvirate consisted of the bishop of Chichester, the earls of Leicester and Gloucester. The bishop, Stephen de Berksted, was an avowed partisan of Leicester's, so much so that after the earl's death he was excommunicated and reconciled only in 1276.[2] Gilbert de Clare, the ambitious, the doubtfully loyal, was to support his colleague up to the day when he found it in his interest to betray him.[3] Simon in fact held the first place when any decision had to be taken or carried out. While respecting the king's person,[4] he was no doubt anxious to restore his personal hegemony, to his own advantage. The part played by the Council of Nine, elected in June 1264, is not characterized [5] and does not appear with any clarity; for the contemporary, Simon de Montfort is always the dominating figure.

The Triumvirs had an immense task to fulfil. They had to secure the country from all intervention from without, to

[1] The *Foedera* are full of acts relating to the purging of the officials. Cf. *C. P. R. 1258–1266*.

[2] *D. N. B.*, *s.v.* Berksted the variant Bisksted is also given.

[3] *Ibid.*, *s.v.* Clare; cf. Jacob, *passim*. See his Index.

[4] In one of his letters Simon speaks of the battle of Lewes, applying to it the epithet *detestabile*. Dr. Round (*The Antiquary*, January–February 1884) explained the word by comparing it with a phrase used by Fairfax, when he was fighting Charles I: 'this unnatural war.' Simon, like Fairfax, may have felt scruples about making war upon his sovereign. The tradition that recommends respect for the royal person while counsellors alone might be attacked may thus have a distant precedent in 1264.

[5] Nowhere, as far as I know, is there any complete list of the Nine. After an analysis of the names of the witnesses to royal acts from 30 May 1264 to the end of July 1265, I reached the following results: frequently mentioned after June 1264, Leicester, the Justiciar Hugh Despenser, Peter de Montfort, Adam de Newmarket (to whom by name is addressed the writ of 4 June instituting the 'custos pacis' and conveying the summons to Parliament); from the beginning of August, Giles de Argentine, Ralph de Camoys, Henry de Sandwich, bishop of London; from January 1265 only, Roger de St. John. Also named, the earl of Gloucester (twice, on 4 and 5 June, 1264), Walter de Cantilupe, bishop of Worcester, John fitz John (once, 25 August), Henry de Barham (16 September), Thomas de Cantilupe (16 February). There may be fourteen names among which the Nine are to be sought; and it is clear that the majority are those of little known persons. In the *Foedera* the names of witnesses are only to be found from January 1265; in all acts before this, Rymer is capable of giving the false impression that the Council was not organized till after the Great Parliament of 1265.

guarantee its tranquillity within, to give the kingdom a definitive constitution—all this while confronted by a conquered but by no means disarmed enemy, and while relying upon a party which its very victory was destined to divide. By his activity, his energy, Simon proved himself efficient at directing the affairs of a great country and justified the hopes that the devotees of a better *régime* had reposed in him.

The battle of Lewes was less a fight than a violent skirmish ending in disbandment. The fugitives went in two directions: the English lords of the Welsh March retired to their own country, while the aliens and their followers had reached the coast, so as the better to escape, if need arose. Simon set about pursuing both contingents. With no other resources but their own, the principal barons of the March, Roger de Mortimer and Roger de Clifford, entered into conversations with the king and delivered him hostages.[1] In the South, the earl of Warenne, Hugh Bigod, and William de Valence had thrown themselves upon Pevensey; then, leaving a strong garrison there, they had crossed over to France. The young Simon, who was told off to besiege Pevensey, failed lamentably,[2] whilst his father laboured to prevent the enemy from returning with reinforcements, and while his elder brother Henry turned 'wool-merchant', so it was said, by seizing that valuable commodity in the ports and putting it up for sale.[3]

Above all, France needed watching. Even after Lewes queen Eleanor had made no interruption in her warlike preparations. To divert the thunder-clouds that were massing across the Straits, the earl, now in control of Henry III's seal and policy, requested Louis IX to forbid any levy of troops and money in his domains (6 July).[4] He reminded him (2 August) that

[1] 25 August; *C. P. R. 1258–1266*, 344, 366, 367.

[2] On 18 September the king ordered the knights and freeholders to be summoned to come with horses and arms to Pevensey, and to place themselves at the disposal of the young Simon in order to capture the king's enemies, 'qui homicidia, incendia, depredaciones et alia enormia perpetrant' (*ibid.*). On 8 November he ordered payment to Simon of 700 marks 'in partem satisfactionis expensarum quas fecit circa obsidionem castri de Pevensey' (*ibid.*).

[3] Wykes, p. 159 'et sic, detractando militiam, de milite strenuo communi nuncupatione lanarius est effectus.'

[4] *Royal Letters*, ii. 257. In the text the letter is dated 'sexto die Julii' and not 10 July, as Shirley erroneously gives in the margin. Cf. Dunstable, p. 233.

Henry III, as his liege, had passed under his protection, that an incursion of aliens into the kingdom would compromise the safety of the hostages and raise the nation in revolt.[1] Simultaneously he sent out in all quarters directions for the country to hold itself ready to repel the expected invasion; he took special contributions from the towns and the clergy, and in the king's name negotiated a loan to equip a fleet;[2] he forbade the import of cloth and of woollens worked abroad, a measure clearly directed against Flanders, the source of potential armed intervention.[3] So it was not long before news came that queen Eleanor's troops had been detained by contrary winds, and had in consequence been disbanded.[4]

This was probably no more than a respite: but to gain time is valuable for any provisonal government. Simon used it for negotiations. In the Treaty of Lewes it had been argued that the Provisions of Oxford should be submitted to the examination of four arbitrators, two French and two English, the legate being charged to give the casting vote, should need arise.[5] But the mistake made at Amiens was not repeated. In asking once more for arbitration (if not from the French king, at any rate from his best councillors), the barons showed plainly that they regarded the Award of Amiens as null and useless; by accepting the role of arbitrators, the French lords implicitly admitted this claim; and by consenting to reopen negotiations Louis IX set at naught his own verdict. To submit their cause to the king of France once again after Lewes was an act of real cleverness on the part of the English. Henry III, from his point of view, would be better able to stomach his own humiliation if he saw a door opened from the side of France. It was therefore decided

[1] *Royal Letters*, ii. 264. Another letter of 4 August (*ibid.*, p. 268) was addressed to the archbishop of Rheims, the bishops of Noyon and Langres, the duke of Burgundy and the countess of Flanders 'tanquam paribus Francie', to Simon de Nesle, Pierre Le Chambellan, the archbishop of Rouen, the bishops of Évreux and Bayeux, 'tanquam consiliariis domini regis Francie.'

[2] Rymer, under 1 and 3 September; *C. P. R. 1258–1266*, 360.

[3] *C. P. R. 1258–1266*, 345. On 7 September the king gave notice that the clergy had consented to give him tithe of all ecclesiastical revenues, and declared (18 October) that this liberality should not be regarded as a precedent (*ibid.*).

[4] *Chronicon de bellis*, p. 38; Wykes, p. 153; Worcester, p. 453. On Simon's commercial policy, see Schanz, *Englische Handelspolitik*, i. 436.

[5] *C. P. R. 1258–1266*, 347; French text and English translation.

that the English king should take up his position at Dover, and the king of France at Boulogne; daily communication by messengers would then be feasible, and it would be possible to co-operate towards the conclusion of peace.[1] This arrangement was doubly advantageous: the two kings were near enough for the negotiations to be free from serious delays, and far enough off from each other to avoid the effect of personal influence. And now as previously it was fully taken for granted that every kind of alien should be excluded from the government, and the fortresses commanded solely by Englishmen.

We may state at once, so as to avoid later discussion, that the negotiations went dragging on without producing any result.[2] The day before Evesham saw matters little more advanced than the morrow of Lewes, and consequently the constitution (*ordinatio*) of 22 June continued in force. We may well believe that neither side pursued the conversations with great fervour, that the English envoys were more anxious to gain time than to conclude peace. Louis IX was never tired of offering his

---

[1] *Royal Letters*, ii. 258.

[2] The first negotiators were R. de Ver, prior of St. John of Jerusalem, Brother Ambélard, master of the Temple, and Master Richard de Mepham, archdeacon of Oxford (*C. P. R. 1258–1266*, 366). Then Henry of Germany was thought of, and liberated from prison specially for the purpose (*ibid.*, 371). On 11 September full powers were given to the bishop of London, Hugh Despenser the Justiciar, Charles of Anjou, and the abbot of Bec; the archbishop of Rouen was given a casting vote, in case of need. Two days afterwards the bishops of Worcester and Winchester were added to the former (Rymer). On 24 September Henry and Ralph of Sandwich were authorized to swear on the king's soul to the peace of Lewes (*C. P. R. ibid.*, p. 372); the king also asked the legate for a safe-conduct on behalf of Peter de Montfort (Rymer). On 30 October he requested a safe-conduct for his ambassadors (*C. P. R.*, p. 485). Three weeks later he sent his clerk Edward de Knolle, dean of Wells, to France, with commission to stop the alienation of feudal rights and revenues which his wife the queen was proposing to make in Gascony to serve the royal cause (Rymer, under 18 November). On 20 January 1265 another safe-conduct was demanded for the English commissioners (*C. P. R.*, p. 476); Henry granted one, lasting till 19 April, to the French king's envoys (Rymer). On 14 April it was Henry of Germany, accompanied this time by the abbot of Westminster, whom the king sent to France (*C. P. R.*, p. 418). On 17 May the French commissioners were due to arrive in England, to convey whom Henry III sent two galleys (Close, 49 Hen. III, m. 6 d). Henry of Germany was then in France, and Henry III asked Louis IX to take in hand the matter which his nephew was to broach to him (*C. P. R.*, p. 425). A safe-conduct was once more issued to the French envoys on 4 June (*ibid.*, p. 433). Then came the catastrophe of Evesham (Aug. 4).

services: neither he nor his brother Alfonse thought for a moment of direct interference in the internal affairs of England. If the barons had had no other end but an agreement, they could have achieved it in full measure.[1]

There was nothing therefore to fear from the French side now. But with Rome it was different. The Holy See could not view with any favour the victory of a hostile party and a hostile leader. Certainly it could not be unaware that if the barons had risen against the Poitevins and the Provençals, the same passionate feelings animated many members of the clergy. Did not the archbishop of Canterbury belong to one of the suspect families which had just been expelled? The prelates, the bishops, and abbots were doubtless attached to the king by the feudal tie, but had they not more than once shown their spirit of independence when Rome was concerned? Earlier we saw the annalist Wykes mentioning statutes made by the upper clergy with the aim of weakening the papal authority. It was in these circles, as we know, that Simon had found the most convinced of his supporters. And then—a more painful fact still—the victory of the barons had caused the complete breakdown of the affair of Sicily. From 1258 the Pope, unable to secure subsidies from England, had been powerless to resist the victorious Manfred in the kingdom of Naples; in 1264 the sudden stroke of Lewes had delivered into Leicester's hands the king of Germany, whom his brother Henry III had advanced to the imperial throne so as to support the rule of Edmund in Naples and Sicily. From 1263 onwards the onerous subsidies that were exhausting the English treasury had to be sacrificed,[2] and it was necessary once again to find a candidate for the crown: the Holy See had indeed found in Charles of Anjou, St. Louis' brother, the man it was looking for, to replace the young and impecunious Edmund;[3] but the preparations made by the French pretender were far from complete; everything was in

[1] According to Primat, it was Simon's obstinacy which made useless the conversations at Boulogne: 'et quant le roi [Louis IX] vit et considéra qu'il ne le povoit fléchir de son propos, il l'en lessa aler, sans faire rien de celi negoce.'; *Historiens de France*, xxiii. 17.

[2] Potthast, nos. 18579, 18693, 18630, 18635, 19037.

[3] Edmund the Crusader (Crouchback) was born on 16 January 1245 (Ramsay, *Dawn*, p. 302).

CLERESTORY WINDOW IN THE CATHEDRAL OF CHARTRES, HERE CONSIDERED
TO REPRESENT SIMON DE MONTFORT

suspense. Manfred peacefully enjoyed his usurpation, and the Pope could with good reason hold Leicester responsible for such a train of disasters.[1]

With its principles attacked, its interests damaged, the papacy was hostile to the revolution in England. Just as in 1260, when Pope Alexander IV condemned the Provisions of Oxford, now after Lewes Urban IV took a line of resolute opposition to the conquerors. The legate, Guy Foucod, arch-bishop of Narbonne and cardinal-deacon of St. Sabina, was dispatched to Boulogne-sur-Mer;[2] but not wishing to be stopped by the dilatory negotiations in process, he tried to cross immediately to England, bearing with him the Papal com-mands. He was forbidden to enter the country. He ordered the two kings and the princes to be set at liberty (12 August); but no one listened to him. He invited the bishops of London, Worcester, Winchester, and Chichester to come over and confer with him, together with the archbishop of Canterbury and the other bishops and clerks in exile overseas;[3] the barons pre-vented their passage. The legate then excommunicated Simon de Montfort, Gilbert de Clare, Roger Bigod, Hugh Despenser, and their followers. The reason? 'Because they forbade him entry into England; because they detain in prison the kings of England and Germany, and keep two princes as hostages, under the vain pretext of the treaty of Lewes; finally because they refuse to abjure the so-called Provisions of Oxford' (20 Octo-ber).[4] The bishops bearing this bull of excommunication did,

[1] He does this expressly in a bull of 18 November 1263, analysed by Posse, *Analecta vaticana*, no. 310.

[2] See the acts in Urban IV's Registers; cf. Dunstable, p. 234; Wykes, p. 155; *Chronicon de bellis*, p. 38; *Flor. hist.*, ii. 500.

[3] Wykes, p. 156; cf. Rymer, under 11 and 13 September.

[4] *Chronicon de bellis*, p. 41. We may add a certain number of acts of public as well as of personal interest: 4 November 1264, mandate to the bishop of Winchester to pay the younger Simon 700 marks to indemnify him for expenses in the siege of Pevensey (B. M. Add. MSS. 6166).—17 November, mandate to sheriff of Surrey and Sussex not to compel the men of these counties to take up arms for the said siege, since they had already expended much money and borne great fatigue in repelling aliens (Close, 49 Hen. III, m. 12 d).—13 Decem-ber, mandate to the free men and others of the county of Devon, to be intendent to the bailiffs of the earl of Leicester, who has the custody of the lands and revenues belonging to the king of Germany in this county (Rymer).—16 Decem-ber, the keepership of Gloucester castle is given to the young Simon (*C. P. R. 1258–1266*, 394).—18 December, mandate to the bailiffs and 'boni homines' of

however, land in England. They were immediately arrested by the police of the Cinque Ports; their baggage was searched, the bull seized, torn in pieces and thrown into the sea.[1] The bishop of Bath nevertheless dared to proclaim the excommunication; as a punishment, his property was destroyed.[2] In the end the prelates who favoured the reforms assembled at Reading, and appealed to a General Council; a great part of the lower clergy approved of this protest, to which the barons attached their seals, side by side with those of the bishops and abbots.[3] It is plain that a considerable part of the English clergy was involved in the revolution.

As the changes ran their course, more simple and more dangerous grew the situation. There were two hostile factors: abroad, the aliens, the queen, and the Pope: at home, the partisans of the fallen king, like the lords of the Welsh March, the avowed enemies of the barons, powerful and irreconcilable. On the contrary, the reformers had many friends among the knights of the shires, among the lower townsfolk and even the poorer elements of the great towns, among that section of the clergy which had crossed swords with Rome, and among the independent Welsh. For the moment, at all events, the danger from without

Bristol to deliver to Leicester the town and its castle, which prince Edward had given into their keeping (*ibid.*, p. 395).—24 December, order relating to the castles and Honour of Chester, exchanged by prince Edward with Simon for other lands and tenures. The prelates must obey the earl of Leicester and his men, as was the usage in the time of Ranulf of Chester (cf. *Annales Cestrenses*, ed. Christie, pp. 90, 131).—24 December, order to Robert de Ferrers, earl of Derby, to deliver to the earl the castle of the Peak with all its dependencies (*C. P. R.*, p. 397); on the next day the king gave him the castle of Portchester (*ibid.*, p. 398).—4 January 1265, mandate to the bailiffs and 'good men' of Great Yarmouth to obey the earl, who has custody of the territories of John de Balliol (*ibid.*, p. 399). This list amply justifies a marginal comment of the *Flores historiarum* (ii. 504): 'Omnia regni negotia in dispositione Symonis comitis.'

[1] Wykes, p. 157.

[2] *Chronicon de bellis*, p. 39; *Flor. Hist.*, ii. 501. After the death of Urban IV (2 October 1264) the same legate, Guy Foucod or the Fat, just referred to, became Pope (5 February 1265) under the name of Clement IV. On his throne, he continued to be the declared enemy of Leicester: on 27 April 1265 he authorized Henry, father of the king of Navarre, to contract any marriage he desired up to the fourth degree of consanguinity 'exceptis tamen filiabus Simonis c. Leycestrie, et omnium eidem Simoni adherentium.' Bréquigny, *Table des Diplômes*, VI. 448; Potthast, no. 19110.

[3] *Chronicon de bellis*, p. 39.

was not particularly formidable, since the king of France and Alfonse of Poitiers were proffering their good offices to the two parties, but denying any really effective assistance to either, while the threat by sea had dissolved of its own accord. But at home England was far from peaceful: the Marcher lords had taken up arms, and had to be brought to heel immediately.

About the end of November Simon de Montfort gathered a great army at Northampton, and taking the king with him marched towards the insurgents in the west. On 13 December he was at Worcester, and although the bridges of the Severn had been destroyed, he crossed the river, joined his ally Llewellyn, prince of Wales, ravaged the lands of Roger de Mortimer and penetrated as far as Montgomery. The rebels were granted peace only on condition of leaving the district for a year.

Simon's visit to Worcester saw the dispatch of the first writs for the holding of a special parliament to crown the victorious work so well begun at Lewes. In each county the text of the articles decreed the preceding June was first published. Then came the writs of summons (14 and 24 December). The prelates —not all, but only the archbishop of York and twelve bishops, a great number of abbots and priors, five deans of cathedral chapters, the heads of the three great military orders (the master of the Temple, the prior of the Hospitallers, and the prior of the English order of Sempringham)—received in the king's name letters addressed to them individually 'asking' them to come 'because of the fealty and affection' [1] they were bound to display towards him. Five earls: Leicester, Gloucester, Norfolk, Oxford, Derby, the Justiciar Hugh Despenser, twenty tenants-in-chief of the crown (*tenentes in capite*) were also summoned, but in their case the formula invoked the fealty and homage [2] to which they were bound. Thus one or the other of these formulae clearly affirmed the feudal obligation to reply to the suzerain's appeal. Apart from these, in each county the sheriff had 'to cause to come' two of the most loyal, honourable, and discreet knights. The cities and boroughs who now, for the first time in history, were to be represented in parliament, had to

[1] 'In fide et dilectione quibus nobis tenemini.'
[2] 'In fide et homagio.' These formulae persisted throughout the Middle Ages.

send two or four deputies. All had to meet at London on the Octave of St. Hilary (20 January 1265).

'Grave discords', wrote Henry III to the bishop of Durham 'have broken out in our kingdom; to secure the re-establishment of peace and to maintain it, Edward, our dearest eldest son, has been given as a hostage. Now that today, thanks to God, these troubles are abated, we need to take counsel with you, and the other prelates and nobles of the kingdom in order to obtain the freedom of our son, to make peace and tranquillity secure, as the honour of God and the interest of our kingdom demand, and to deliberate upon certain other business; we therefore command you, in the name of the fealty and affection wherein you are bound to us, to be present at London on the said day, without excuse or delay, in such manner as to prove that you value our honour and your own, as well as the peace of the country in general.' [1]

All did not respond to the call. The obligation to be present was undoubtedly a heavy charge upon some, in particular upon the deputies of cities and boroughs regularly accustomed to the ordinary sessions of their shire courts. Others may have been prevented by local circumstances. The king, for example, expressed (23 February 1265) his surprise that the counties of Shropshire and Stafford had not sent in time the two knights summoned by the sheriff; [2] he was anxious that they should be before him on the *quinzaine* of St. Peter's Chair (which is 22 February) 'to confer upon the business of the kingdom and the setting at liberty of prince Edward'; but these two counties bordered upon the Welsh frontier, a particularly troublesome area at the time. At all events many were absent on the day when

---

[1] *S. C.*, p. 403. Rymer. The facsimile of these documents, celebrated among all English historical records, is to be found in *National Manuscripts*, series 1. The bishop of Norwich, who was not named in the Charter of 14 December, nor in that of the 24th, was addressed by letters close, dated Woodstock, 26 December. An assembly of nobles and prelates, says the letter, has been summoned for the Octave of St. Hilary, 'in order to deliberate upon the conditions under which Edward shall be set free and on the means of stabilizing the peace so happily concluded at Lewes' (Close, 49 Hen. III, m. 11 d). See D. Pasquet, *An Essay on the Origin of the House of Commons*, tr. R. G. D. Laffan (1925), pp. 53–6.

[2] Close, 49 Hen. III, m. 9 d. On 16 February the king forbade Simon de Montfort and his sons, Gilbert de Clare &c. to assemble at Dunstable for a tournament; he ordered them to come and discuss with him the setting at liberty of his son (Rymer).

proceedings opened, and the deliberations took place without them, an eventuality foreseen in the Provisions of Oxford. On 14 February, parliament was informed that the king was ready to swear to observe the charters of liberty and the *Ordinatio* of June 1264, and to promise a full and entire amnesty to those who had taken arms against him.[1] Then the elected deputies were free to depart, after a longer stay than they had anticipated;[2] but the nobles pursued the thorny discussion upon the sanctions they desired to obtain. On 10 March, Edward promised to recognize the Ordinance of 1264 and to accept the conditions which, with his father's agreement, were to be laid down for his liberation.[3] Consequently he ceased to be under the custody of his cousin Henry de Montfort and passed accordingly into his father's keeping.[4] Finally on 14 March, in the Chapter House at Westminster, the king renewed his oaths, with the express addition 'that he would never raise any accusation against those he had defied as enemies, that is the earls of Leicester and Gloucester, the citizens of London and the barons of the Cinque Ports'. If he or his son failed to keep their engagements, 'it should be permitted to all members of his kingdom to rise in revolt without running the risk of forfeiture. If on the other hand any other person were to contravene the settlement, his goods and those of his heirs should be confiscated.' These resolutions were to be proclaimed in each county by the agency of special commissioners, the letters patent to be publicly read in open county court,[5] at least twice a year, after Easter and after Michaelmas.[6]

The parliament of January–March 1265, sometimes called the Great Parliament to distinguish it from the Model Parliament of Edward I, is celebrated much less for the importance of

---

[1] *Chron. maj. et vic. Lond.*, p. 71.

[2] Such is the inference from a mandate to the sheriffs to pay the knights of the counties which they represented in Parliament compensation for long absence: 'moram diuturniorem quam credebant' (Close Roll). It is not a question of compensation to the deputies of the towns.

[3] Rymer (Rec. Com. ed. 1816).

[4] Rymer, under 14 March. *S. C.*, p. 464.

[5] 'In pleno comitatu.' For this controversial expression see *E. H. R.* xxxvii. 493, and xxxix. 401. It should be remembered that the word *comitatus* means county tribunal or court as well as the county considered as an administrative unit.

[6] *Statutes of the Realm, Charters of Liberties*, pp. 32–3; *S. C.*, p. 404. Cf. Waverley, p. 358; *Chron. maj. et vic. Lond.*, p. 71.

its decisions than for its composition. For the first time, we need
not hesitate to repeat, representatives of the urban populations
were summoned, and for the second time those of the rural
nobility. It was an innovation pregnant with future consequences, but to contemporary eyes no extraordinary nor far-
reaching event. No one imagined then that a House of
Commons was to arise side by side with what was later called
the House of Lords. The elected deputies of the counties and
boroughs had long been co-operating with the sheriffs in their
administration and with the itinerant justices. But it was without any doubt due to Simon de Montfort's influence that the
representatives of the boroughs were in December 1264 associated with those of the counties, and consequently in later
ages people went so far as to entitle him the Founder of the
House of Commons. Nobody to-day would commit such an
error. Simon thought solely of strengthening the coalition
whose leader he was, and he had met with too much sympathy
in some of the towns not to appeal for their collaboration. For
it was really among his own partisans that he chose, or secured
the choice of, the members of *his* parliament,[1] as it may rightly
be called. It was perfectly natural that, of the two archbishops,
he should only summon (*semondre*) York, Boniface of Canterbury having gone into exile on the continent, whence he did
not return till March, after having accepted the severe terms
obviously dictated by the real master of the government.[2]
Taking the list of prelates, one can find no more than twelve
bishops, nearly half consisting of those who administered the
Anglo-Welsh dioceses. Similarly there is only a bare majority
of earls; five, composed of Simon and his allies. Furthermore
we should note that the writs ordering the borough representation were not addressed in the first instance to the sheriffs, the
natural intermediaries between central and local administration, but directly to the mayors (and doubtless to the mayors
of towns favourable to the barons), as if the loyalty of the
sheriffs, even after the purge following Lewes, was doubtful.

---

[1] Ramsay, *Dawn*, p. 234: 'A parliamentary assembly of the supporters of
the existing government.'

[2] Rymer, dated 'anno Domini 1264, mense Martii', but this Act should be
attributed to 1265; cf. *C. P. R. 1258–1266*, 413.

And finally the great assembly of January–March was in Simon's eyes vested with such an exceptional character, that in the ensuing parliament (June) the prelates and the upper nobility alone were summoned. It was under Edward I and upon his initiative that the institution became more regular and definite: it was then that Leicester's opportunist measure, first adopted and then abandoned, was to become a principle of government. At all events he created the precedent, the regular application of which in the end gave England and the world what is now called the parliamentary system. That should be enough to justify the renown enjoyed in England by the memory of a modest French lord, who became one of the most characteristic types of the English aristocracy and contributed extensively towards the establishment of the principal political institution in his adopted country. Master or, to use a more ambitious expression, protector of the kingdom, his desire was to tie the hands of arbitrary power by imposing on the sovereign a council composed of the greatest ecclesiastical and lay figures. After Evesham the smaller folk, who had placed their hope in him, honoured him as a martyr; yet he was none the less representative of the higher nobility.[1]

A revolution, even a successful revolution, must be built in some way upon the past. Nothing is ever constructed upon a *tabula rasa*. Simon had to make profitable use of his gains, if he was going to dominate both the intransigents among the royalists and also the moderates of his own party. He appointed as Chancellor Thomas de Cantilupe, the nephew of his friend the bishop of Worcester (22 February 1265). He put Ralph of Sandwich in charge of the Wardrobe, and gave him as subordinates two other devoted partisans, Adam de Newmarket and Walter de Crepping, most probably with orders to keep the king under strict surveillance. The privy seal was entrusted to Peter de Montfort and Ralph de Sandwich. They were his own men; but by maintaining the unity of the Wardrobe and the Chancery, Simon continued one of the practices of royal policy most open to criticism.[2]

[1] Blaauw's attempt (*Barons' War*, p. 364 f.) to reconstruct the list of baronial supporters does not inspire confidence.

[2] Tout, *Chapters*, i. 309–12.

As soon as the treaty of peace was concluded (14 March),[1] and the parliament had been dissolved, it became necessary to bring its results to the knowledge of all; it was a needful formality, but one which was carried out only three months later. During this period the situation assumed a more and more disquieting aspect, for relations became more and more strained between Henry and his brother-in-law; back came the aliens to the aid of the royalists, the earl of Gloucester failed him and prince Edward escaped; these were the principal acts of the drama which was to find its culmination in the blood-bath of Evesham.

The existence of any sort of tolerable relationship between Henry III and Simon was an impossibility. The king was maintained in his rank of supremacy, official acts were drawn up in his name ('per regem'); his Household had suffered no changes offensive to his dignity,[2] but he lived in a kind of isolation far away from his wife, who never ceased her labours in France to find him arms and money,[3] and he was separated also from his son, who was now being maintained in prolonged detention, in spite of the terms of the treaty of 14 March.[4] Can the king's heart have been behind the order he issued enjoining respect for the person of the earl of Leicester, now under the

[1] On 5 March, Henry III sent the king of Scotland a copy of the treaty of peace concluded 'with the unanimous consent' of the barons. He asked him to send ambassadors to swear observance to it in his name, 'ne liberatio dicti filii nostri retardetur per defectum alicujus rei que per vos fieri posset in hac parte'; he asked him to arrange that the great Scotch lords 'unanimiter velint et concedant nobis et magnatibus nostris impendere succursum et juvamen, ad tranquillitatem regni nostri et conservationem pacis ejusdem' (Close, 49 Hen. III, m 8 d): words clearly inspired by the barons who had every interest in preventing Scotch intervention. On 10 March the mayor of London and the Aldermen took the oath of fealty to the king at St. Paul's; the Sunday following (15 March) the citizens had to follow suit, all above the age of twelve; but the mayor in front of everybody was bold enough to give the king a warning: 'Domine rex, quamdiu vos volueritis esse nobis bonus rex et dominus, nos erimus vobis fideles et devoti' (*Chron. maj. et vic. Lond.*, p. 73). On the vigil of St. Gregory (11 March) the princes Edward and Henry of Germany were set at liberty 'coram omni populo in magna aula Westmonasterii'; nine bishops excommunicated all violaters of the charters of liberties (*ibid.*, p. 71).

[2] Tout, *Chapters*, i. 300.

[3] Rymer, under 13 and 14 February 1265.

[4] In actual fact Edward merely changed his prison. If we are to believe the *Liber de antiquis legibus*, p. 72, his cousin Henry of Germany went in person to surrender to Henry de Montfort.

menace of his insolent enemies? [1] At all events he lived in fear of the earl, and put all his hope in his continental friends. These friends had not ceased to be active during the winter, and the queen's efforts had borne fruit in the end. Henceforward from March 1265 the aliens began to trickle back. Peter of Savoy was at Pevensey, which the younger Simon had never succeeded in taking: John de Warenne was at Lewes; the refugee Hugh Bigod at Bosham; William de Valence at Pembroke. Summoned on 19 March to appear before the next parliament,[2] they preferred to let fighting settle their cause.

It was a bold challenge; energetic measures were needed to meet it. At the order of Leicester and his sons the men of the Cinque Ports equipped galleys and other vessels, and carried out raids with cruelty and ardour, arresting and pillaging foreign merchants, and drowning the crews.[3] The younger Simon, governor of Portchester, had seizure made of all merchandise landed at Portsmouth and Southampton; shortly afterwards he was put at the head of the military levies of

[1] On 23 February 1265, mandate was sent to John Fitz John to imprison William de la Zouche, who had uttered threats against Simon de Montfort and other barons; he was to be kept in detention until the day that the barons had got satisfaction from him (Close, 49 Hen. III, m 9). Cf. four letters of 11 April, 'de securitate capienda a Roberto Aguilon, inimico Simonis de Monteforti' (Rymer). Cf. *C. P. R. 1258–1266*, 419–20; *Liber de antiquis legibus*, p. xxiv.

[2] Close, 49 Hen. III, m 7.

[3] *Chron. maj. et vic. Lond.*, p. 73.—The Close and Patent Rolls provide a commentary on this passage. 2 March 1265, mandate to the younger Simon, constable of the royal castle of Portchester, to seize the wine, cloth, wax, and spices recently arrived at Southampton and Portsmouth, and keep them safely until all the king's needs had been realized (Close, 49 Hen. III, m. 9).—9 May, mandate to the faithful subjects of the ports of Dover, Winchelsea, Romney, Rye, Hythe, Sandwich, Faversham, Portsmouth, and Southampton, to watch the coast and prevent any band of adventurers coming from the continent from joining John de Warenne and William de Valence at Pembroke; these had left the country without licence and had just re-entered it with four ships and a hundred and twenty men, foot-soldiers and cavalry (*ibid.*, m. 6 d). On 10 May Henry III communicated this order to all sheriffs and commanded them to read in public, and in addition to the charters of liberties, the articles of the peace recently concluded at London (*Royal Letters*, ii. 282). On 20 May he ordered Ralph Bassett of Drayton 'keeper of the peace' and the sheriffs of Shropshire and Staffordshire to proclaim that peace and concord ('pax et unanimitas') reigned between Simon de Montfort and Gilbert de Clare. As Roger de Clifford 'et alii commarchiones', who had been exiled 'juxta provisionem apud Wygore niam nuper factam', had refused to obey, he commanded the sheriff to capture them (Rymer, Rec. Com. ed.).

3463 H h

Surrey and Sussex, and bidden to besiege Pevensey castle for the third time.[1] The king's faithful subjects in the Channel ports were exhorted to watch the coast with the greatest attention (9 May); the countess of Leicester went herself to Dover, with a numerous suite,[2] took command of the place in the absence of her son Henry,[3] and made her contribution towards the defence by cultivating the friendship of the burgesses and buying arms. These preparations obliged the enemy to modify his plan of attack. On 10 May news came that earl William de Valence, accompanied by the earl of Surrey, had disembarked on the extreme south-western end of Wales, at Pembroke which was his own possession.

In Wales Simon was to find a useful ally and a formidable foe. The country of Celtic race, language, and customs had been for several centuries a prey to the acquisitive designs of its Anglo-Saxon and Anglo-Norman neighbours. William the Conqueror had succeeded in establishing himself all along the Severn and the sea-shore, where the nature of the ground placed few obstacles in the way of invasion and the more fertile plains were

---

[1] Oseney, p. 165; Waverley, p. 363.

[2] Information is given about the movements of the earl, the countess of Leicester, and their children from the end of February to the end of July by the household accounts of the countess and Tanner's comment thereon in his introduction. The countess arrived at Odiham on 22 February. On 17 March prince Edward and Henry of Germany, the earl's prisoners, were taken to Wallingford under the guardianship of Henry de Montfort. Leicester was there on 19 March. There must have been a great assembly at the castle, for as many as 334 horses were stabled there. Prince Edward left with Simon on 1 April. The countess departed from Odiham on 1 June, and rejoined her younger son Simon at Portchester, where she remained till the 12th; then travelling via Chichester and Battle, she reached Winchester on the 14th, and Dover the next day. 84 horses were used by her luggage and her suite; her son Simon who accompanied her had an escort of 111 horses.

[3] Three acts of a purely biographical interest may be added here: on 2 March 1265, letter close mentioning the last born of Simon and Eleanor's children: 'Mandatum est Johanni de Eyvill, justiciario forestarum ultra Trentam, quod in forresta de Sirewod (Sherwood Forest, co. Notts.) faciat habere Ricardo de Montforti, filio S. de M., comitis L., decem damas et quinque damos vivos ad quemdam parcum suum instaurandum, de dono regis' (Close, 49 Hen. III, m. 9). On 14 March, Leicester witnesses a charter granted by Henry III to the men of Middlesex (*Monumenta Guildhallae Londoniensis*, ii. 2nd part, 665). The same day the king confirms the grant of four manors made to his nephew Henry de Montfort by his parents, and abandons his claims upon the lands and revenues which Richard Cœur de Lion had sometime given to Baldwin of Béthune (*C. Ch. R.*, ii. 54).

to be found. Along the eastern frontier, defended by rugged mountains and deep valleys, he had stationed a certain number of vassals with the task of organizing and continuing the work of invasion to their own advantage, but at their own risk and responsibility.[1] Some of them succeeded in forming powerful lordships along an extended front and with uncertain boundaries, these constituting the Welsh March. There they ruled as sovereigns. Although subjects of the English king and bound to do feudal service, they administered their domains without the intervention of the central government or its officials. Bigods, Cliffords, Mortimers, Clares had fixed themselves there. To the west of the March the Celtic tribal system persisted in its primitive barbarity. There were frequent wars between the chiefs of independent tribes. One of them, Llewellyn son of Griffith, whose authority extended along the Irish seaboard, had recently with some justification taken the title of prince (1258).[2] He claimed the power of forcing the other chiefs to do homage to him, and was actuated by feelings of nationalism crudely hostile to any domination from without. Henry III had thought fit to confront him with his own son Edward, who received as an appanage the Welsh domains of the crown. Rhuddlan in the north, Montgomery, Carmarthen, and Cardigan in the south provided a powerful barrier against the incursions of this dangerous neighbour. Upon these territories Edward strove to implant English institutions: as in England, the country was divided into hundreds and counties, administered by sheriffs and bailiffs; English law on the subject of justice and police was introduced, and even a capitation tax levied. These innovations, particularly the latter, exasperated the Welsh. Llewellyn had recourse to arms, and in two fortunate campaigns reconquered part of the annexed territories, drove his plundering expedition as far as the earldom of Pembroke (1257) and was only hurled back after severe efforts. It could be foreseen that he might ally himself with Leicester, and this took place for the first time in 1264; during the next year this became a valuable asset to the earl, when his final rupture

[1] See J. E. Lloyd, *A History of Wales, from the earliest time to the Edwardian conquest* (1911) and W. Rees, *South Wales and the March* (1924).
[2] See J. E. Lloyd, *op. cit.*, p. 723.

with Gilbert de Clare put him in a position of cruel embarrassment.

The earl of Gloucester, we saw above, was Simon's colleague from the beginning of the civil war; he had been armed knight by him on the eve of Lewes and had made his contribution to the victory. He had then become a member of the Triumvirate; in the Treaty of 14 March 1265, his name comes immediately after Leicester's. But in his youthful impatience he could not bear playing second string. Doubtless he shared his elder colleague's idea of the necessity of imposing some check on royal despotism; this is clear from the fact that, after joining the king's side before Evesham, he came back again into opposition after Leicester's death; yet, as long as Simon lived, he had no chance of leading the reforming party. Gilbert reproached his rival with keeping the king still a prisoner, and governing the kingdom in lonely state;[1] with maintaining knights from abroad at his beck and call and even entrusting them with the command of important fortresses like Dover, Windsor, and Wallingford.[2] The revolution had been directed against such; was it therefore fitting for Simon himself to keep them in England? And had not Simon reserved to himself the ransom of prisoners which ought to have been divided equally between them? Leicester had done this, had refused to surrender the king of Germany and the other combatants taken by Gilbert at Lewes, prisoners whose ransoms he should have acquired.[3] And then Gilbert was discontented at seeing Simon's sons occupying increasingly important positions in the government, and had taken the course of 'secretly or openly detracting from their glory'.[4] On two occasions, perhaps more, these

[1] Rishanger, *Chronica*, p. 32: 'disponens pro libito suo regnum totum.'

[2] *Chronicon de bellis*, p. 41. On 26 April 1265 (Rymer, under the erroneous date of 16 April; cf. *C. P. R. 1258–1266*, 420), the younger Simon was authorized 'pro securitate pacis in regno assecurande et firmande' to take as a hostage the son of John Fitz Alan in his castle of Arundel. Here was another castle which was to fall into the earl's hands.

[3] Rishanger, *Chronica*, p. 32. Cf. *Chron. maj. et vic. Lond.*, p. 73; *Chronicon de bellis*, p. 41; *Flor. Hist.* iii. 1; Oseney, p. 162. According to the *Annales Londonienses*, p. 65, the conflict between the two earls took place 'occasione Willelmi de Zuzthe (Zouche), quem inter se contendebant habere captivum.'

[4] Waverley, p. 358; Battle (*Simon de Montfort*, p. 378): 'Comes vero Glovernie, videns filios comitis in immensum efferri, invidet, quia nec clam nec palam eorum gloriam detrahere non cessavit.'

young lords all but came to blows, in tournaments held first at Dunstable,[1] then at Northampton.[2] Only with difficulty had Simon succeeded in preventing these dangerous armed encounters, often the prelude to serious military operations. But when he learned that the barons of the Welsh March, now the allies of Gilbert, had penetrated into his lands, he ordered the latter to drive them out. Gilbert refused. Simon thereupon took the field, with the king and prince Edward in his train. Nominally free, they were in fact prisoners. On 11 April he reached Northampton, which Gilbert had evacuated; he crossed the Severn and entered Hereford, where he remained till Whitsun (24 May). An attempt made to heal the quarrel by means of arbitration broke down. Gilbert took up a defensive position and raised troops.[3] War was now inevitable. Gilbert de Clare's change of front was ominous for the campaign that was to open against the royalists. Simon, however, had already taken his precautions. From Hereford he informed the sheriffs (10 May) that he had completed his measures to prevent the aliens who had reached the west coast from joining William de Valence and John de Warenne; he told them to contradict the false rumours current about the expedition directed against the rebels of the Welsh March. The king, he said, had no other designs against the Marchers than to constrain them to carry out the decision taken at Worcester, i. e. that they should go into exile.[4] He

[1] According to the *Chronicon de bellis*, p. 42, Gilbert had the 'proclamation' made for the tournament where he and Henry de Montfort, 'utriusque partis capitanei', were to meet. Simon got the king to forbid the tourney. Gilbert having refused to obey, Simon brought force to bear upon him by mobilizing the militia of London. According to Rishanger's *Chronica*, p. 32, the provocation came from Simon's sons, who were blamed by their father.

[2] Wykes, p. 162: the earl's two sons invited to Northampton 'omnes nobiles regni' on the *quinzaine* of Easter (about 20 April) 'ad ostentationem virium de genere confligendi quod vulgo torneamentum consueverat appellari'. Gloucester did not appear, because he was afraid, so the chronicler assures us; but the writer was hostile to Leicester.

[3] *Chron. maj. et vic. Lond.*, p. 73. The date is given between Easter (5 April) and Whitsuntide (24 May). The point to be settled turned on certain aspects of the Provisions of Oxford and the treaty of Lewes which Simon was accused of not observing; 'quos articulos dictus comes [Gloucester] posuit in scriptis;' but the arbitration 'ad effectum non venit'. According to *Flor. Hist.*, iii., 1, the earl went towards Hereford 'cum rege sibi supplici et acclini, cui necesse fuerat de necessitate facere virtutem'.

[4] *Royal Letters*, ii. 282. On 20 May the king ordered Ralph Basset of Dray-

summoned parliament for 1 June,[1] not, we may remember, an extraordinary assembly as in the previous winter, but one composed solely of the prelates and barons. This parliament, which was due to be held at Winchester, certainly never met, for on 1 June the king was still on the frontier of Wales, waiting for chance to intervene and change his pitiable, paradoxical situation. The son made the effort of which his father the king was incapable. Edward felt humiliation at having to subscribe to the revolutionary projects of Simon, his uncle and godfather. He was then twenty-six years of age, and on more than one occasion he had had reason to complain of him, whether in Gascony or after Lewes. In spite of the treaty of 14 March, he was still kept under supervision at Simon's side. He had only one thought, to escape, to rally the members of the royalist party from their dispersion and to make Leicester pay the price of his victories by force of arms. The prince had in his own service the brother of his friend Gilbert, Thomas de Clare, upon whose loyalty Simon still believed he could count.[2] On Thursday in Whitsun week (28 May), while the king was at Hereford, Edward and Thomas left the town to go hunting; they were accompanied by a large following which probably contained some accomplices. They first pretended to be drawn off well ahead in pursuit of the deer; then when they saw they were at a sufficient distance from their keepers, they made a dash at full speed into the open country. They were vigorously pursued, but at a place

ton, keeper of the peace, and the sheriffs of Shropshire and Staffordshire to publish the news that peace and complete understanding (*unanimitas*) existed between the earls of Leicester and Gloucester; but as Roger de Clifford and his partisans ('alii commarchiones'), who ought to have left the kingdom in pursuance of the convention recently made at Worcester, had neglected to do so in contempt of the king, the sheriffs were bidden to arrest him 'si animos fidelium regis a rege avertere satagerint ad pacem perturbandam' (*Foedera*, Rec. Com. ed., 1816).

  ·S. C., p. 406. On 15 May at Gloucester, the king ordered the dean and chapter of York to send two canons to him at Winchester on 1 June as representatives, with full powers to treat of public business, in conjunction with the prelates and nobles of the kingdom (*ibid.*). This was the formula used in the writs of summons to Parliament sent to the cathedral clergy.

  [2] Wykes, p. 163, calls Thomas de Clare 'adolescens ingenuus tanquam familiaris et cubicularius domini Edwardi'; further on he says that Edward escaped 'cum dicto cubiculario suo et paucis aliis militibus.'

agreed upon fell in with the retainers of Clifford and Mortimer, who were in hiding not far from the town with the object of projecting their flight. Edward crossed the Wye with two knights and four squires, and reached Wigmore. He was free! [1] On the morrow Gilbert joined him at Ludlow; there he made the prince swear to maintain the good charters and customs, to expel the aliens and to admit none but Englishmen to the Council. Herein he showed that if he had separated from Leicester, it was not the earl's principles, but his overpowering ambition that he repudiated.[2]

From this moment fortune that long had wavered came to rest in the royalists' camp. Success brought them a continual increase of numbers.[3] In vain Simon made the king give orders for the pursuit of the fugitives (30 May), or ask the bishops of the Southern province to excommunicate Gilbert de Clare and his adherents (8 June); [4] in vain he set his 'keepers of the peace' upon the rebels.[5] He was soon in a desperate position, for the

[1] Rishanger, *Chronica*, p. 33; *Chronicon de bellis*, p. 43; *Flor. Hist.*, iii. 2; *Chron. maj. et vic. Lond.*, p. 73; Wykes, p. 163. The monk of Battle (*Simon de Montfort*, p. 378) gives another version of the escape: according to him Edward, who had gone out walking from Hereford, found a diversion in trying some good hunters, and then, when he had discovered one that was sufficiently nimble and strong (Edward with his long limbs was above the ordinary in weight), he escaped. Cf. the account given by Henry de Silgrave, ed. Hook, p. 104. The annalist of the *Chron. maj. et vic. Lond.*, is too official a narrator when he writes, p. 73, that Edward 'recessit de Herefordia sine licentia'.

[2] Wykes, p. 165; cf. Jacob, *Studies*, pp. 172–3.

[3] In a private letter addressed to Henry de Mauley by one of his vassals, dated by Shirley between 15 and 18 June 1265, it is said that the earl of Gloucester, prince Edward, and William de Valence were at Gloucester, besieging the castle which was resisting energetically; but the king and Simon arrived with a large force, and the arrival of the younger Simon with his army was expected (*Royal Letters*, ii. 288). This, then, was how the concentration of the royalist armies took place, William de Valence's coming from Pembroke to join the prince and Gilbert de Clare. On Leicester's relations with Llewellyn and with Gilbert de Clare, as well as on the military operations taking place in Wales, see the excellent article by Professor Tout in *Owens College Historical Essays* (Manchester, ed. 1907), 'Wales and the March during the Barons' War', with two maps.

[4] Rymer. The act of 8 June is interesting because it enumerates among the witnesses: 'comitem Leicestrie, Justiciarium, Petrum de Monteforti,' &c. For long it was thought that the title *Justiciarium* applied to Leicester. It is now known that he was never anything but Steward of England, and that the Justiciar then was Hugh Despenser.

[5] Rymer. The order is addressed to the younger Simon, keeper of the peace

enemy, in command of the crossings of the Severn, cut off his line of retreat towards his supporters, who were still holding the southern counties of the kingdom. He first attempted a bold stroke which, had it succeeded, would once more have changed the appearance of things: he proposed to make for Bristol, which was his own and might enable him to resume contact with his friends. So all of a sudden he turned his back on prince Edward, and picked his way into the Welsh districts under the control of his enemies. On his path he destroyed Monmouth.[1] Then with his baggage he crossed hill and valley, marching for Newport, the place where the Usk enters the estuary of the Severn. There he was opposite Bristol, which was sending him vessels of transport; but the convoy was surprised and partly destroyed by three warships belonging to Gloucester. At this moment the enemy which had been looking for him was on the point of entering Newport. Simon escaped under cover of night and crossed the Usk by the bridge at Abergavenny.[2] He got to Glamorgan and joined Llewellyn, who a little while previously had secured from Henry III recognition of his title of prince by promising him homage.[3] But his troops could get no bread, a form of food then unknown to the Welsh,[4] and he returned to Hereford after suffering irreparable losses and severe fatigue. Reinforced by several Welsh contingents he succeeded in crossing the Severn at a point unknown by the enemy,[5] and marched

in the counties of Surrey and Sussex; to Brian de Gouiz, keeper in the counties of Somerset and Dorset; to Hugh Peverel, warden of Dorset.

[1] A patent of Henry III is dated Monmouth, 28 June (*C. P. R. 1258–1266*, 434).

[2] *Flor. Hist.*, iii. 3, and Wykes, pp. 167–71 are the two principal sources. *C. P. R. 1258–1266*, 431 mentions the date 9 June in a letter asking 'quod homines, major et ballivi de Bristoll eis (the earl of Leicester and his partisans) sint auxiliantes, mandatis Edwardi, qui se ad rebelles transtulit, in nullo obtemperantes'; on 9 June the king assured the people of Bristol that he 'conservabit (eos) indempnes de custodia castri Bristoll contra Edwardum filium suum et alios rebelles, dum se erga regem et Simonem de Monteforti, custodem dicti castri, fideliter se habebunt.'

[3] Waverley, p. 363; Battle (*Simon de Montfort*, p. 379). On 12 June at Hereford, the king empowered earl Simon and Roger of St. John, the king's secretary, to treat with Llewellyn; on 22 June he granted Llewellyn his pardon in return for 30,000 marks, recognized his title of prince, and granted him several castles and hundreds, on condition that in the future he fulfilled all his feudal obligations (Rymer).   [4] Wykes, p. 168.

[5] According to Rishanger's *Chronica*, the crossing took place at 'Clive' (p. 35).

to meet his younger son, whom he had recalled from the siege of Pevensey. The young Simon did not carry out the order diligently. He started from Tonbridge on 24 June, but wasted time in taking and pillaging Winchester (16 July).[1] Finally he arrived at Kenilworth on the evening of 31 July. His troops, tired out, went to rest in the houses of the village and the priory, and slept without suspecting that the enemy was near. On the next day (1 August), very early, Edward and Gilbert suddenly fell upon them. In the twinkling of an eye they captured about thirteen bannerets in their beds, and a large quantity of men, horses, and baggage. Simon, who ought to have been on guard, but was probably drunk, was awakened by the noise, and escaped practically naked in a small bark to shut himself up behind the thick walls and flooded moat of the castle.[2] The conquerors returned to Worcester on the Severn, with their prisoners and their booty.

On the next day (3 August) Simon de Montfort reached Evesham, the bridge-head on the Avon. There he learned of the disaster at Kenilworth, while his scouts warned him of a converging movement now being undertaken by the two army corps commanded by Edward and Gilbert. He saw that he was going to be surrounded, and prepared, like a Christian hero,

[1] Some of the dates are given us by Eleanor's household accounts. In a letter of 21 July dated at Winchester the younger Simon acknowledged the receipt of 300 marks from the bishop, and promised to obtain an acquittance from the king in the shortest possible time (B.M. Add. MSS. 6166). Cf. Wykes, p. 171; *Chron. maj. et vic. Lond.*, p. 74. In the pillage of Winchester the mayor's account rolls and tallies were destroyed. On 25 February 1266 the king ordered the barons of the Exchequer 'in recompensationem dampnorum quae dilectus noster Stephanus Fromond, major civitatis nostre Winton', occasione . . . depredacionis facte in eadem civitate per Simonem de Monteforti filium quondam comitis Leycestrie' not to require the mayor to furnish accounts for this period of office (*Exerpta e rolutis finium*, ii. 434).

[2] *Flor. Hist.*, ii. 489, describe the castle 'quod [L.] mirabili structura atque reparatione firmaverat et machinis multis hactenus inauditis apud nos et invisis mirabiliter instauraverat.' See iii. 3, for the account of the surprise. The Annals of Waverley present the facts in a very different light: the young Simon, they relate (p. 363), remained six days at Kenilworth, full of confidence in the number of fighting men whom he was leading. Prince Edward announced his visit. Simon, full of delight, left the place and awaited his guest without taking the accustomed precautions during the night. He was suddenly attacked, defeated, and only escaped with difficulty. This story is contradicted by all the others.

for the final struggle. In the morning, about the third hour (9 a.m.)[1] having heard mass with the king,[2] he left the town. In front of him and about two miles from Evesham, Edward had drawn up his troops,[3] and in such good order that Simon, it was said, could not refrain from remarking how well Edward had profited from his lessons.[4] Gilbert had the task of making a turning movement.[5] The earl had with him no more than a handful of men, tested by two months of difficult soldiering. Bravely with his advance-guard he received the shock of Edward's army that cried as it charged: 'Death to the traitor!'[6] But the Welsh enrolled under his banner broke and scattered, and Gilbert appeared on the scene attacking in the rear. With a little group of his sons, Henry and Guy, the Justiciar, Hugh Despenser, and Peter de Montfort around him, Simon several times pierced the enemy's first line; his horse was killed under him and he continued to fight on foot. In the end, pierced with blows[7] he fell commending his soul to God.[8] His body, which not even his

---

[1] *Flor. Hist.*, iii. 5 n.: 'bellum intulit hora diei tertia, qui vere dies Martis fuit et dici potuit.' The day was in fact Tuesday, the martial day of the Calendar. Rishanger, *Chronica*, p. 35: 'feria ergo tertia, que nonis August occurrit.'

[2] Wykes, p. 172: 'audita missa, modicum pransi.' Cf. Lanercost, p. 76 'audito officio et accepto viatico.'

[3] See the plan of the ground and the position of the forces given in Ramsay *Dawn*, facing p. 242.

[4] *Chronicon de bellis*, p. 45. Gilbert de Clare and his friends had originally ignored the very elements of tactics: 'omnem disciplinam bellicae congregationis ab eo [Simone] susceperant, qui in experientia militari, temporibus illis omnibus anteponendus erat.'

[5] On this point the chroniclers differ, and it is difficult to reconcile their accounts. Wykes says that the royalist army was divided into two corps and that Gilbert, in command of the second, had to sight the enemy by marching in from a flank (p. 172). Oxenedes, who apparently gives rein to his imagination, exhibits (p. 229) the earl refusing to wait for reinforcements before the battle, 'dicens se nusquam fugere, quamvis esset in mortis discrimine.' Then when leaving Evesham, he saw two armies, and asked who was in command of the corps marching towards him. 'It is Edward's army,' came the reply. 'And the other?' 'It is Gloucester's.' 'Yes,' he said, 'the traitor! I see clearly that today I shall die.'

[6] Oseney, p. 170. According to Oxenedes, p. 299, this taunt was hurled at Simon 'qui tam violenter et ignominiose nunquam aliquid verbum locutus est quamvis dicerent ei: Traditor, redde te, non respondit, sed in ultimo spiritu constitutus dixit *Dieu merci* et sic spiritum emisit.'

[7] Rishanger, *Chronica*, p. 47.

[8] Oseney, p. 170. Wykes, p. 175, gives the date of the battle with a great wealth of synchronism: 'gestum est hoc praelium extra oppidum Eveshamia

hair shirt [1] could save from violation, was stripped and hideously mutilated. His head and limbs were hacked off and the trunk thrown to the dogs.[2] The monks of Evesham came after the battle to collect the mournful remains; they covered them with a torn coat, and bearing them upon a portion of an old ladder, laid them in the conventual church. Later they were placed in a decent shroud and interred in a new tomb.[3] But there were complaints: The man who died excommunicate and a traitor to his king did not deserve Christian burial, some said. They succeeded so well that the corpse was exhumed and cast into the common sewer.[4]

The companions of the vanquished leader received no quarter. Henry de Montfort, whom Edward might have been willing to save, fell dead by his father's side; his brother Guy, who was picked up a mass of wounds, was spared. The others were massacred pitilessly. The royalists lost few dead, though some may have perished in the *melée* because they had neglected to wear the sign of their party on their arms.[5] The king was

die martis proxima post festum S. Petri in Vincula, quarto die mensis Augusti, pridie scilicet nonas ejusdem mensis.'

[1] Battle Chronicle (*Simon de Montfort*, p. 379): 'atque sic cilicio proprio quo carnem artius domuerat, ut dictum est, martyrisatur.' Cf. Waverley, p. 365: 'martyrium pro pace terrae et regni reparatione et matris ecclesiae, ut credimus, consummavit gloriosum.'

[2] Wykes, p. 174. Oseney, p. 171: 'caput ejus amputabant, manus, pedes et membra virilia, quod dictu horribile est, abscidebant.' *Annales Londonienses*, p. 69: 'dicta virilia ori ejus imponentes.' *Chron. maj. et vic. Lond.*: 'testiculi sui abscissi fuerunt et appensi ex utraque parte nasi sui et ita missum fuit capud suum uxori domini Rogeri de Mortuomari apud castrum de Wiggemora. Pedes vero et manus sue abscissi fuerunt et missi per diversa loca inimicis suis, ad magnum dedecus ipsius defuncti.' The young Simon, who was bringing help, saw the head pass him, as it was being borne on the end of a long pike to Wigmore (Wykes, p. 175). In his edition of the *Chronicon de bellis* Halliwell collected much evidence of the mutilation.

[3] Oseney, p. 178.

[4] Oseney, p. 178: 'tantum elaborabant quod fuit extumulatum et in loco remotiori projectum; qui quidem locus, nisi paucissimis, usque hodie est occultus et incognitus.' Waverley on the other hand says: 'tumulata sunt corpora Symonis de M. et Henrici, filii sui, et domini Hugonis Dispensatoris, per licentiam domini regis, in ecclesia conventuali de Evesham, ante magnum altare, scilicet ante gradum inferius.' *Chron. maj. et vic. Lond.*, p. 76: 'truncus autem corporis sui datus est sepulture.' Cf. Wykes, p. 175. The Oseney chronicler perhaps did not know of the sort of posthumous reparation probably made a long while afterwards.

[5] *Flor. Hist.*, iii. 5: 'namque omnes hi [the royalists] rubeo signo in brachiis

wounded, doubtless lightly, by a chance arrow; [1] but he had the joy of being delivered by the son of his affection.[2]

ambobus cruce signati, ac caeteri partis adversae omnes cruce alba ante et retro insigniti.'

[1] *Flor. Hist.*, *ibid.*; Rishanger, *Chronica*, p. 35: 'in praesenti bello dominus Rex extitit vulneratus et pene morti vicinus, jaculo in eum ex improviso dijecto.' No other evidence supports this statement on the gravity of the wound.

[2] Wykes, p. 174, says that the king re-entered Evesham 'tubis pro triumpho resonantibus', delivered 'probitate filii quem tenerrime diligebat.' We may add in conclusion that a great storm broke out when the battle was over; most of the chroniclers note the fact, some in terms reminiscent of the gospel story of the death of Christ. Cf. Barth. de Cotton, *Historia Anglicana*, p. 140.

IX

REPRISALS AND RESTORATION OF PERSONAL GOVERNMENT

THE fury with which the royalists glutted their passions on the battle-field heralded the reprisals to be taken against the dead earl's family, friends, and followers.[1] They occurred immediately, and in the early stages were violent and arbitrary. Gilbert de Clare was among the first to wreak vengeance upon the former allies whom he had betrayed.[2] The king annulled at a blow all the measures taken by Simon while he was in control of the royal seal.[3] Finally Parliament, assembled at

[1] The second part of Mr. Jacob's *Studies*, entitled 'Some legal records of 1264–70 relating to the period of disturbance', is of the greatest interest in this connexion. The work is divided into three chapters: 1. 'The territorial settlement after the rebellion'. 2. 'Some characteristics of the rebellion'. 3. 'The support given to Simon de Montfort'. Cf. *C. P. R. 1258–1266*, 436, 441, 444, 457, 467, &c.; and also *Hist. MSS. Comm., Report on MSS. of Lord Middleton* (1911), p. 72.

[2] From 6 August, two days after the battle, Gilbert was ordering his tenants by letter to help his officers in seizing the goods of the defeated party. The inquest made after his father's death shows the importance of the property possessed by the de Clare family and the number of officials who administered it (Jacob, *Studies*, p. 246). Later on Gilbert was to fight against the king together with the Disinherited from their refuge in Ely; but he began by absorbing what he could before taking up the role of his former rival.

[3] Rymer, under 1 October 1265: *C. P. R. 1258–1266*, 459. In the *Foedera* (*Rec. Com. ed*. i. 463), we read: 'Edwardus, filius regis, XXVIII° die mensis Maii e custodum manibus elapsus, summa diligentia contendit ad liberandum patrem suum captivum. Quod factum est quarto die Augusti mensis, in prelio apud Evesham occisis, captis aut fugatis Simone de Monteforti et ceteris rebellibus. Et rex jam sui compos, litteras et concessiones sub sigillo regis, quo, non Rex sed Simon de Monteforti pro suo utebatur arbitrio nullas esse declarat.' It should be noted that these words are not discoverable upon the Patent Roll. They were the comment of the editor of the *Foedera*, who printed them in large type. So too in the case of the heading over the acts printed as following the battle of Lewes, 'rege captivo'. I owe this correction to the kindness of Mr. Stamp, Deputy Keeper of the Public Records. In the *Calendar of County Court . . . Rolls of Chester*, 1259–97, ed. by R. Stewart-Brown (Chetham Society, 1925), an analysis is to be found on pp. 59–60 of a suit brought by the abbot of Basingwerk against the abbot of Chester. The demandant in 1286–7 claimed possession of a manor, with the right of advowson. The tenant recalled that in 49 Hen. III (1264–5) the abbot of Basingwerk had already lost his case as the result of a patent of prince Edward and of a judgement pronounced by the justice Luke de Thaney, to which the abbot replied that at that time the prince was a prisoner at Wallingford and that he had dispatched the letter patent in order to obtain his

Winchester (14 September) decided that seizure was to be made throughout the country of the lands of the 'Rebels'.[1] *Seisitores* were called upon to execute this Draconian sentence, and the government authorized and even encouraged the royalists to despoil their enemies. Their operations were carefully entered upon the rolls that record in cold official language evictions shattering the relations between lords and vassals, frequent grants made to strangers, &c. Even numerous subjects who had remained loyal were victims of iniquitous plundering, and were obliged to come and prove their innocence before the king and council, if they were to obtain restitution of their goods at all.[2] Yet it was some benefit that justice could be appealed to at all, and it has been found possible to conclude, paradoxically enough at first sight, that the tribunals of the crown contributed to the general pacification of the country from the moment that these cases began to be heard at law.[3]

This repressive policy was at first supported by the Holy See, which before as after Lewes made numerous efforts to encourage the king in his struggle against the party of reform, and later, when he had won his liberty, to secure him sovereign power.[4] On 23 August 1263 Urban condemned and annulled the 'alliances, leagues and conspiracies' made by the nobles;[5] on 16 September

liberty, the royal seal being then at the entire disposal of Simon de Montfort; that Luke de Thaney, appointed by the earl, was a rebel and that if he, the abbot of Basingwerk, had obeyed the judgement condemning him, it was against his will.—A charter of Henry III, sealed with the Great Seal and dated Northampton 5 January 1266 enumerates a certain number of lands and possessions confiscated from the partisans of Simon de Montfort and granted to Roger 'de Molis' in recompense for faithful service. Cf. *Report on the Manuscripts of the late Reginald Rawdon Hastings*, i. 279. (Hist. MSS. Commission, 1928).

[1] For the history of this Parliament and for the whole question of the Disinherited see Joseph Hunter, *Rotuli selecti ad res Anglicanas et Hibernicas spectantes* (Rec. Com. 1834). In particular Hunter reproduced the text of an Exchequer roll entitled 'Terre rebellium date fidelibus tempore regis Henrici III in diversis comitatibus Anglie.' Mr. Jacob makes a close analysis of others besides, pp. 153–6.

[2] Jacob, p. 170. Wykes, whose pen has been frequently hostile to Simon de Montfort, blames this vindictive policy (p. 184) in a passage reproduced and commented on by Mr. Jacob, p. 170.　　　　[3] Jacob, p. 155.

[4] The *précis* in Bliss's *Papal Letters* is a first-rate source, but it should be supplemented by the *Registres d'Urbain IV* (ed. École française de Rome) with the text verbatim.

[5] *Reg. Urbain IV*, no. 345: 'Egressus Sathan a facie Domini et mittens ventum validum a regione deserti, regnum Anglie concussit acriter' (Job i. 12, 19).

he sent to Henry's court his chaplain William, archdeacon of Paris, with commission to absolve him from every illicit oath which he might have been compelled to take.[1] Later it was Cardinal Guy, bishop of St. Sabina, whom he appointed legate with full powers of bringing ecclesiastical censure to bear upon all prelates, clerks, barons, and others who contributed to the prolongation of the civil war (November–December 1264).[2] On 16 March 1264 he gave approval and confirmation to the Award of Amiens.[3] On 2 June he suspended Richard, bishop of Lincoln, who, not content with disregarding the orders of the Holy See, had striven in his diocese and elsewhere to obstruct their application through putting pressure upon the notaries and other officials of the Curia.[4] On 5 February Cardinal Guy, recalled to Rome, became pope under the name of Clement IV.[5] The new pontiff was not going to forget the insults he suffered when the barons forbade him to enter the country, and threw into the sea the apostolic letters he was bearing. The legate whom he now appointed (4 May 1265). Ottoboni, cardinal of St. Adrian, was instructed to work for the re-establishment of the king and his family in their former estate.[6] He was to compel the prelates, barons, and others, under pain of suspension and deprivation of office, to give the king (then a prisoner) his cities, castles, lands, towns, goods, and rights,[7] he was allowed to preach the crusade against all ' heretics ' &c.[8] On 13 September, while

---

[1] *Reg. Urbain IV*, no. 718. A bull of the same date (no. 724) states the rumour that the storm now shaking the kingdom was partly the work of Henry III's own brother: ' te permittente ac dissimulante ne dicam procurante, commota.' The pope exhorted Richard, king-elect of the Romans, to bring assistance to the English monarch.

[2] *Ibid.*, no. 581. Then follows a long list of bulls relating to the legation of Cardinal Guy in November, December, and January (pp. 396–400).

[3] *Ibid.*, no. 708.   [4] *Reg. Urbain IV*, no. 647 ; cf. Bliss, 400–1

[5] The new pope's letters should be studied in the *Registre de Clément IV*, ed. E. Jordan ; they add many particulars to Bliss. Those anterior to the moment when the pope learned (between 13 and 24 September) of the disaster of Evesham, fall into two large groups: the first runs from 4–15 May, comprising nos. 40–60 ; the other, running from 1–6 July, consists of nos. 115–19 and 122 : In all 26 letters or bulls for less than four weeks. This will indicate the bitter determination with which the pope pursued Simon de Montfort and his ' complices'.

[6] *Reg. Clément IV*, nos. 40 and 42 (4 and 11 May).

[7] *Ibid.*, no. 45 (5 May).

[8] *Ibid.*, nos. 58 and 59 (5 and 6 May) ; no. 122 (6 July) ; no. 955, 'sicut

still in ignorance of the result of August 4, Clement IV exhorted prince Edward to deliver his father, and ordered the publication in France of the sentences of excommunication he had himself uttered during his legation against the earls of Leicester and Norfolk, against the Justiciar Hugh Despenser &c. The legate was to warn Llewellyn, under the same penalty, that he must abandon Simon; and he was to take all useful measures to suppress the enthusiasm of the bishops and monastic clergy who in their sermons had represented Simon and his accomplices as zealots for the good cause.[1] Finally on 17 September, having learned of the offences of 'the perverse men' who died without thinking upon God or the salvation of their souls, he ordered the legate to support the royal cause with all his power. Three bishops,

---

ethnicus et publicanus'. Ralph of Coggeshale notes at exactly the same period, 'error quorundam haereticorum qui vulga appellantur publicani' (Du Cange, *i.e.* populicani). 'Ethnico' is evidently used in the same sense. The Crusade was to be preached in England, Scotland, Wales, and Ireland; in Denmark and Norway, in France, but not in the lands of the counts of Poitou and Anjou (brothers of Louis IX), in Germany or other parts of the Empire.

[1] *Reg. Clément IV*, no. 231; Bliss, p. 431. Of the bishops summoned by Simon to the Great Parliament of 1265, eight—Durham, Lincoln, Winchester, London, Worcester, Chichester, Ely, and Salisbury were cited *coram rege* to answer for their misdoings against the peace and for other acts of hostility against the king (Jacob, p. 293). Of the abbots, Bury St. Edmunds was accused of having participated in an attack on Robert de Tattershall's properties and had to purchase the royal favour by paying a sum of 266*l.* 13*s.* 4*d.* into the Wardrobe (Jacob, p. 293). The abbot of Waltham was sued by Peter of Savoy for an attack on his demesne at Cheshunt (*ibid.*, p. 293). The connexion of the abbey of Notley with the Leicester interest also emerges: the abbot, accused of having sheltered the king's enemies, recalled the fact that his house had been founded by the Marshals of England (*sic*) and that an earl of Leicester had some time married the heiress of one of these high dignitaries, so that consequently the abbey could not have refused to receive its patron's retainers. The verdict of the jury was that in fact Simon of Leicester was the *advocatus et superior domus* (*ibid.*, p. 295). The abbot of Reading, charged with having sent his men against his lord the king, and with having subsidized the cause of the rebels, served the earl upon an embassy, and revealed to him a plot to get prince Edward away from Wallingford where he was a prisoner, took shelter behind the royal order to bishops and abbots to provide him with help and subsidies. His case was adjourned to come before next parliament (*ibid.*, p. 295). A chapter of the inquiry of 1267 touching the members of the clergy suspected of having aided Simon, is thus conceived: l'em enquerra ausi bien des erceveskes, eveskes, de tutes gens de religion, de quel ordre ke il seient, cum de persones [lat. *personae*, Eng. *parsons*] et prestres et de clers, e de tute autre manere de genz, ki apertement procurerent de busunies de cunte de Leicestre et de cels ke tindrent od lui, en atreant le gent par mençonges et par faucetés (p. 184).

London, Worcester, and Lincoln, were suspected of complicity with Simon de Montfort; if the fact were proven, they were to be suspended, while on the other hand the legate was to reinstate in their possessions and dignities all clerks, prelates or otherwise, who had been robbed by the king's enemies.[1] On 15 September 1266 he exhorted the king of France not to allow the earl's widow and her son Simon to recover the goods of which their deceased husband and father had been justly despoiled.[2] Clement IV's resentment against Leicester still breathes in a letter of November 1265; he recalled how, when he came as legate, Simon stopped his messengers from crossing the Channel. The bishops of London, Worcester, and Winchester, accompanied by several barons, had, he said, come to find him at Boulogne, the place where they had been summoned; but on receiving from him the order to publish, and secure in England the observance of, the sentences against Simon and his accomplices, they treated the order with scorn. The legate Ottoboni had therefore to cite the guilty to appear before him, and secure their appearance, to receive punishment for their misdeeds.[3] This correspondence is in the highest degree instructive. Naturally it reveals nothing unexpected on the part of papal policy, always hostile to novelties that might shake the existing order of things in the Church; but the insistence with which the help given by a notable

---

[1] *Reg. Clément IV*, no. 986; Bliss, p. 435, with reference to Dom Martène, *Thesaurus novus anecdotorum*, ii. 115, 211, 247, 250. For the tribulations of the bishop of Lincoln after Evesham, see Rotuli Ricardi Gravesend (C. & Y.S.), p. x, and Miss Rose Graham, *E. H. R.*, xv. 87–400; *Reg. Clément IV*, no 1197. The bishop extracted himself after heavy payment, and died reconciled with the king.

[2] *Reg. Clément IV*, no. 425, 426. See *ibid.*, no. 1820, 1828, for congratulations to Henry and Edward on liberation.

[3] Bliss, p. 419; Wykes, p. 185; Oseney, p. 181. Among the legate Ottoboni's letters, one, undated, but probably of 1266, is addressed to the Chapter of Worcester. The legate reminds them that Simon and his followers were excommunicated by the then legate, now Pope Clement IV, and that their lands and possessions were placed under interdict. Now he has ascertained that in the town of Worcester, which has been placed under interdict for the same reason, divine offices continue to be celebrated 'publice et sollempniter'. Consequently the legate forbids the members of the Chapter 'ne vos, quos ex causis predictis constat esse suspensos, ad electionem episcopi in ecclesia Wigorniensi, nunc pastore vacante (Walter de Cantilupe died on 12 February 1266) absque nostra licencia vel speciali mandato, procedere aliquatenus presumatis' (Rose Graham, *E. H. R.*, xv. 108–9.).

section of the clergy to Simon's policy and action [1] was both characterized and condemned is too significant not to be brought out in full relief.

The peace which Urban IV and Clement IV constantly desired to see established required several years of labour from a government now restored to its traditional position of authority. During this time troubles never ceased to agitate the country: there were four principal points of vexation.

First, there was London. We noticed above the demagogic movement raised by Thomas FitzThomas, mayor-elect during three consecutive years.[2] We saw how the city militia fought at Lewes under Leicester's orders. After Evesham the king, doubtless with the approval of the Winchester Parliament, suspended the municipal privileges and replaced the popularly elected mayor and sheriffs [3] by a keeper drawn from the nobility, Sir Hugh Fitz-Otes. The town tried its hand at resistance; but it was blockaded by the royalists and had to capitulate (6 October), surrender the keys of the gates, and break the chains stretched across the roads to stop the king's forces.[4] The former mayor and six leading citizens who were compromised by their alliance with Simon were brought before the royal tribunals. The names of all who took flight after Evesham were entered on a roll deposited in the Wardrobe, and this roll was read in public at Christmas 1269, with a prohibition to the criminals from ever coming back on pain of death. As the

[1] In a letter addressed by the legate, 23 August 1266, to a convent of Franciscans (unnamed), occurs the phrase: 'hoc de vobis querimus ut . . . simpliciter ambuletis, nemini dantes occasionem contra ministerium vestrum qua vituperari possit[is]' (*E. H. R.* xv. 99).

[2] *Chroniques de Londres*, ed. Aungier, pp. 3–6; cf. *Chron. maj. et vic. Lond.*, pp. 47–50.

[3] *Chroniques de Londres*, p. 50: 'Sire Hugh Fitz-Otes fu fait gardein de Loundres, et le meir et les viscontes abatuz pour .v. ans pur ceo qe le cité tint ove les barons.' Cf. Waverley, p. 366. Forty citizens, sent to Windsor to make peace with the king, were first imprisoned, and then released, all but seven, on 20 November (*ibid.*, p. 367).

[4] Letter addressed to the king, 6 October 1265, to announce the submission of the place (*Royal Letters*, ii. 294). Waverley (p. 366) relates that towards Michaelmas the king summoned the burgesses of London to submit at their own discretion. They then deputed ('inito consilio communi' (about forty of the more distinguished to enter into friendly negotiations on behalf of all. The king had them cast into prison. It was then that they gave up the keys of the town. A little later the king had the gates and the road-chains cleared away (p. 367).

inquisitors saw it, every citizen was *ipso facto* labelled as an enemy of the king and could be reduced to the pitiable condition of an outlaw.[1] When one adds to this the legal measures taken against other towns guilty of the same mistakes, one can appreciate how strong had been Simon de Montfort's influence upon the middle and lower classes of the population,[2] just as upon the heart of the clergy.

In the Cinque Ports Leicester had always found most valuable assistance.[3] The confederation remained in the early stages loyal to his wife and her son. The countess Eleanor, now disinherited and in deep mourning for husband and son alike,[4] had found in Dover a place a refuge which seemed safe enough.[5] But she took her precautions, e. g. she sent over to France the 'party chest' which she had in her keeping, together with her two youngest sons, Richard and Amaury.[6] Fourteen nobles, captured in the war, whom she held imprisoned in the fortress, succeeded with the complicity of the keepers in gaining possession of the dungeon, and then took measures to resist the garrison. The news of this happy stroke brought Edward with an army to besiege the place: its defenders surrendered after obtaining the honours of war. The countess was treated with much respect by her nephew and allowed to cross over to France, safe and sound, with her daughter Eleanor.[7] The

---

[1] Jacob, *Studies*, pp. 284–5.   [2] *Ibid.*, p. 290.

[3] *Reg. Clément IV*, no. 122.

[4] Wykes, p. 178, is cruel enough to remind us here of the first widowhood of the countess: 'quae, deposita purpura, habitum vidualem quem, voto castitatis temere violato, per carnis petulantiam indiscrete reliquerat . . .' For long, he adds, she wore nothing but woollen garments and abstained from flesh. In Eleanor's household accounts there are entries of alms given twice for the repose of her husband's soul, once in 12s. 9d. (e. g. August 1265), the other time in 7s. (3 September). Was this all?

[5] On 28 September the king ordered the barons and bailiffs of Dover not to allow Eleanor or any of her people to depart without special licence (*Royal Letters*, ii. 292).

[6] On 10 October Henry III wrote to Louis IX: 'Cum nuper vos rogaverimus quod de illa pecunia que fuit quondam S. de M., inimici nostri, et que in manibus diversorum prelatorum et magnatum regni nostri extitit, mercatoribus vestris in partem recompensationis dampnorum que sustinuerunt in regno nostro tempore turbationis habite ibidem, satisfieri faceretis, ac jam pro certo intelleximus quod Alienora, comitissa Leycestrie, nuper Almaricum de Monteforti et Ricardum fratrem ejus . . . cum XI millibus marcarum ad partes destinaverit transmarinas . . .' (Close, 49 Hen. III, m. 2 d). Cf. Wykes, pp. 178–9.

[7] 26 October 1265; *Royal Letters*, ii. 294.

sailors of the other ports in the confederation received so rude
a lesson from prince Edward under the walls of Winchelsea
(7 March 1266) that they submitted in the end (29 March).[1] By
the close of May peace was established in the south.

After Evesham the young Simon had prudently shut himself
in at Kenilworth. He had been keeping there several prisoners
taken at Lewes, notably his uncle the king of Germany. Richard
of Cornwall he now released unconditionally.[2] Then, leaving a
strong garrison in the place, he took the field once more, and
rejoined the rest of his followers, called by the chroniclers 'the
Disinherited', in the island of Axholm, a vast marshy region
watered by the numerous tributaries of the Humber.[3] Edward
caught him there in the course of the winter. On 25 December,
exactly a year after the royal festivities given by Leicester at
Kenilworth, his son promised to appear before the council, now
reorganized by Henry III.[4] The next day he came under safe-

[1] Waverley, p. 369.

[2] On 6 September 1265, Richard promised always to be a loyal friend to his
sister and all hers: 'A toz ceus qui cest escrit orunt u verunt, Richard, par la
grace de Deu rey des Romeins, toz jors cressaunt saluz en Deu. Sache vostre
université nos estre tenuz a ma dame Aleanor, nostre swer, cuntese de Leycestre, a toz ses enfaunz e a tote lor gent, a estre lor leal ami e enterin ; e lor serom
eydaunt e cunseylaunt a tote nostre poer a lor dreyture porchacer en Engleterre e a totes lor bosoynes fere envers tote gent, sauve la foy nostre seynur le
rey de Engleterre e la monseur Edward soen ffiuz. Et de ce voloms a nostre swer
e leautement premettons a fere luy nostre lettre overte dedesoz les octaves de
la Seint Michel prochein suant. E de ce fere luy baylom en pleiage nos honor-
ables peres en Deu Water, par la grace de Deu evesqe de Wirecestre, et Roger
evesqe de Cestre, e mon seur Warin de Bassingburne, qi par nos prieres en cest
escrit unt mis lor seaus. Doné en la priorie de Kenillewrthe, le dimeinche
prechein avaunt la feste de la Nativité Nostre Dame, en l'an du rengne le rey
quarante nevime (Archives Nationales, J 1024, no. 45. Original sealed on
doubled end of parchment, seals missing. Printed, but with numerous inaccuracies, by Blaauw, *Barons' War* p. 361). Cf. Waverley, p. 365. Rishanger
(*Chronica*, p. 43) says that later, when the younger Simon was obliged to
surrender, the king of Germany entreated his brother for their nephew's life,
'dicens quod apud Kenelworthe fuisset occisus eo tempore quo Simon, pater
ejus, ceciderat, nisi hujus Simonis ope fuisset ereptus.'

[3] See Alan G. Ogilvie, *Great Britain. Essays in regional geography*, 1928,
p. 190.

[4] 'Et a teus choses tenir come avant est contenu, ad le une partie e le autre
fianté en la mayn frere Olyver de Eyncourt, ke poer a ce out du legat sire
Ottebon. E en tesmoignage de cestes choses ont sire Symon de M., sire Baude-
win Wake, sire Adam de Everigeham, S. Jon de Eyvile, sire Richard de Vernon
pur eus e tute lur compagnie selée la partie de cest escript endentée, ke demeure
vers la partie nostre sire le roy ; e mi sire Edward, le cunte de Seint-Pol, le c. de

conduct to Northampton and agreed to evacuate the island with his followers, to give up Kenilworth, to retire to the continent for the rest of his life, where he was to receive the insignificant annuity of 500 marks sterling (26 December).[1]

Simon only accepted these conditions to win his freedom. As soon as he had reached London, he fled to Winchelsea, which still held out; thus he broke the agreement of Northampton, and put himself out of legal protection. Henceforward he could only lead the restless and tedious existence of an outlaw. For the time being his escape reopened hostilities. Kenilworth especially, which Simon had been promising to relieve, offered a prolonged and energetic opposition to the royalists. As clear proof that he had decided to conduct its defence to the very last extremity, the governor of the place, Henry de Hastings, had the barbarity to cut off the hand of the royal messenger sent to summon the place to surrender.[2] The garrison he commanded was fully 1,200 men.[3] Protected as it was both naturally and artificially, the fortress was practically impregnable. Consequently prince Edward, to spare the lives of his men, decided to convert the siege into a blockade.

While he waited for starvation to overcome such obstinate resistance, the king took measures to reform the state. What was to remain of the reforms inaugurated at Oxford and confirmed by the Great Parliament of 1265? What should be the legal condition of the Disinherited? In the camp before Kenilworth Henry III put the solution of these two questions into the hands of twelve commissioners.[4] The plan of reform drawn up by them was approved by a Parliament which met at Northampton on 20 October 1266, and was sanctioned on the 31st by the king. This famous Act, known as the *Dictum de Kenilworth*, is both the epilogue to, and the solution of, the long

Warenne, e mi sire Henri de Alemaine, unt fet seeler la partie de le escript ke demeure vers sire Symon e sa compagnie.' (Copy in Clair., 1188, fol. 28).

[1] Clair., 1188, fol. 26. Further on, on fol. 75 of the same volume, there is another promise made by the younger Simon (original act dated 15 January 1266, old style).

[2] *Chronicon de bellis*, p. 54.

[3] *Ibid.*, p. 52. The siege of the castle involved considerable expense, as did the military operations of 1266–7; the sheriffs' accounts are of great interest in this connexion (Jacob, *Studies*, pp. 251, 253).

[4] Their names are in *Flor. Hist.*, ii. 12.

and troubled period filled with the glamour of Simon de Montfort's triumphs and defeats.[1] 'We pronounce,' declared the commissioners (article 7), 'that all written documents drawn up by the king, prince Edward and the nobles of the kingdom by reason of the Provisions of Oxford, and during the Civil War at the instigation of Simon de Montfort and his accomplices, shall be annulled.' 'We pronounce' (article 1) 'that his serene highness prince Henry, king of England, shall recover in entirety and exercise in full freedom his power and authority; . . . that all must answer, when summoned to justice, in the king's court, as was the custom before the recent disturbances. . . . That our lord the king shall maintain all grants which up to now he has made of his own will and without constraint.' In other terms, a return is made to the ninth year of Henry III, when the king swore to observe the Great Charter and the Charter of the Forest. 'There shall be,' says article 5, 'an amnesty for all rebels who shall have made their submission before forty days.' 'There shall be no disherison (article 12), but re-purchase. Those who have fought against the king in the ranks of the earl of Leicester, his bailiffs, his officials of every degree, must pay five years' revenue of their lands. At this price, they will be given back full enjoyment of their goods. If they only find the half or the third of the penalty, the half or the third of their land shall remain in confiscation.' What was the fate of those unwilling to submit to these conditions? Article 21 states that they must submit to the judgement of the king's court before the Hilary parliament; all refusing to appear 'will be treated as disinherited, as they are called, and their goods confiscated for ever' (article 39). Undeniably, it was a severe judgement, and none found it too lenient; but it put an end to arbitrary spoliation, to reckless grants, and substituted the reign of justice for the *régime* of private vengeance. The formula of article 12, 'no disherison, but re-purchase' was found beneficial, in spite of its rigour.[2]

---

[1] The text of the *Dictum* is printed by Stubbs, *S. C.* pp. 407–11.

[2] Jacob, *Studies*, p. 174. The author both indicates the record sources for the application of the *Dictum* (Chancery Inquests, the *Coram rege* and Assize Rolls, Sheriffs' Accounts &c.), and also brings criticism to bear upon them, because, briefly speaking, the evidence they contain does not exhaust the truth. A judicial circuit in 1267 applied the principles laid down at Kenilworth. Mr.

Article 17 of the *Dictum de Kenilworth* specially concerned the garrison: 'they shall all have the benefit of the peace, save Henry de Hastings and those who mutilated the king's messenger. These last must pay seven years of their annual rental or shall be at the king's mercy. The besieged repudiated these conditions. The legate, who was honestly working for general pacification,[1] desired to intervene; but he was rebuffed, and laid upon the inflexible defenders a sentence of excommunication which did not disturb them in the least. Starvation alone could defeat them. On 8 November they requested and obtained a truce of forty days at the end of which they promised to surrender, if they were not rescued. They still hoped that the younger Simon would come to their aid; but the unfortunate man was in no position to keep the promises he had made them,

Jacob compiles a list of the justices and gives the text of the commissions which they received (17 and 23 November). His closely documented commentary should receive careful attention. Rishanger well summarizes the working of the re-purchase system, p. 45. He adds that Leicester's sons and Robert, earl of Derby, were excluded from its advantages. Those not in a position to buy back their lands, were obliged to leave them in the hands of the present tenants until they were in a position to do so. The Disinherited had their possessions returned to them in 1276 (Waverley, p. 386).

[1] See his letters published by Miss Rose Graham in *E. H. R.*, xv (1900), 87–120. In August 1266 the legate informed the pope that after the Easter festivities the king and his sons had left London to march 'contra illos qui castrum de Kenillworde detinent.' He himself had remained in London at the request of all who had the interests of the king and kingdom at heart, and he was staying in the Tower ('castrum regis quod in extrema civitatis ipsius parte . . . situm habet satis amenum et spatia lata domorum'), p. 97. He wrote to the king (letter undated):'licet illi qui in castro [Kenilworth] contra vos manent multa et magna commiserint, . . . nichil magis elucet in principe quam in justicia servare clementiam': this is why he calls upon Henry III 'quatinus . . ., misericordiam et clemenciam vestro prospectui proponentes, ipsos clementer admittatis ad veniam et misericordiam regie pietatis' (p. 103). Similar expressions were used by him in a letter to the pope written after 12 June 1266: 'Post hec ad locum exercitus regis A. contra alios rebelles ipsius congregatos in castro de Kenilworth proposui me trans[portare?], ut de reconciliatione dictorum rebellium . . . tractem et deliberem pro statu et negociis dicti regni . . ., quia in rebus tanta subversione commotis ad reformationem ipsarum opus est clementia, non rigore (p. 107). Cf. Jacob, *Studies*, p. 171. The king of France also counselled moderation. In a letter dated Vincennes 5 May (1266), Louis IX wrote to Henry III: 'ad procurandam pacem et amicitiam liberorum Simonis, quondam comitis L., nepotum vestrorum, ac comitisse, genetricis eorum, vestre sororis, et aliorum de terra vestra, quorum pax et concordia vobis ac toti regno vestro, sicut vobis, videtur esse plurimum fructuosa' (*Royal Letters*, ii. 304).

and the fortress had to open its gates (end of December 1266). The defenders were granted their lives, and could take their personal belongings away with them.[1]

It still took the whole of 1267 to reduce the last of the 'discontented' who had taken refuge in the island of Ely, a locality better defended even than Axholm. They received encouragement from Gilbert de Clare, who secretly, it appears, egged them on, after assuring the king that he would help him in extinguishing the remains of the great conflagration.[2] That peace did not require a longer time for its definite establishment was due to the personal efforts of prince Edward, who in the process succeeded in learning how a king should act.[3]

Article 8 of the *Dictum de Kenilworth* was framed thus: 'We humbly beg the legate to prevent, by constraint of the Church, Simon de Montfort from being regarded as a saint or a just person by any man, since he died excommunicate,[4] and the miracles which some attribute to him, but which are vain or fictitious, being published abroad by any mouth. Let our lord the king consent to make the same prohibition, under threat of corporal punishment.' Most contemporary chroniclers (Wykes excepted) speak of the fallen hero of Evesham as a martyr; they relate that miracles were done at his tomb and on the spot where he had been so horribly mutilated. One relates that he wore a hair shirt; another employs these significant phrases: 'So died

---

[1] *Chronicon de bellis*, pp. 53–59; Rishanger, *Chronica.*, p. 43; Wykes, pp. 194–6; Oseney, pp. 194–7; Waverley, p. 103. According to the Annals of Winchester the castle capitulated on 15 December (p. 104). The king immediately gave it to his younger son; then he went off to keep joyful Christmas at Woodstock (Wykes, p. 196).

[2] Jacob, *Studies*, p. 236. The earl of Gloucester was obliged to give security for his future good behaviour. The pope acting as arbitrator, decided, that he must pay a heavy sum (10,000 marks, liable to be doubled), and deliver up his castle of Tonbridge (now handed over to the bishop of Rochester to be maintained at the earl's cost) or alternatively give up his eldest daughter as a hostage into the queen's tutelage for three years. (*Reg. Clément IV*, no 569; 11 January 1268).

[3] On 15 July 1267 the pope ordered the legate to publish abroad in the kingdom the prohibition 'ne quis regnum Angliae turbare presumat' (*ibid.*, no. 583), so uncertain was the state of peace.

[4] On the fifth of the Ides of May (11 May 1267) the pope informed Ottoboni that he had received a petition from Amaury de Montfort that called for an inquiry and report. Amaury asserted that his father before Evesham had asked for and obtained absolution, and that before death he had given signs of repentance. *Reg. Clément IV*, no. 452; Bliss, p. 434.

this illustrious man, earl Simon, who spent not only his property, but his life, to deliver the poor from oppression, to establish justice and liberty.' He adds this curiously idealized
portrait: 'he was well instructed in letters; he rejoiced in the
divine office; he was sober and kept vigil at night longer than
he slept.[1] His words were measured, his face was austere. He
attached great weight to the words of the religious, and showed
a great respect towards priests. He was wholly devoted to
blessed Robert, called Grosseteste, bishop of Lincoln. The latter,
it is said, commanded him to struggle and die for the cause of
the English Church; he foretold to him that peace could not be
established therein by the material sword, and that the martyr's
crown would recompense all who died for her. They say that
after his death Simon shone by many miracles which were
operated in secret, for fear of the royal power.'[2]

The quotation is touching. Simon's portrait is not complete,
but some of its lines are true. Above all else it has the merit of
faithfully reflecting popular feeling. A pious hand has gathered
and preserved for posterity a circumstantial and carefully dated
account of more than two hundred of these miracles.[3] An office
was even composed in honour of the 'new Maccabaeus'.[4]

It is fitting that we should not allow the sympathetic impression made upon the reader by this naïve testimony to vanish.
The portrait, although transformed by popular credulity, is
perhaps more accurate in its main outlines than any we might
pen in the light of after-events with the aid of archives and the
evidence of persons directly concerned. We ought not to
see in Simon merely the party leader or the egoist. We
cannot say exactly why his name became dear to English
people; it may be that his tragic death contributed at least as
much as his eventful life to his posthumous popularity; but
these are the facts and they tell in his favour. The people's love
for the victim of Evesham obliterates his errors and his failings;
in the eyes of posterity it is the best guarantee that his memory
is worthy to live.

[1] To pray and sing hymns during the night is a very ancient Christian custom. See Le Blant, *Inscriptions de la Gaule Chrétienne*, i. 100.
[2] *Chronicon de bellis*, p. 6; see also Halliwell's Introduction.
[3] Printed by Halliwell at the end of the *Chronicon*.
[4] Published by Sir George Prothero at the end of his *Life of Simon de Montfort*.

X

DISPERSAL OF SIMON DE MONTFORT'S FAMILY

THE family of Montfort had a strange destiny. At the dawn of the thirteenth century it was scarcely known. In a few years' time the victories won by Simon III over the Albigenses and the conquest of Languedoc had given him a European reputation. Twenty years more, and his younger son had by his marriage mounted the very steps of the throne of England. Friend or enemy of Henry III, in proportion as he progressed in his career of honour and riches, triumphs and misfortunes, he drew upon himself the attention, concentrated upon himself the hope of his adopted country. With a numerous family about him, the proud father of five sons and two daughters, he touched the height of power for a moment, and was struck down from it by a single blow. But worse was to be. Not only was his house fallen, but it was swiftly to disappear in contempt or oblivion.

The countess Eleanor had retired to France, and there passed into the convent of Augustinian nuns of St. Dominic at Montargis.[1] No dwelling could more befit that mother in mourning for her husband and her eldest son. The house had been founded in 1207 by her sister-in-law, Amicia, countess of Joigny, who had several times journeyed to the Roman Curia to secure its incorporation in the Order of St. Dominic.[2] For long the church had sheltered the tombs of several ladies of the de Montforts: Amicia herself,[3] and her mother Alice de Montmorency,[4] another Alice, countess of Bigorre, niece of the earl of Leicester,[5]

[1] Rohault de Fleury, *Les Couvents de Saint Dominique*, ii (1903), has given the place of the couvent drawn in 1854; for its history, he refers to Dom Morin, *Histoire du Gastinois*, 1630, reprinted 1883 and to Dom Chapotin, *Études historiques sur la province dominicaine de France* in *l'Année dominicaine* 1896; from the latter he borrows the impression of the seal of the founders.

[2] Dom Mortier, *Histoire des maîtres généraux de l'Ordre des frères prêcheurs*, i. 536, analyses at length the bulls of 18 April 1245 and 25 January 1257 giving definitive organization to the monastery according to the wishes of the foundress.

[3] Epitaph deciphered in Dom Morin: 'Amicia, daughter of Simon, count of Montfort, close friend of St. Dominic, who died in the Albigeois, and wife of Gaucher I de Joigny, foundress of this church, who passed away in 1252, 20 February' (p . 25).

[4] According to Expilly, *Dictionnaire*, *s.v.* Montargis.

[5] Ibid.: 'Alice some time countess de Bigorre, lady of Chabanais, and

&c. The dead there spoke to the countess Eleanor of those she had lost. She was anxious in her turn to perpetuate the earl's memory by placing a memorial slab with her husband's name upon it in the church.[1] From her retreat, where she was to pass nine more years, she never ceased claiming and pleading for the recovery of the remnants of her fortune. She died somewhere about May 1275, occupied to the last moment with her little disputes and material interests.[2] She was about sixty-three. She had lived too long, for she survived to see the glorious name of Montfort dragged in the dust by two of her sons.

The four whom she still possessed after the disaster of Evesham, together with her daughter Eleanor, followed her into exile. One of them, Richard, an esquire, finds a mention in a charter

daughter of the noble count, Monseigneur Gui, second son of Simon, count of Montfort, who died for the Christian faith against the Bougres in the Albigeois, who passed away in the year of grace 1255.'

[1] Expilly speaks of two stones under which, he says 'repose the ashes (sic) of the count of Montfort and Amaury de Montfort, both brothers, as well as those of the earl of Leicester, nephew of the foundress.' It is quite certain that no part of our Simon's body was ever buried at Montargis or anywhere in France. In the *Bulletin de la Société de l'histoire de Paris* (1917, p. 80) M. Max Prinet draws attention to a funeral monument in the abbey of St. Antoine-des-Champs, which Father Menestrier attributes to Eleanor de Montfort, 'whose heart was laid, after her death, in the church of St. Antoine. She was married to Simon de Montfort after having taken a vow of widowhood, which is perhaps the reason why she wanted to be represented on her tomb clothed as a religious, holding her heart in her hands, as if she was offering it to heaven. At the side of this representation are the armorial bearings of her four sons . . . all without ornament.' M. Prinet supposes that Eleanor's heart was separated from her body so as to be transported to Paris. See Bonnardot, *L'abbaye royale de St.-Antoine-des-Champs* (1882). In the *Issues of the Exchequer* (ed. Devon), p. 98, mention is made of an act of king Edward I ordering payment to the abbess of this house in 63*l.* 1*s.* 8*d.* on account of the 220*l.* 16*s.* left to it by Eleanor; he has this sum paid because of his obligation to the countess in the matter of the earl Marshal's inheritance.

[2] On 23 September 1266 Henry III asked the French king to settle all the disputes between him, the countess Eleanor and the young Simon (*C. P. R. 1258–1266*, 641, 678). The countess was perpetually claiming her dower; before the Parlement of Paris she brought an action against her half-brothers to make them restore to her part of the goods possessed by Hugh of La Marche and the countess queen Isabella, *Royal Letters*, ii. 317. A verdict in 1269 decided that the count of Angoulême was bound to give the countess 40 librates of land in appanage. See Du Cange, s.v. *Apanagium*; Beugnot, *Olim*, i. 871; Boutaric, *Actes du Parlement de Paris*, i. 1743; Giry, *Établissements de Rouen*, i. 322.

of 1266, along with his brother Amaury, the clerk;[1] after this he disappears and leaves no trace behind. Further on, we shall deal with Guy and Simon who murder Henry of Germany at Viterbo; for the moment we must follow Amaury and his sister Eleanor.

Simon de Montfort's youngest son Amaury had been destined for the church; in January 1264 his father had secured for him a stall in the cathedral of York, with the title of Canon and Treasurer of the Chapter;[2] but immediately after Evesham the king stripped him of this prebend in favour of Edmund de Mortimer,[3] probably the younger son of earl Roger, one of Leicester's bitterest enemies; none the less he kept his title of Treasurer[4] in spite of the intruder, whom he had no scruple in charging before the Official of Paris.[5] Finally, after taking orders,[6] he was successful, doubtless with the aid of his brother Guy, in obtaining the honorary, yet none the less useful title, of papal chaplain. He is next found in Italy; for about four years he lived at Padua and apparently studied medicine there.[7] Though suspected of complicity in the tragedy of Viterbo he was able to prove that at the time he was lying fever-stricken in Padua, and that he was at the point of death on the very day that the assassination took place.[8]

Four years later he left for Wales with his sister Eleanor, who earlier had been betrothed by her father to prince Llewel-

[1] Clairembault, 1188, fol. 25v.: 'Et volons et octroyons que, se Amauri de Montfort, clerc, et Richard de Montfort, escuyer, frères, fils de devant dite comtesse de Lyncestre. . . .'

[2] Bliss, i. 417, 28 January 1264.

[3] On 7 August 1265 (three days after Evesham), the king commanded the Chapter of York to give Amaury's prebend to Edmund de Mortimer (*C.P.R.* 1258–1266, 451; Rymer, under 7 August and 17 September.

[4] The title is given him in a bull of 19 March 1267 (Bliss, i. 434).

[5] Clairembault, 1188, fol. 31. Amaury grants Masters Nicholas de Marlborough and Nicholas de Waltham, full power to plead on his behalf before the Official of Paris all suits, especially that of the Treasurership of York, that are pending between him and Edmund de Mortimer and other persons. By a bull (undated) the Pope, at Amaury's request, declared himself fully authorized to take cognizance of the fact that Edmund had been excommunicated by the legates of the Holy See.

[6] On 4 December 1267 the archbishop of Rouen (Eudes Rigaud, a friend of Leicester's) authorized Amaury to take the subdiaconate and major orders from any bishop on the continent (Clairembault, 1188, fol. 26).

[7] *Simon de Montfort*, p. 367.　　　　　　　　[8] *Ibid.*, p. 365.

lyn; the vessel taking them there was stopped not far from Bristol[1] a little before Christmas. Eleanor was taken to court and kept under observation there because Llewellyn was in a chronic state of revolt; Amaury was shut up in Corfe castle, a state prison of sinister memory, where after forty years of captivity the sister of the unfortunate Arthur of Brittany had died.[2] Llewellyn finally submitted (1276) and on 13 October 1278 he married the granddaughter of John Lackland amid great pomp, but she died soon afterwards in childbirth (21 June 1282).[3] At the same period Amaury also won his freedom: but not without difficulty; three Popes, John XXI,[4] Nicholas IV,[5] and Martin IV[6] had for several years petitioned in vain for his release. Edward I was not convinced that Amaury was innocent of the murder of Henry of Germany. He was angry with him for intriguing with Llewellyn, whose hostility was a permanent danger to the English crown.[7] He was indignant that Amaury should be endeavouring to get the Holy See to withdraw the excommunication upon his father, the earl.[8] But in the end tired of warfare, importuned by the archbishop of Canterbury, John Peckham,[9] and softened by the promise of the Pope made that Amaury should leave England for ever,[10] Edward I gave in. On 21 April 1282 at a fully-attended council in the New Temple

[1] To be more precise, near the little island of Sulley on the coast of co. Glamorgan, and not near the rock of that name in the extremity of Cornwall. See J. Dallaway in *Archaeologia*, xxi. 79.

[2] Worcester, p. 469; Oseney, p. 266. Amaury was later transferred to Taunton (*C. P. R.* 1281–92, 403).

[3] Waverley, p. 388; Wykes, p. 277; Worcester, p. 476.

[4] *Reg. Jean XXI*, no. 79; Bliss, p. 452; Posse 883, 884 (28 January 1277).

[5] Bliss, p. 461 (17 February 1280).

[6] *Reg. Martin IV*, nos. 18–20; Bliss p. 463.

[7] *Hist. MSS. Comm. 4th Report* (Ormsby-Gore archives), p. 396.

[8] Already in 1267 Clément IV (11 May) was instructing his legate 'ut, cum Amalricus asserat ejus patrem in morte signa penitentie dedisse, et ob id petat eum ecclesiastice sepulture tradi', to make inquiry into the point. The same day, he ordered him to publish in certain places the sentences against Simon de Montfort and his followers, 'prout viderit esse necessarium, ne contemnatur, ut fiebat ab aliquibus' (*Reg. Clément IV*, no. 452; Bliss, p. 434). In a letter to the Pope (*Report* cited, p. 396; undated and erroneously addressed to Alexander IV), Edward complained that Amaury had secured a promise that the excommunication should be withdrawn. He asked that, on the contrary, it might be maintained.

[9] Letter of the archbishop to the king, 7 June 1281, cited by Blaauw, p. 335.

[10] *Reg. Martin IV*, nos. 18–20; Bliss, p. 463; Posse, no. 1040.

at London the bishop of Winchester asserted that on a visit to the prison, he had made inquiry of his gaolers and that all, 'lifting their hands to heaven and stretching them out towards the church of the castle', had sworn that Amaury's words had never been abusive nor menacing to the king.[1] The archbishop declared that his friends had brought him a similar report. These efforts eventually succeeded. Amaury was released,[2] but he never secured reconciliation with the English monarch nor did he regain his stall in the chapter of York.[3] It is worth noting that he never did anything to deserve a return to favour. Two years after his release he aroused Edward I's lively indignation by having the king's brother, Edmund, earl of Leicester and Lancaster, cited before the court of Rome on the subject of the hereditary succession to his father's lands. At this Edward tartly recalled the papal privileges many times granted to his predecessors, in virtue of which suits concerned with fiefs, dower and money claims were to be decided exclusively by English tribunals, without ever being carried out of the country. In a dry and acrimonious letter he forbade Amaury to pursue the case any farther (28 December 1284). Amaury protested that his intentions were sincere, and complained that the king had omitted any and every mark of politeness in his letter, declaring, however, that he would give up the suit, not because he had been forbidden to continue, but because he would have been grieved to vex his good cousin, the king of England (1 March 1285).[4] This letter of withdrawal was sent from Paris. Amaury seems to have spent some further time there;[5] then he

---

[1] *Simon de Montfort*, p. 368. Cf. Rymer, under 30 September 1280, and 7 June 1281. Blaauw, p. 335.

[2] Oseney, p. 287.

[3] On 29 September 1282 Amaury's proctor, Matthew de Essartis, canon of York, presented to John of Pontoise, bishop of Winchester, a certain Richard de 'Cerminstre' chaplain of Amauri, for the church of 'Burchonia' (Clairembault, 1188, fol. 31). The name of Amaury's chaplain is not to be found in the *Register* of bishop Pontissara of Winchester (Cant. and York Society). On 21 December Matthew de Essartis handed over his proctorial powers to Nicholas de Waltham (*ibid*).

[4] Rymer, under 28 December 1284 (in the Rec. Com. ed.). Amauri's letter, which is very singular in tone, survives also in Archives nationales, J 918, no. 32.

[5] *Simon de Montfort*, p. 369.

CASTLE OF MONTFORT L'AMAURY. THE KEEP

retired to Italy. There, the story is, he put off the garb of a churchman for the mailed tunic of a knight.[1] We are even shown him fighting side by side with his brother Guy, in the battle in which the latter was taken prisoner. He served as tutor to Guy's two daughters and died in 1292. Before the century was out, there doubtless survived not a single male[2] descendant of Simon de Montfort, the illustrious and unhappy earl of Leicester.

After Kenilworth had capitulated, the younger Simon had withdrawn to France. He made several fairly successful efforts to interest St. Louis' compassionate soul in his favour. Henry III was not averse from Simon's returning to England; but the conditions he laid down were hard: Simon might come with a safe-conduct to justify himself of the misdeeds (*excessibus*), wrote Henry III to Louis; all that could be granted was that he would not be charged with his father's crimes 'for which he well deserves to lose his father's inheritance'.[3] In March 1268 he was safe in France. Later on we shall find him with his brother Guy in Italy.[4]

[1] In the *Flores historiarum*, iii. 67, we read: 'quo defuncto [Guy de Montfort] Emericus, frater ejus, clericus eminentis litteraturae, qui ultimus fuit de progenie Guenelonis, factus est miles, abjecto habitu clericali.'

[2] An old friend once showed me an extract from the paper *L'Événement* (11 August 1887), giving the strange information appended here—I print it for what it is worth:

'Un descendant du célèbre Simon de Montfort, qui dirigea la croisade contre les Albigeois, vient de mourir a Naples, le mois dernier.

'Les lettres de faire-part portent, que le 20 juillet est décédé le prince Philippe-Léopold de Montfort d'Aquino Pico, duc de Laurito, Comte de Leicester, duc de Grande-Bretagne, grand connétable de France, prince de Jéroleto, Sanza et Castiglione, prince du Saint-Empire, comte de Squillace, Campobasso et Morcone, marquis de San-Giuliano, comte de Grettier y Mennos, seigneur du château de Trifone, deux fois grand d'Espagne, etc.'

I shall make no attempt to correct the gross blunders in this paragraph; but will merely add a remark made by the Comte de Franqueville (*Le gouvernement et le Parlement britanniques*, ii. 168): 'See the curious work of Sir Bernard Burke, *Vicissitudes of Families*. Among the descendants . . . of Simon de Montfort a saddler is to be found.' Cf. *D. N. B.*, *s.v.* Montfort, Guy de.

[3] *Royal Letters*, ii. 314 (6 September 1267).

[4] On 26 March 1268 Simon de Montfort and Renaud de Picquigny nominated two arbitrators to decide certain matters in which they were interested in the presence of the Official of Paris, before next St. John's day (Clairembault, 1188, fol. 29). See *C. Ch. R. 1266–1272*, p. 130. The Chron. of Bartholomew Cotton relates, p. 146, that in 1271 Simon came to England 'ut sepulchrum

Guy, who had been carried off (a wounded man) from the field of Evesham, was first confined to Windsor, later imprisoned at Dover. Having corrupted one of his gaolers there, he succeeded in escaping,[1] and the two brothers made off to take refuge in France. Guy lost no time in enrolling in the service of his cousin Charles, count of Anjou, who had just received the crown of Naples and Sicily (6 January 1266), and was then preparing an expedition for the conquest of the kingdom that had had no governor since the death of Manfred, killed at Benevento (26 February 1266). Already Charles's eldest son, the prince of Salerno, had made intercession to Henry III (27 February 1267) asking for his royal favour upon the fugitive who so earnestly desired it.[2] Was it intended to impose upon him conditions like those which Simon had already repudiated? There is nothing to tell us; we only know that from this moment onwards Guy attached himself to the king of Naples.[3] On 12 April 1267 he occupied Florence at the head of eight hundred French knights so as to block the road against the Germans;[4] the following year he took part along with his brother in the decisive battle of Tagliacozzo (23 August 1268), and they both received their fair share in the spoils of the unfortunate Conradin: Guy secured the castles of Monteforte, Atripalda and Nola, and Simon the county of Avellina in the Campagna.[5] In the same year Guy also received from the king an annual

venerabilis Symonis patris sui, quondam comitis Leycestrie, et Henrici, fratris sui, visitaret.' This visit cannot have taken place before 13 March 1271, the day on which Henry of Germany· was assassinated by Guy and Simon de Montfort.

[1] The date of this escape has not been fixed precisely. The Continuator of Gervase of Canterbury (ii. 245) says St. George's day (23 April) and Wykes (p. 190) puts it in Whitsun week, i. e. between 16 and 23 May. Cf. *D. N. B.*, s.v. Montfort, Guy de.

[2] Rymer, under this date.

[3] Villani (*Scriptores Rerum Italicarum*, ed. Muratori, xiii. cols. 226, 232) makes out that in 1265 Guy had already been nominated captain of 1,500 French knights by Charles I, that he left France in June and that he was present at the battle of Benevento; but as Charles only became king of Naples on 6 January 1266, as the battle of Benevento was fought on 26 February and as Guy did not escape till the following April or May, the testimony of the Italian chronicler is here valueless.

[4] Malespini (*Script Rer. Ital.*), ed. Muratori, viii, col. 1008.

[5] Cherrier, *Luttes des papes et des empereurs*, iii. 265, 266, 284. These four places are in the Campagna, quite close to each other.

pension of 400l. (of Tours) out of the revenues of the county of Anjou (28 September).[1] Then he departed to make war in Sicily along with his brother[2] on the king's behalf. Two deeds (4 April 1270)[3] show him holding an administrative function of a confidential character; as vicar of Charles I he authorizes the mayor of the commune of Siena, Jacopo Bagliaresi, to choose a podestà; and (the same day) he receives from the lips of the new mayor the oath of fealty due to the king. On 10 August Guy married the only daughter and heiress of Count Aldobrandino Rosso (Rufus) dell' Anguillara.[4]

Thus in four years two surviving sons of the 'martyr' of Evesham had rebuilt their house on new foundations. Its base was soon to be shaken by a crime which may have been long premeditated.

The murder of Henry of Germany.[5] Henry, son of Richard of Cornwall, king of the Romans (or of Germany), had left England for the crusade upon Tunis in the company of his first cousin Edward (the future Edward I). When they arrived the French king had just died and peace had been made with the Infidel. So he returned with the new king of France, Philip III, and on 9 March 1271 reached Viterbo, where a conclave was being held to determine the choice of a successor to Clement IV (d. 29 November 1268). The two Montforts cherished a bloodthirsty hatred against their cousin; they held him responsible for the

---

[1] The deed is printed by A. de Boüard, *Actes et lettres de Charles I roi de Sicile, concernant la France, 1257–1284* (1920), no. 87. In the charter Guy is called 'the king's cousin' (*Regis Sicilie consanguineus*).

[2] Villani calls his brother by the name of Philip!

[3] Printed by Count Alexander de Saint-Priest, *Histoire de la conquête de Naples par Charles d'Anjou, frère de Saint Louis* (1847–9), iv. 247. In the first act Guy is termed 'comes Montisfortis, vicarius domini Karuli regis Sicilie.' It is dated 'apud Lucignanum' [Lucignano]. Witnesses, the archbishop of Tours and Simon: 'domino Symone, comite Montisfortis, fratre dicti vicarii'. But how could the two brothers be simultaneously called 'Count of Montfort'? Probably Guy should be considered as Count of Montefiore, not of Montfort [l'Amaury]. Simon's title here is perhaps purely honorary, given out of 'courtoisie'. Saint-Priest remarks that the two charters emanate from the archives of Naples. They may have been mis-copied. According to the discoveries made by Paul Durrieu in these archives, Guy bears the official title of 'conseiller et chevalier-terrier de l'hôtel du roi' (*Les archives angevines du royaume de Naples*, 1886, ii. 352). [4] Cf. *M. G. H. SS.* xvii. 512.

[5] On this see the admirable dissertation of Robert Davidsohn, *Forschungen zur Geschichte von Florenz*, iv. (1908) 201–11. Cf. Boehmer, *Regesta Imperii*, Regesten V, no. 14159.

hideous mutilation which had defaced their father's body. The occasion was favourable, and they resolved to take their revenge. On 13 March the young prince was praying in one of the churches of the town,[1] when the two brothers suddenly sprang upon him, covered him with violent blows, and dragged him out of the church. Henry with hands clasped cried 'mercy, for God's sake, kill me not'. But Guy replied: 'You had no mercy on my father nor on my brother.' Then having slain his victim, he cried, 'I have taken my revenge', and fled with his brother and his father-in-law, the Conte Rosso, who acted as an accomplice in the plot.[2]

This repulsive outrage excited the liveliest indignation among the princes and lords present. The kings of Sicily and France spoke in horror of the crime.[3] But the vacancy of the Holy See (29 November 1268–1 September 1271), the death of Richard of Cornwall (9 April 1272) and of his brother Henry III (16 November), the absence of Edward I in the Holy Land, protected the murderers for a while. Simon died in obscure circumstances shortly after the tragedy of Viterbo.[4] When Edward I, on his return from Accon, had a meeting with Gregory X at Orvieto (14 February 1273), he probably took steps against Guy,[5] who had found refuge in the monastery of San Galgano near Siena; for on 1 March the Pope summoned the murderer and his accomplices to appear before him in a fortnight's time, and, in order that the date and summons might be generally known, the documents of the process were affixed to the doors of the cathedral at Orvieto.[6] Guy tried subterfuges; he attempted to justify himself;[7] demanded a safe-conduct for his

---

[1] The church of San Lorenzo, according to Guillaume de Nangis and Primat, *Historiens de France*, xxiii. 86; according to *Flor. Hist.*, iii. 21, it was the Church of St. Sylvester. Cf. Davidsohn, p. 202.

[2] Malespini in Muratori, *SS. Rer. Ital.*, viii, col. 1087.

[3] Minieri-Riccio, *Saggi di codice diplomatico* (1878), p. 77.

[4] In his bull of 1 April 1273, the Pope spoke of him as already dead: 'dicto Symone fatali morte rebus humanis exempto'. According to *Flor. Hist.* (iii. 22), he died in a castle near Siena, the same year as the murder.

[5] Davidsohn, p. 204.

[6] Rymer, under 1 March. Pope Gregory X's bulls relating to the process against Guy de Montfort have been printed by Jean Guiraud: *Registres du pape Grégoire X*, nos. 209–17. Cf. Potthast, no. 20682; Posse, *Analecta Vaticana*, nos. 746–54, and 763–9.

[7] *Reg. Grég. X*, no. 218. This item contains three letters by Guy. In the

brother Amaury, who was to be his advocate; pretended that it was unsafe for him to approach the Pope while the king of England was in Italy, for, as he said, Edward had taken an oath to kill him if he set foot outside his father-in-law's territories.[1] The Pope would hear none of this, and as Guy did not appear on the prescribed day, he pronounced the condemnation of the contumacious in most solemn fashion in his palace at Orvieto: 'let him lose the esteem of men, let him be branded with the eternal mark of infamy; let him be incapable of making a will, unfit to receive anything by will or from an intestate person; let his ignominy follow his children to the fourth generation; let him be excommunicate, and his goods placed under interdict.' Then he outlawed him, and commanded all governors of provinces, podestas, consuls, &c., to seize him and bring him to the court of Rome, to be thrown into prison (1 April).[2]

The following June Gregory X left Orvieto to go to Lyons where a General Council was due to be held.[3] While he was at Florence (June–July) Guy de Montfort tried to soften the Pope's just indignation by dint of supplications and promises of humble submission. His wife came also to ask for favour, but without effect. When the Pope left Florence, Guy, attended by several of his friends, followed him more than two miles in the dress of a penitent, with bare feet and a rope round his neck, and falling prostrate before him declared with the tears streaming from his cheeks that he put himself entirely 'alt et bas' at his mercy, and asked to be sent to prison, it mattered not where, or besought him to give him the benefit of absolution and thus

third he is bold enough to write: 'si dicatur delictum meum a me commissum fuisse, nego; et notorium esse, nego. Immo dico ipsum prorsus ignotum vobis, Peter Sancte, qui tunc fuistis in partibus transmarinis; nec est qui vere dicere possit se vidisse quod ego illud homicidium commiserim, quia non commisi.' He adds: 'Scilicet quod ipsum non occiderim, et quod tamen *justam causam habuerim ipsum occidendi* . . .' The italics are, of course, my own. In his bull (1 April) the Pope retorts: 'tam ipse Guido quam memoratus Symon ceterique eorum satellites . . . nec mortuo pepercerunt, sed et post mortem illatam vulnera inferentes eidem, ipsum traxerunt ad hostia dicte parrochialis ecclesie jam extinctum.' Cf. Davidsohn, p. 205.

[1] Cf. Davidsohn, p. 205.

[2] This eloquent document should be read in Rymer and in *Reg. Grég. X*, no. 220, where it fills no less than four columns. Cf. Potthast, no. 20712.

[3] Simultaneously Edward I left Italy, crossing the Mont-Cenis on 7 June. See Henry Gough, *Itinerary of king Edward I throughout his reign*.

to leave him a door open to mercy.[1] Touched by these marks of
repentance which may have been sincere, the Pope relaxed his
stern attitude a little; he ordered Guy to be placed in close
confinement in church territories, and entrusted to the keeping
of the king of Sicily.[2] Guy feared nothing so much as to be
delivered into the hands of Edward I; an ecclesiastical prison
for him was salvation. But the king of England found his
punishment far too lenient, and appears to have complained
about it with some vigour to the Pope.[3]

   The king of Sicily did not feel the same grievances as the
English monarch. His Italian schemes, based on the support
of the Guelfs, fully warranted his taking into his service a
man notorious for the unscrupulous use of his talents;[4] but it
had to be done very quietly. It appears that a secret interview
took place in which a plan for treating the prisoner with greater
kindness and latitude was worked out. Pope Gregory X consented to treat Guy as a sort of free captive in the fortress of
Lecco, on lake Como.[5] Later at Lyons, where he was presiding
over the Council, he gave orders that the excommunication
should be lifted (23 July 1274).[6] Guy himself performed the last
act in the intrigue by escaping, once again, and thanks to the
connivance of his gaolers, from the 'tour forte et haute', where
he was confined.[7] For four years nothing is known of him.

   He reappears in 1278. One of his French cousins, John de
Montfort, Count of Squillace and Montescaglioso in Campagna,[8]

   [1] Davidsohn p. 205. *Reg. Grég. X*, no. 326.
   [2] Bull of 29 November 1273. Rymer, under this date. *Reg. Grég. X*, no. 814:
'in terra Ecclesie romane, in aliqua arce tuta assignari et . . . ipsum Guidonem
per . . . Sicilie regem illustrem . . . custodiri.' Cf. Potthast, no. 20767.
   [3] This is suggested by the tone of the bull just analysed.
   [4] I am unable to utilize, in this connexion, a charter published by Rymer as
of 28 February 1274. For reasons which will be stated below (p. 272), this letter
must surely be attributed to 1289.
   [5] Davidsohn, p. 206.
   [6] *Reg. Grég. X*, no. 383. Cf. Bliss, *Papal Letters*, i. 446; Potthast, no. 20880.
   [7] Primat, *Historiens de France*, xxiii. 36.
   [8] Jean and Guy belonged to two branches of one common stem: Montfort
and La Ferté-Alais (both in Seine-et-Oise). The first lord of La Ferté-Alais who
was also called Guy, had a son, Philip I, lord of Castres in the Albigeois.
Philip II, who succeeded him, was the father of John, who acquired through
inheritance the county of Squillace in the Campagna. In a letter addressed by
Charles I of Anjou, king of Sicily, to Philip III of France, John and his brother
Simon are described thus: 'Johannem de Monteforti, comitem Squillacensem,

having been nominated captain of Bologne, Charles I was anxious to place Guy in command of the garrison;[1] but the new Pope Nicholas III[2] declared roundly that any town giving him such a position would be excommunicated.[3] The following year Charles of Salerno made efforts (27 February 1279) to reconcile Guy with the king of England;[4] Edward at first replied (11 April) that there were serious difficulties in the way;[5] it seems however that the correspondence continued for a certain while, though its enduring was a fruitless one: the king had demanded that Guy should either go 'outremer', i. e. to Palestine, and remain there as long as he was not recalled by himself, or that he 'demeurât outremonts', i. e. in Italy, without coming to France, unless he was duly authorized to do so. Guy replied that the alternatives seemed to him 'trop griés et mesmement cele d'outre-mer': he consented however to remain in Italy, so long as he was not officially recalled.[6]

Under these conditions there seem many difficulties in the way of asserting, as has been done,[7] that Guy went to France; but is Norway a possibility? Several documents, which are

et Symonem fratrem ejus, dilectos familiares nostros' (A. de Boüard, *Actes de Charles I d'Anjou*, no. 677). This shows us a scion of the Montforts in the service of the Angevins in Italy.

[1] Davidsohn, p. 207.

[2] Gregory X (d. 10 January 1276) was succeeded by 1. Innocent V, who reigned from 21 January–22 February; 2. Honorius V, 11 July to 18 August; 3. John XXI, 8 September 1276 to 20 May 1277. Nicholas III was elected on 25 November 1277. This rapid succession of pontiffs greatly contributed to the growth of political anarchy in Italy.

[3] Davidsohn, p. 207.

[4] This letter is in Rymer, ed. 1739, among the 'Omissa', of the fourth part, p. 79, with the marginal dating 1267, which is manifestly a misprint. The indication 'An. 7 Ed I' proves that it belongs to the year beginning 20 November 1278. The text itself gives both date and place: 'Escrit à Paris, le lundi après la chaiere de seint Pere', the festival celebrated on 22 February. Davidsohn introduces unnecessary confusion when he writes, p. 207: 'dennnoch im denselben Monat Februar 1277 [*sic*], le lundi apres la chaiere de Seint Pere, also 1280, 26 Februar, richtete Prinz Karl von Salerno . . .' The true date is given in Hardy's *Syllabus*.

[5] Rymer: 'Datum apud Brehull, XI° die Aprilis, anno regni nostri 7°.' Brehull is Brill in Buckinghamshire.

[6] See Rymer for the two letters in French, ed. of 1739, 2nd part, p. 187, and fourth part, p. 82, among the 'Omissa'; in the Record edition, i. 536. These letters are of 8 Edward I and noted with precision as such in Hardy's *Syllabus* (1280).

[7] This is what Davidsohn, p. 208, seems to imply.

difficult to date, but which apparently belong to 1280, have preserved the rumour of this. What in fact do they reveal? That a friar named Richard, Abbot of Lyse in Norway, informed Edward I that the king of Norway[1] had had a knight suspected of being Guy de Montfort put under arrest; that the king's steward,[2] when in Scotland, had been informed about his capture by several persons, by Abbot Richard in particular; but that on return to his own country it was discovered that the individual suspected had not been imprisoned at all.[3] We have the text of a contract between Abbot Richard and two Norwegian barons,[4] in which the latter, though well aware that king Edward's enemy had been able to escape secretly,[5] none the less swore to employ all their efforts, in return for a large sum of money, in effecting his capture. The English king asked Eric to deliver the prisoner over to him, if he was still in safe keeping.[6] After this all is silence. One fact emerges very forcibly from the mystery: Edward I's hatred for Guy de Montfort. This was not the last occasion he had for displaying it.

Let us return to our chronological narrative. In 1281 Guy de Montfort represented the king of Sicily at Orvieto, where the

---

[1] Rymer gives three letters, two in French, one in Latin, relating to this business. For the purpose of clarity I shall distinguish them as A, B, and C, in the order in which they stand in the *Syllabus*. Letter A is dated 'in octabis Epiphanie', 13 January [1280]; letter B, is immediately posterior and letter C was written in November. The letters in French have not been very correctly reproduced. At my request Mr. A. E. Stamp, the Deputy Keeper of the Public Records, kindly sent me several corrections; but they concern the orthography, not the interpretation of the text. The Norwegian Abbot (letter A) was head of Lyse, a Cistercian house, founded in 1164 in the island of Halmö near Bergen (Chr. Lange, *De norske klostershistorie in Middelalderen*, p. 350; cf. Janauschek, *Origines Cistercienses*, i. 83).

[2] Letter B, January. The steward is called 'Augustinus [Einstein], illustris regis Norwegie senescallus.'

[3] 'Percipiens militem quendam, de quo suspitio habebatur quod inimicus vester existeret Guido de Monteforti, hoc anno [?1279] me existente in Scotia, latenter ad partes Norwegie declinasse. . . .'

[4] Letter A.

[5] 'Circa captionem Guidonis de Monteforti, prefati regis Anglie inimici, qui de Norwegia, antequam comprehendi posset, latenter evasit. . . .'

[6] Letter C: 'quendam nobilem, pro eo quod ipse inimicus noster Guydo de Monteforti esse suspicatur . . . Militem ipsum, si adhuc in potestate vestra teneatur arrestatus, ad nos sine delatione mitti faciatis. . . .' This letter is not dated; but it is addressed to Eric, king of Norway, who succeeded his father Magnus in June 1280, and so is certainly subsequent to this date. I do not understand why Hardy puts it in November.

pope was staying,[1] at the reception given for princess Clémence, the fiancée of Charles Martel, grandson of Charles I.[2] About this time a daughter was born to him,[3] but it was from 1283 that his active life seems to have begun again. The Pope appointed him (11 May) captain of the papal army in Romagna against the attacks of the Ghibelline Guido di Montefeltro, 'the persecutor of the Church'.[4] Scarcely had the siege of Urbino been begun, when, to the Pope's great indignation, he made peace with his adversary.[5] This was because he had just learned of the death of his father-in-law, and was in a hurry to betake himself into Tuscany in order to defend his wife's inheritance; and this new struggle ended by an agreement made with the count of Santa Fiora, the chief of his rivals.[6] After this, he was free to return to the service of the Angevins, which the death of Charles I and the captivity of Charles II had disorganized;[7] but the fleet which was to transport him and his troops to the relief of Catania, then beleaguered, was captured at sea by Roger de Loria (23 or 24 June 1287). A prisoner for the third time, Guy was destined to meet death in irons.

He was to suffer two cruel deceptions. Naturally he had negotiated for his ransom. The burdensome conditions offered to him we know from a document, the date of which has until now perplexed historians. This is the letter printed by Rymer

[1] The Pope was in residence at Orvieto from 23 March 1281 till 27 June 1284 (Potthast).

[2] Davidsohn, p. 208.

[3] *Ibid.*, p. 209. The marriage had taken place eleven years before.

[4] Potthast, no. 22022. In this bull Guido di Montefeltro is termed 'pravitatis alumnus, persecutor Ecclesie manifestus.' A little later (4 October) the Pope congratulates Malatesta di Verocchio, podestà of Rimini, on having, with his forces, brought effective aid to Guy de Montfort against the men of Urbino, 'hostes Ecclesiae antiquatos' (no. 22065). Posse here confuses Guy de Montfort and Guido di Montefeltro.

[5] *Reg. Martin IV*, no. 472 jj: 'licet dilectum filium virum Guidonem de Monteforti postmodum illuc [Romagna] miserimus ut ibi gereret duntaxat capitaniam exercitus ibidem pro Romana ecclesia existentis, ipse tamen Guido sine conscientia nostra, motu proprio, cum Guidone, dicto comite de Montefeltro, et sequacibus suis certos tractatus concordie asseritur habuisse . . .' Nangis (ed. Géraud, i. 260) was therefore mistaken when he wrote that Guy abandoned the siege of Urbino 'de licentia domini Pape'.

[6] Davidsohn, p. 208.

[7] Charles of Salerno had been made prisoner by this same Roger di Loria on 5 June, 1284; he did not regain his liberty till 1289; he was crowned at Rieti on 29 May. His father Charles I had died at Foggia on 7 January 1285.

under 21 May 1274; in actual fact it belongs to 1289.[1] In it John de Montfort, count of Squillace, the prisoner's cousin,[2] makes known to Raoul de Clermont, constable of France and to Amaury, Guy's last surviving brother, the terms on which he could be liberated for the sum of 8,000 ounces of gold, a considerable price; the contributors were to be the *Parte Guelfa* of Florence, Siena, Orvieto, the communes of Montepulciano, Porto and Pistoia, and perhaps also certain Tuscan vassals, though in the district of Reggio people, it was said, were too poor and exhausted to give any help. This list allows us to form some more or less approximate idea of the count's friends and vassals in Italy. But scarcely had these promises of financial aid been put forward, when Guy was told of further conditions imposed by Don Jayme (of Aragon), which brought his ransom up to the figure of 10,000 ounces of gold, 4,000 to be paid on the spot, and the balance in six months. If this were not done, the count's person would be in danger.[3] For reasons that are unknown, but may be guessed, these last terms were not put into execution, and the suspicion arises, not unreasonably, that Edward I may have used his influence with the king of Aragon in order to maintain his detested cousin in captivity.[4]

[1] This letter, which exists in two versions, French and Latin, is given in Rymer. It is dated 'Dat. Neapoli XX die Maii, indictione secunda', without the year. Rymer and the successive editors of the *Foedera* attribute it to 1274, which fits the second indiction perfectly. Davidsohn on the contrary thinks (p. 206) that it should be referred to 1289, which suits the second indiction equally well. He is certainly right; but I believe that the point can be proved with greater precision than this. Don Jayme (Jame in the French text, Jacobus in the Latin) is undoubtedly James, king of Aragon; but which James? James I died in 1276; James II began to reign in Sicily in 1285 and in Aragon in 1291. The choice has to be made, and cannot be difficult if it is realized that Raoul de Clermont, lord of Nesle, was created constable of France in 1287 (cf. Father Anselme, *Histoire Généalogique*, vi. 90 and viii. 491). It is clear then that the king of Aragon is in fact James II and that the letter should be dated 1289, which makes it of special importance.

[2] We showed above (p. 268) that this lord was Guy de Montfort's cousin. In the latin text he is termed 'Johannes de Mountforte, comes de Squillacio et de Monte Scaggioso'.

[3] 'Et si in hoc deficitur, prorsus dubito quod de persona sua sit periculum.'

[4] Nangis, ed. Géraud, i. 273: 'solus Guido de Monteforti periit in carcere, nec potuit deinceps prece vel pretio, quamvis multum pro eo offerretur, redimi, dolo, ut a multis suspicatur, Eduardi regis Angliae detentus'. King Edward was at the time in Gascony (see *Rôles Gascons*, iii. 14) keeping an attentive eye upon the course of events on the other side of the Pyrenees. The previous year (1288) he had secured from the king of Aragon the treaty of Campofranco

We do not know what Guy's wife, Margarete d'Anguillara did in these tragic circumstances. A letter of 11 July or 2 August[1] tells us that she had put herself under the protection of the Holy See, and that Nicholas IV had appointed a cardinal[2] with the special duty of guarding all her property, especially the county of Soana, a fief held from the Papacy.[3] We do not know if it was before or after this date that she arranged the marriage of her eldest daughter, Thomasse, scarcely ten years old, to Piero di Vico, the owner of large properties near Viterbo and prefect of Rome a few years later. The marriage took place under wholly irregular circumstances: not only was the father not consulted, but the mother herself brought her own daughter to her future husband's house, without her suzerain the Pope knowing anything about it.[4] Later Guy protested, but in vain, though shortly afterwards death came to deliver him from all his troubles (1292).[5]

It would be interesting to know what effect so disturbed an existence had upon the development of Guy's mind and character. What part would he have played in England, had Edward ceased to ostracize him? Would the experience which he must inevitably have gained in anarchical Italy with her vain aspirations after national unity, have been of any advantage to him in the council of a centralized and powerful organized monarchy like England? So strong a contrast might have been a powerful lesson for a statesman. Would Guy have been capable of taking it to heart?

surrendering Charles of Salerno. Could he now fail to take advantage of so favourable an opportunity for avenging Henry of Germany?

[1] *Reg. Nic. IV*, no. 5752; cf. Davidsohn, p. 210.

[2] Benedetto Gaetani, cardinal deacon of St. Nicolas in Carcere, the future Boniface VIII.

[3] 'Considerantes quod, cum dilectus filius, nobilis vir Guido de Monteforti, carceralibus vinculis ab hostibus teneatur, regimen et custodiam comitatus Soane, qui ab Ecclesia romana tenetur in feodum, quique ad dilectam in Christo mulierem Margaretam, uxorem suam, de paterna successione devenit, personaliter exercere non potest. . . .'

[4] These details are taken from a charter (6 January 1295) of Charles II, king of Sicily; Davidsohn has published the crucial passage, p. 210. The king, now seized of the facts, consents, at the request of the wife, to pardon the fault committed by the omission to ask the father's consent.

[5] Davidsohn quotes (p. 210) from the Angevin Registers a deed of 21 March 1292 wherein Guy is referred to as already dead, and a passage from a Sicilian chronicle to the effect that he committed suicide.

CONCLUSION

SIMON DE MONTFORT has been very variously judged by historians. Extolled by some, severely criticized by others, he has at any rate been considered by all alike a man far above the ordinary. Called by circumstances to play his part at a critical moment in the destinies of a great country, his character and his talents bore him aloft to meet the greatest of issues. Although he was brought up in France and never reached England till he was a mature man, he did not remain for long a stranger to the passions, the ideas, the needs of his adopted country. Like other 'aliens' he could have founded his fortune upon royal favour, could have maintained it by dint of servile devotion. He began as a successful courtier, but he was made to dominate, not to serve. Breaking with the king his brother-in-law, he declared against arbitrary power, and in a brief while, especially after his government in Gascony, became its most convinced opponent. His relations with several of the loftiest and purest spirits of his day exercised a salutary influence upon him. Originally his hostility to Henry III had seemed to derive from immoderate egoism or ill-satisfied ambition; later it drew its inspiration from a nobler passion, regard for the public weal. Before the June parliament of 1258 several of his special friends had already placed all their hopes in him; these belonged to the sanest, the most high-minded section of the clergy. After the reforms imposed upon the king by the heads of the lay nobility had met with their rebuff, he entered the political arena and soon became the leader of the reformers, a party in which the most varied collection of people were seen to figure, members of the local squirearchy, the democracies of the towns, the mendicant orders, the lower parochial clergy; a party which had as its object to limit and control the king's arbitrary power by means of aristocratic councils elected by their peers. The monarchy might keep its feudal, its sacred character, but it must rely upon the highest classes in the nation. The baronial victory in 1258–9 and in 1264–5 tended to establish a more and more oligarchical régime; and at the head of this Leicester in the end placed himself. In the Constitution made at Oxford he was but a unit; in 1264 he became the soul and the right arm of the Triumvirate. Parliament, scarcely yet separated from the *Curia regis*, was still no more than an instrument in the service of the royal power. Normally it did not comprise more than the prelates and the nobles of the kingdom summoned by the king, to assist him whether by their advice or by their swords and their purses. In December 1264 in order to strengthen more closely the bond uniting the smaller nobility and the urban bourgeoisie to his cause, Simon summoned in addition the elected representatives of the counties and the boroughs. The need of the moment led him to take this extraordinary step, and it was wholly impossible for him to have seen its prodigious developments; for he was a man of the past and it was all unwittingly that he laid foundations for the future.

Yet whatever narrowness may have characterized his reforming ideas, he served the cause of political liberty. Like Thomas Becket, for that end he died. His 'martyrdom' certainly did more for his triumph than his schemes might ever have effected, had he enjoyed the leisure to bring them to completion. His rivals, even his enemies, carried on his work. Two years after Evesham the Statute of Marlborough embodied part of the Provisions of Oxford, which consequently became the law of England, instead of being the militant programme of a narrow, self-centred party. This was the real, the true path to follow: the monarchy was to cede to the demand for reform, couched though it might be in imperious and offensive language, in order that it might continue to direct the movement in its own person and to reap the profits. It was not the factious barons, but Edward himself, who, schooled by his rough experience, turned to lasting profit the precedent created by his uncle, Simon de Montfort. The parliaments he summoned on the morrow of his return in 1275 and above all at the beginning of 1295 were but framed upon the ephemeral model of 1265; in fact it is from this experiment that the English parliament, such as it existed throughout the Middle Ages and thereafter, dates. There is no doubt that we must attribute part of the initiative for this step to Simon de Montfort. He was not the sole creator, but the fact is enough to give him glory, and he fully deserved that in far later years his statue should be erected in front of the entrance to the House of Commons.

APPENDIX A

It may be thought useful to give the text of Montfort's will, reproduced on Plate VIII. This was printed in my thesis, pp. 328–30. I may now add four new items. Not long ago a certain number of documents concerning Leicester's administration in Gascony came to light in the Public Record Office. These serve to complete the selection which I published (ibid., pp. 279–320). They are in a very bad condition, but four of the more legible have been photographed and are reproduced below, thanks to the courtesy of the P.R.O. authorities. Three of them, drawn up in Latin, are complaints against Leicester's arbitrary actions. The fourth, on the other hand, is a declaration made by the Earl's steward, William Pigorel, on the subject of the violent outrages committed by the partisans of Arnaud de Ladils at Bayonne. They are to be found in the Miscellanea of the Chancery, 24/1, nos. 12, 13, 14, and 16.

I. *Will of Simon de Montfort: 1 January 1259.*

Au nun du Pere, e du Fil et du Seint-Esperit. Je, Simon de Munfort, cuens de Leycestre, faz mon testament, e comant et devis ke li tort ke je e fet en quel maniere, uo an quel païs ke ço sait ke l'en puisse savoir, sayent amendé, e mes detes saient paiées ausi par tuot, e noméement les detes des servises ke l'en m'a fez saient rendues a ceus qui m'unt servi, a qui je sui tenuz por leur servise, kar ce tyen-je a la greyneur dete; e totes ces choses saient fetes selunc ce ke l'en mieuz le porra savoir ou par mes lettres ou par temoinz; e veil ke asez legierement saient les genz creuz qui riens me demanderunt, por qaie ke il dient teles resuns par kaie il sanble mieux ke il dient voir ke mançonge, quar je veil ke la ou il aura aucune dote, ke ele sait bien fete clere par devers moie, ke que il cuot, si ke je an saie bien delivres, kar je ne vuel demorer an dete ne an supeçun de dete vers nuli.

E totes ces choses qui apartienent a mon testament, je les, e devis a fere, e en charche la cuntesse ma fame, e faz de lui mon aturné, e lui pri e requier e comant an la faie ke ele me dait, ke ele le face en tele maniere come bone dame le dait faire pur son segneur qui en lui se fie; e ce ke ele fera de ces choses, face par le cunseil le eveesque de Nicole Richart,[1] e de frere Adan des Marais.[2] E se ele morayt avant ke ces choses fusent acunplie(e)s, je faz mon aturné de fere ou de

---

[1] Richard de Gravesend, elected bishop of Lincoln, 23 September, approved by the king 13 October, consecrated 3 November, 1258; d. 13 December, 1279 (*D.N.B.*, *s.v.* Gravesend, Richard de).

[2] Adam Marsh, frequently mentioned above. Dr. Little (*De adventu fratrum minorum in Angliam*, pp. 14, 63, 131), puts his death on 18 November, 1258; but the present document shows him to be still alive on 1 January, 1259.

parfere ce ke ele n'aurait fet, de Henri mon fyuz, en tel manyere ke tut ce ke il an fera face par le conseil monseur Piere de Monfort e monseur Hue le Despansier, e monseur Ernaut du Bois,[1] ne en nule maniere riens ne face de ce, se par le cunseil nun de ces trais, se il en nule maniere les i puet avoir; e se il ne puet toz, ne face riens sanz les deus ou sanz l'un, se plus n'en puet avoir. E par desus tuz voeil e comant ke il craie le cunseil aus devant diz le eveesque et frere Aden, e en nule maniere ne sayt riens fet sanz le conseil de ces deus, se il vivent, e, se li uns morait, de celi qui demurra. E se Hanris morait avant ke cete chose fut tote parfete, je voeil e devis ke icic (*sic*) traie (*sic*) qui sunt desus nomé, P., H., E., aient autel poer cume Henris eust, se il vesquit. E se il tuit traie (*ms.* tarie) n'i poeient estre ou por mort ou por grief esoyne, les deus ou l'un aient ou ait le puair ke tuz trais aurient s'il estaient ensanble, mes ke tutes choses saient fetes par le conseil e l'ordenement des deus desus diz, le eveesque e frere Aden, ou de l'un d'eus, se li autres morait, ou de leur atornez a ceste chose fere se il moraient, les qieus atornez je veil qu'i aient leur puer a ceste chose fere.

Je les, e ator toz mes muebles, e toz mes chatieus, e totes mes gardes, e ce ke a moie apartient de la valuue de ma terre treque a l'aage de mun ayr, selounc l'otraie qe li rais m'en a fet, si come l'en puet voeir en ses lettres;[2] e ce ke demorra de ces chatieus e de totes ces choses ke je les por fer mon devis, quant ce sera acunpli qui est ci devisié desus, ou ke l'en trovera par epres ou epecial comandemant ke je en aie fet ou face uncore ou par lettres ou en autre certeine maniere, je veil ke tot le remenant sait gardé par l'ordenement la cuntesse ma fame e par sa volenté. E ele par le conseil aus devant diz le eveesque et frere Adan, premierement purvaie de ço ke la povre gent de ma terre saient porveu du mien, si ke il ne saient an perilieuse defaute, e nomement les gaaneuors de qui biens je e eu meinte foyz e je dot bien k'aucune partie mal (*sic*),[3] e deu remenant face et devist

---

[1] Peter de Montfort and Hugh Despenser find frequent mentions above. See Dugdale, *Baronage*. The family of Ernaut du Bois were former dependents of Leicester. They derived their name from Bois-Arnaud, c. Rugles, arr. Evreux (Eure). See Delisle, *Cart. Normande*, no. 790, notes. Ernaut I, who lived in king Stephen's day, was steward of Robert the Hunchback, earl of Leicester: Dugdale, *Warwickshire*, i. 8, 60. Matthew Paris notes the death of an Ernaut du Bois under 1255, *Chron. maj.*, v. 487, cf. p. 379. He was judge of the forest south of Trent. Clark, *Arch. Journal*, xxxv. 209.

[2] By letters patent of 20 February 1257 the king permitted the earl to dispose by will of all his goods and revenues. Shirley, *Royal Letters*, ii. 392. Cf. *C.P.R.* 1247–1258, 542.

[3] As one of my young colleagues, M. A. de Boüard suggests to me, we ought to give these words the following sense: 'and I suspect that in the eyes of some I have done harm', i.e. have behaved unjustly.

a fere ce ke ele verra ke mieuz sait. E je veil ke ele ait plein poair ke tot ce ke ele en fera ou ordenera ou devisera a fere apres li par le conseil de ces deus preudes homes devant dyz ou de l'un, sait ferm e estable ausi cume se je le avoie fet. E il me senble ke, se il i avait chose de remenant qui geres de lieu peut tenir a nos enfanz, boen serait ke la mere leur fait selonc ce ke ele quiderait ke bon fut, si ke par ce leur fut, en leur venir a terre, l'achesun detorbée de grever leur genz ; ce di-je ou por tuz ou por une partie ou por l'un, se l'en vaait ke il covenist ke il fust charcyz des autres. E je pri mon chier pere Richart, par le grace de Dieu eveesque de Nicole, ke il, por greneur seurté de ceste chose, mete sun seel an cest escrit ;[1] e je, por ce meemes, i met le mien. *E je, Henris, fiuz au devant dit Simon, ai escrites ces lettres de ma mein,* e otraie e promet a mon segneur mon pere ke je a bone faie e a tot mon poer tendré ce ke est ci escrit.

Ce fu fet le jor de la circuncision Nostre Segneur, en l'an Nostre Seigneur millesimo cc° l^{mo} viij. en l'amur de Nostre Segneur Jesu Crist. Amen.[2]

[1] The original still bears a fragment of the bishop of Lincoln's seal, though of Simon de Montfort's nothing remains.

[2] Printed, with several errors, in *Bibliothèque de l'École des Chartes,* t. xxxviii. This interesting document was reproduced by heliographic process in *Recueil de fac-similés à l'usage de l'École des Chartes,* premier fascicule, no. 75.

II. *Complaints of Amanieu d'Albret.*[1]

Chancery Miscellanea, 24/1 (12).

In modum denunciationis . . . . insinuat regie maiestati nobilis vir Amaneuus de La [breto]/ . . . . quod dominus Symon comes Leyc' suus (?) in Vasconia senescallus, construxit quoddam castrum de nouo in parochia / de Perissols Vasatensis diocesis, quod castrum vulgariter appellatur la Crote, quod quidem castrum est infra limites et terminos districtus . . . . / seu castellarie . . . . de Sora et pro parte in suo proprio solo constructum et eciam situatum. Super quo iste comes / a predicto Amaneuo [h]umiliter requisitus in presentiam [*sic*] venerabilium patrum . . [2] Archiepiscopi Burd. et episcopi Vasatensis et . . . . / utrum vellet tam manifestam injuriam inrogare, promisit quod a predicta prejudiciali constructione desisteret donec / [p]lenius de . . . . / liqueret, ad quam inquirendam mitteret dictum dominum . . .[2] episcopum Vasatensem et dictum patrem archiepiscopum./ Quibus non missis contra promissionem suam non tantum opus quod inceperat construendum, immo homines suos servos et alios / s[cilicet] militum suorum ibidem recipit et deffendit in ejusdem nobilis et suorum grave dispendium et gravamen. Item / proponit quod in forma pacis seu compositionis eo mediante facte inter Geraldum de Armaniaco et predictum . . comitem / de voluntate partium fuerit taliter ordinatum quod duo castra, scilicet Auxitanum et de Lavardens, que quidem duo castra idem . G. per homines suos [tene]bat, [cum][3] eidem domino Amaneuo traderentur tenenda et / custodia[4] ab eo ad expensas comitis, quousque matrimonium esset in facie ecclesie celebratum inter Es/quivatum, nepotem ipsius comitis, [et] Markarosam, filiam vicecomitis Altivilaris et dicti Amaneui / consanguineam et dicti Esquivati sponsam, quousque dictus G. secundum formam superius annotatam uellet castrum Auxitane diocesis tradere Amaneuo. Comes contra premissam . . . . paccionem [dictum?] castrum in ipsius eciam / presentia irrationabiliter occupavit et adhuc detinet occupatum, licet super hoc in multis curiis eundem / conquisiuerit et judicium sue curie postulauerit, quod sibi extitit omne jus[esse?] denegatum. Item proponit / quod cum de pace seu composicione facienda inter ipsum, ex una parte, et Bernardum, fratrem ipsius ex altera, super portione / paterne hereditatis quam idem B. petebat, comunes amici inter-

---

[1] Cf. the Querele de Saltu, *Simon de Montfort*, pp. 297–300.
[2] Two dots indicating name, and so throughout.
[3] 'cum' struck out.
[4] Possibly for 'custodienda'.

ponerent partes suas, idem . . comes ad cuius / officium pertinebat discordantes ad viam concordie revocare nec eos debebat permittere ad arma uel injuriam uenire, quos quidem poterat juridictione compescere, domino Helie Rudelli, auunculo et tutori dicti B., pre/-cepit, sub incriminatione sententie sue, ne ulterius aliquatenus de pace tracta[tum]¹ admitteret./ Item proponit quod ipse castrum Fronciaci quod idem comes obsederat cum quibusdam aliis magnis acris in finibus / predicte compositionis ascriptis tradidit dicto . . comiti pro bono compositionis et pacis sub forma inferius inuenta[?]./ [Item?] proponit quod, cum ipse obtulisset dicto . . comiti iusticiam pro se et domino Gastone, vicecomite Bearnie / uenit² Vascon' coram dominis S. . . . . et B. de Valencia super hoc a nobis in Vasconiam destinatis / Idem comes, oblacione justicie non admissa, quandam domum suam fortam [*sic*] que vocatur Ylon fecit comburere per milites suos quibus imperavit et hoc pluraliter. In quo quidem loco iiijᵒʳ agricultores fuerunt³ occisi ab / eis et alia dampna . . . . et postea collata multitudine armatorum et cum exercitu magno / . . . . si posset sibi suisque nocere oblatione justicie non admissa / . . . . in testimonio predictorum et archiepiscopi Burdegalensis.

III. *Complaints of the mayor and commune of Bordeaux on the change in the Bordeaux coinage.*

Chancery Miscellanea, 24/1 (13).

Notum sit vestre majestati quod, cum ad preces majoris et com-munie Burdegalen' in primo adventu domini Symonis de Monteforti in Vasconia dedissetis dicto Symoni vestris litteris in mandatis quod supersederet facere monetam tunc, pro eo quod toti terre in mutatione monete maximum dampnum et gravamen imminebat, d[ictus] Symon, vestris inhobediens litteris, monetam cudi fecit contra vestram et proborum hominum voluntatem [propter quod] terra [nostra] dampnificata fuit graviter et depauperata. Et etiam modo grauius periculum imminet toti terre, [et v]alde monetam deterio-ravit. Cum enim moneta illa Burdegalensis que currebat antequam fecisset istam . . . . quatuor denarios pogesia⁴ que est quarta pars denarii in lege et de decem et novem sol. in pondere, ipse diminuit eam et reduxit ad quatuor dynarios pogesia, et de decem et novem sol. in pondere reducta fuit in principio ad viginti solidos . . . .

---

¹ Altered from 'tractare'.
² The sense requires 'et venisset'.　　　　　　　³ 'occidit' struck out.
⁴ On the *pogesia* see Du Cange and Adrien Blanchet, *Études numismatiques.*

IV. *The complaints of the citizens of Dax.*

Chancery Miscellanea 24/1 (14). The beginning of every line is missing.

Line 1. . . . . Cives . . . . Aquenses [quoddam] homicidium perpetra-
tum fuisset [1] in / . . . .

2. . . . . ante adventum domini Simonis comitis Leycestrie in
Vasconiam et juxta

3. . . . . in quo observatur de dicto homicidio salvo jure domini
regis par

4. . . . . dictus comes prout voluit et noluit non ut licuit et debuit

5. . . . . vocavit promittens quod ipse bonam pacem faceret de
predicto homicidio

[*The remainder is too fragmentary to give any coherent sense.*]

V. *Declaration by William Pigorel, Seneschal of Gascony, on the deeds of violence committed at Bazas by Arnaud de Ladils and his companions.*[2]

Sabchen tut aquid qi aquestes letres presents ueiran ne auziram
qe / jo W. Pigorel, senesqualc de Gascunha, portans les uezadas d'En/
Simon de Montfort Comte de Lisestre, arei a Bazars lo dimars
apres la p[?] so es asaber als . . . . Etremotin (?), per En W. Ar. / de
Lad[ils], quim mostrad ab gran areneure en qual maneire Ar. de
Lad[ils], en P. de Lad[ils]e ab lor amys li auen plegads sos sirbents /
en l'auer corud la ab armes e la careire ou En W. Ar. e Lad[ils] este / e
jo per. . . . .

i. 309. As regards the coinage of Bordeaux, Henry III when in Gascony
1253–54 gave orders for a new issue to be struck; the details are in *Rôles
Gascons*, i. no. 2139, 26 September 1254.

[1] Cf. *Simon de Montfort*, p. 301 : . . . conqueruntur quod comes pro inter-
fectione cujusdam clerici de quo pax facta fuerat, detinuit quendam qui aliquando major fuerat dicte ville et tandem demisit eum super corpus et
catalla sua. . . .

[2] See *Simon de Montfort*, pp. 309–12.

APPENDIX B

I. *The families of Beaumont [-le-Roger] and Leicester.*

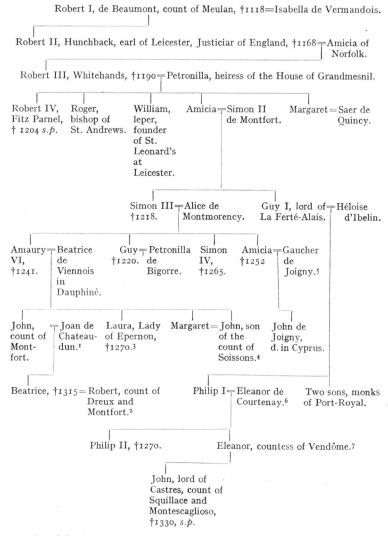

Robert I, de Beaumont, count of Meulan, †1118=Isabella de Vermandois.

Robert II, Hunchback, earl of Leicester, Justiciar of England, †1168⊤Amicia of Norfolk.

Robert III, Whitehands, †1190⊤Petronilla, heiress of the House of Grandmesnil.

Robert IV, Fitz Parnel, † 1204 *s.p.*

Roger, bishop of St. Andrews.

William, leper, founder of St. Leonard's at Leicester.

Amicia⊤Simon II de Montfort.

Margaret=Saer de Quincy.

Simon III⊤Alice de Montmorency. †1218.

Guy I, lord of⊤Héloise La Ferté-Alais. d'Ibelin.

Amaury VI, †1241.

Beatrice de Viennois in Dauphiné.

Guy †1220.

Petronilla de Bigorre.

Simon IV, †1265.

Amicia⊤Gaucher de Joigny.[5]

John, count of Montfort.

Joan de Chateaudun.[1]

Laura, Lady of Epernon, †1270.[3]

Margaret=John, son of the count of Soissons.[4]

John de Joigny, d. in Cyprus.

Beatrice, †1315=Robert, count of Dreux and Montfort.[2]

Philip I⊤Eleanor de Courtenay.[6]

Two sons, monks of Port-Royal.

Philip II, †1270.

Eleanor, countess of Vendôme.[7]

John, lord of Castres, count of Squillace and Montescaglioso, †1330, *s.p.*

[1] *Cartulaire de Porrois*, no. 251; charter of July 1241, calling the count John and his wife Joan. The necrology of Port-Royal, transcribed here by A. de Dion, records, under 5 December, 1275, the death of Petronilla, d. of Amaury

Notes 2–8 on next page.

II. *The descendants of Simon IV, Earl of Leicester.*

Simon IV⊤Eleanor of England.[8]

| Henry de Montfort †1265, s.p. | Simon †about 1271, s.p. | Guy †1292. | Margaret, daughter of Count Rosso dell' Anguillara. | Richard †after 1266, s.p. | Amaury, Treasurer of York, †1295. | Eleanor = Llewelyn, prince of Wales, †1276. |

Thomassia = Pierre dei Prefetti.   Anastasia = Romanellus dei Ursi de Urbe.

de Montfort and of Beatrice de Viennois, abbess of Porrois [after her husband's death]. 'On the same day we remember John, count of Montfort, his brother, and his sister Alice, lady of Houdan' (no. 329).

² A. de Dion, *Le Cartulaire de Béatrice de Montfort.* This is only the introduction to a text that was never published. The original, which perished in the fire in the Chambre des Comptes (1737), contained a list of the fiefs of the county (scriptum feodorum), drawn up in 1230, and many charters of Amaury VI, his son John, and his daughter-in-law Joan, &c.

³ *Cartulaire de Porrois*, no. 270. Charter of 'Lora, filia bone memorie Almarici, quondam comitis Montefortis' (July 1256). *Cartulaire de Vaux-de-Cernay*, ii. 238 n.; Charter of February 1257: 'karissimus pater Almaricus quondam comes Montisfortis.'

⁴ *Ibid.*, no. 269. John, son of the count of Soissons and his wife Margaret confirm a donation made by their father to Porrois.

⁵ Amicia de Joigny, Leicester's sister, foundress of the convent of Austin nuns at Montargis. See p. xxiv, and Dom Chapotin, *Histoire des Dominicains de la province de France*, p. 348; her epitaph is on p. 363: 'laquelle trespassa l'an 1252, le 20 février.'

⁶ *Cartulaire de Porrois*, no. 218. Charter of March 1232, new style: 'Amauricus, comes Montisfortis, Francie constabularius,' confirms a gift made to the religious of Porrois by his cousin Philip of 15 l. of rent drawn 'de prepositura mea de Feritate Aales' (La Ferté-Alais).

⁷ In an early obituary of N.D. de Port-Royal (Clairembault, 1188, fol. 28 v.), we find: '9 May, the memory of Eleanor de Montfort, daughter of Philip de Montfort, lord of La Ferté Alept, grand-niece of Simon, count of Montfort, our benefactor, and wife of the count of Vendôme, who on the same day of 1314, gave 600 l. to the monastery.'

⁸ From a letter of Eleanor, dated the year of the Incarnation 1266, December, we may extract the passages enumerating the five children still surviving (four sons and one daughter): 'A touz ceus qui ces lettres verront, Aliénor, contesse de Lyncestre, Symon et Guy de Montfort, frères, chevaliers, et Aliénor de Montfort, leur soer, saluz en nostre Seigneur. . . . Volons et otrions que, se Amauri de Montfort, clerc, et Richart de Montfort, escuier, frères, fils de devant dite contesse de Lyncestre. . . .' (Copies in Clairembault, 1188, fol. 25 v., and in Dupuy, 804, fol. 145; cf. above p. 260 n. 1).

III. *Descendants of Guy I, brother of Leicester.*

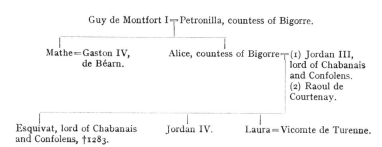

Guy de Montfort I ⊤ Petronilla, countess of Bigorre.

Mathe = Gaston IV, de Béarn.

Alice, countess of Bigorre ⊤ (1) Jordan III, lord of Chabanais and Confolens. (2) Raoul de Courtenay.

Esquivat, lord of Chabanais and Confolens, †1283.

Jordan IV.

Laura = Vicomte de Turenne.

APPENDIX C

Seals of the Montfort family

A. *Simon de Montfort (1181–1218).* *Copy* in Clairembault, 1188, fol. 2 v.; charter dated Montpellier, the 8th of the kalends of December (24 November) 1209. The original had four seals attached. The seal and counterseal of Simon III alone remain. Lettering: SIGILL [SIM]ONIS DE MONTEFORTI.

B. *Amaury VI de Montfort (1191–1241).* The *original* is inserted in Clairembault 1188 between fols. 65 and 66; a fragment of a seal in green wax, with nothing more than the effigy of a knight galloping to the right. A further *original* (in green wax and fragmentary) exists in Archives Nationales S 4373, dated April 1234; Grant to the abbey of St. Antoine, Paris.

Counterseal: standard empaled, on either side fleur-de-lis. Lettering: 'Veritas' *(Cartulaire des Vaux de Cernay).*

Copy in Clairembault 1188, fol. 3 r., June 1218. Amaury and Guy, count of Bigorre, confirm the grant of 10 *l.* (of Paris money) made to the abbey of Val by their mother, Alice, Comtesse of Toulouse: 'Concesserunt etiam fratres nostri Symon et Robertus.' Amaury's seal, reproduced here, Plate IV, is a shield with a lion. The counterseal shows a shield with a fork-tailed lion rampant.

C. *Simon de Montfort (1208–65).* *Originals*: (i) Birch, *Catalogue of Seals,* vol. ii, indicates five original charters of the earl in the British Museum; four in *Additional Charters,* no. 11294–7, and one in the Harleian MSS., no. 11296, published by him in *Journal of the British Archaeological Association,* 1876. The last is the deed whereby Simon de Montfort and Peter of Savoy, Henry III's proctors, announce that upon their representations the king of France has prolonged the truce to the *quinzaine* of Easter, 1258; the seal hangs by a strip of parchment. Birch describes it thus: 'Bronze green, very fine. In a dress girded at the waist; blowing a horn held to the mouth by the right hand. Horse galloping on a hilly mount replenished with flowers and herbage. Below in the foreground, a hound at speed. On the right, a tree of two branches in the background.' By the charter in MS. Harl. (83, O. 45), Simon confirms to Richard Suard 'pro homagio suo et servitio', 20 marks annual rent 'in prepositura mea Leycestrie . . . , reddendo mihi et heredibus meis, pro omni servitio, unum esparvarium sorum.'

(ii) Archives Nationales JJ 629, no. 10 and 10 bis: ratification of the Treaty of Paris, 1259. Cf. Douët d'Arcq, no. 10162: 'Type de chasse; personnage galopant à gauche; tête nue, sonnant du cor. Au second plan, deux touffes d'arbre.' *Copies.* Clairembault, 1188, fol. 10 r., 20 r. The copy on fol. 20 r. is upon a charter issued in January 1261: 'Symon de Monteforti, comes Leicestrie, et Alienora, comitissa Leicestrie, conjuges,' declare that they hereby resort to the queen of France to settle all their disputes with the king of England on matters touching their interests. Two seals in yellow wax.

Simon de Montfort's Chancery employed two seals, as we can gather from a remark in a letter of the duke of Burgundy, 28 May 1256 (Archives Nationales, JJ 26, no. 287): 'cum vestris majori vel minori sigillo sigillatis.'

D. *Eleanor of England (1215–75).* Copy in Clairembault, 1188, fol. 17 r. and 25 v.: charter dated December 1266. This is an agreement between Eleanor, her sons Simon and Guy, and her daughter Eleanor, on the one hand, and the king of France on the other, on the subject of an annual rent of 500l. paid by Louis IX to her late husband. The four consenting parties apposed their seals. All four are in green wax.

E. *Henry de Montfort (1238–65).* Copy in Clairembault, 1188, fol. 24 r.: Charter of the morrow of the festival of SS. Peter and Paul (30 June) 1264: 'Nus, Henris de Montfort, fiuz le comte de Leycestre, Hugues le Despenser justice de Engleterre et Henris de Hastinges,' are charged with the duty of 'amender les damages, huntages e despiz foiz par lui et par les soens a Sire Simon de Montfort, fiuz le conte de Leicestre [Simon the younger] et a soens.'

F. *Simon the younger (1240–71?).* Copy in Clairembault, 1188, fol. 28 r. Cirograph indented by A.B.C. dated Northampton, January 1266, giving details of an agreement, made the previous 25 December, between the younger Simon and Prince Edward at Bikerdike (? Bicker Dyke, Lincs.), settling the conditions of the capitulation of the defenders in the Isle of Axholm: 'E, en tesmoin de ces choses l'avant dit sire Symon, sire Johan de Eyvill, sire Baudwyn Wake, sire Hue de Neville et sire Ric. de Vernun, pour eus et pour lur compainie avant dite, unt seele la partie [that remained with the king]. E mun sire Edward, le cunte de Seint Pol, le cunte de Warene e mun sire Henri de Alemaigne unt fet seeler de lur sceaus l'autre partie ke demuere vers mun sire Symon e sa companie.' Simon's seal is partially destroyed. A portion of a knight only remains.

Fol. 250: Charter of December 1266 (See above, D). Lettering, partly effaced: '[sigillu]m Simonis de Monteforti.'

G. *Guy de Montfort (1243-92)*. *Copy* in Clairembault, 1188, fol. 28 r. This is one of four seals *sur double queue* parchment, on a deed of December 1266 attested by Eleanor, her two sons, and her daughter (above D).
Fol. 25 v.: seal incomplete: with four branches, only three of which remain. Counterseal is lettered '[G]uidonis de Mo[nteforti].

H. *Amaury (1244?-95?)*. *Copy* in Clairembault, 1188, fol. 17 October 1274. Letter of the official of Paris notifying that in his presence Amaury de Montfort, Treasurer of York, has appointed Nicholas de Marlborough and Nicholas de Waltham his proctors in his suit relating to the treasurership of York. Seal in green wax, representing a clerk standing, holding up his right hand open, with keys hanging from his wrist. His left holds an open book.

I. *Eleanor (1252-82)*. *Copy* in Clairembault, 1188, fol. 25 v. See above, D. A woman standing between two small shields bearing the rampant lion of Montfort. Lettering: 'Sigillum Secreti.'

J. *Henry of Germany (1235-71)*. *Copy* in Clairembault, 1188, fol. 14 r.: London, 15 October 1259: deed whereby prince Edward promises to aid and counsel the earl of Leicester; 'Et en tesmognage de cest chose, a cest escrit avons mis nostre seel ensemblement avec les sceus nos chers amis mon seignur Henry, fiuz le roy d'Alemagne, et monsegnur Jehan, conte de Warenn, et monsegnur Roger de Leyborne.' Sealed with four seals.
A good reproduction of the seal and counterseal of Henry of Germany. He is represented mounted, holding a sword in his right hand, and with the left a targe bearing a fork-tailed lion. Lettering: 'Sigillum Henrici [filii regis] Romanorum.'
Counterseal: targe with image of a lion, bordered by three eagles, one above, the others at the sides. Lettering: 'Secret. Henrici filii regis Romanorum.' The counterseal is reproduced on fol. 26 r. (deed relating to the capitulation of the Isle of Axholm, 25 December 1265).

INDEX

P p

PRINTED IN GREAT BRITAIN AT THE UNIVERSITY PRESS, OXFORD
BY JOHN JOHNSON, PRINTER TO THE UNIVERSITY